Bill & Ted's most EXCELLENT adventures

volume one

Evan Dorkin
and friends

Amaze Ink, San Jose CA

Bill and Ted's Most Excellent Adventures Volume 1

Originally Published by Marvel Comics as *Bill and Ted's Bogus Journey #1* and
Bill and Ted's Excellent Comic Book #1-4, September 1991-March 1992

Published by Amaze Ink/Slave Labor Graphics
P.O. Box 26427, San Jose CA 95159-6427

President & Publisher - Dan Vado
Editor-in-Chief – Jennifer de Guzman
Director of Sales – Deb Moskyok
Production Assistants – Eleanor Lawson & Traci Hui

Reprint Credits

Tone art:
Rusty Drake
Jennifer de Guzman
Traci Hui
Eleanor Lawson
Tom Malmin
Rikki Simons
Diana X. Sprinkle
Tavisha

Book design, pre-press and cover colorist:
Sarah Dyer

For further information:
Amaze Ink/SLG - www.slavelabor.com
Evan Dorkin and Sarah Dyer – www.houseoffun.com

Printed in Canada

First Printing – February, 2005

ISBN: 0-943151-98-8

BILL AND TED'S SOMEWHAT EXCELLENT INTRODUCTION

In 1991 I was hired by Marvel Comics to adapt the film sequel to Bill and Ted's Excellent Adventure into a one-shot comic book. I was also offered the job of writing and pencilling a monthly Bill and Ted comic book series that Marvel was spinning off from the franchise. I was grateful for the job, but not overly excited about it.

The reason? Well, as I'm sure you know, Bill and Ted's Excellent Adventure was about two less-than brilliant heavy metal dudes who use a time-traveling phone booth to collect famous historical figures for a high school history project. I hadn't seen the first movie. I was not a heavy metal fan, and to this day I really, really hate the word "dude". So it didn't seem like the ideal project for an angry young New Yorker who dressed in black and listened to punk bands. Still, I needed the work, the money, and the exposure (not necessarily in that order), so I agreed to work on the series up until issue #4. I figured I could stick it out that long, even if the book turned into a disaster.

But a funny thing happened on the way to issue #4. I found myself thoroughly enjoying working on the comic. I was given almost total freedom by my editors to make fun of whatever I wanted, and to draw the goofiest crap I could think of. And despite everything, I had also become fond of the characters. Bill and Ted were polar opposites to the angst-ridden misfits in my own comics. Stupid as hell, to be sure, but also upbeat, happy, and refreshingly un-neurotic. I found myself saying "excellent" and "yes, way" all the time. I may even have let loose a "dude" once or twice, as much as I hate to admit it. And while I never did get around to seeing Bill and Ted's Excellent Adventure, I ended up staying on the book until its cancellation with issue #12, missing only issue #8 because of deadline problems. Who knew I'd be totally bummed when the series ended?

I hope you have as much fun reading these comics as I had making them.

Later, dudes.
—Evan Dorkin
December, 2004

A note regarding the Bogus Journey adaptation: Several scenes didn't make it into the final cut of the movie, leading to some differences between the film and the comic. The film's ending was cut down quite a bit, with the car chase and appearance of Bill and Ted's childhood fears removed completely. Another discrepancy is the depiction of the Grim Reaper. My impression from the script was of the classic skeletal figure, but halfway through drawing the book we received production stills showing the movie Death as a pale-skinned, hollow-eyed Bergman parody. We didn't have time to change it, so the skull and bones Death stayed in the book. I prefer him that way, to be honest.

Thanks to: Fabian for the gig, Stephen and Marie for the much-needed embellishing, David for the one page surprise, Kurt and Tom for all the choice words, original series colorist Robbie Busch, Nat Gertler for suggesting the reprint project to SLG, Dan at SLG for taking him up on it, Jennifer at SLG for all her hard work, all the folks who spent so many hours toning the pages, and of course, to Sarah, for being so excellent.

TABLE OF EXCELLENT CONTENTS

Scripts and pencil art for all stories by Evan Dorkin
Script for *Bill and Ted's Bogus Journey* adapted
by Evan Dorkin from the original screenplay

Original series editor – Fabian Nicieza
Assistant editor – Evan Skolnick

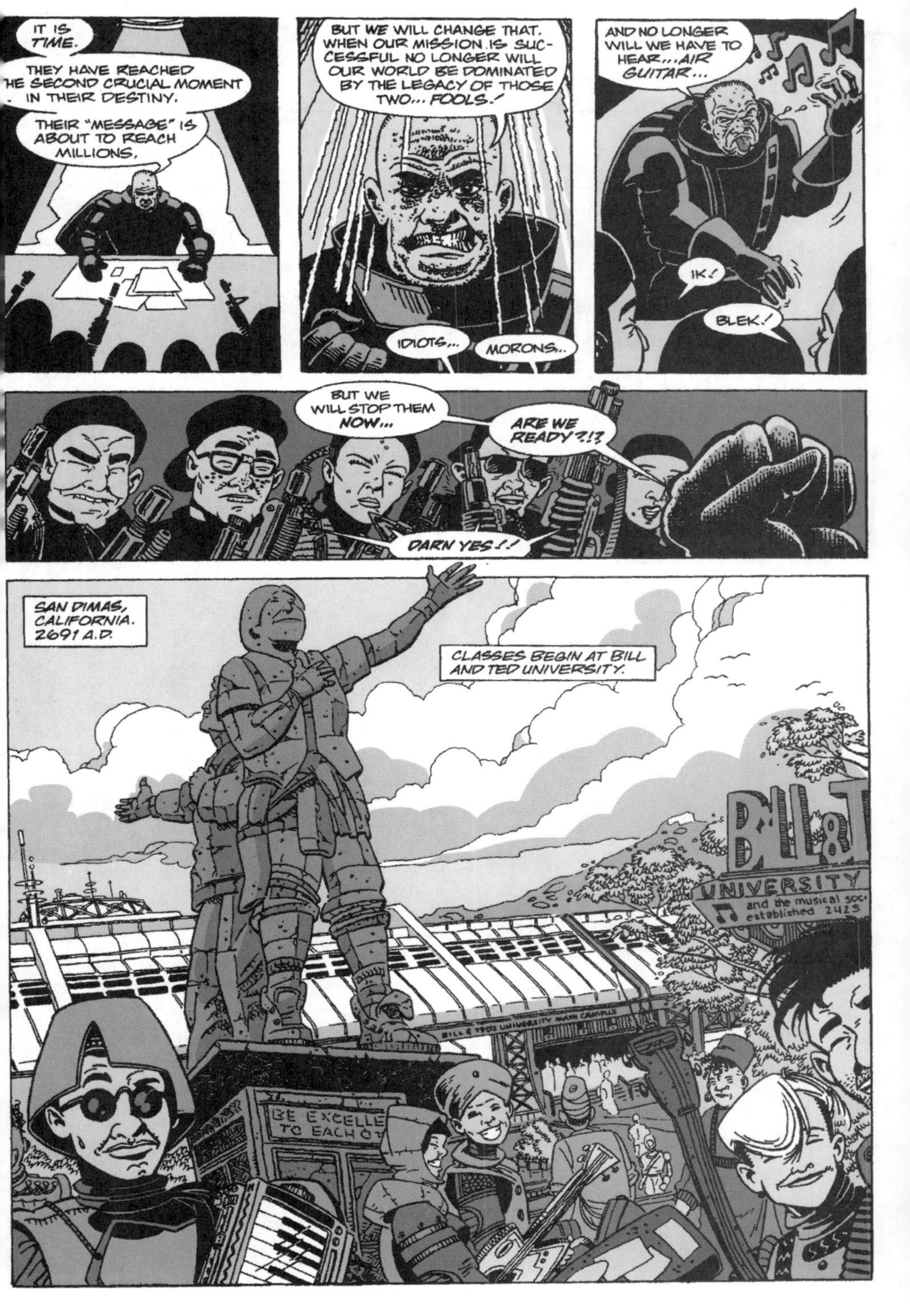
IT IS TIME.
THEY HAVE REACHED THE SECOND CRUCIAL MOMENT IN THEIR DESTINY.
THEIR "MESSAGE" IS ABOUT TO REACH MILLIONS.
BUT WE WILL CHANGE THAT. WHEN OUR MISSION IS SUCCESSFUL NO LONGER WILL OUR WORLD BE DOMINATED BY THE LEGACY OF THOSE TWO... FOOLS.!
IDIOTS...
MORONS...
AND NO LONGER WILL WE HAVE TO HEAR... AIR GUITAR...
IK!
BLEK!
BUT WE WILL STOP THEM NOW...
ARE WE READY?!?
DARN YES!!
SAN DIMAS, CALIFORNIA. 2691 A.D.
CLASSES BEGIN AT BILL AND TED UNIVERSITY.
UNIVERSITY
established 2425
BE EXCELLE
TO EACH O

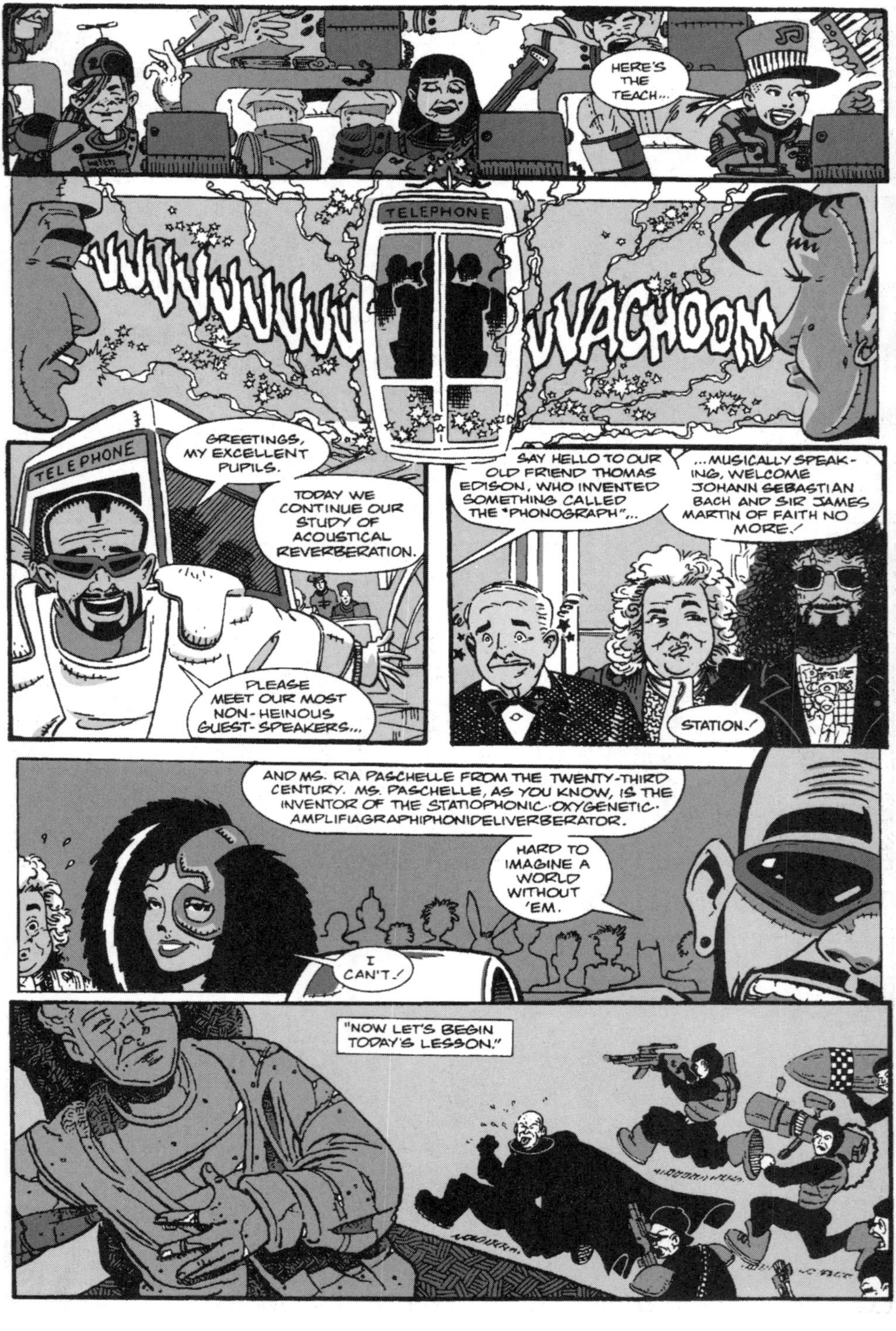
HERE'S THE TEACH...
VVVVVVVVV VVACHOOM
TELEPHONE
GREETINGS, MY EXCELLENT PUPILS.
TODAY WE CONTINUE OUR STUDY OF ACOUSTICAL REVERBERATION.
PLEASE MEET OUR MOST NON-HEINOUS GUEST-SPEAKERS...
SAY HELLO TO OUR OLD FRIEND THOMAS EDISON, WHO INVENTED SOMETHING CALLED THE "PHONOGRAPH"...
...MUSICALLY SPEAKING, WELCOME JOHANN SEBASTIAN BACH AND SIR JAMES MARTIN OF FAITH NO MORE!
STATION!
AND MS. RIA PASCHELLE FROM THE TWENTY-THIRD CENTURY. MS. PASCHELLE, AS YOU KNOW, IS THE INVENTOR OF THE STATIOPHONIC-OXYGENETIC-AMPLIFIAGRAPHIPHONIDELIVERBERATOR.
HARD TO IMAGINE A WORLD WITHOUT 'EM.
I CAN'T!
"NOW LET'S BEGIN TODAY'S LESSON."

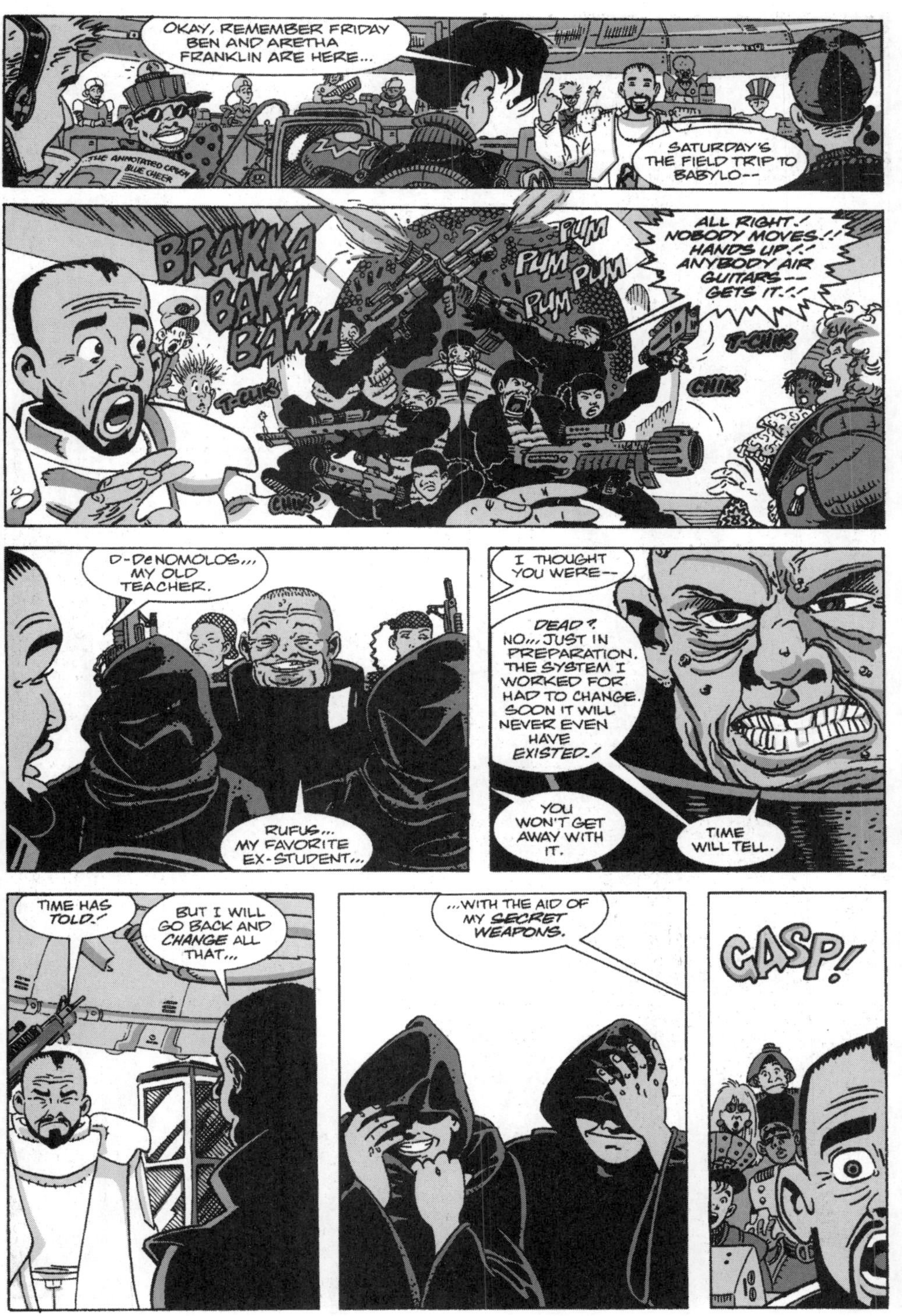
OKAY, REMEMBER FRIDAY BEN AND ARETHA FRANKLIN ARE HERE...
THE ANNOTATED CREEP BLUE CHEER
SATURDAY'S THE FIELD TRIP TO BABYLO--
BRAKKA BAKA BAKA
PUM PUM PUM PUM PUM
ALL RIGHT! NOBODY MOVES!! HANDS UP!! ANYBODY AIR GUITARS-- GETS IT!!
T-CHIK
CHIK
T-CHIK
CHIK
D-DeNOMOLOS... MY OLD TEACHER.
RUFUS... MY FAVORITE EX-STUDENT...
I THOUGHT YOU WERE--
DEAD? NO... JUST IN PREPARATION. THE SYSTEM I WORKED FOR HAD TO CHANGE. SOON IT WILL NEVER EVEN HAVE EXISTED!
YOU WON'T GET AWAY WITH IT.
TIME WILL TELL.
TIME HAS TOLD!
BUT I WILL GO BACK AND CHANGE ALL THAT...
...WITH THE AID OF MY SECRET WEAPONS.
GASP!

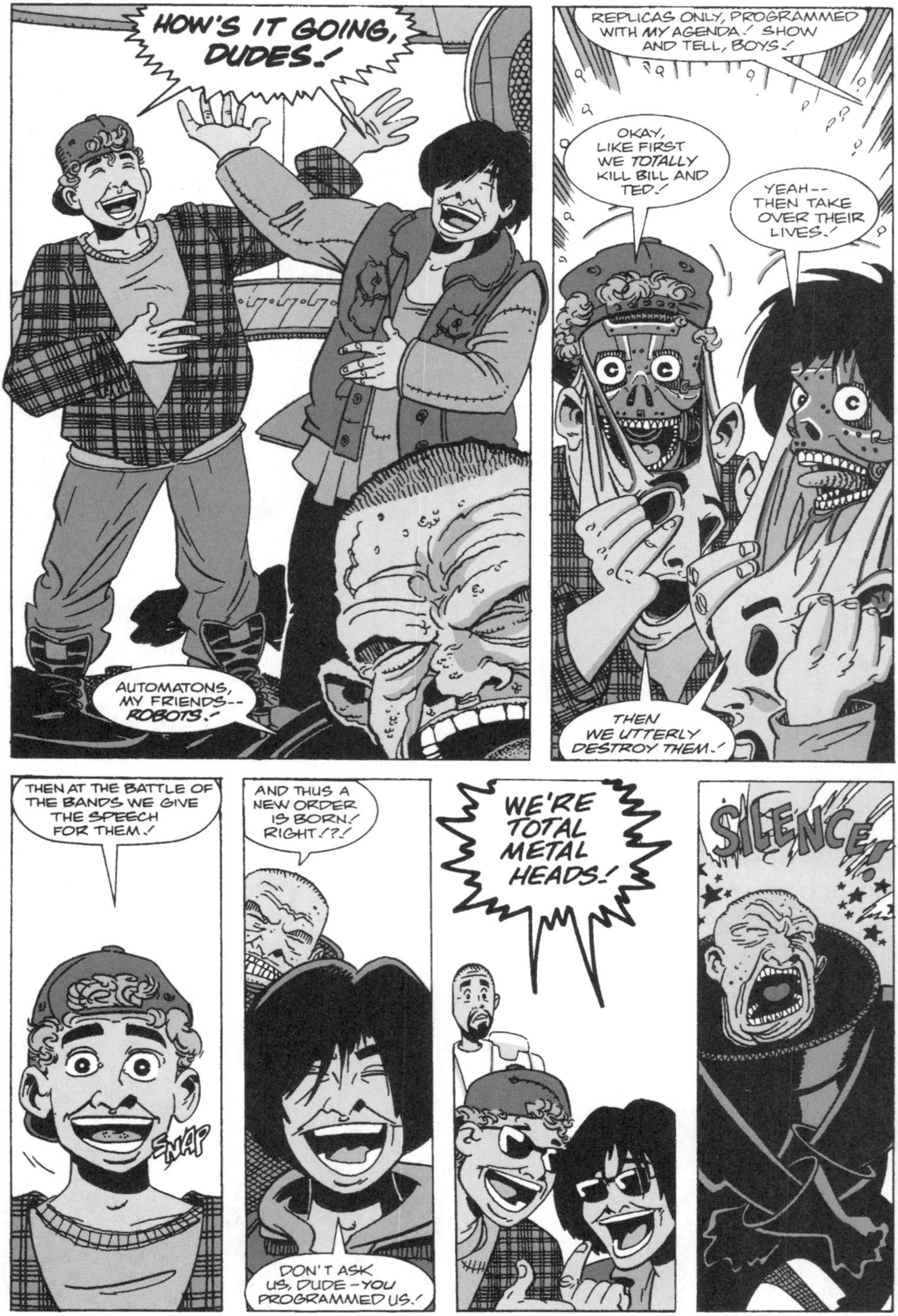
HOW'S IT GOING, DUDES!
AUTOMATONS, MY FRIENDS-- ROBOTS!
REPLICAS ONLY, PROGRAMMED WITH MY AGENDA! SHOW AND TELL, BOYS!
OKAY, LIKE FIRST WE TOTALLY KILL BILL AND TED!
YEAH-- THEN TAKE OVER THEIR LIVES!
THEN WE UTTERLY DESTROY THEM!
THEN AT THE BATTLE OF THE BANDS WE GIVE THE SPEECH FOR THEM!
SNAP
AND THUS A NEW ORDER IS BORN! RIGHT!?!
DON'T ASK US, DUDE - YOU PROGRAMMED US!
WE'RE TOTAL METAL HEADS!
SILENCE!

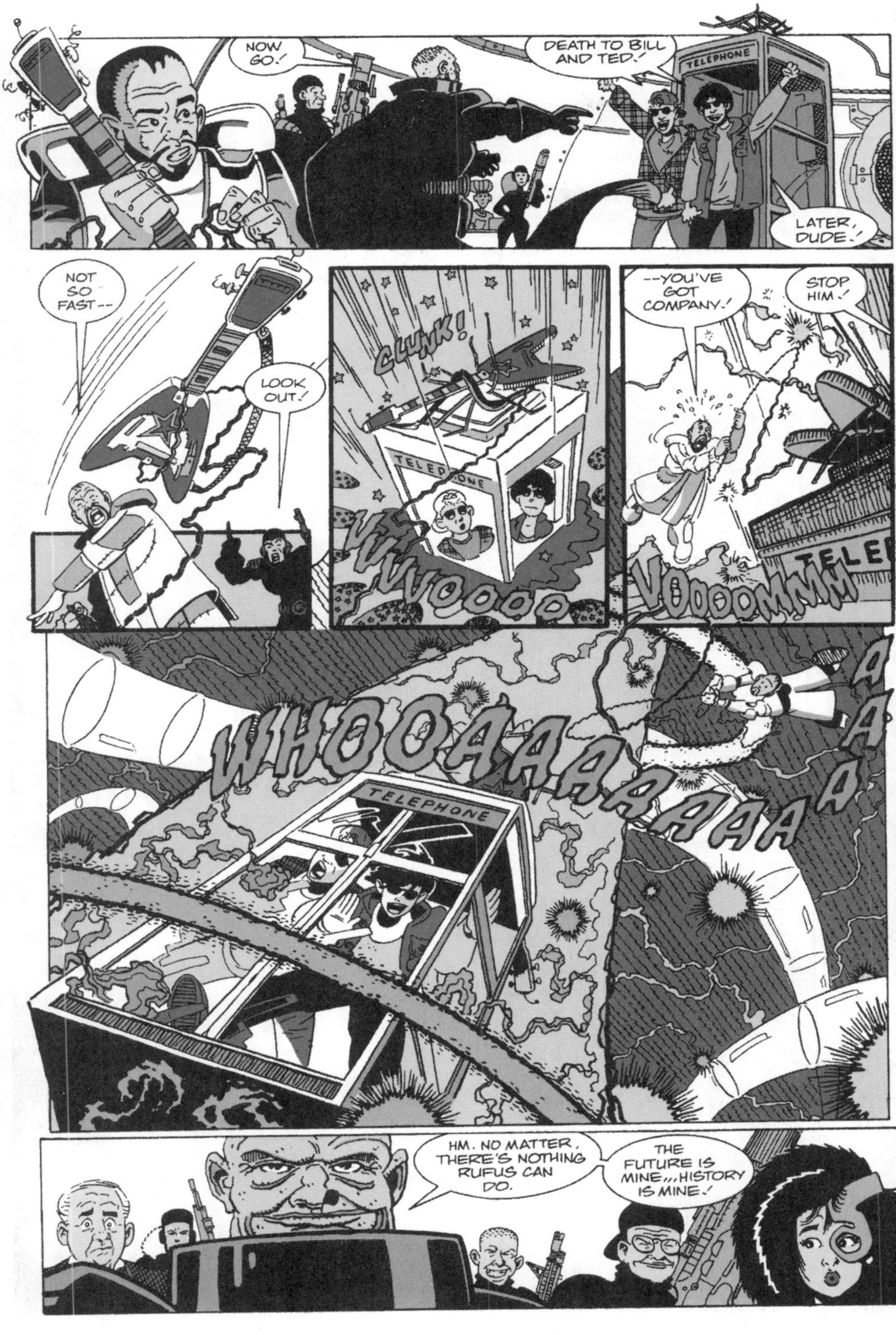
NOW GO.!
DEATH TO BILL AND TED.!
TELEPHONE
LATER, DUDE.!
NOT SO FAST--
LOOK OUT.!
CLUNK!
TELEPHONE
VVVVOOOOO
--YOU'VE GOT COMPANY.!
STOP HIM.!
VOOOOMMM
WHOOAAAAAAAAAAAA
TELEPHONE
HM. NO MATTER. THERE'S NOTHING RUFUS CAN DO.
THE FUTURE IS MINE,,, HISTORY IS MINE.!

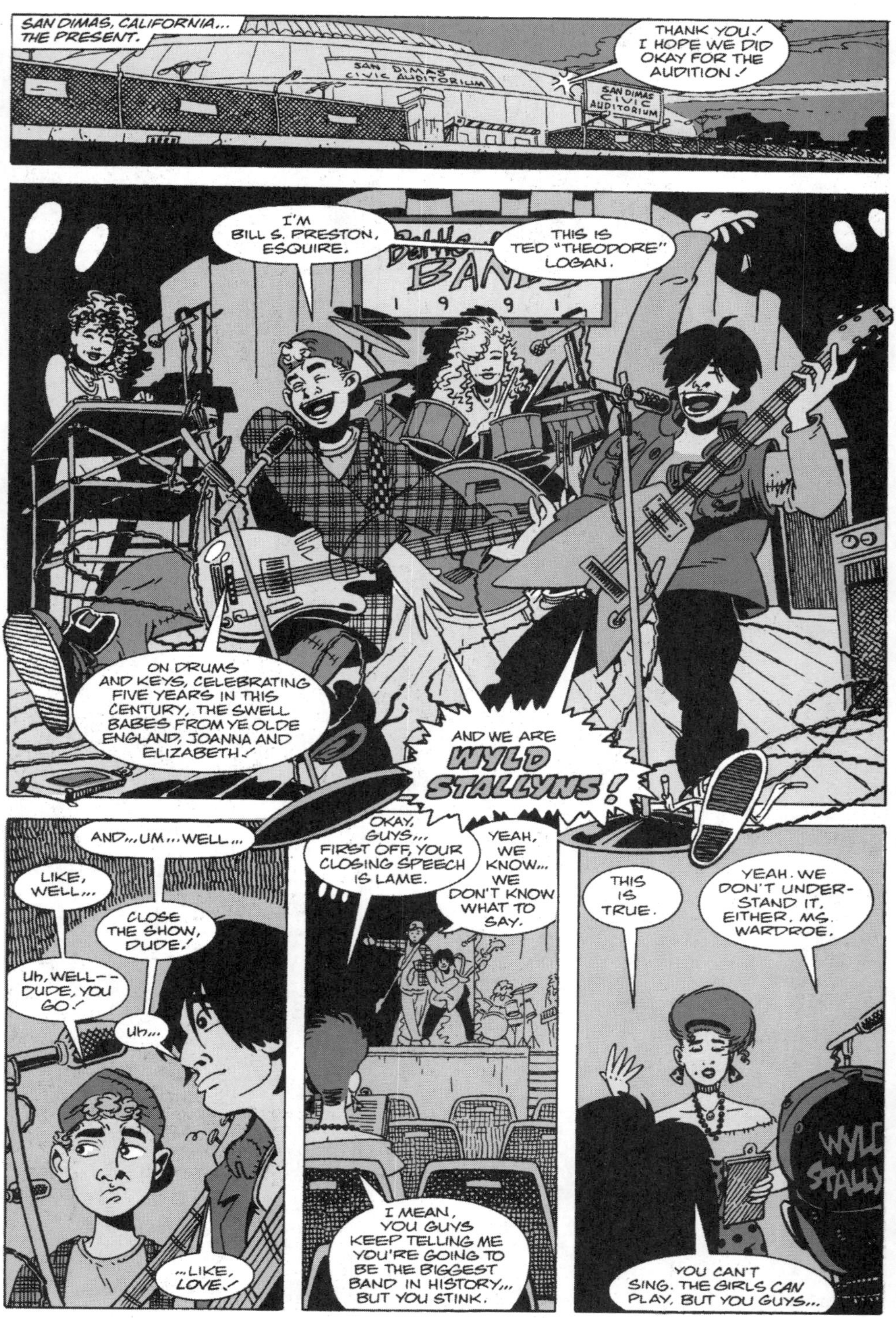
SAN DIMAS, CALIFORNIA... THE PRESENT.
SAN DIMAS CIVIC AUDITORIUM
THANK YOU! I HOPE WE DID OKAY FOR THE AUDITION!
I'M BILL S. PRESTON, ESQUIRE.
THIS IS TED "THEODORE" LOGAN.
BANDS 1991
ON DRUMS AND KEYS, CELEBRATING FIVE YEARS IN THIS CENTURY, THE SWELL BABES FROM YE OLDE ENGLAND, JOANNA AND ELIZABETH!
AND WE ARE WYLD STALLYNS!
AND... UM... WELL...
LIKE, WELL...
CLOSE THE SHOW, DUDE!
Uh, WELL-- DUDE, YOU GO!
Uh...
...LIKE, LOVE!
OKAY, GUYS... FIRST OFF, YOUR CLOSING SPEECH IS LAME.
YEAH, WE KNOW... WE DON'T KNOW WHAT TO SAY.
I MEAN, YOU GUYS KEEP TELLING ME YOU'RE GOING TO BE THE BIGGEST BAND IN HISTORY... BUT YOU STINK.
THIS IS TRUE.
YEAH. WE DON'T UNDER-STAND IT, EITHER, MS. WARDROE.
YOU CAN'T SING. THE GIRLS CAN PLAY, BUT YOU GUYS...

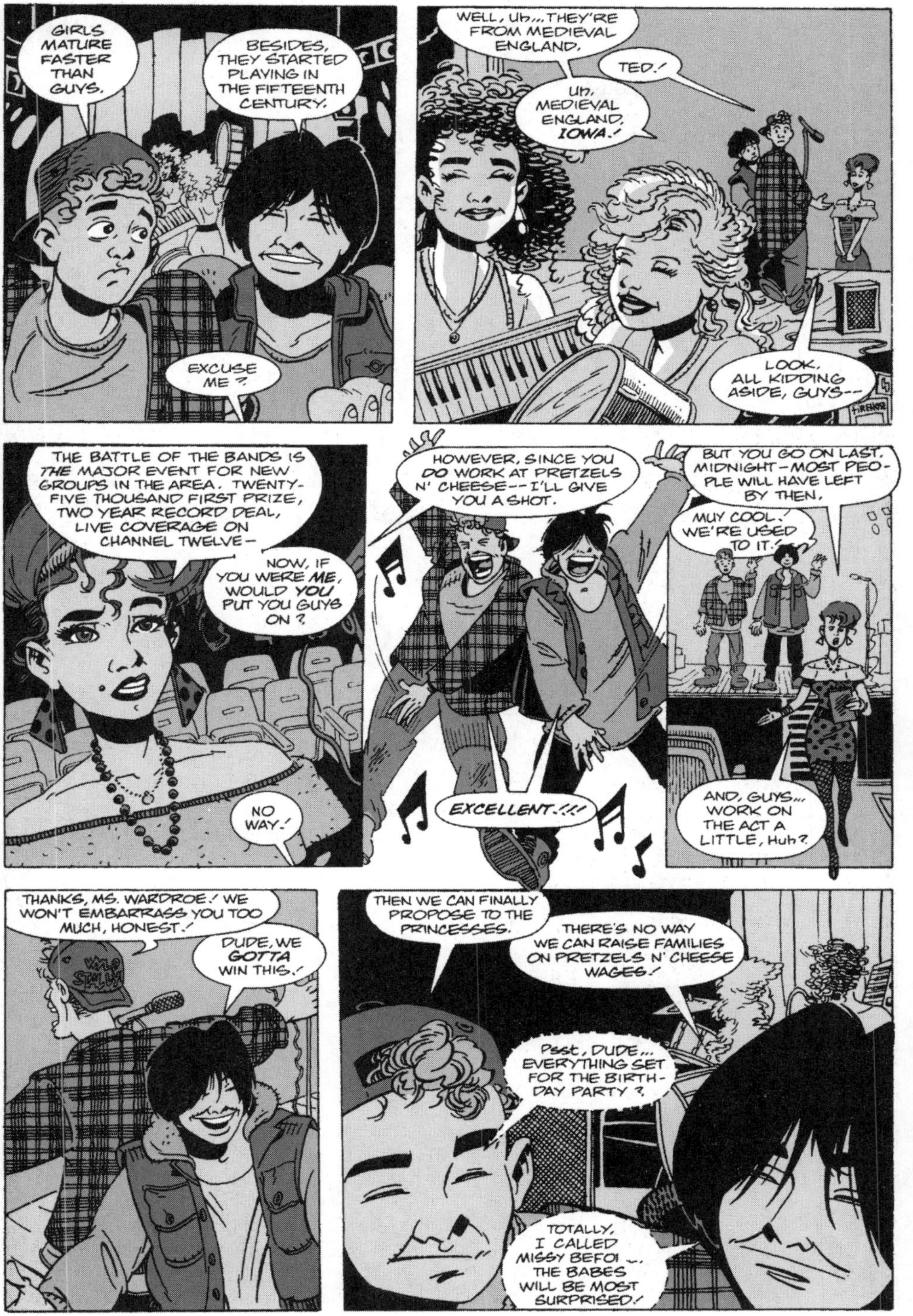
GIRLS MATURE FASTER THAN GUYS.
BESIDES, THEY STARTED PLAYING IN THE FIFTEENTH CENTURY.
EXCUSE ME ?
WELL, Uh... THEY'RE FROM MEDIEVAL ENGLAND.
TED!
Uh, MEDIEVAL ENGLAND, IOWA!
LOOK, ALL KIDDING ASIDE, GUYS--
THE BATTLE OF THE BANDS IS THE MAJOR EVENT FOR NEW GROUPS IN THE AREA. TWENTY-FIVE THOUSAND FIRST PRIZE, TWO YEAR RECORD DEAL, LIVE COVERAGE ON CHANNEL TWELVE-
NOW, IF YOU WERE ME, WOULD YOU PUT YOU GUYS ON ?
NO WAY!
HOWEVER, SINCE YOU DO WORK AT PRETZELS N' CHEESE-- I'LL GIVE YOU A SHOT.
EXCELLENT!!!
BUT YOU GO ON LAST. MIDNIGHT-MOST PEOPLE WILL HAVE LEFT BY THEN.
MUY COOL! WE'RE USED TO IT!
AND, GUYS... WORK ON THE ACT A LITTLE, Huh?
THANKS, MS. WARDROE! WE WON'T EMBARRASS YOU TOO MUCH, HONEST!
DUDE, WE GOTTA WIN THIS!
THEN WE CAN FINALLY PROPOSE TO THE PRINCESSES.
THERE'S NO WAY WE CAN RAISE FAMILIES ON PRETZELS N' CHEESE WAGES!
Psst, DUDE... EVERYTHING SET FOR THE BIRTH-DAY PARTY ?
TOTALLY, I CALLED MISSY BEFO... THE BABES WILL BE MOST SURPRISED!

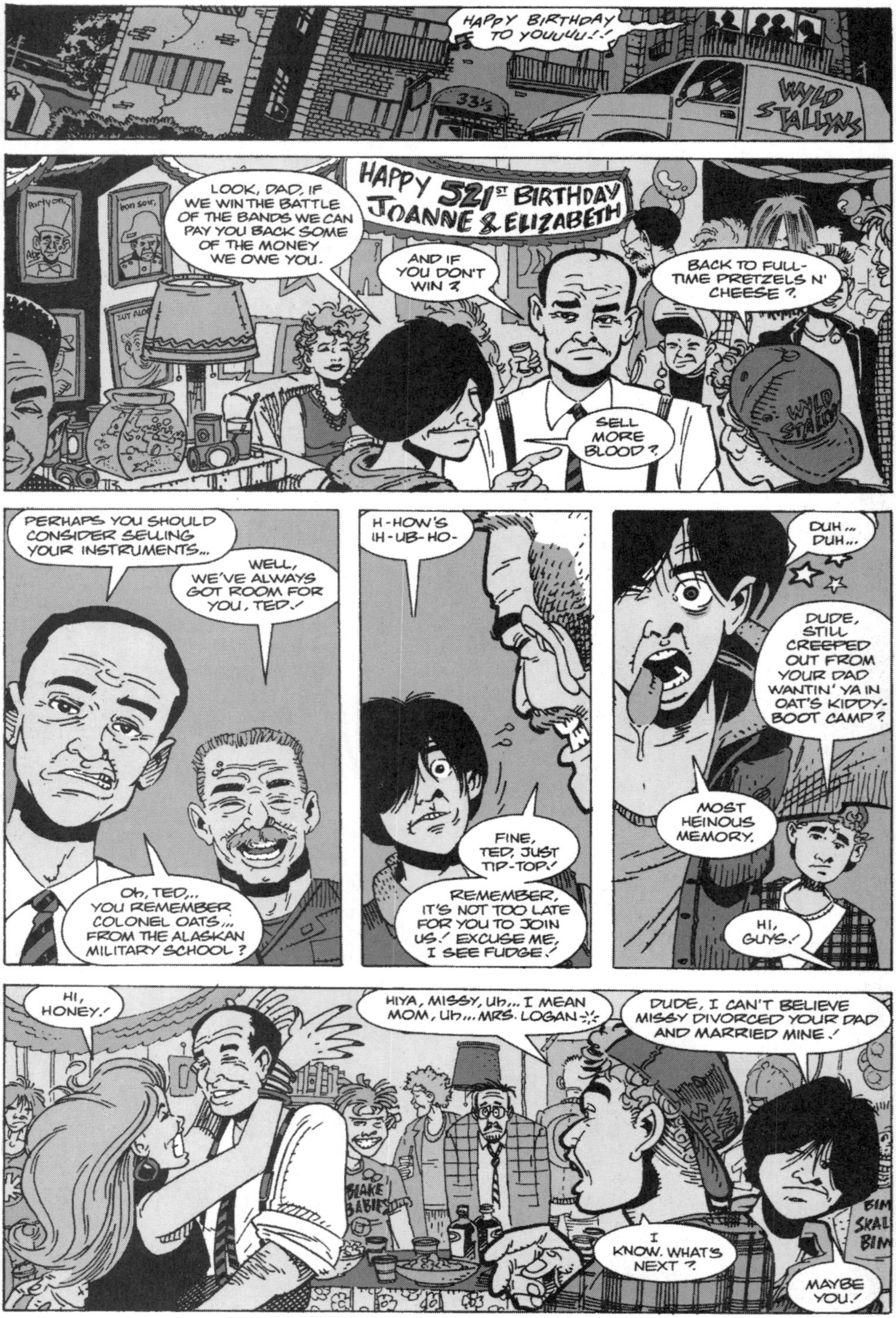
HAPPY BIRTHDAY TO YOUUUU!!
33½
WYLD STALLYNS
HAPPY 521ST BIRTHDAY JOANNE & ELIZABETH
LOOK, DAD, IF WE WIN THE BATTLE OF THE BANDS WE CAN PAY YOU BACK SOME OF THE MONEY WE OWE YOU.
AND IF YOU DON'T WIN ?
BACK TO FULL-TIME PRETZELS N' CHEESE ?
SELL MORE BLOOD ?
WYLD STALLYNS
PERHAPS YOU SHOULD CONSIDER SELLING YOUR INSTRUMENTS...
WELL, WE'VE ALWAYS GOT ROOM FOR YOU, TED!
Oh, TED,.. YOU REMEMBER COLONEL OATS... FROM THE ALASKAN MILITARY SCHOOL ?
H-HOW'S IH-UB-HO-
FINE, TED, JUST TIP-TOP!
REMEMBER, IT'S NOT TOO LATE FOR YOU TO JOIN US! EXCUSE ME, I SEE FUDGE!
DUH... DUH...
DUDE, STILL CREEPED OUT FROM YOUR DAD WANTIN' YA IN OAT'S KIDDY-BOOT CAMP ?
MOST HEINOUS MEMORY.
HI, GUYS!
HI, HONEY!
HIYA, MISSY, Uh... I MEAN MOM, Uh... MRS. LOGAN
DUDE, I CAN'T BELIEVE MISSY DIVORCED YOUR DAD AND MARRIED MINE!
BLAKE BABIES
I KNOW. WHAT'S NEXT ?
MAYBE YOU!

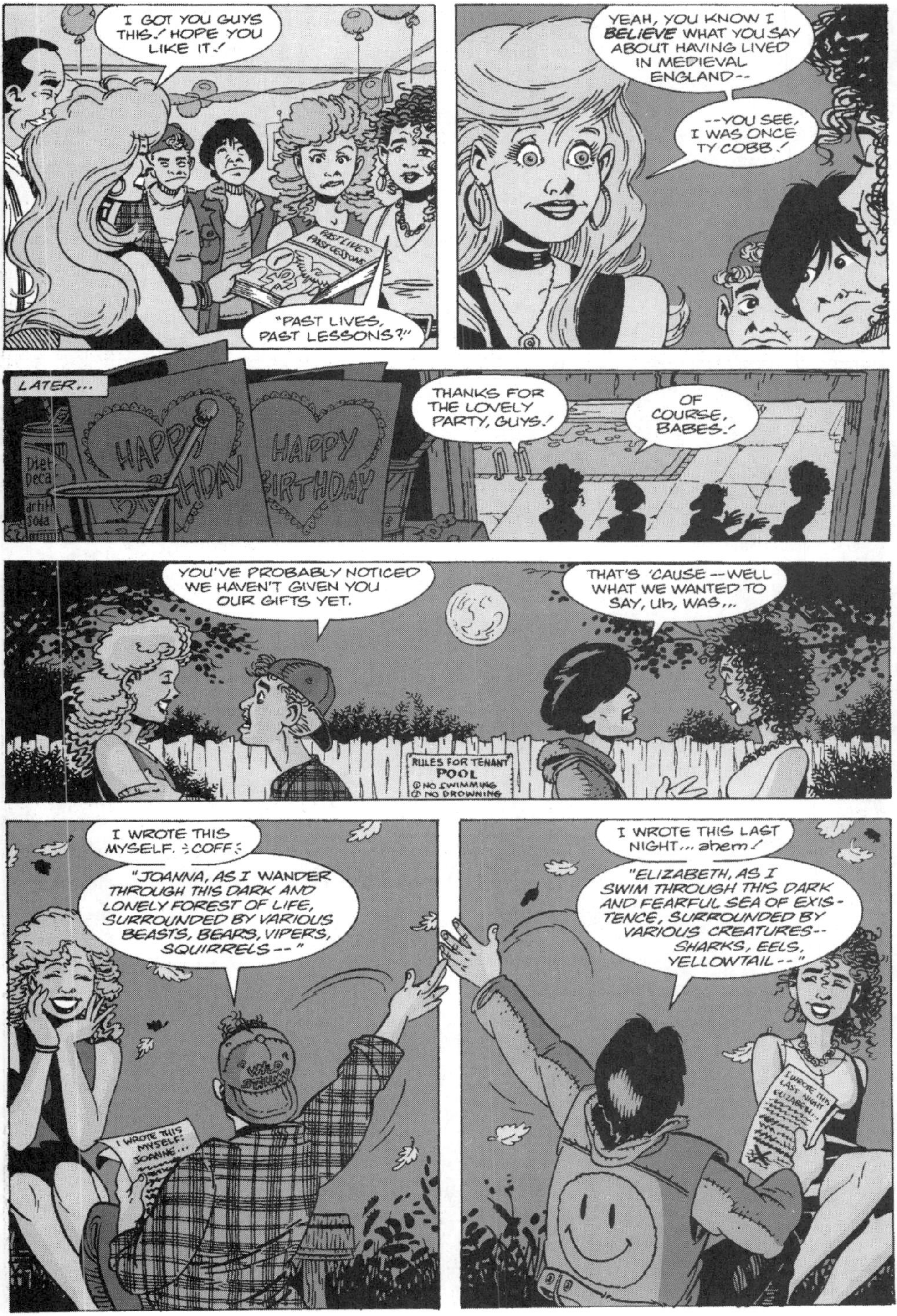
I GOT YOU GUYS THIS.! HOPE YOU LIKE IT.!
PAST LIVES PAST LESSONS
"PAST LIVES, PAST LESSONS?"
YEAH, YOU KNOW I BELIEVE WHAT YOU SAY ABOUT HAVING LIVED IN MEDIEVAL ENGLAND--
--YOU SEE, I WAS ONCE TY COBB.!
LATER...
HAPPY BIRTHDAY
HAPPY BIRTHDAY
Diet Deca artifi soda
THANKS FOR THE LOVELY PARTY, GUYS.!
OF COURSE, BABES.!
YOU'VE PROBABLY NOTICED WE HAVEN'T GIVEN YOU OUR GIFTS YET.
THAT'S 'CAUSE --WELL WHAT WE WANTED TO SAY, uh, WAS...
RULES FOR TENANT POOL
① NO SWIMMING
② NO DROWNING
I WROTE THIS MYSELF. COFF
"JOANNA, AS I WANDER THROUGH THIS DARK AND LONELY FOREST OF LIFE, SURROUNDED BY VARIOUS BEASTS, BEARS, VIPERS, SQUIRRELS --"
WILD STALLYNS
I WROTE THIS MYSELF: JOANNE...
I WROTE THIS LAST NIGHT... ahem!
"ELIZABETH, AS I SWIM THROUGH THIS DARK AND FEARFUL SEA OF EXIS-TENCE, SURROUNDED BY VARIOUS CREATURES-- SHARKS, EELS, YELLOWTAIL --"
I WROTE THIS LAST NIGHT ELIZABETH...

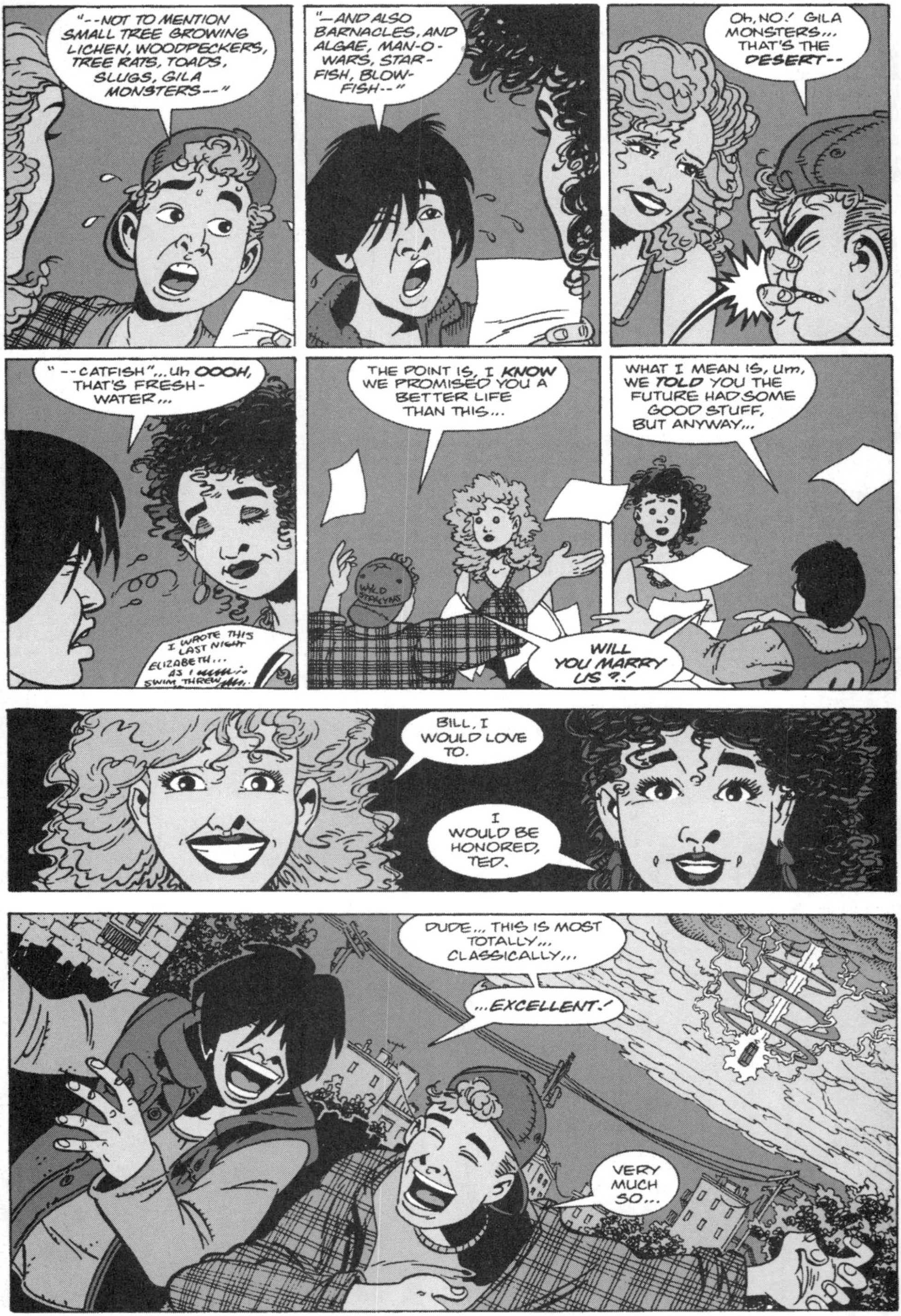
"--NOT TO MENTION SMALL TREE GROWING LICHEN, WOODPECKERS, TREE RATS, TOADS, SLUGS, GILA MONSTERS--"
"--AND ALSO BARNACLES, AND ALGAE, MAN-O-WARS, STAR-FISH, BLOW-FISH--"
Oh, NO! GILA MONSTERS... THAT'S THE DESERT--
"--CATFISH"... Uh OOOH, THAT'S FRESH-WATER...
I WROTE THIS LAST NIGHT ELIZABETH...
THE POINT IS, I KNOW WE PROMISED YOU A BETTER LIFE THAN THIS...
WHAT I MEAN IS, Um, WE TOLD YOU THE FUTURE HAD SOME GOOD STUFF, BUT ANYWAY...
WILL YOU MARRY US ?.!
BILL, I WOULD LOVE TO.
I WOULD BE HONORED, TED.
DUDE... THIS IS MOST TOTALLY... CLASSICALLY...
...EXCELLENT!
VERY MUCH SO...

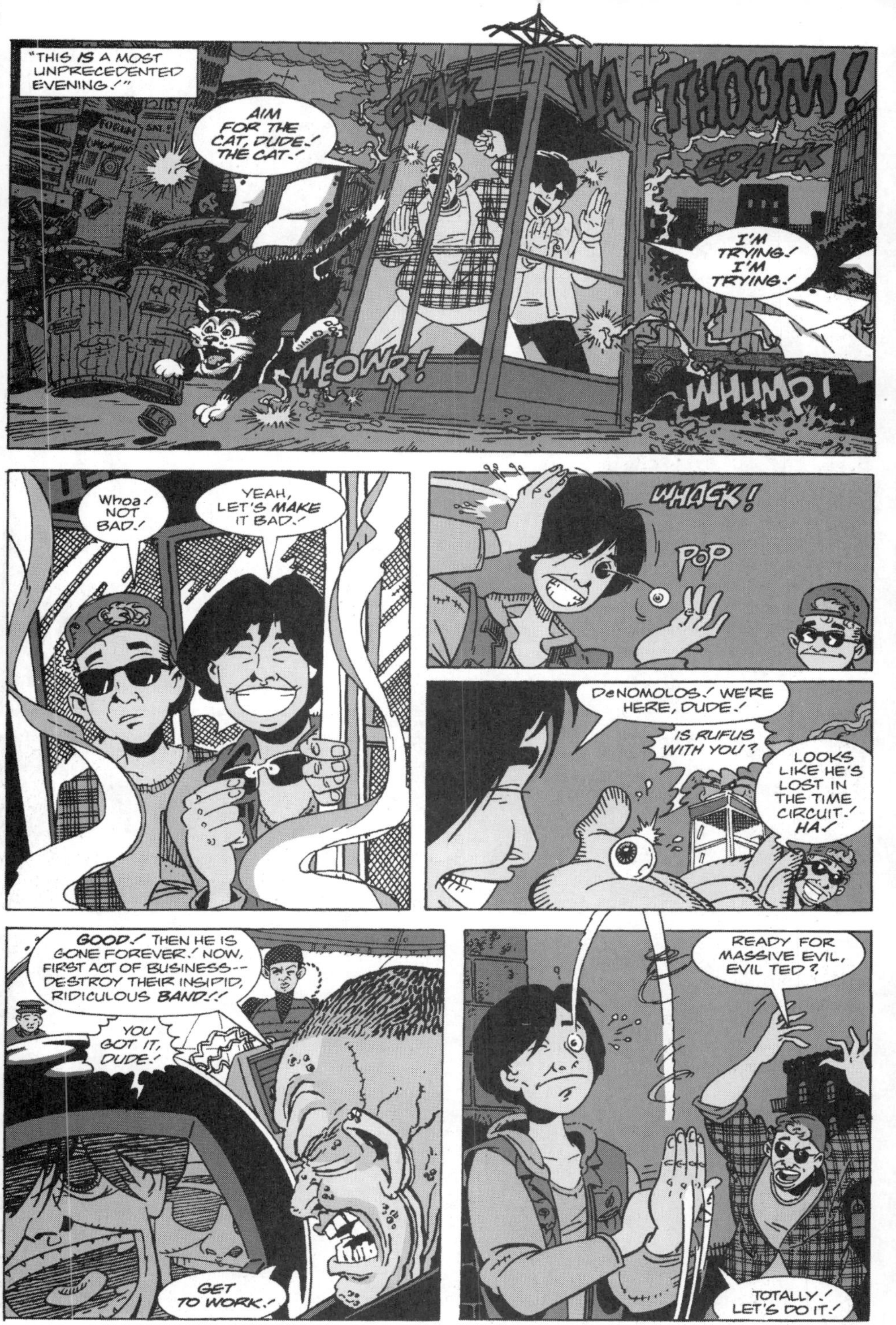
"THIS IS A MOST UNPRECEDENTED EVENING!"
CRACK
VA-THOOM!
AIM FOR THE CAT, DUDE! THE CAT!
CRACK
I'M TRYING! I'M TRYING!
MEOWR!
WHUMP!
Whoa! NOT BAD!
YEAH, LET'S MAKE IT BAD!
WHACK!
POP
DeNOMOLOS! WE'RE HERE, DUDE!
IS RUFUS WITH YOU?
LOOKS LIKE HE'S LOST IN THE TIME CIRCUIT! HA!
GOOD! THEN HE IS GONE FOREVER! NOW, FIRST ACT OF BUSINESS-- DESTROY THEIR INSIPID, RIDICULOUS BAND!!
YOU GOT IT, DUDE!
GET TO WORK!
READY FOR MASSIVE EVIL, EVIL TED?
TOTALLY! LET'S DO IT!

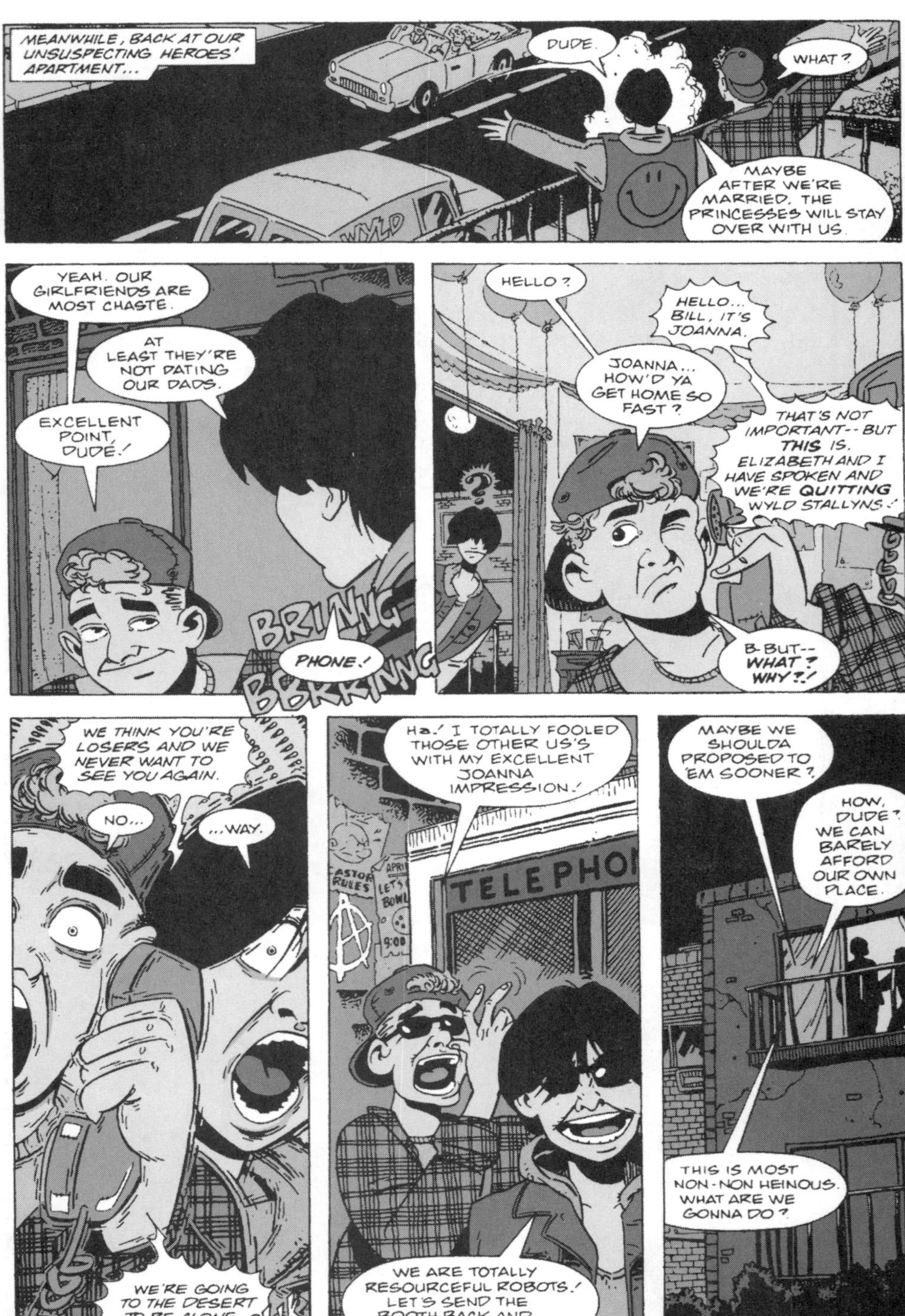
MEANWHILE, BACK AT OUR UNSUSPECTING HEROES' APARTMENT...
DUDE.
WHAT?
MAYBE AFTER WE'RE MARRIED, THE PRINCESSES WILL STAY OVER WITH US.
YEAH. OUR GIRLFRIENDS ARE MOST CHASTE.
AT LEAST THEY'RE NOT DATING OUR DADS.
EXCELLENT POINT, DUDE!
BRINNG
PHONE!
BBRRINNG
HELLO?
HELLO... BILL, IT'S JOANNA.
JOANNA... HOW'D YA GET HOME SO FAST?
THAT'S NOT IMPORTANT-- BUT THIS IS. ELIZABETH AND I HAVE SPOKEN AND WE'RE QUITTING WYLD STALLYNS!
B-BUT-- WHAT? WHY?!
WE THINK YOU'RE LOSERS AND WE NEVER WANT TO SEE YOU AGAIN.
NO...
...WAY.
WE'RE GOING TO THE DESERT TO BE ALONE. GOODBYE.
CLIK
Ha! I TOTALLY FOOLED THOSE OTHER US'S WITH MY EXCELLENT JOANNA IMPRESSION!
TELEPHO
WE ARE TOTALLY RESOURCEFUL ROBOTS! LET'S SEND THE BOOTH BACK AND START... PHASE TWO.
MAYBE WE SHOULDA PROPOSED TO 'EM SOONER?
HOW, DUDE? WE CAN BARELY AFFORD OUR OWN PLACE.
THIS IS MOST NON-NON HEINOUS. WHAT ARE WE GONNA DO?

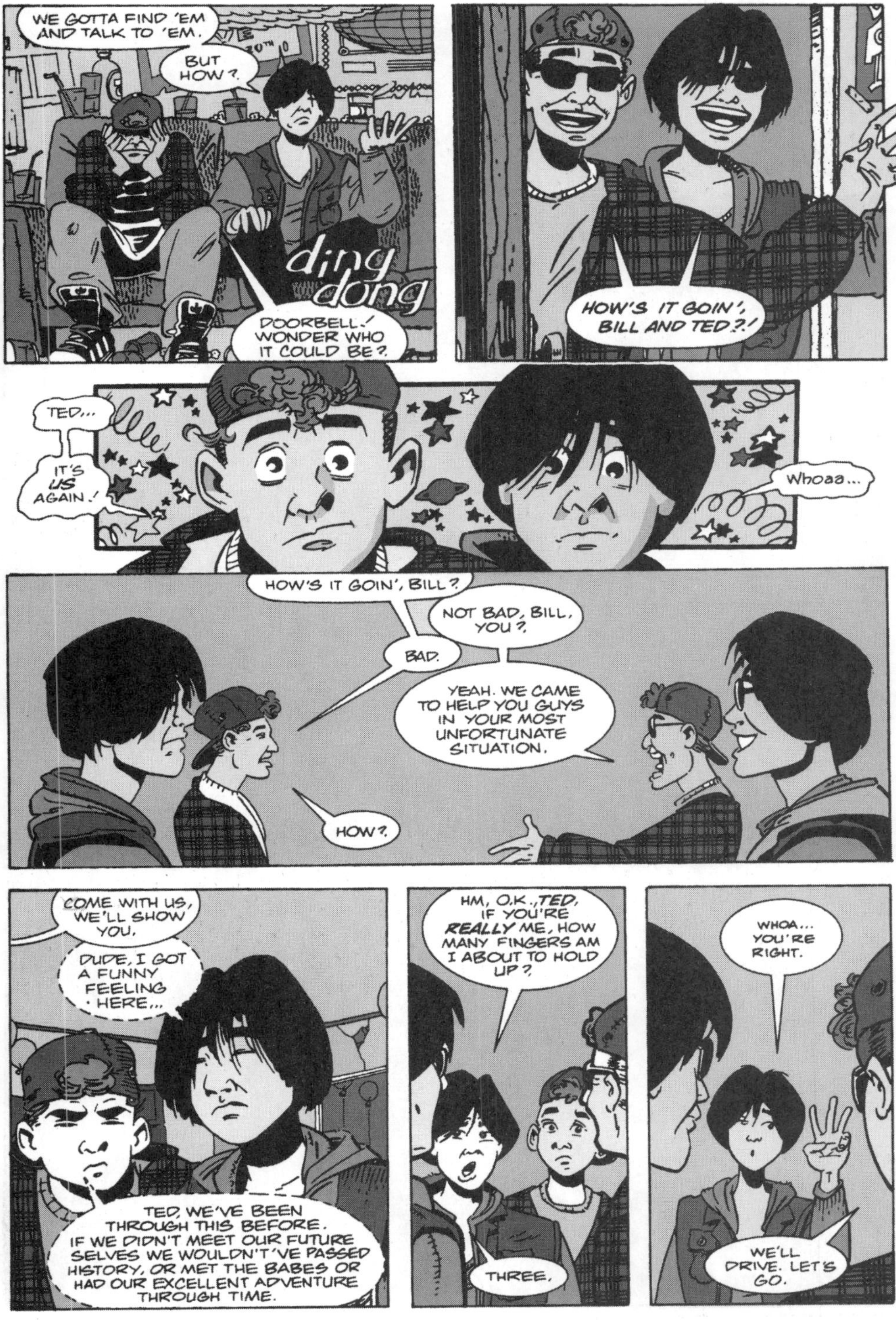
WE GOTTA FIND 'EM AND TALK TO 'EM.
BUT HOW ?.
ding dong
DOORBELL.! WONDER WHO IT COULD BE ?.
HOW'S IT GOIN', BILL AND TED ?.!
TED,...
IT'S US AGAIN.!
Whoaa...
HOW'S IT GOIN', BILL?
NOT BAD, BILL, YOU ?.
BAD.
YEAH. WE CAME TO HELP YOU GUYS IN YOUR MOST UNFORTUNATE SITUATION.
HOW ?.
COME WITH US, WE'LL SHOW YOU.
DUDE, I GOT A FUNNY FEELING HERE...
TED, WE'VE BEEN THROUGH THIS BEFORE. IF WE DIDN'T MEET OUR FUTURE SELVES WE WOULDN'T'VE PASSED HISTORY, OR MET THE BABES OR HAD OUR EXCELLENT ADVENTURE THROUGH TIME.
HM, O.K., TED, IF YOU'RE REALLY ME, HOW MANY FINGERS AM I ABOUT TO HOLD UP ?.
THREE.
WHOA... YOU'RE RIGHT.
WE'LL DRIVE. LET'S GO.

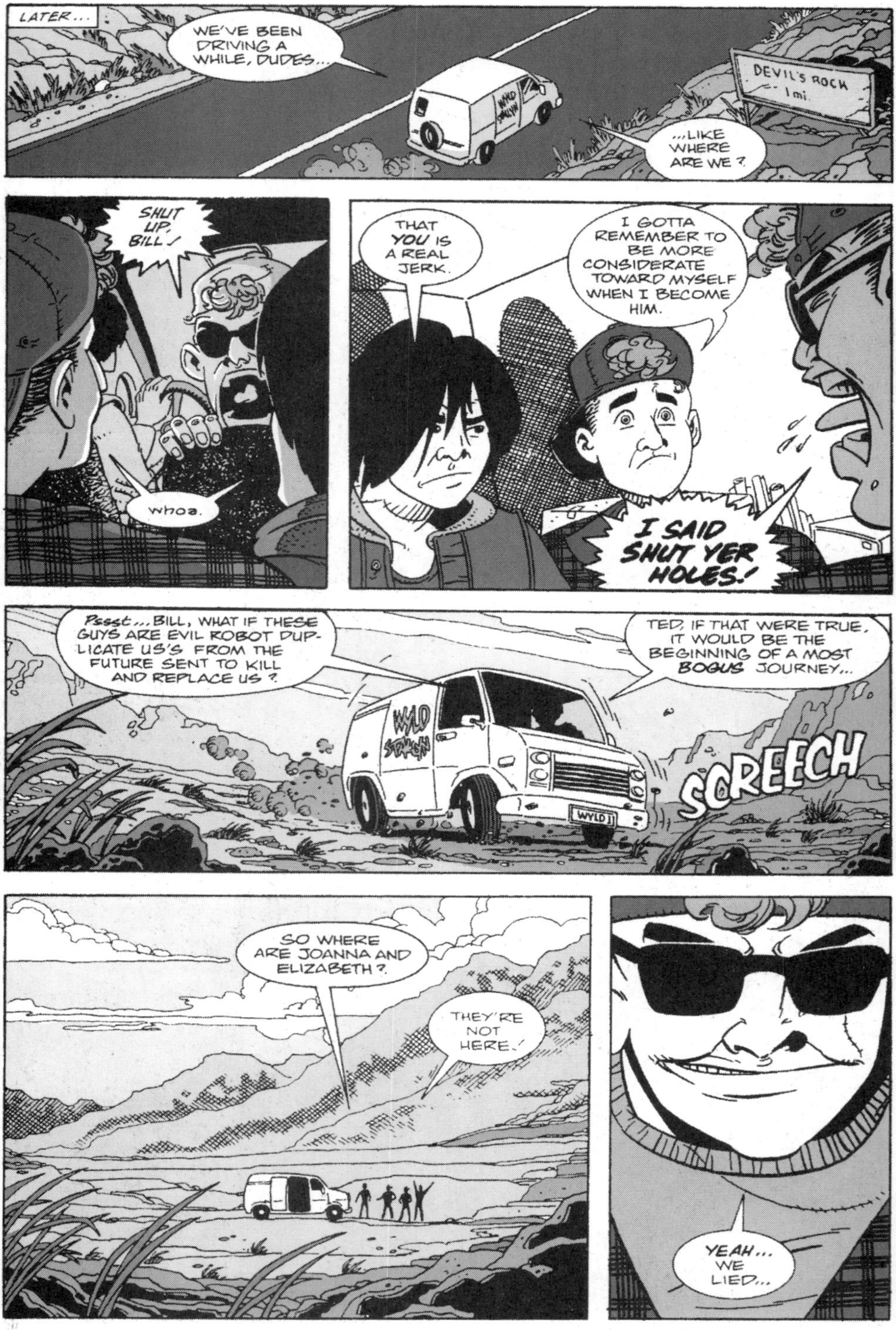
LATER...
WE'VE BEEN DRIVING A WHILE, DUDES...
DEVIL'S ROCK 1 mi.
...LIKE WHERE ARE WE?
SHUT UP, BILL!
whoa.
THAT YOU IS A REAL JERK.
I GOTTA REMEMBER TO BE MORE CONSIDERATE TOWARD MYSELF WHEN I BECOME HIM.
I SAID SHUT YER HOLES!
Pssst... BILL, WHAT IF THESE GUYS ARE EVIL ROBOT DUPLICATE US'S FROM THE FUTURE SENT TO KILL AND REPLACE US?
TED, IF THAT WERE TRUE, IT WOULD BE THE BEGINNING OF A MOST BOGUS JOURNEY...
SCREECH
SO WHERE ARE JOANNA AND ELIZABETH?
THEY'RE NOT HERE!
YEAH... WE LIED...

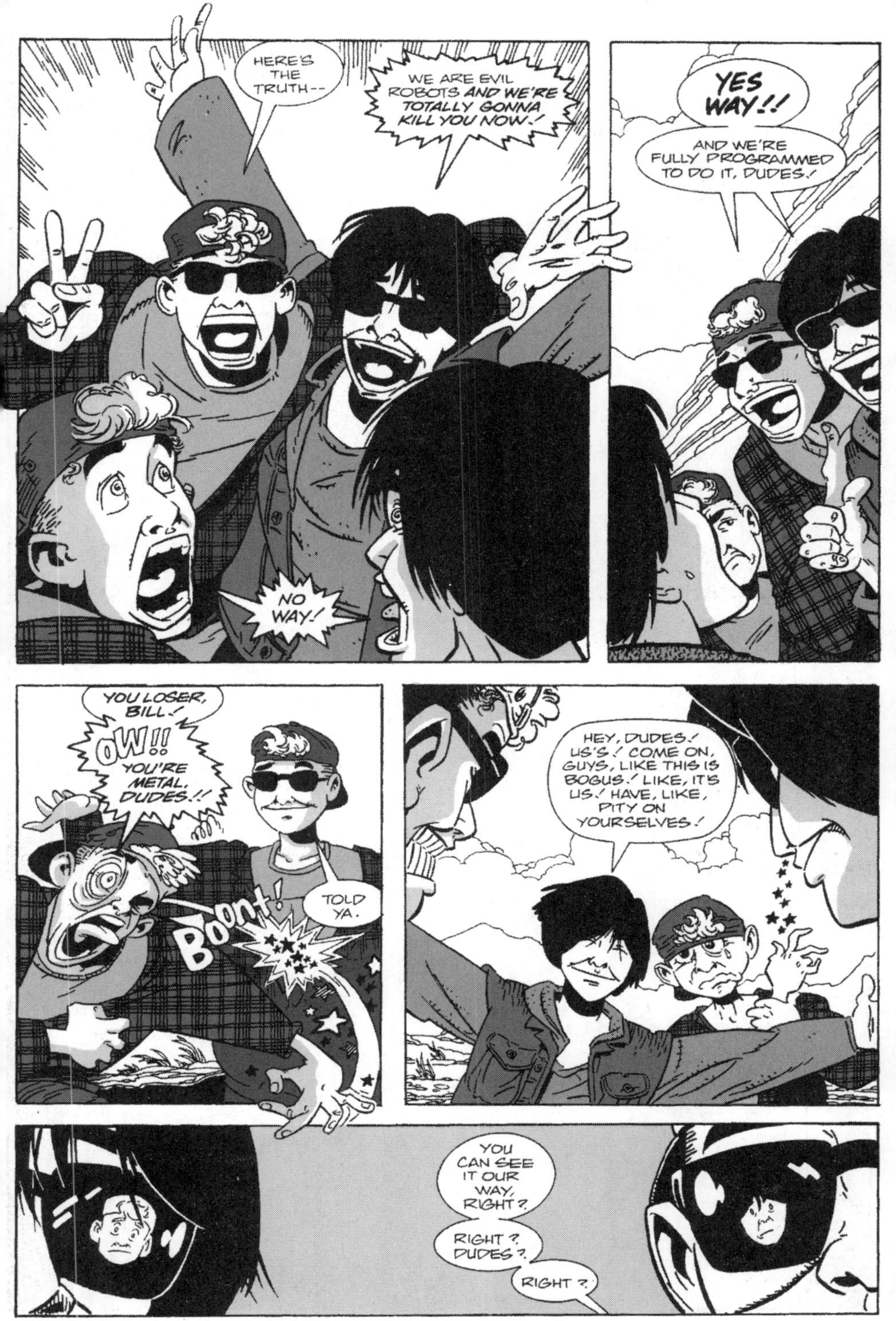
HERE'S THE TRUTH--
WE ARE EVIL ROBOTS AND WE'RE TOTALLY GONNA KILL YOU NOW!
NO WAY!
YES WAY!!
AND WE'RE FULLY PROGRAMMED TO DO IT, DUDES!
YOU LOSER, BILL!
OW!!
YOU'RE METAL, DUDES!!
BOONT!
TOLD YA.
HEY, DUDES! US'S! COME ON, GUYS, LIKE THIS IS BOGUS! LIKE, IT'S US! HAVE, LIKE, PITY ON YOURSELVES!
YOU CAN SEE IT OUR WAY, RIGHT?
RIGHT? DUDES?
RIGHT?

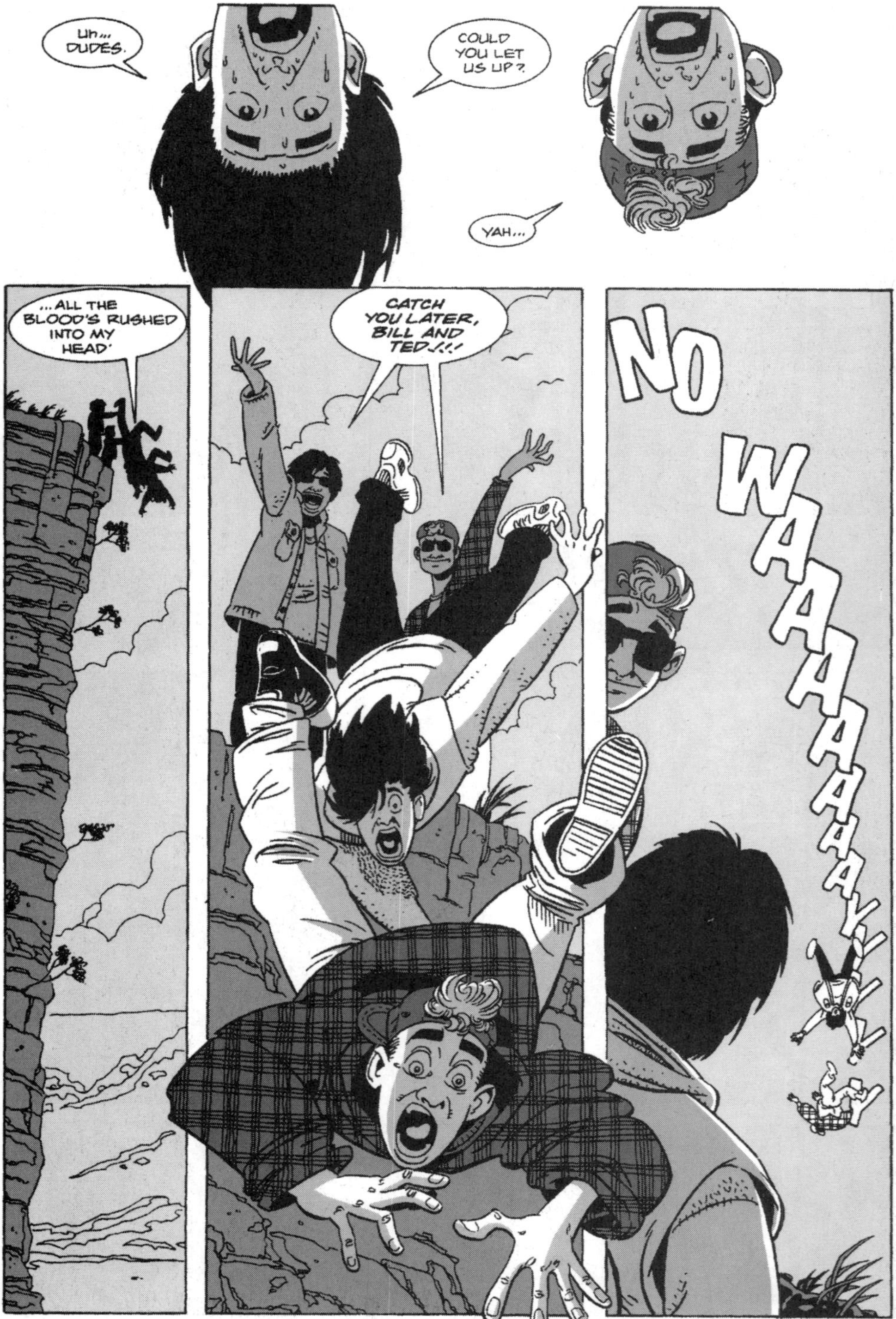
UH... DUDES.
COULD YOU LET US UP?
YAH...
...ALL THE BLOOD'S RUSHED INTO MY HEAD!
CATCH YOU LATER, BILL AND TED!!!
NO WAAAAAAAAY!

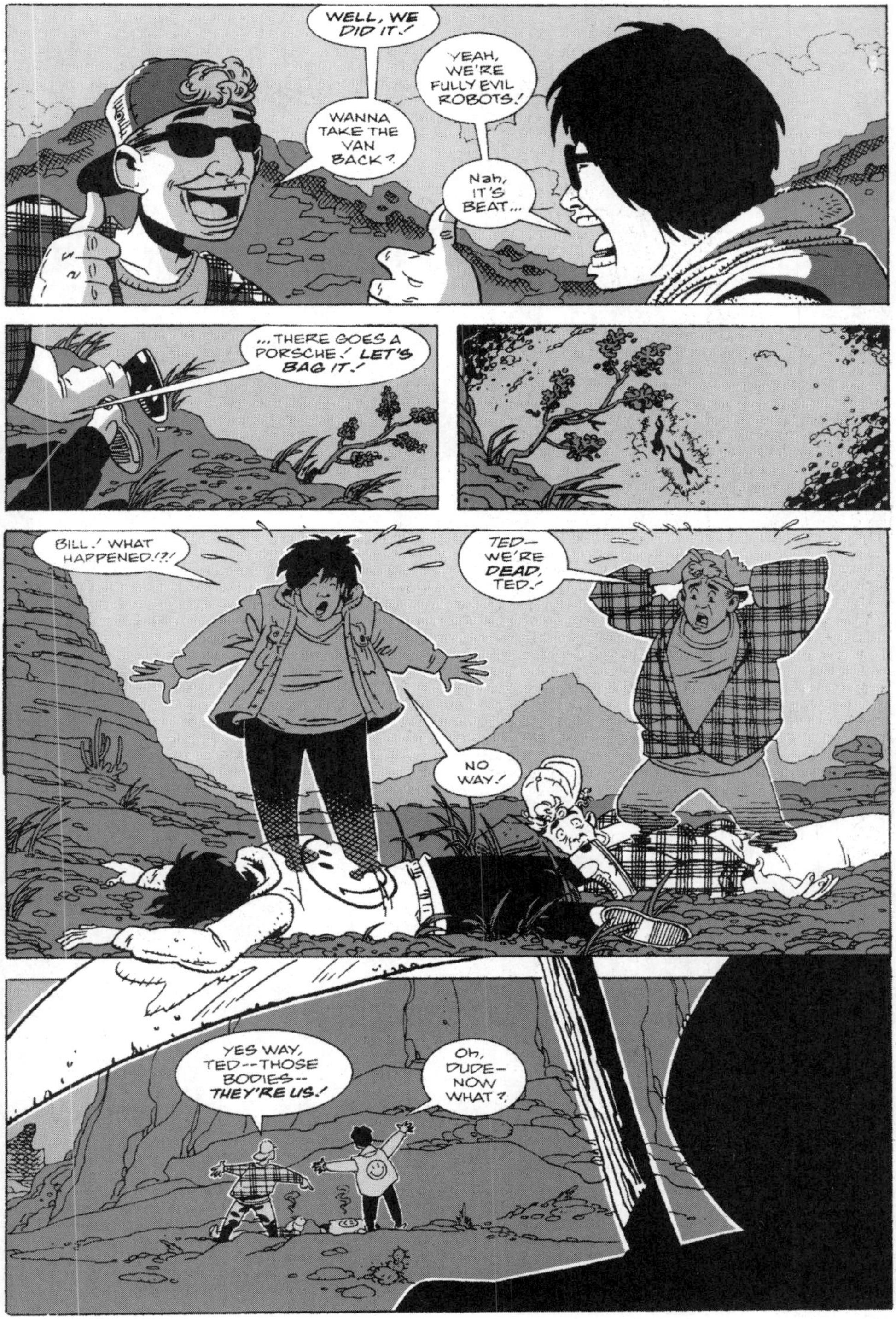
WELL, WE DID IT!
WANNA TAKE THE VAN BACK?
YEAH, WE'RE FULLY EVIL ROBOTS!
Nah, IT'S BEAT...
...THERE GOES A PORSCHE! LET'S BAG IT!
BILL! WHAT HAPPENED!?!
TED— WE'RE DEAD, TED!
NO WAY!
YES WAY, TED--THOSE BODIES-- THEY'RE US!
Oh, DUDE— NOW WHAT?

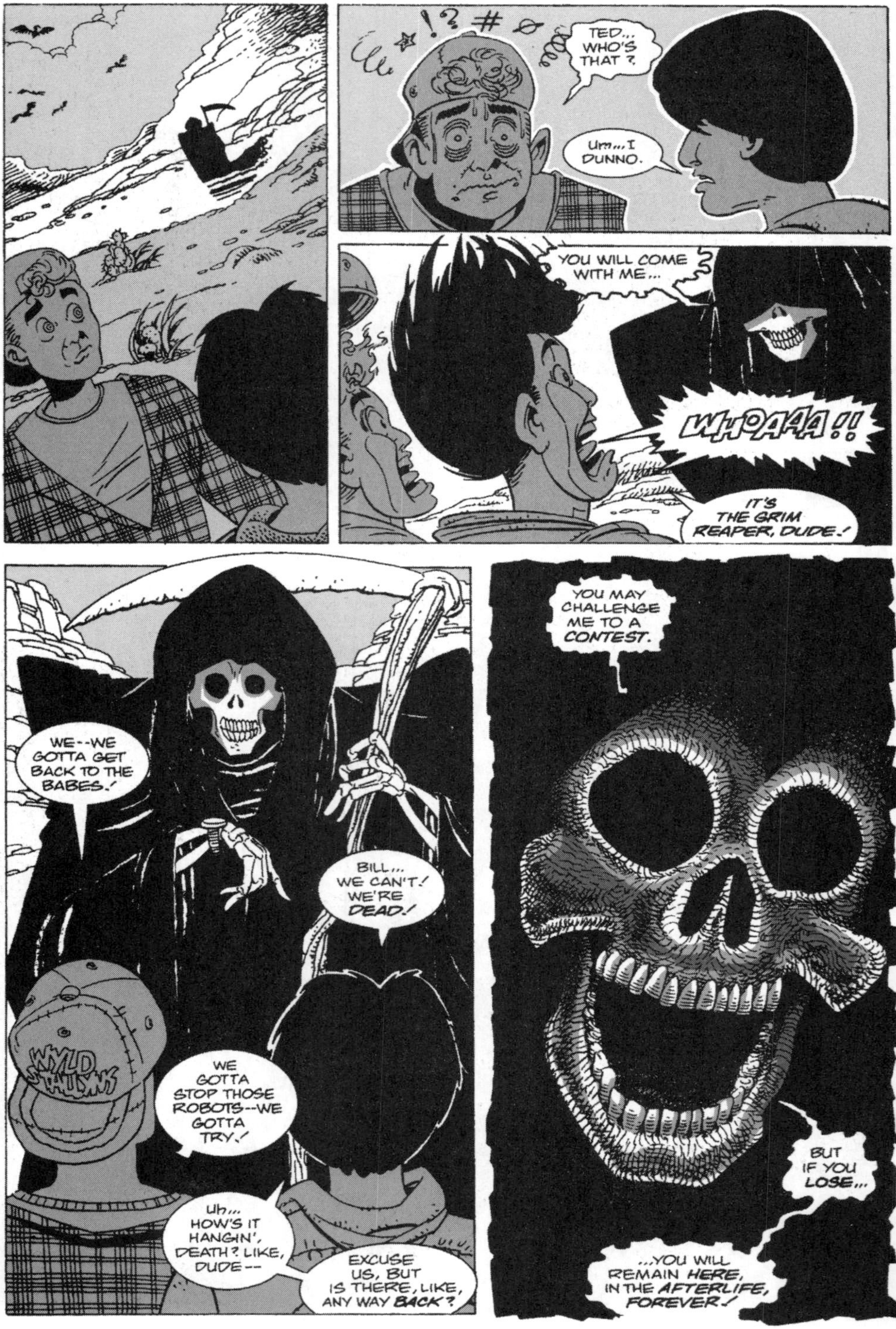
TED... WHO'S THAT ?
Um... I DUNNO.
YOU WILL COME WITH ME...
WHOAAA !!
IT'S THE GRIM REAPER, DUDE !
WE--WE GOTTA GET BACK TO THE BABES !
BILL... WE CAN'T! WE'RE DEAD!
WYLD STALLYNS
WE GOTTA STOP THOSE ROBOTS--WE GOTTA TRY !
Uh... HOW'S IT HANGIN', DEATH? LIKE, DUDE--
EXCUSE US, BUT IS THERE, LIKE, ANY WAY BACK ?
YOU MAY CHALLENGE ME TO A CONTEST.
BUT IF YOU LOSE...
...YOU WILL REMAIN HERE, IN THE AFTERLIFE, FOREVER !

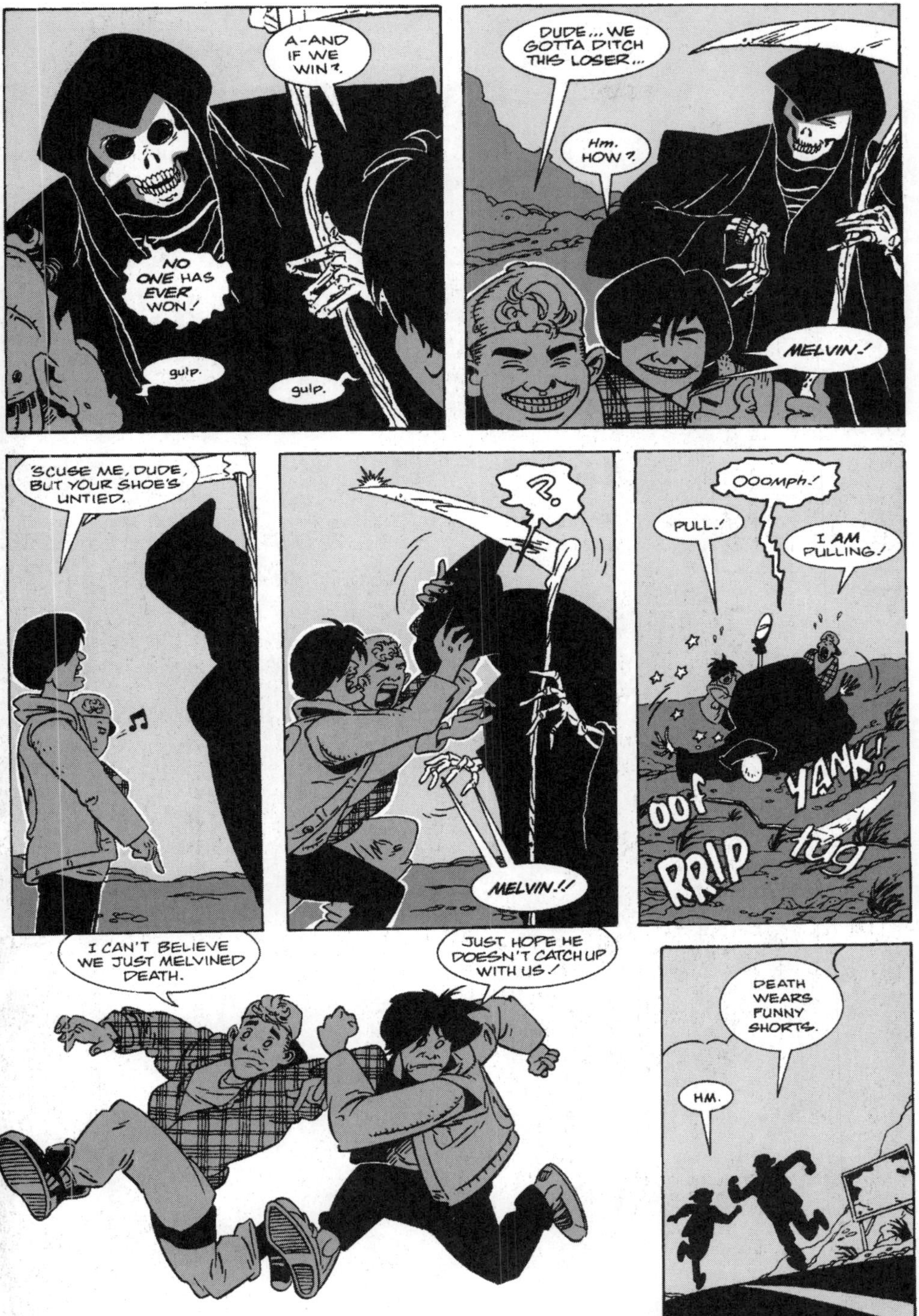
A-AND IF WE WIN?
NO ONE HAS EVER WON!
gulp.
gulp.
DUDE... WE GOTTA DITCH THIS LOSER...
Hm. HOW?
MELVIN!
'SCUSE ME, DUDE, BUT YOUR SHOE'S UNTIED.
?
MELVIN!!
Ooomph!
PULL!
I AM PULLING!
YANK!
oof
RRIP
tug
I CAN'T BELIEVE WE JUST MELVINED DEATH.
JUST HOPE HE DOESN'T CATCH UP WITH US!
DEATH WEARS FUNNY SHORTS.
HM.

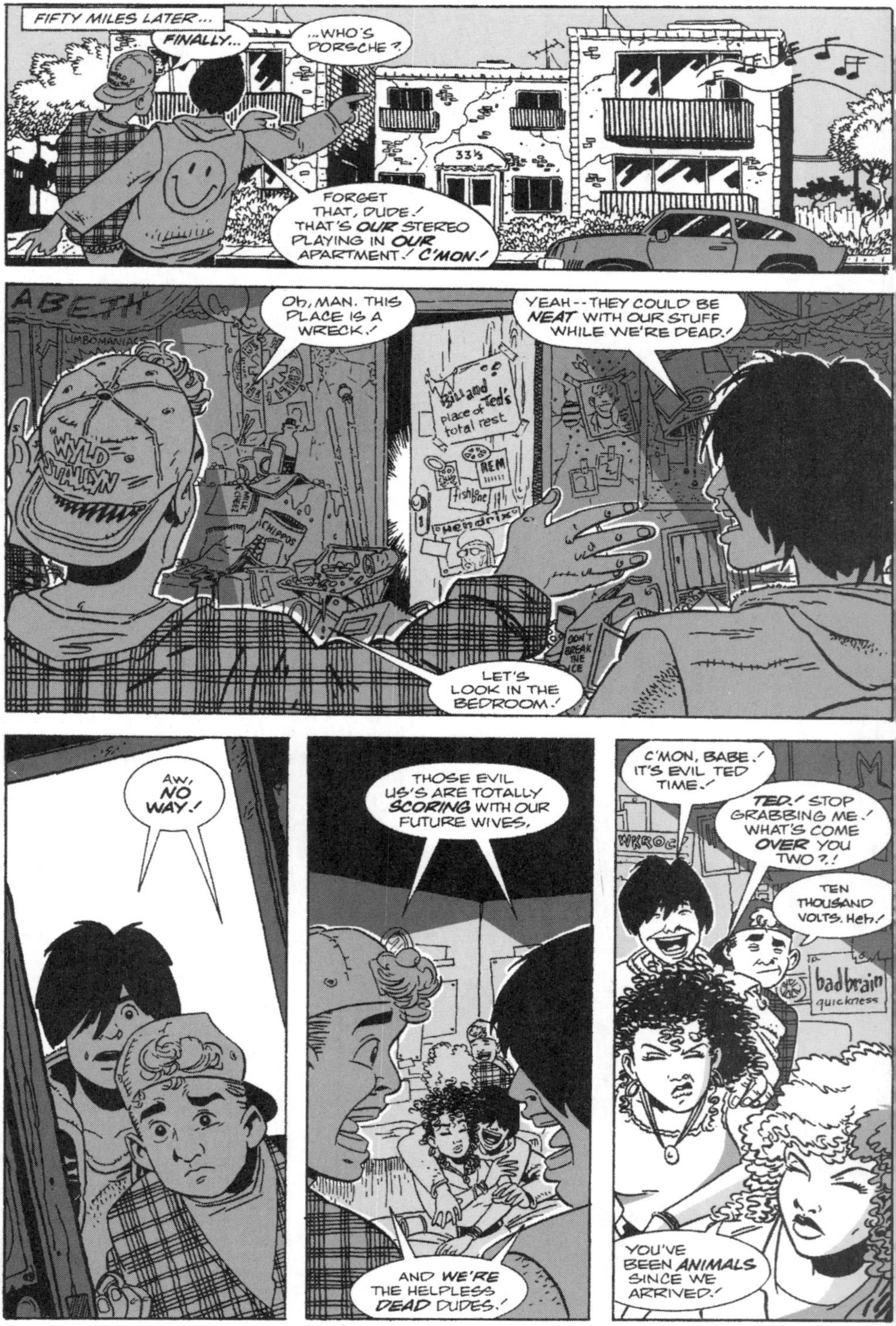
FIFTY MILES LATER...
FINALLY...
...WHO'S PORSCHE?.
FORGET THAT, DUDE! THAT'S OUR STEREO PLAYING IN OUR APARTMENT! C'MON!
Oh, MAN. THIS PLACE IS A WRECK!
YEAH--THEY COULD BE NEAT WITH OUR STUFF WHILE WE'RE DEAD!
Bill and Ted's place of total rest
REM
Hendrix
DON'T BREAK THE ICE
LET'S LOOK IN THE BEDROOM!
AW, NO WAY!
THOSE EVIL US'S ARE TOTALLY SCORING WITH OUR FUTURE WIVES,
AND WE'RE THE HELPLESS DEAD DUDES!
C'MON, BABE! IT'S EVIL TED TIME!
TED! STOP GRABBING ME! WHAT'S COME OVER YOU TWO?!
TEN THOUSAND VOLTS. Heh!
badbrain quickness
YOU'VE BEEN ANIMALS SINCE WE ARRIVED!

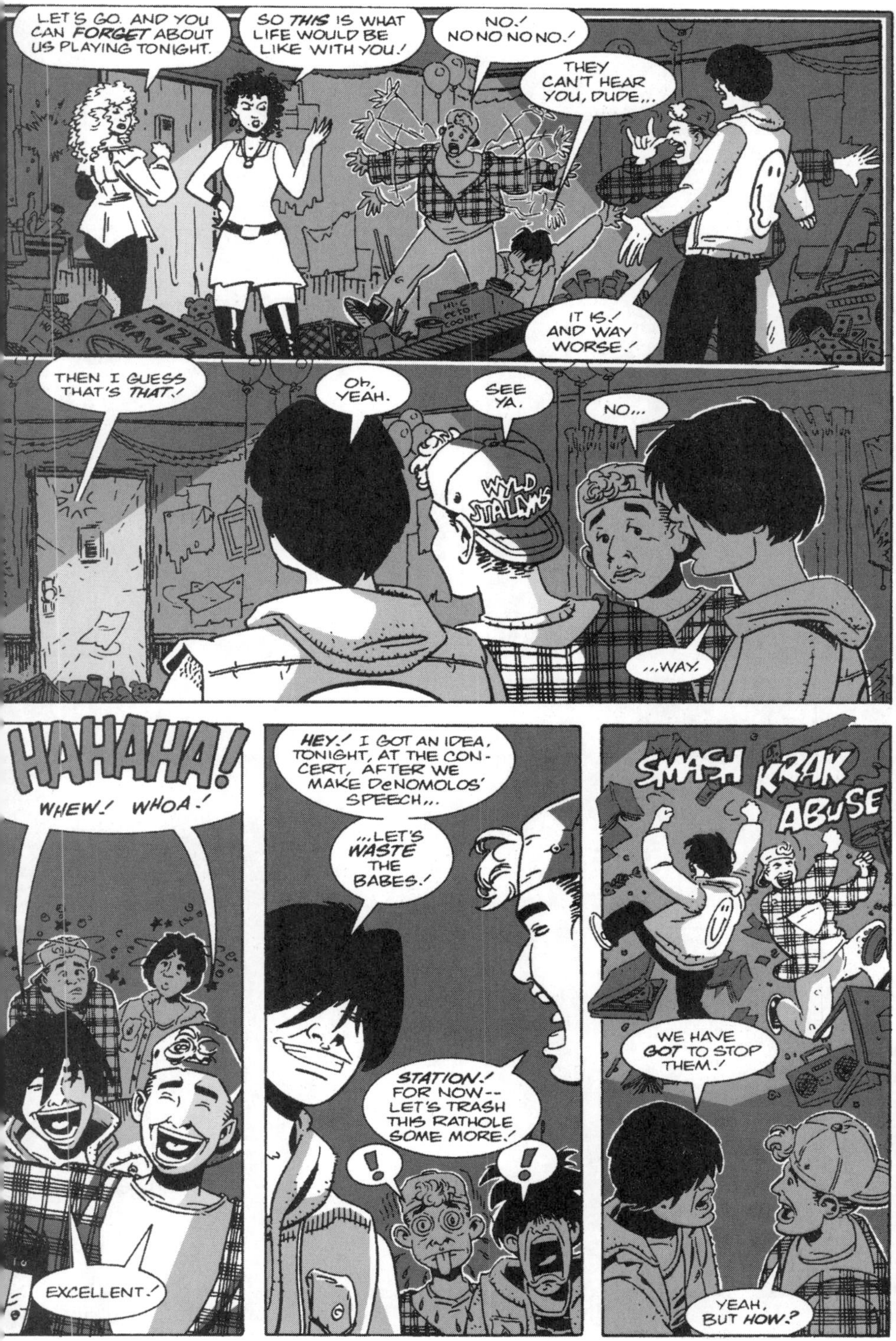
LET'S GO. AND YOU CAN FORGET ABOUT US PLAYING TONIGHT.
SO THIS IS WHAT LIFE WOULD BE LIKE WITH YOU.!
NO.! NO NO NO NO.!
THEY CAN'T HEAR YOU, DUDE...
IT IS.! AND WAY WORSE.!
THEN I GUESS THAT'S THAT.!
Oh, YEAH.
SEE YA.
NO...
...WAY.
WYLD STALLYNS
HAHAHA!
WHEW.! WHOA.!
EXCELLENT.!
HEY.! I GOT AN IDEA. TONIGHT, AT THE CON-CERT, AFTER WE MAKE DeNOMOLOS' SPEECH...
...LET'S WASTE THE BABES.!
STATION.! FOR NOW-- LET'S TRASH THIS RATHOLE SOME MORE.!
!
!
SMASH KRAK ABUSE
WE HAVE GOT TO STOP THEM.!
YEAH, BUT HOW?

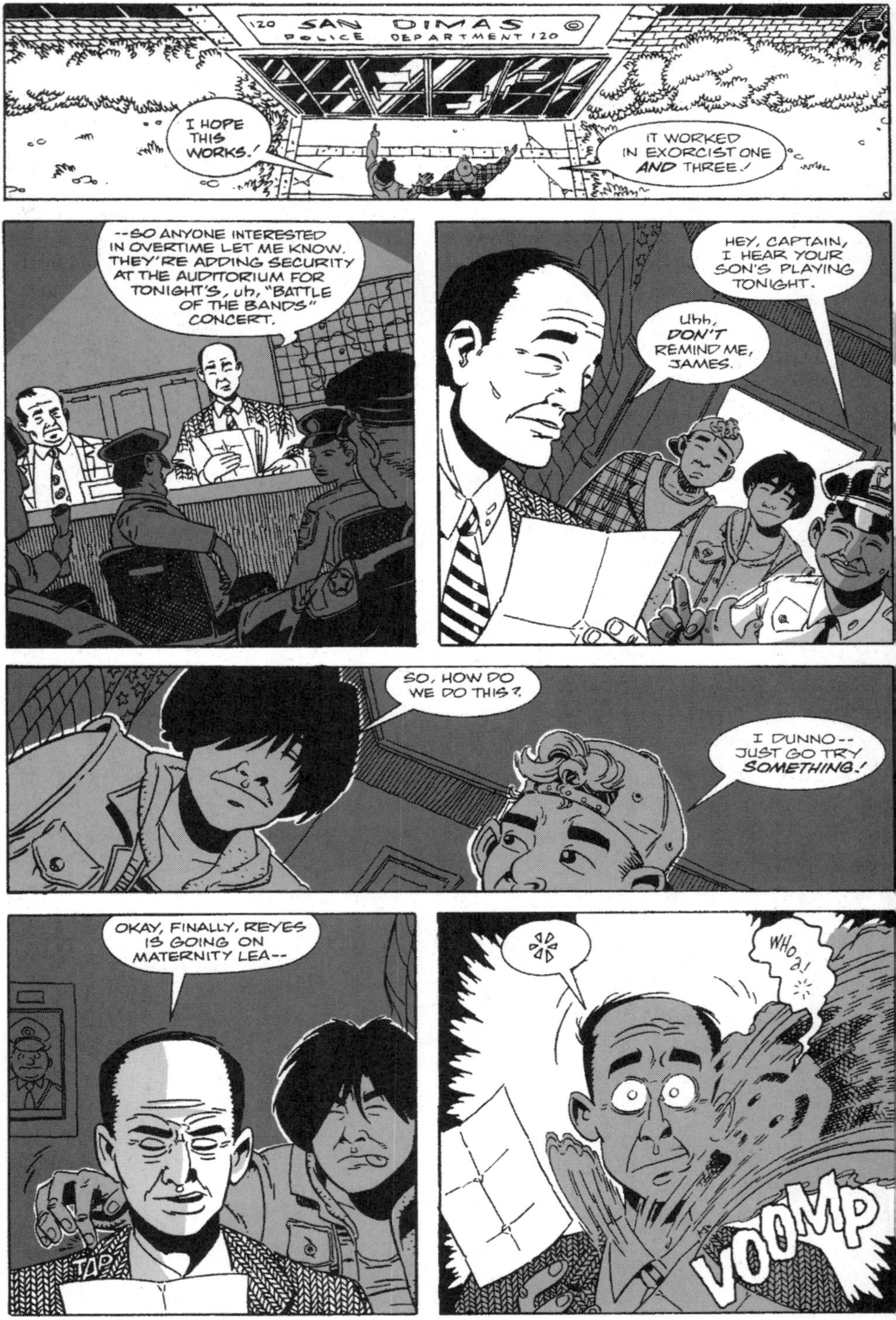
120 SAN DIMAS POLICE DEPARTMENT 120
I HOPE THIS WORKS.!
IT WORKED IN EXORCIST ONE AND THREE.!
--SO ANYONE INTERESTED IN OVERTIME LET ME KNOW. THEY'RE ADDING SECURITY AT THE AUDITORIUM FOR TONIGHT'S, uh, "BATTLE OF THE BANDS" CONCERT.
HEY, CAPTAIN, I HEAR YOUR SON'S PLAYING TONIGHT.
Uhh, DON'T REMIND ME, JAMES.
SO, HOW DO WE DO THIS?
I DUNNO-- JUST GO TRY SOMETHING!
OKAY, FINALLY, REYES IS GOING ON MATERNITY LEA--
TAP
WHOa!
VOOMP

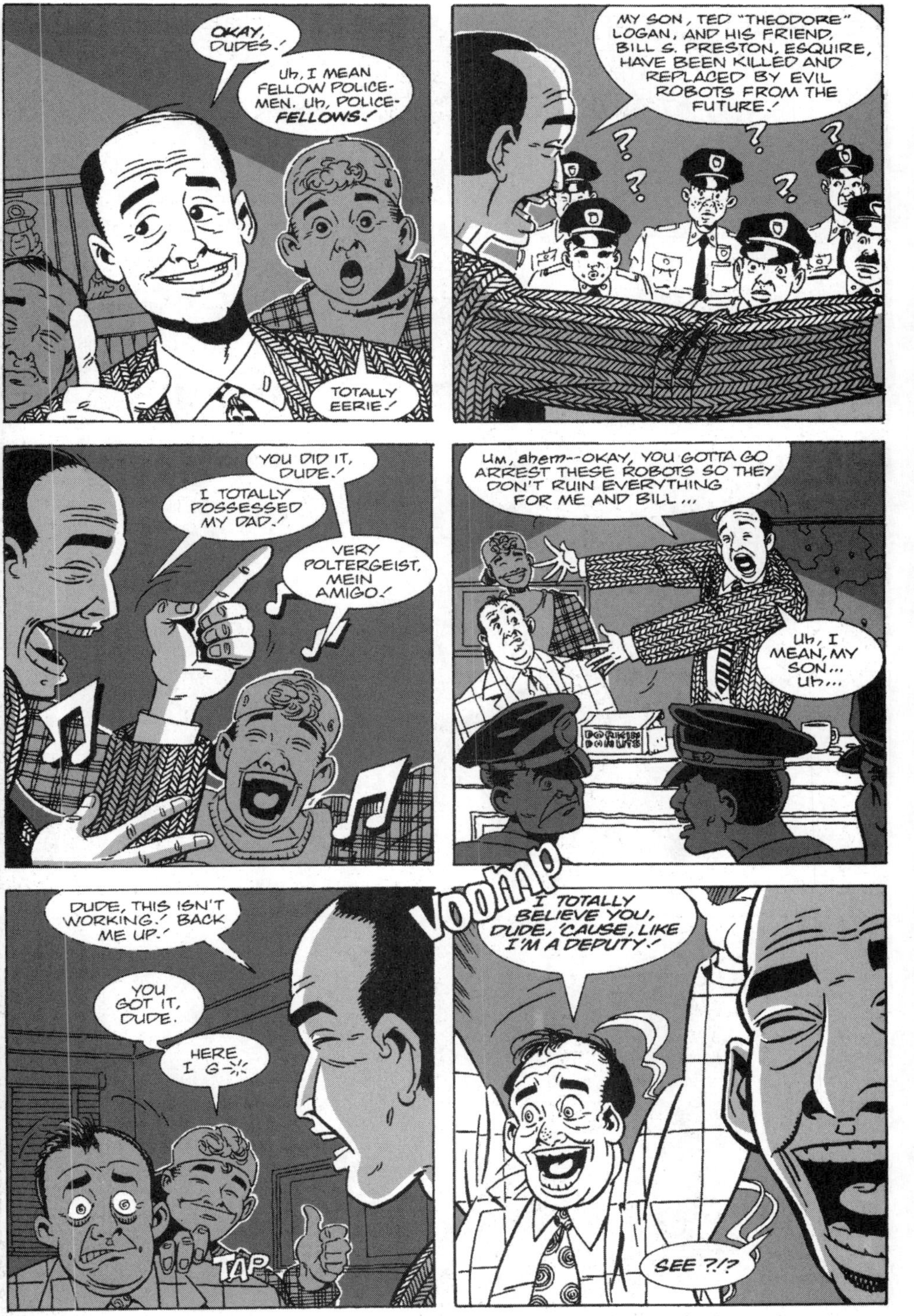
OKAY, DUDES.!
Uh, I MEAN FELLOW POLICE-MEN. Uh, POLICE-FELLOWS.!
TOTALLY EERIE.!
MY SON, TED "THEODORE" LOGAN, AND HIS FRIEND, BILL S. PRESTON, ESQUIRE, HAVE BEEN KILLED AND REPLACED BY EVIL ROBOTS FROM THE FUTURE.!
YOU DID IT, DUDE.!
I TOTALLY POSSESSED MY DAD.!
VERY POLTERGEIST, MEIN AMIGO.!
Um, ahem--OKAY, YOU GOTTA GO ARREST THESE ROBOTS SO THEY DON'T RUIN EVERYTHING FOR ME AND BILL ...
Uh, I MEAN, MY SON... Uh...
DUDE, THIS ISN'T WORKING.! BACK ME UP.!
YOU GOT IT, DUDE.
HERE I G-
TAP
VOOMP
I TOTALLY BELIEVE YOU, DUDE, 'CAUSE, LIKE I'M A DEPUTY.!
SEE ?!?

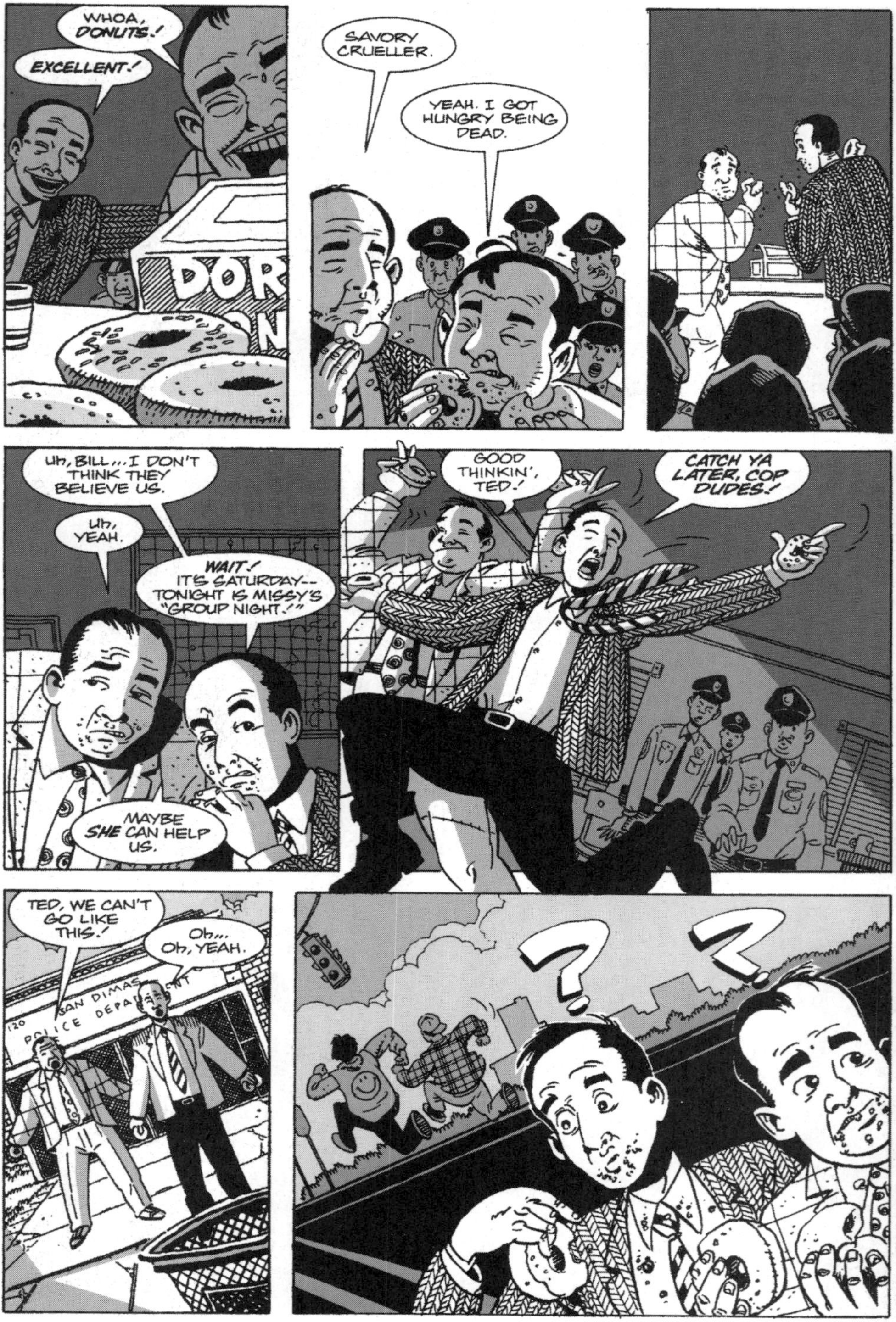

WHOA, DONUTS.!
EXCELLENT.!
SAVORY CRUELLER.
YEAH. I GOT HUNGRY BEING DEAD.
uh, BILL... I DON'T THINK THEY BELIEVE US.
uh, YEAH.
WAIT.! IT'S SATURDAY-- TONIGHT IS MISSY'S "GROUP NIGHT."
MAYBE SHE CAN HELP US.
GOOD THINKIN', TED.!
CATCH YA LATER, COP DUDES.!
TED, WE CAN'T GO LIKE THIS.!
Oh... Oh, YEAH.
SAN DIMAS
POLICE DEPARTMENT
120
? ?

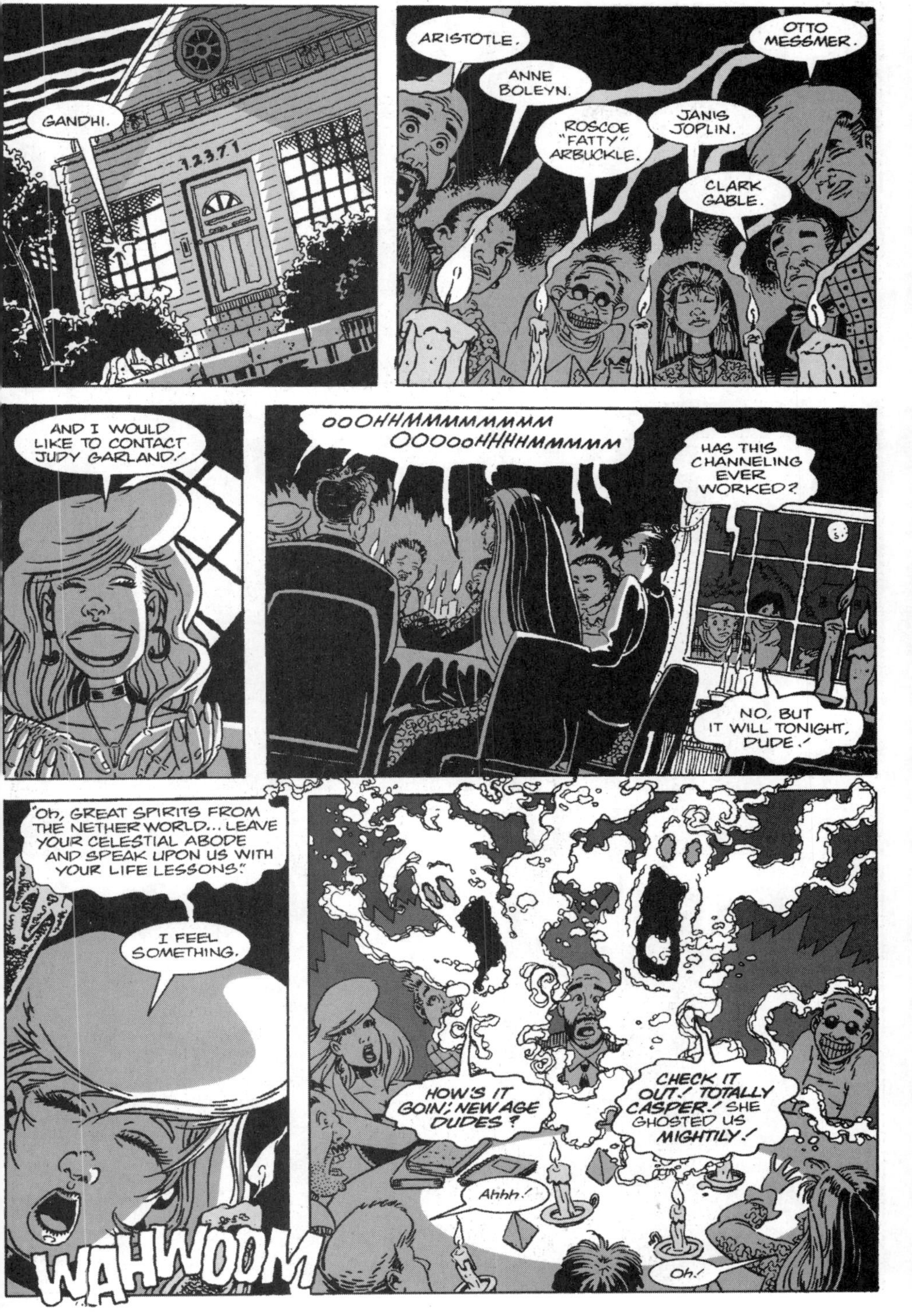
GANDHI.
1.2.3.7.1
ARISTOTLE.
ANNE BOLEYN.
ROSCOE "FATTY" ARBUCKLE.
JANIS JOPLIN.
OTTO MESSMER.
CLARK GABLE.
AND I WOULD LIKE TO CONTACT JUDY GARLAND!
oooHHMMMMMMMMM OOOOoHHHHMMMMMM
HAS THIS CHANNELING EVER WORKED?
NO, BUT IT WILL TONIGHT, DUDE!
"Oh, GREAT SPIRITS FROM THE NETHER WORLD... LEAVE YOUR CELESTIAL ABODE AND SPEAK UPON US WITH YOUR LIFE LESSONS."
I FEEL SOMETHING.
WAHWOOM
HOW'S IT GOIN', NEW AGE DUDES?
CHECK IT OUT! TOTALLY CASPER! SHE GHOSTED US MIGHTILY!
Ahhh!
Oh!

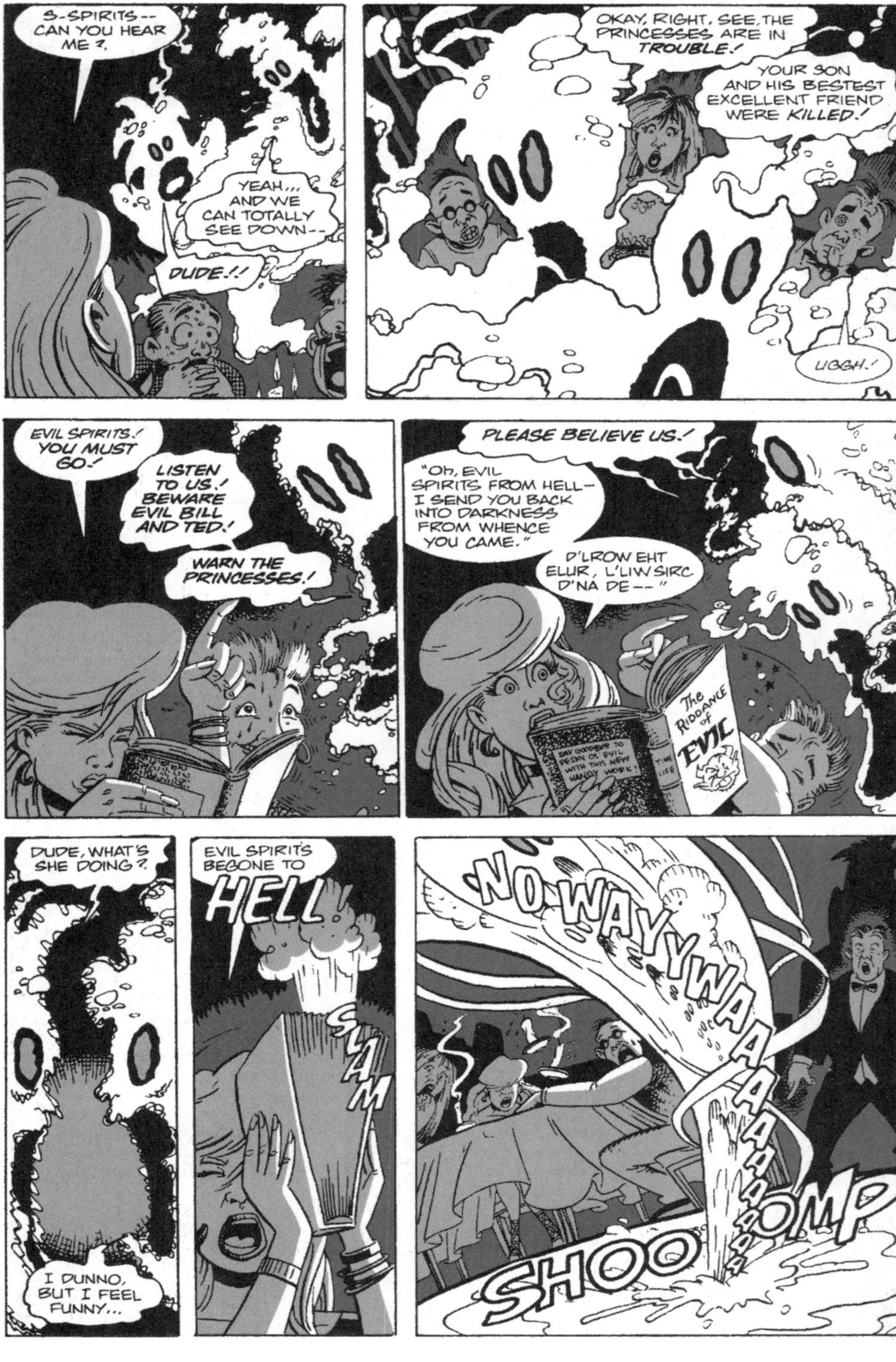
S-SPIRITS-- CAN YOU HEAR ME?.
YEAH,,, AND WE CAN TOTALLY SEE DOWN--
DUDE.!!
OKAY, RIGHT. SEE, THE PRINCESSES ARE IN TROUBLE.!
YOUR SON AND HIS BESTEST EXCELLENT FRIEND WERE KILLED.!
UGGH.!
EVIL SPIRITS.! YOU MUST GO.!
LISTEN TO US.! BEWARE EVIL BILL AND TED.!
WARN THE PRINCESSES.!
PLEASE BELIEVE US.!
"Oh, EVIL SPIRITS FROM HELL-- I SEND YOU BACK INTO DARKNESS FROM WHENCE YOU CAME."
D'LROW EHT ELUR, L'LIW SIRC D'NA DE --"
The RIDDANCE of EVIL
DUDE, WHAT'S SHE DOING?
I DUNNO, BUT I FEEL FUNNY...
EVIL SPIRITS BEGONE TO HELL
SLAM
NO WAYYWAAAAAAAA
SHOOOMP

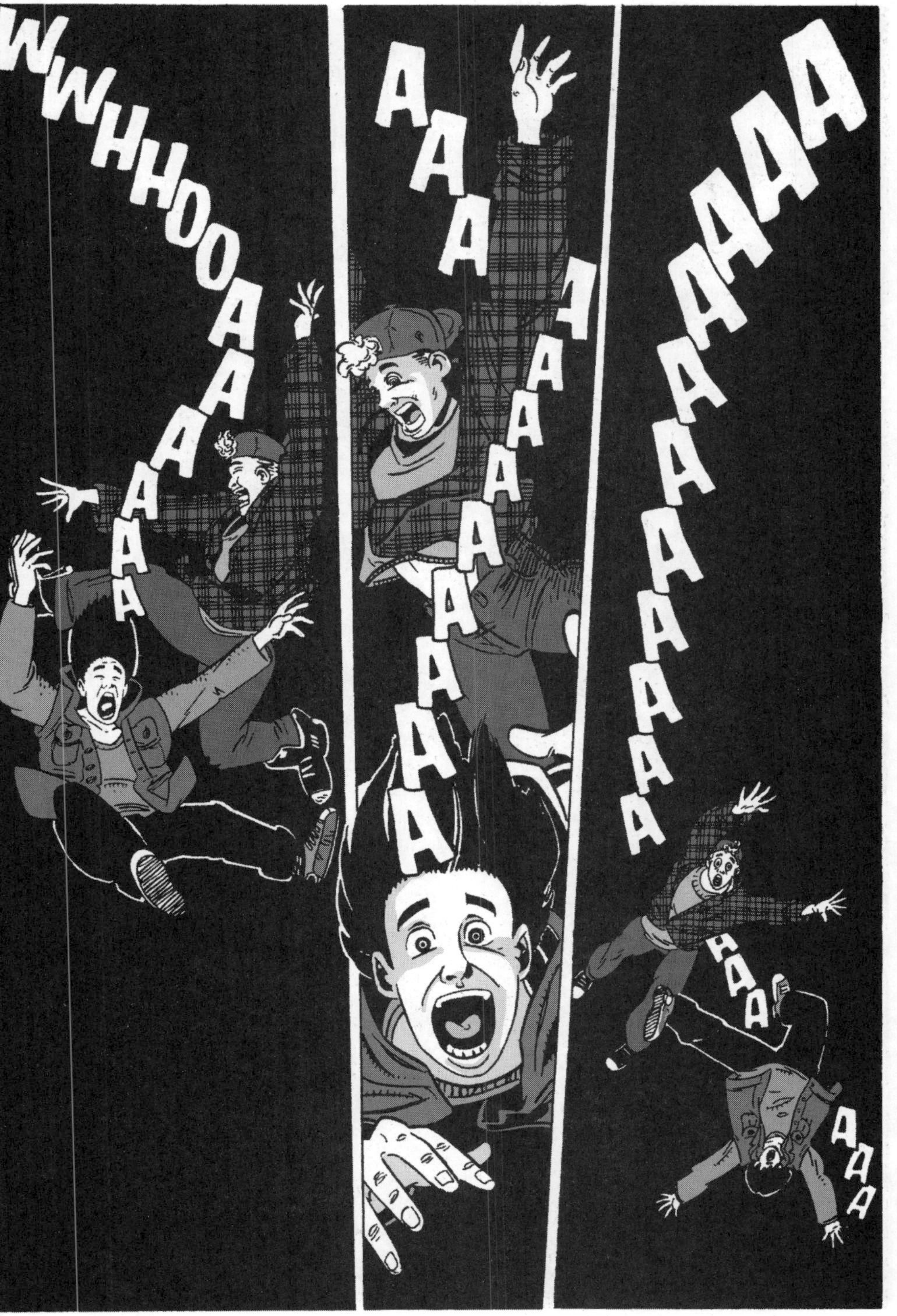
WWHHOOAAAAAA
AAAAAAAAAAAA
AAAAAAAAAAAAA
AAA
AAA

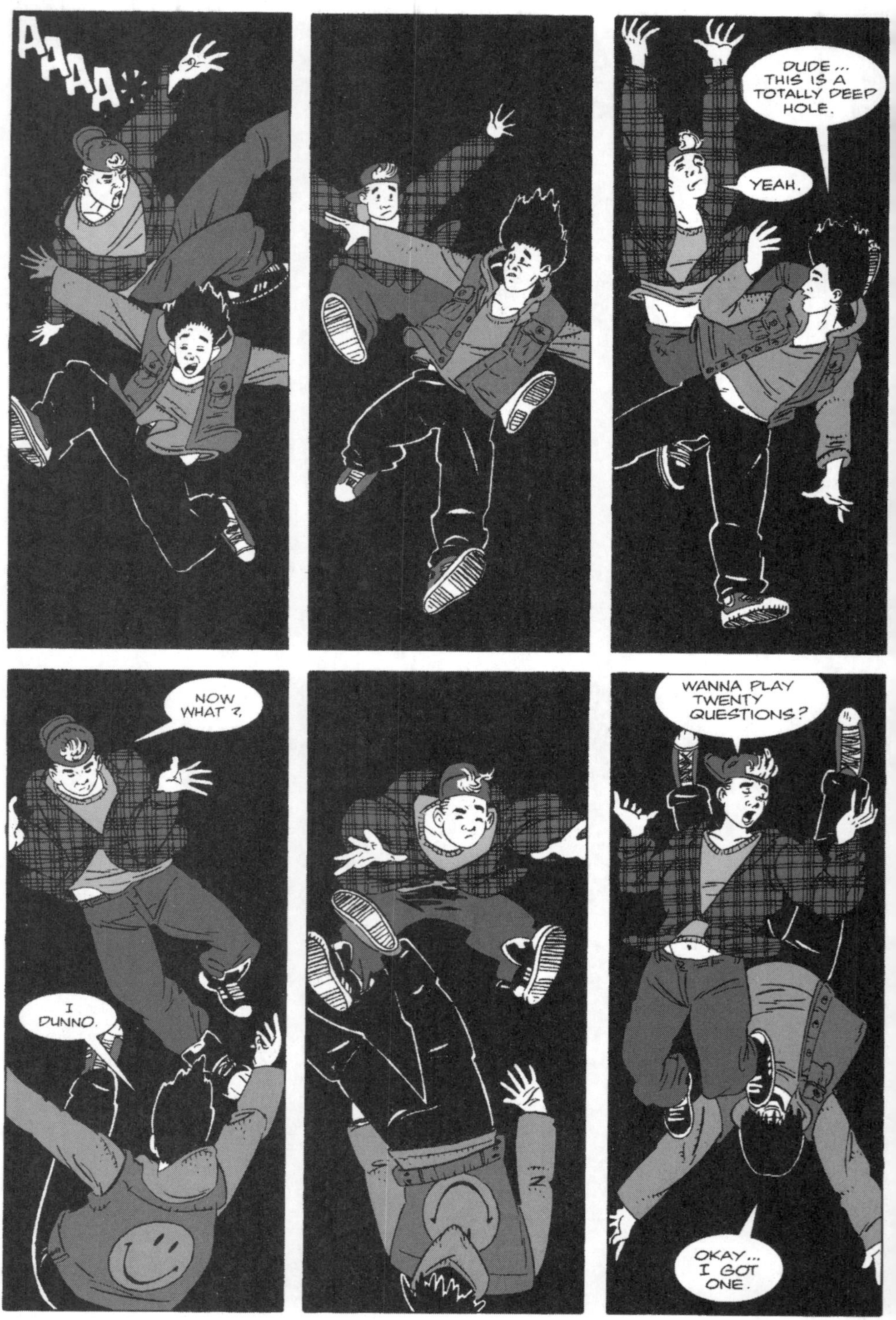
AAAA!
DUDE... THIS IS A TOTALLY DEEP HOLE.
YEAH.
NOW WHAT ?,
I DUNNO.
WANNA PLAY TWENTY QUESTIONS?
OKAY... I GOT ONE.

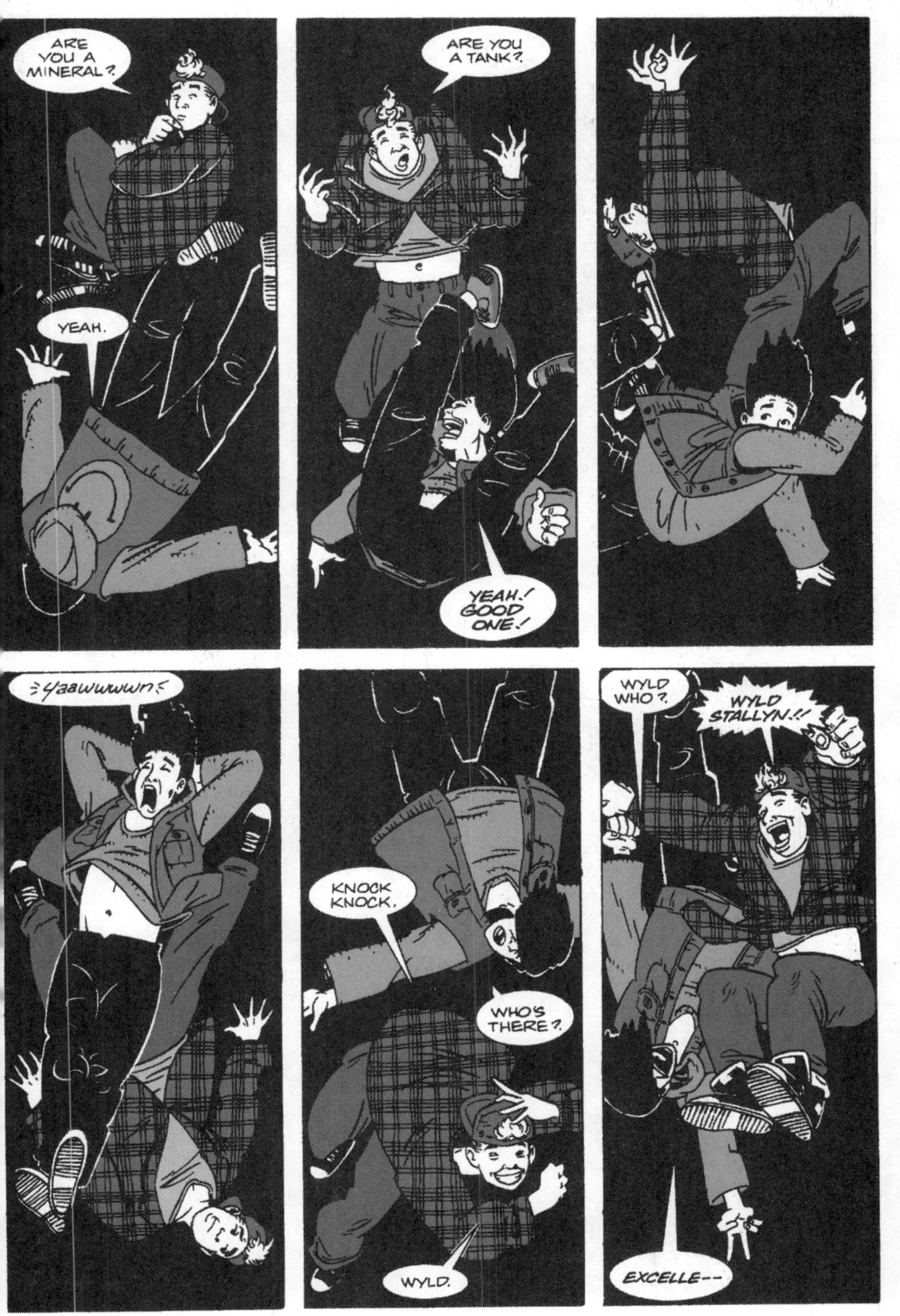
ARE YOU A MINERAL?
YEAH.
ARE YOU A TANK?
YEAH! GOOD ONE!
yaawwwwn
KNOCK KNOCK.
WHO'S THERE?
WYLD.
WYLD WHO?
WYLD STALLYN!!
EXCELLE--

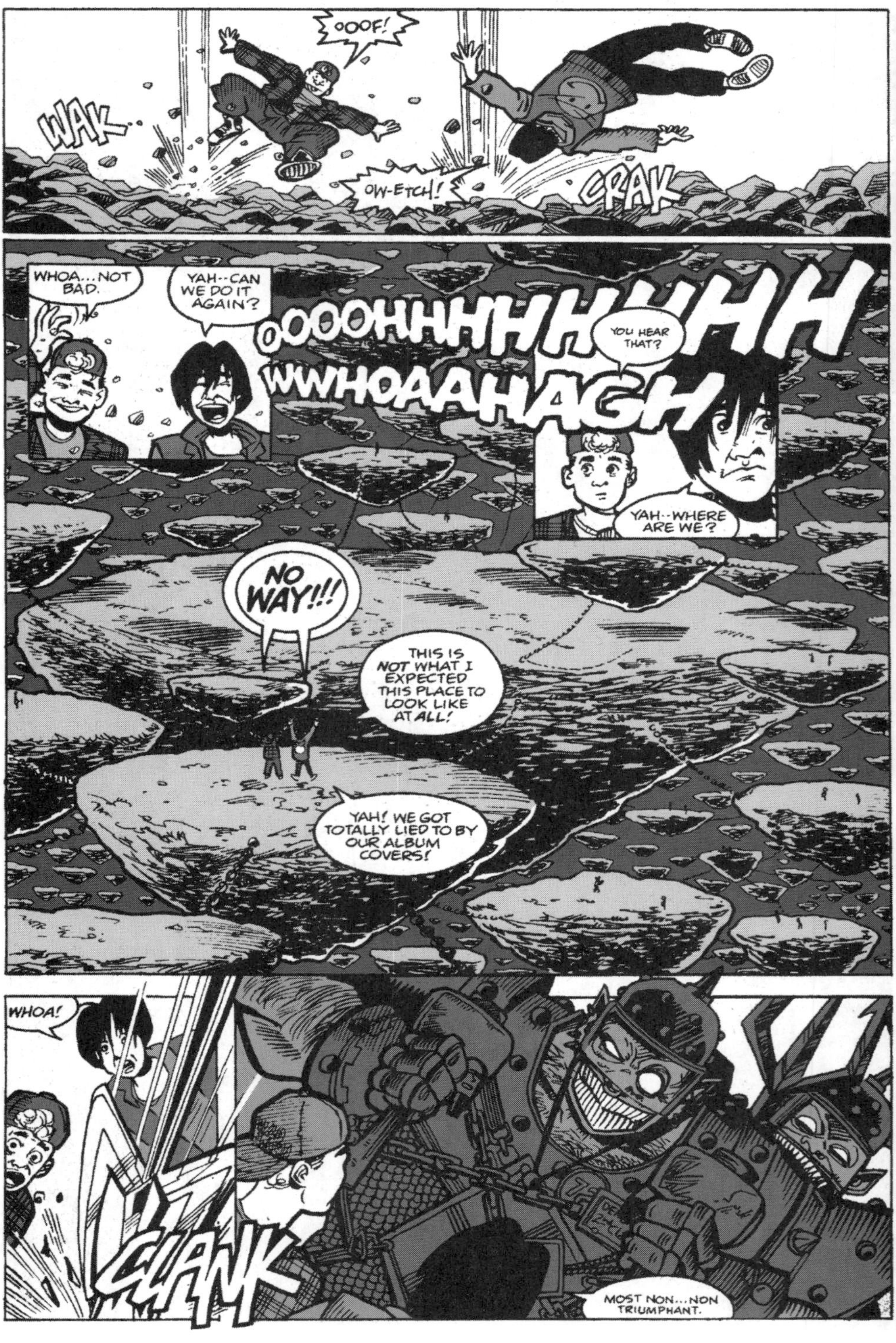

WAK..
OOOF!
OW-ETCH!
CRAK
WHOA...NOT BAD.
YAH--CAN WE DO IT AGAIN?
OOOOHHHHHHHH
WWHOAAAHAGH
YOU HEAR THAT?
YAH--WHERE ARE WE?
NO WAY!!!
THIS IS NOT WHAT I EXPECTED THIS PLACE TO LOOK LIKE AT ALL!
YAH! WE GOT TOTALLY LIED TO BY OUR ALBUM COVERS!
WHOA!
CLANK
MOST NON...NON TRIUMPHANT.

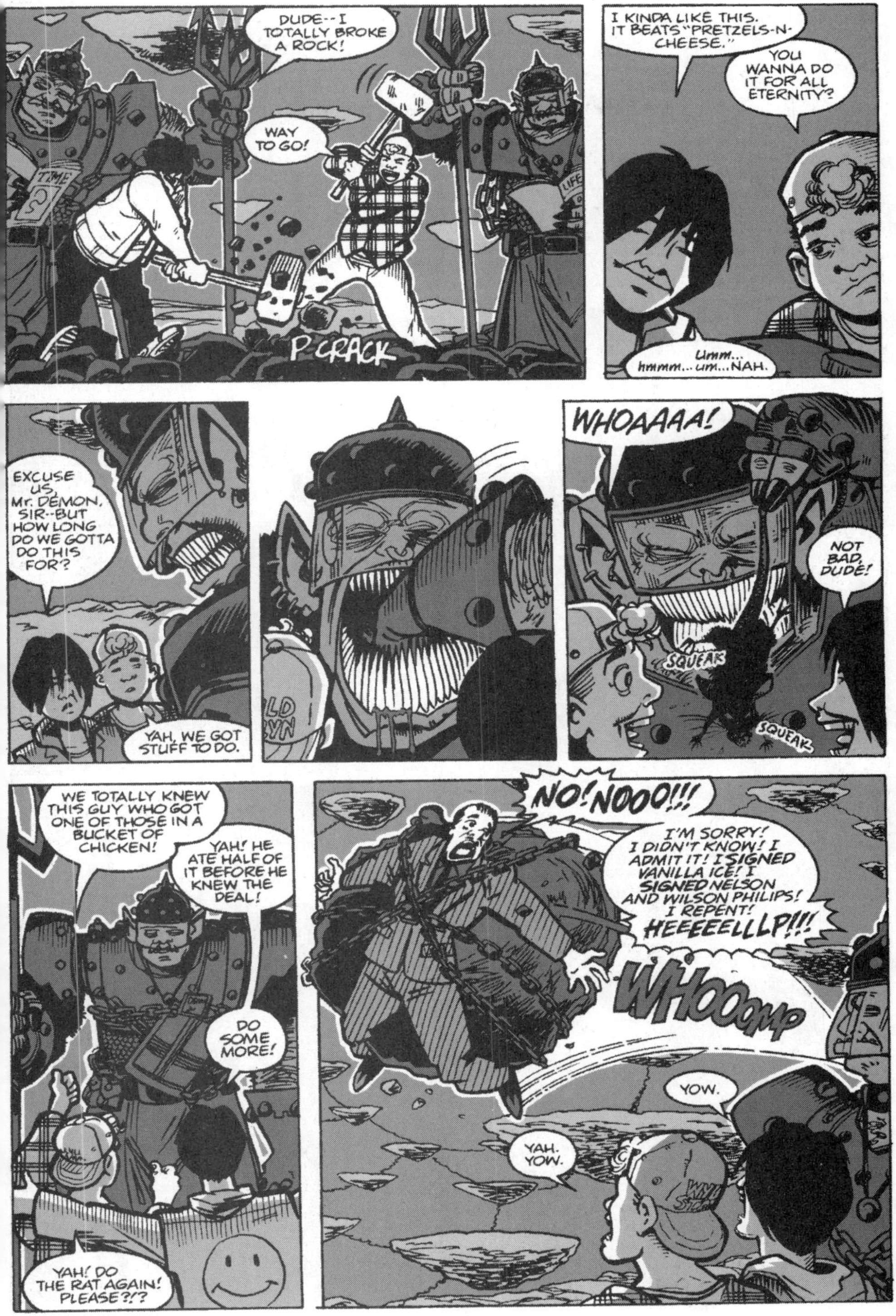
DUDE--I TOTALLY BROKE A ROCK!
WAY TO GO!
TIME
LIFE
P-CRACK
I KINDA LIKE THIS. IT BEATS "PRETZELS-N-CHEESE."
YOU WANNA DO IT FOR ALL ETERNITY?
Umm... hmmm... um... NAH.
EXCUSE US, Mr. DEMON, SIR--BUT HOW LONG DO WE GOTTA DO THIS FOR?
YAH, WE GOT STUFF TO DO.
WHOAAAA!
NOT BAD, DUDE!
SQUEAK
SQUEAK
WE TOTALLY KNEW THIS GUY WHO GOT ONE OF THOSE IN A BUCKET OF CHICKEN!
YAH! HE ATE HALF OF IT BEFORE HE KNEW THE DEAL!
DO SOME MORE!
YAH! DO THE RAT AGAIN! PLEASE?!?
NO! NOOO!!!
I'M SORRY! I DIDN'T KNOW! I ADMIT IT! I SIGNED VANILLA ICE! I SIGNED NELSON AND WILSON PHILIPS! I REPENT! HEEEEELLLP!!!
WHOOOMP
YOW.
YAH. YOW.

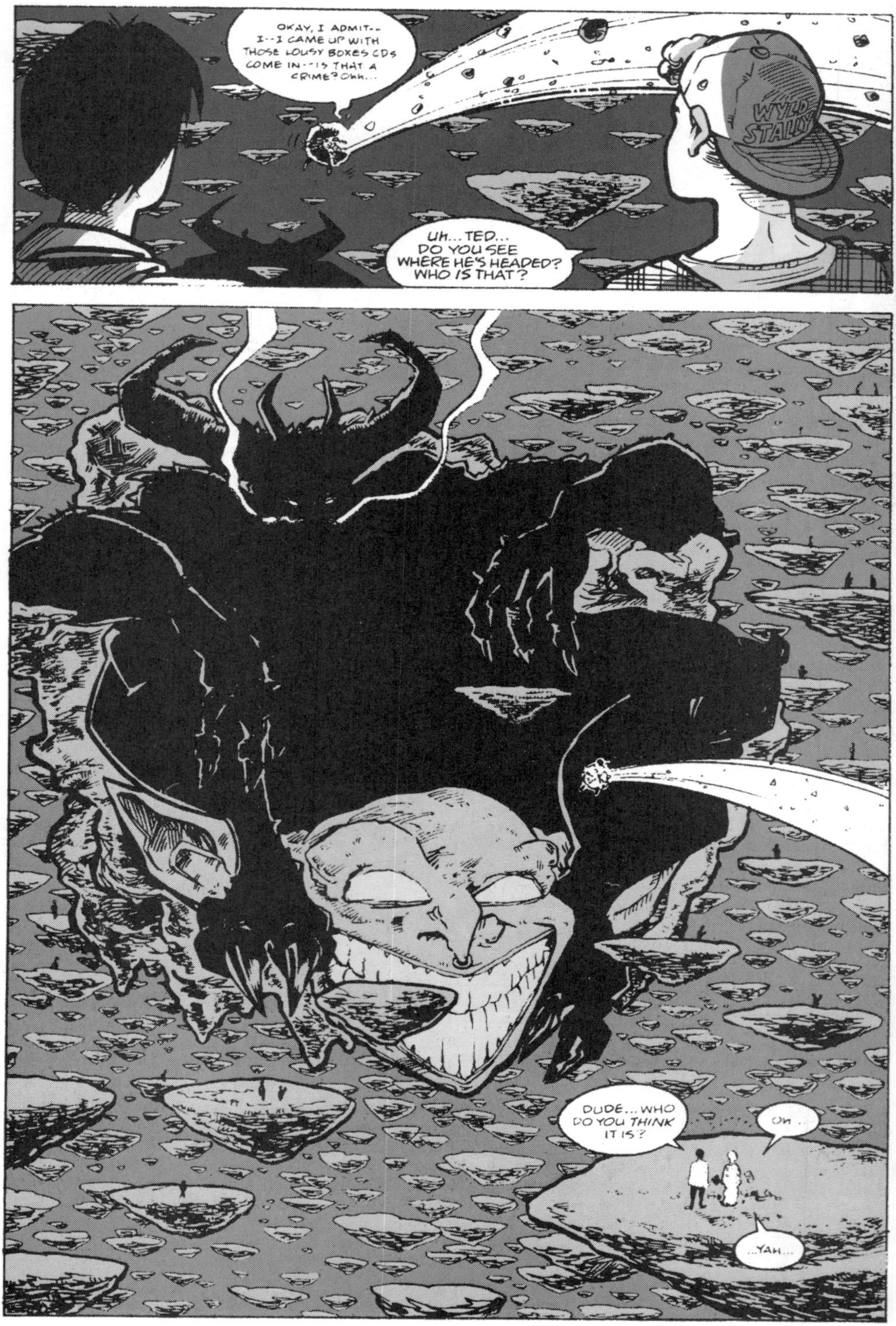
OKAY, I ADMIT-- I--I CAME UP WITH THOSE LOUSY BOXES CDs COME IN--IS THAT A CRIME? OHH...
WYLD STALLY
UH... TED... DO YOU SEE WHERE HE'S HEADED? WHO *IS* THAT?
DUDE... WHO DO YOU *THINK* IT IS?
OH..
...YAH...

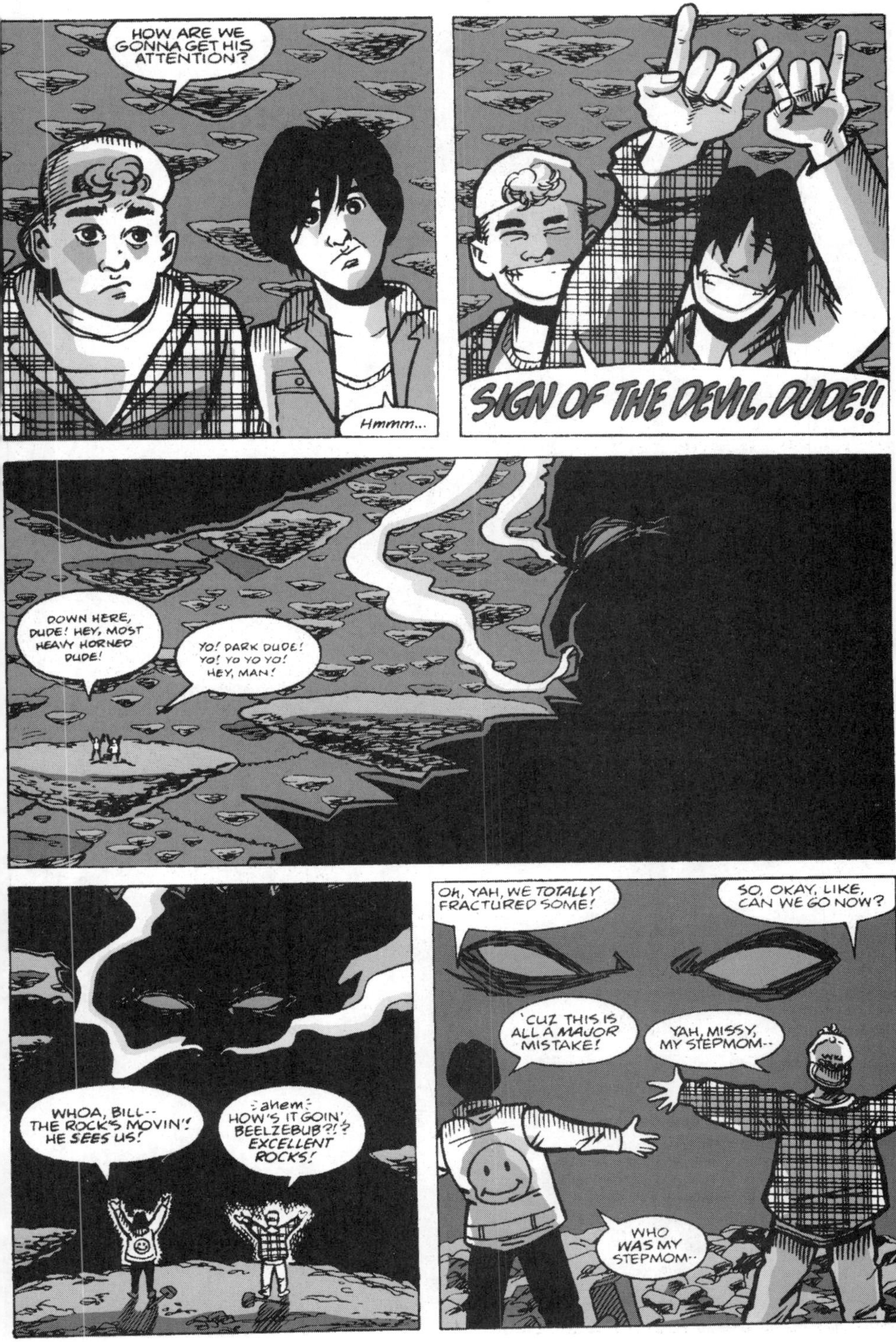
HOW ARE WE GONNA GET HIS ATTENTION?
Hmmm...
SIGN OF THE DEVIL, DUDE!!
DOWN HERE, DUDE! HEY, MOST HEAVY HORNED DUDE!
YO! DARK DUDE! YO! YO YO YO! HEY, MAN!
WHOA, BILL-- THE ROCK'S MOVIN'! HE SEES US!
ahem HOW'S IT GOIN', BEELZEBUB?!? EXCELLENT ROCKS!
Oh, YAH, WE TOTALLY FRACTURED SOME!
SO, OKAY, LIKE, CAN WE GO NOW?
'CUZ THIS IS ALL A MAJOR MISTAKE!
YAH, MISSY, MY STEPMOM--
WHO WAS MY STEPMOM--

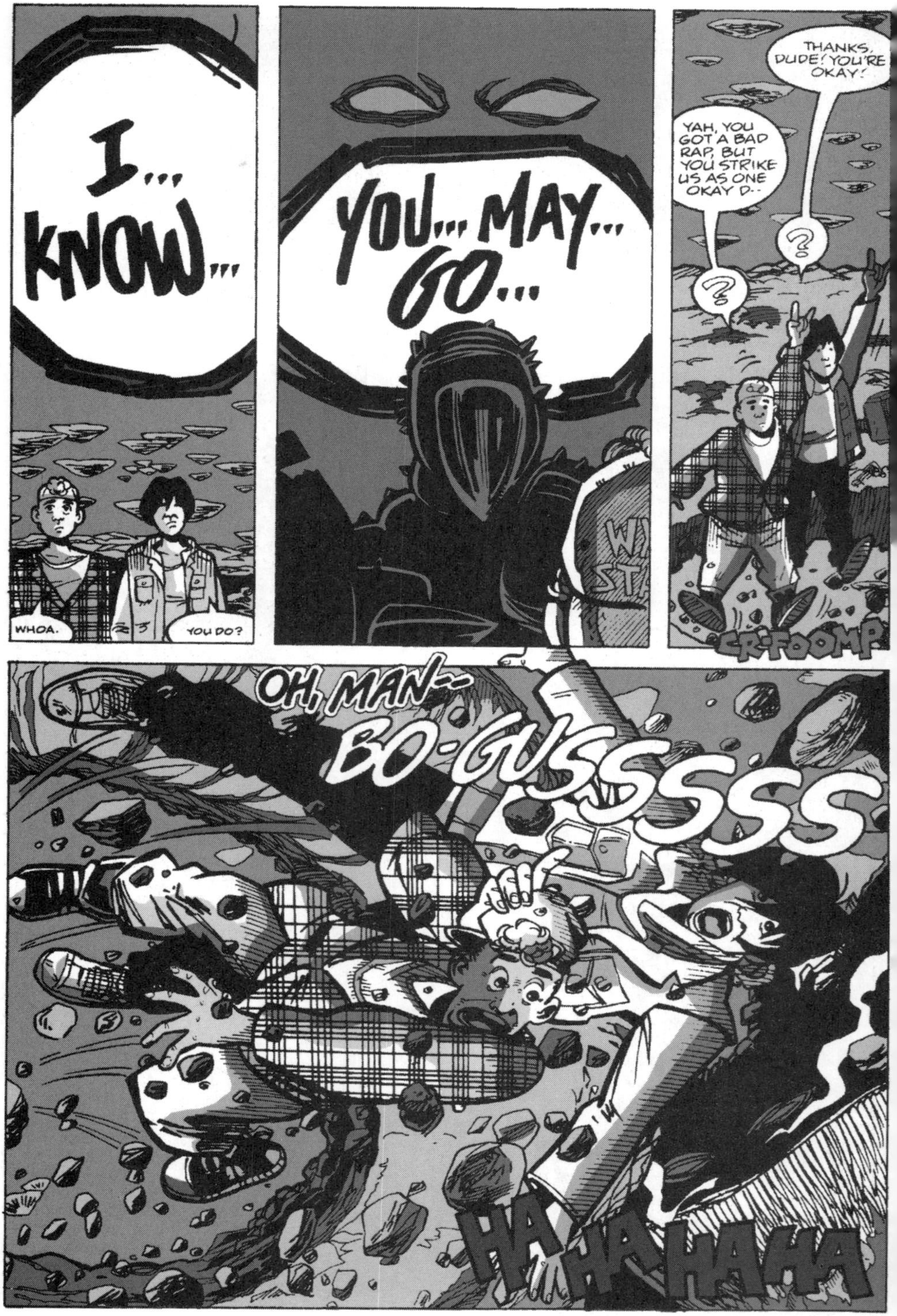
I... KNOW...
WHOA.
YOU DO?
YOU... MAY... GO...
THANKS, DUDE! YOU'RE OKAY!
YAH, YOU GOT A BAD RAP, BUT YOU STRIKE US AS ONE OKAY D--
?
?
CR-FOOMP
OH, MAN--
BO-GUSSSSSS
HAHAHAHAHA

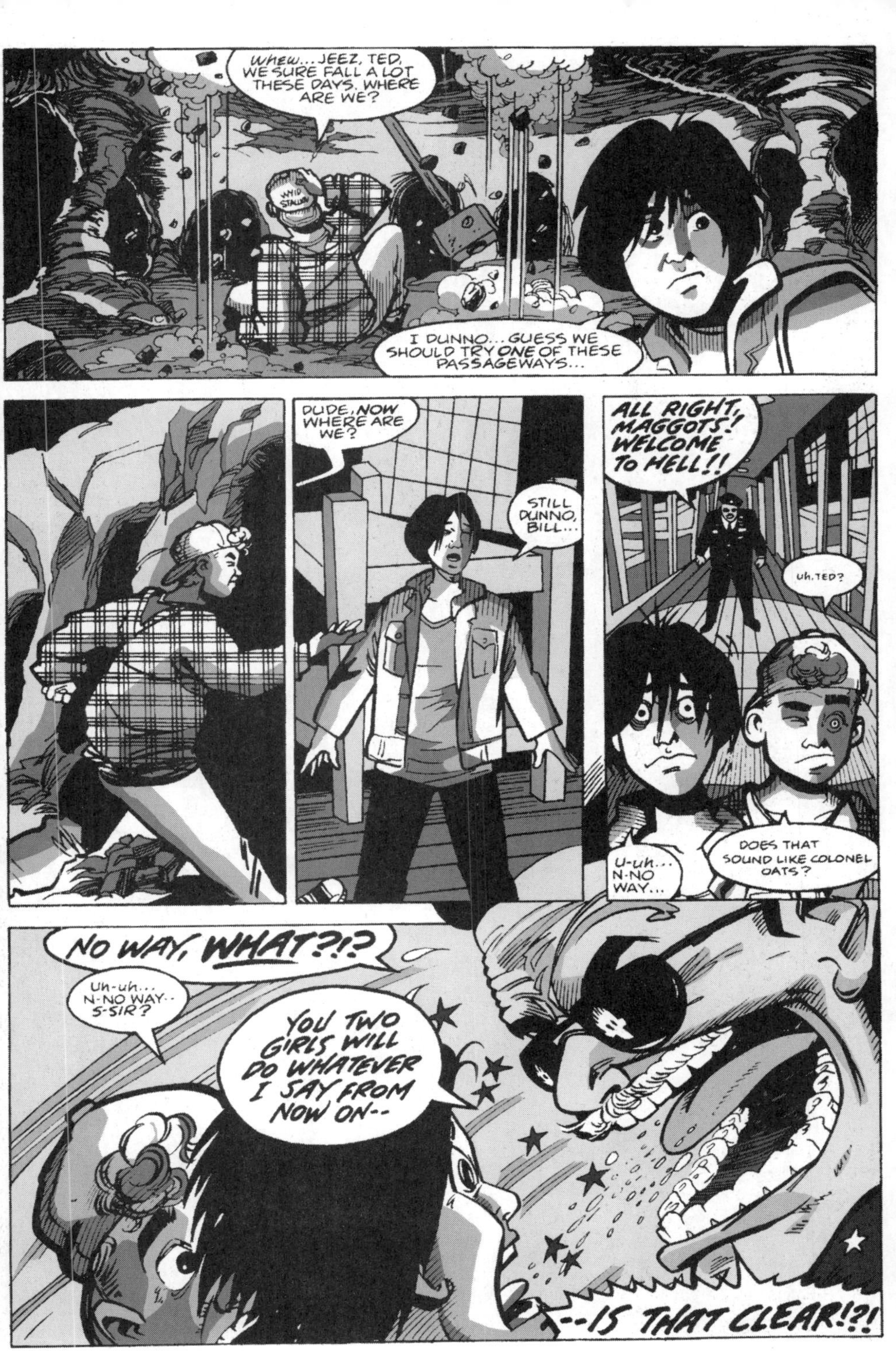
WHEW... JEEZ, TED, WE SURE FALL A LOT THESE DAYS. WHERE ARE WE?
WYLD STALLYN
I DUNNO... GUESS WE SHOULD TRY ONE OF THESE PASSAGEWAYS...
DUDE, NOW WHERE ARE WE?
STILL DUNNO, BILL...
ALL RIGHT, MAGGOTS! WELCOME TO HELL!!
UH, TED?
DOES THAT SOUND LIKE COLONEL OATS?
U-UH... N-NO WAY...
NO WAY, WHAT?!?
UH-UH... N-NO WAY.. S-SIR?
YOU TWO GIRLS WILL DO WHATEVER I SAY FROM NOW ON--
--IS THAT CLEAR!?!

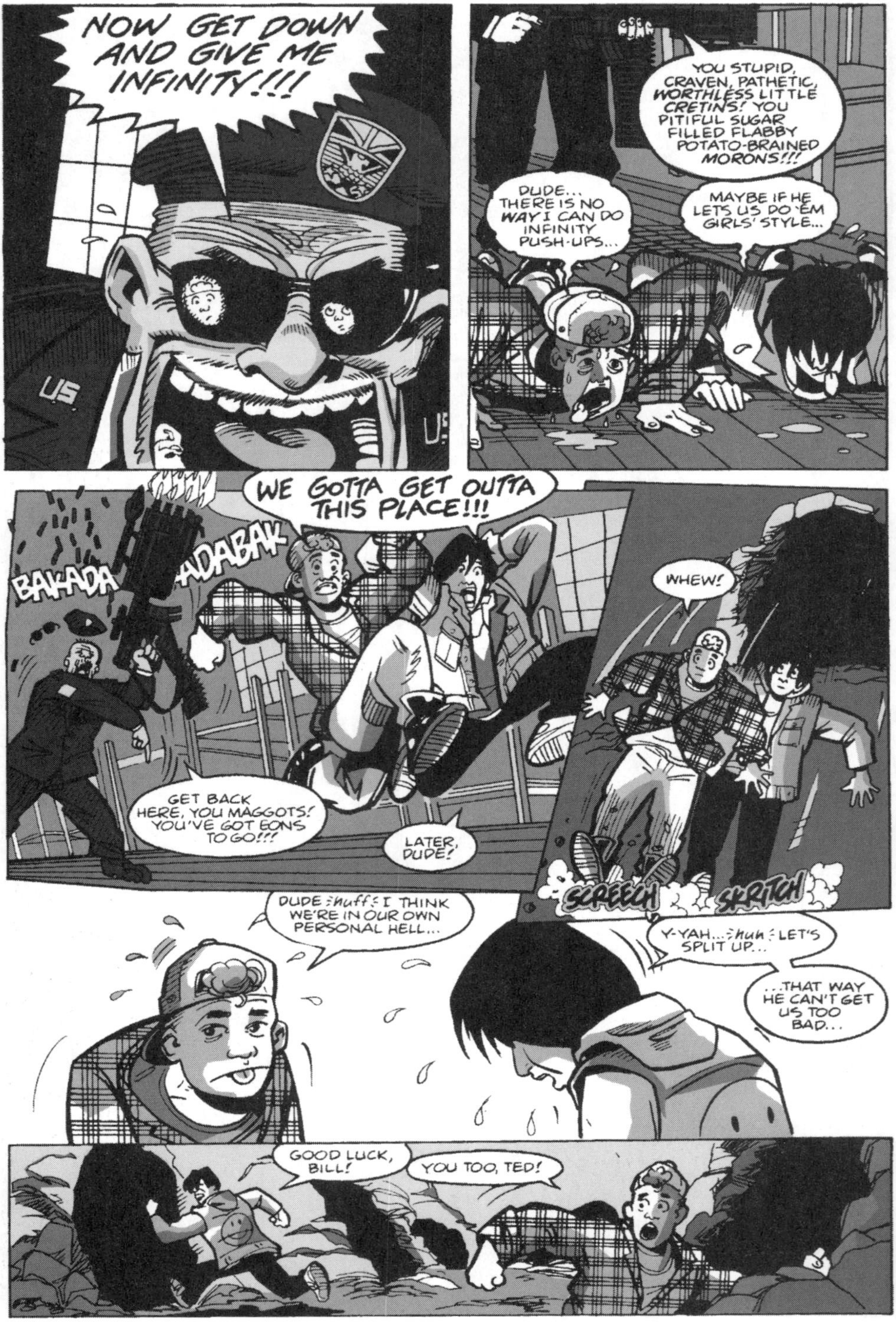
NOW GET DOWN AND GIVE ME INFINITY!!!!
YOU STUPID, CRAVEN, PATHETIC, WORTHLESS LITTLE CRETINS! YOU PITIFUL SUGAR FILLED FLABBY POTATO-BRAINED MORONS!!!
DUDE... THERE IS NO WAY I CAN DO INFINITY PUSH-UPS...
MAYBE IF HE LETS US DO 'EM GIRLS' STYLE...
WE GOTTA GET OUTTA THIS PLACE!!!
BAKADA
ADABAK
GET BACK HERE, YOU MAGGOTS! YOU'VE GOT EONS TO GO!!!
LATER, DUDE!
WHEW!
SCREECH
SKRITCH
DUDE huff I THINK WE'RE IN OUR OWN PERSONAL HELL...
Y-YAH... huh LET'S SPLIT UP...
...THAT WAY HE CAN'T GET US TOO BAD...
GOOD LUCK, BILL!
YOU TOO, TED!

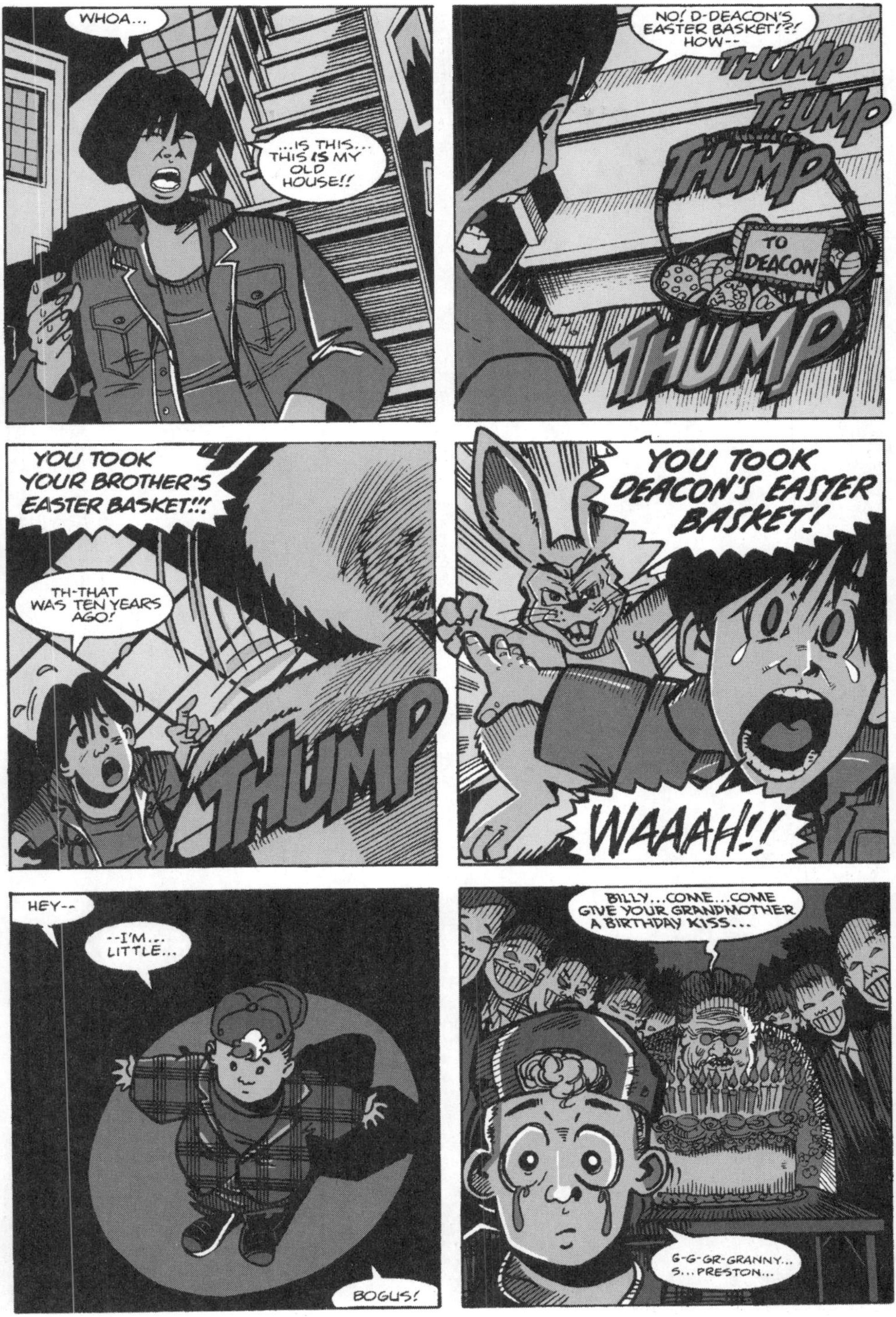
WHOA...
...IS THIS... THIS IS MY OLD HOUSE!!
NO! D-DEACON'S EASTER BASKET!?! HOW--
THUMP
THUMP
THUMP
TO DEACON
THUMP
YOU TOOK YOUR BROTHER'S EASTER BASKET!!!
TH-THAT WAS TEN YEARS AGO!
THUMP
YOU TOOK DEACON'S EASTER BASKET!
WAAAH!!
HEY--
--I'M... LITTLE...
BOGUS!
BILLY...COME...COME GIVE YOUR GRANDMOTHER A BIRTHDAY KISS...
G-G-GR-GRANNY... S...PRESTON...

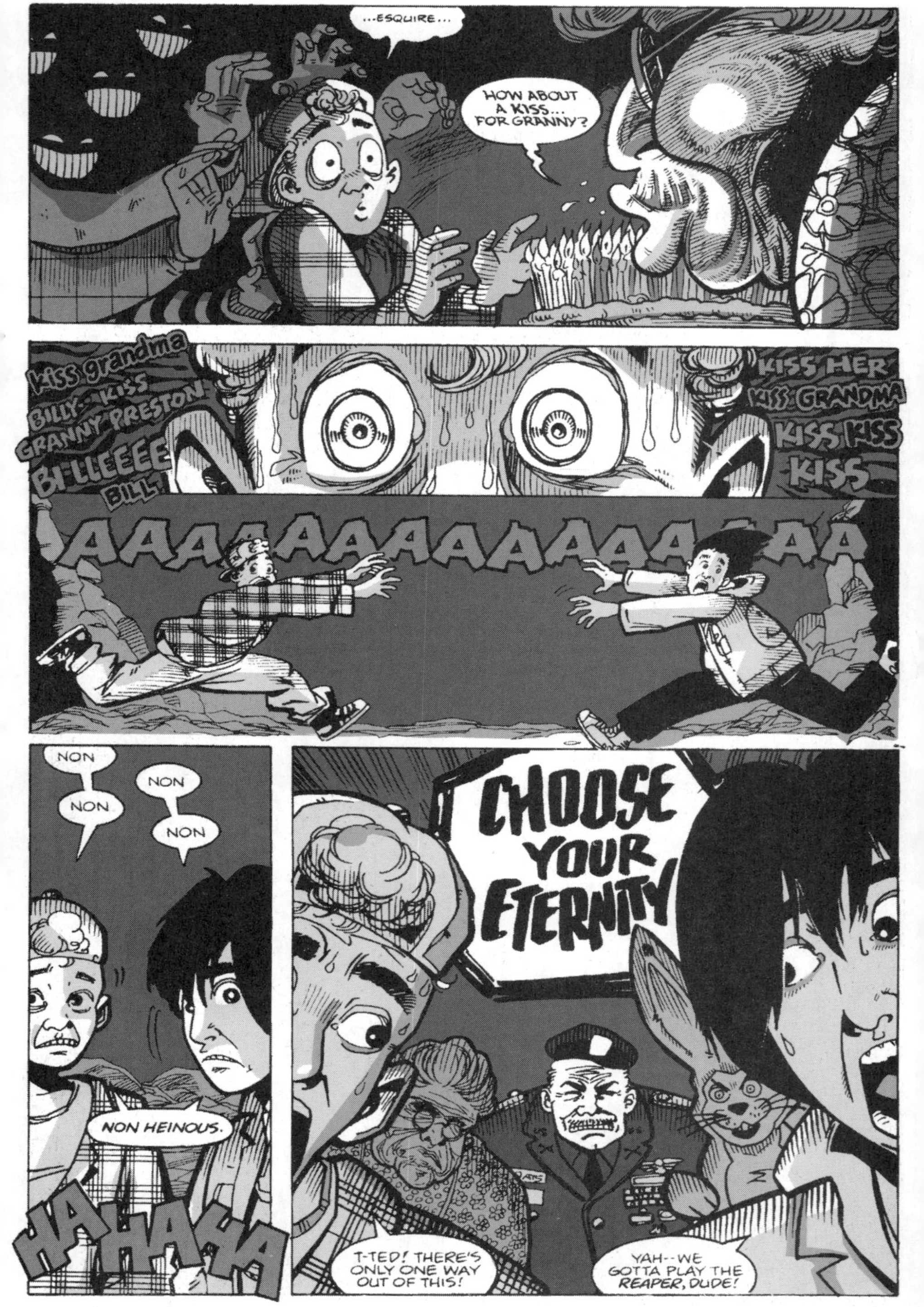
...ESQUIRE...
HOW ABOUT A KISS... FOR GRANNY?
kiss grandma
BILLY-- KISS
GRANNY PRESTON
BI LLEEEE
BILL
KISS HER
KISS GRANDMA
KISS KISS
KISS
AAAAAAAAAAAAAA
NON
NON
NON
NON
NON HEINOUS.
HAHAHA
CHOOSE YOUR ETERNITY
T-TED! THERE'S ONLY ONE WAY OUT OF THIS!
YAH--WE GOTTA PLAY THE REAPER, DUDE!

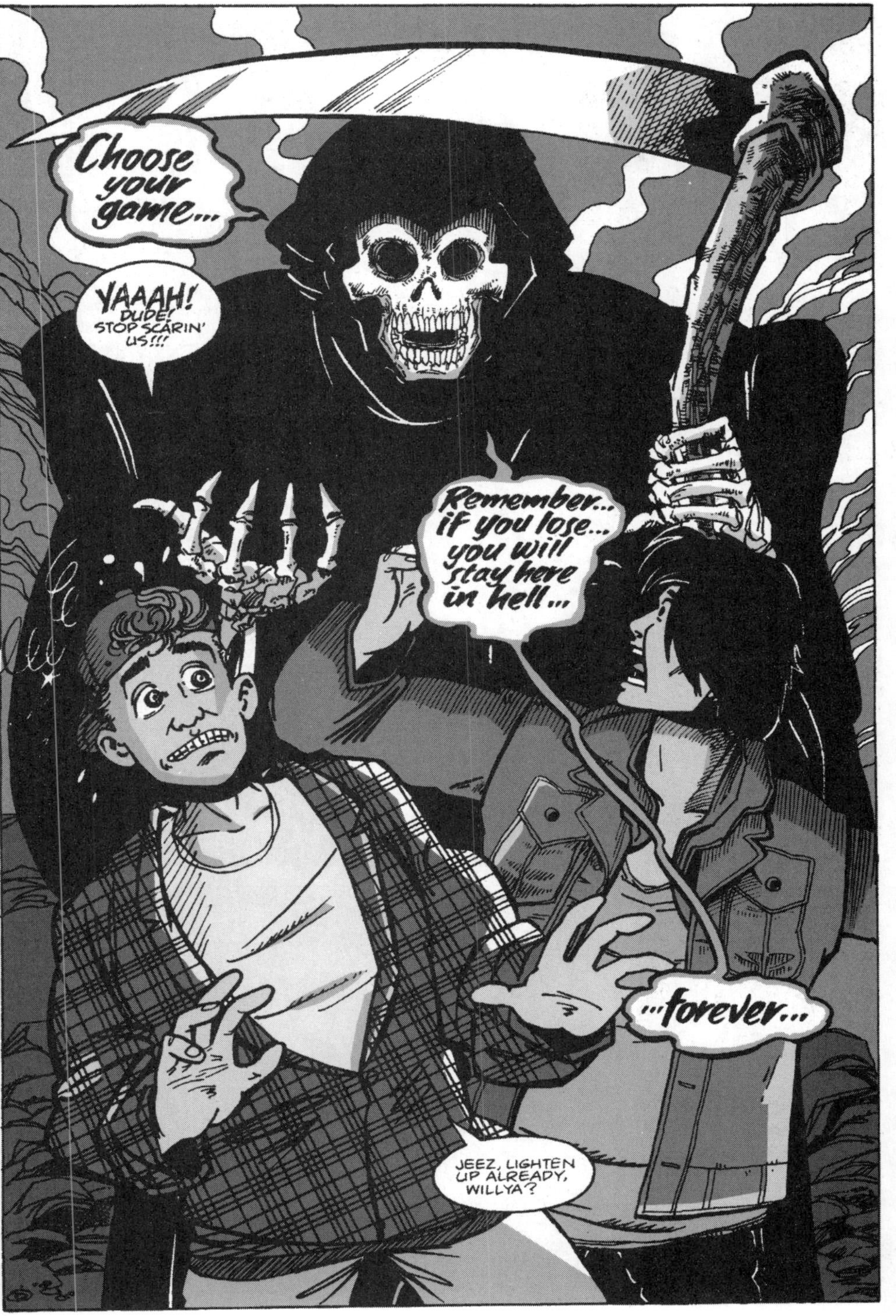
Choose your game...
YAAAH! DUDE! STOP SCARIN' US!!!
Remember... if you lose... you will stay here in hell...
...forever...
JEEZ, LIGHTEN UP ALREADY, WILLYA?

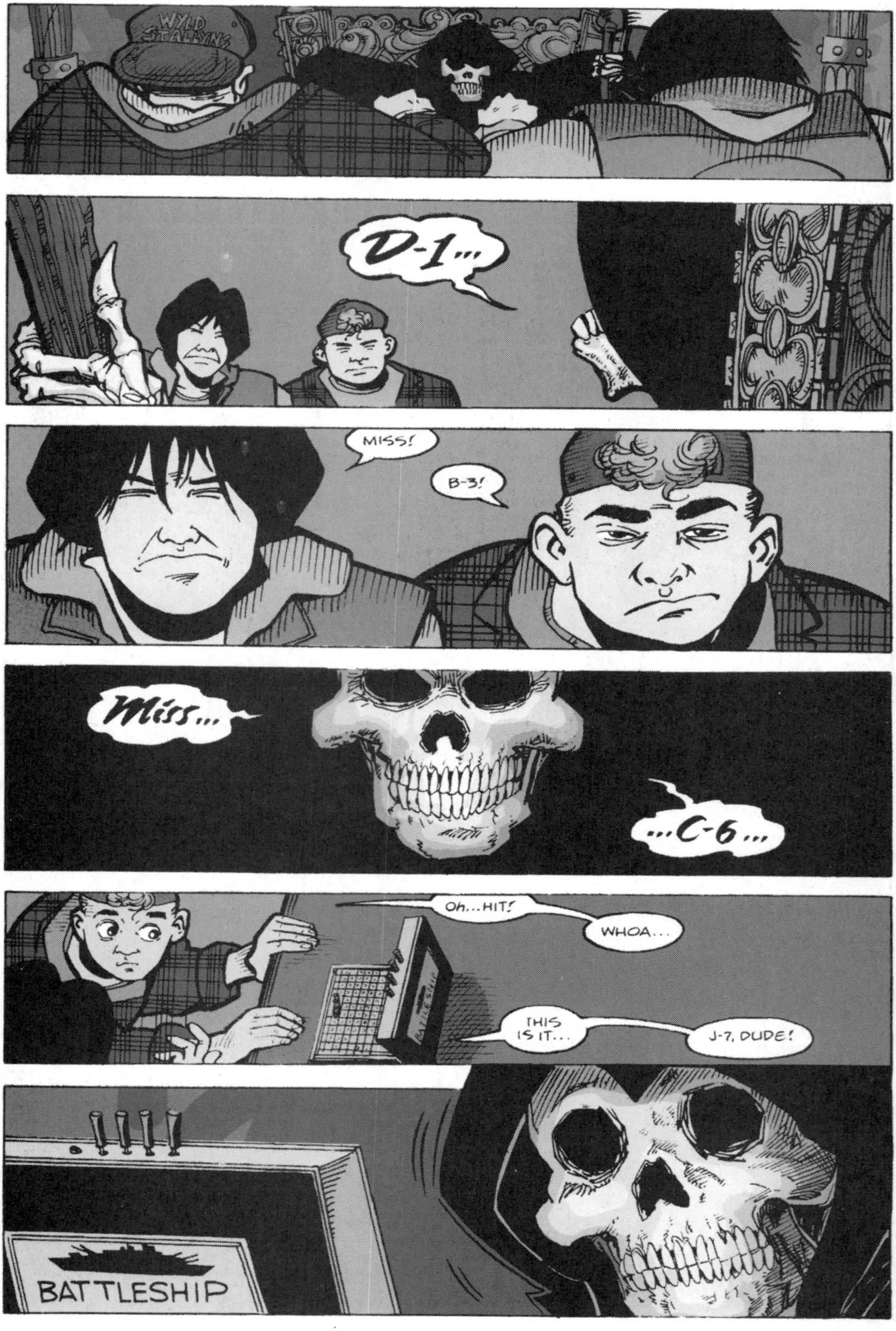
WYLD STALLYNS
D-1...
MISS!
B-3!
Miss...
...C-6...
Oh...HIT!
WHOA...
THIS IS IT...
J-7, DUDE!
BATTLESHIP

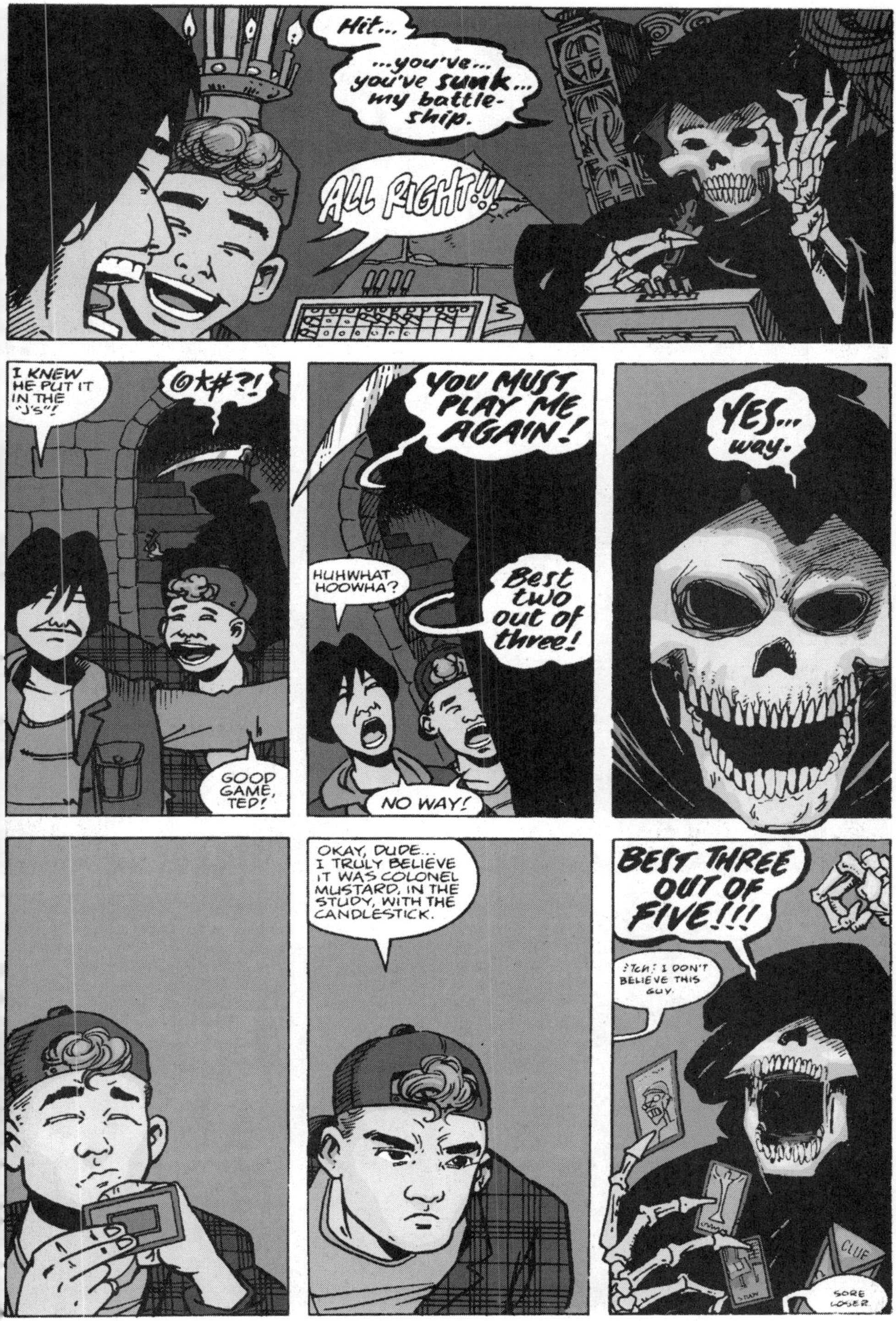
Hit...
...you've... you've sunk... my battle-ship.
ALL RIGHT!!!
I KNEW HE PUT IT IN THE "J'S"!
@*#?!
YOU MUST PLAY ME AGAIN!
HUHWHAT HOOWHA?
Best two out of three!
GOOD GAME, TED!
NO WAY!
YES... way.
OKAY, DUDE... I TRULY BELIEVE IT WAS COLONEL MUSTARD, IN THE STUDY, WITH THE CANDLESTICK.
BEST THREE OUT OF FIVE!!!
Tch! I DON'T BELIEVE THIS GUY.
SORE LOSER.

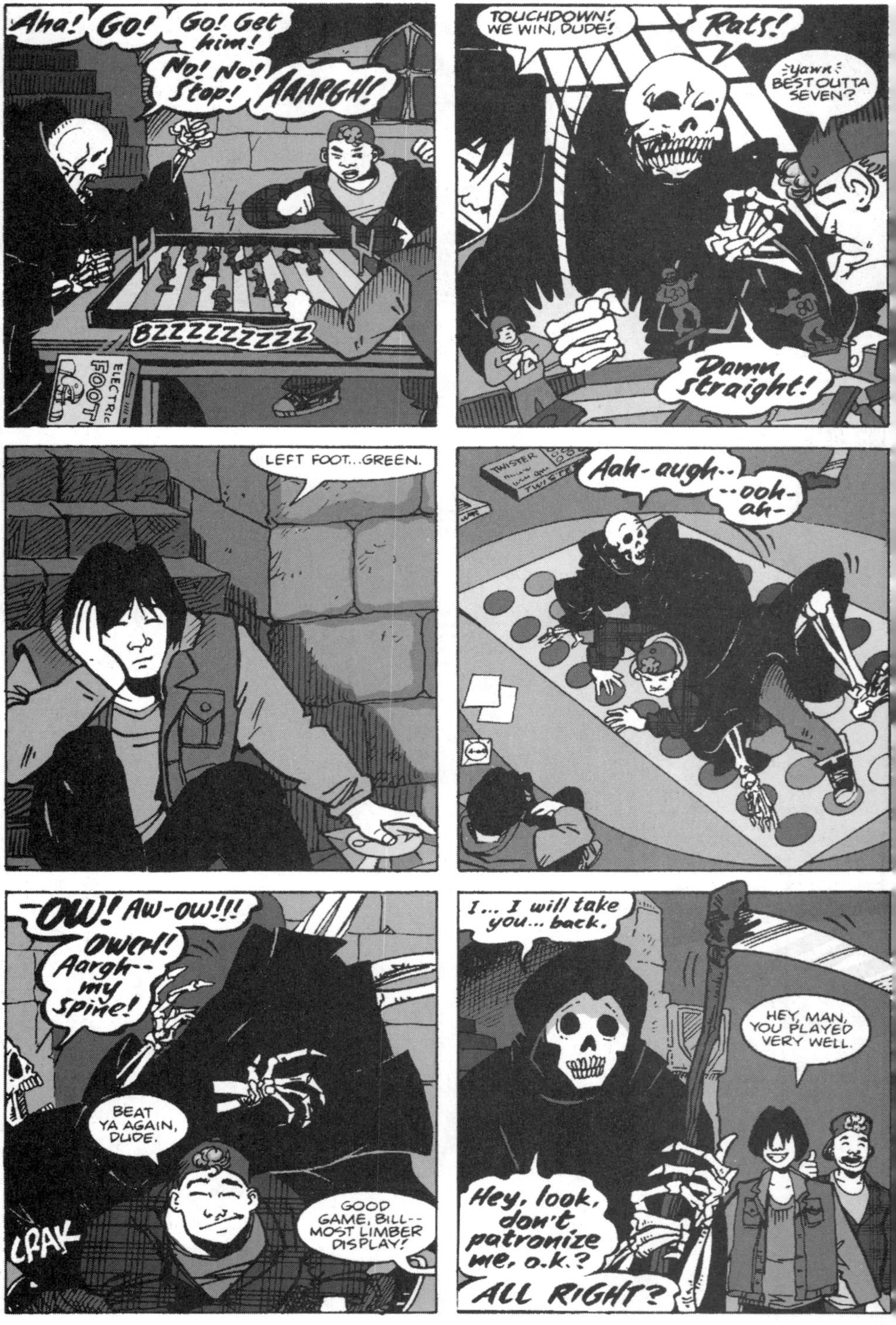
Aha! Go!
Go! Get him!
No! No! Stop!
AAARGH!
BZZZZZZZZZZ
ELECTRIC FOOT
TOUCHDOWN! WE WIN, DUDE!
Rats!
Yawn BEST OUTTA SEVEN?
Damn straight!
LEFT FOOT...GREEN.
TWISTER
Aah-augh-- --ooh-ah-
-OW! AW-OW!!!
OWCH! Aargh-- my spine!
BEAT YA AGAIN, DUDE.
CRAK
GOOD GAME, BILL-- MOST LIMBER DISPLAY!
I... I will take you... back.
HEY, MAN, YOU PLAYED VERY WELL.
Hey, look, don't patronize me, o.k.?
ALL RIGHT?

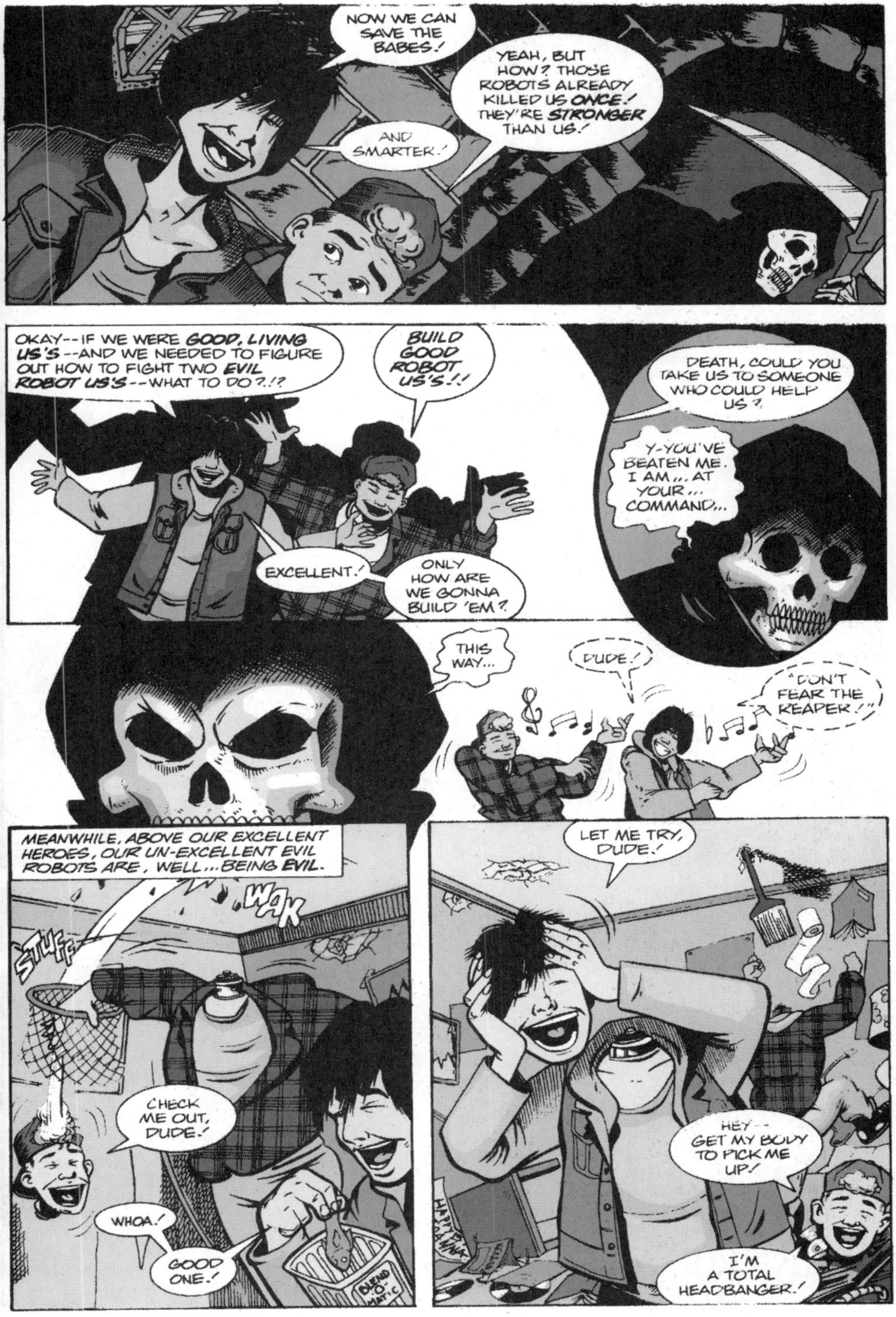
NOW WE CAN SAVE THE BABES!
YEAH, BUT HOW? THOSE ROBOTS ALREADY KILLED US ONCE! THEY'RE STRONGER THAN US!
AND SMARTER!
OKAY--IF WE WERE GOOD, LIVING US'S--AND WE NEEDED TO FIGURE OUT HOW TO FIGHT TWO EVIL ROBOT US'S--WHAT TO DO?!?
BUILD GOOD ROBOT US'S!!
EXCELLENT!
ONLY HOW ARE WE GONNA BUILD 'EM?
DEATH, COULD YOU TAKE US TO SOMEONE WHO COULD HELP US?
Y-YOU'VE BEATEN ME. I AM... AT YOUR... COMMAND...
THIS WAY...
DUDE!
"DON'T FEAR THE REAPER!"
MEANWHILE, ABOVE OUR EXCELLENT HEROES, OUR UN-EXCELLENT EVIL ROBOTS ARE, WELL... BEING EVIL.
STUFF
WAK
CHECK ME OUT, DUDE!
WHOA!
GOOD ONE!
BLEND-O-MATIC
LET ME TRY, DUDE!
HEY--GET MY BODY TO PICK ME UP!
I'M A TOTAL HEADBANGER!

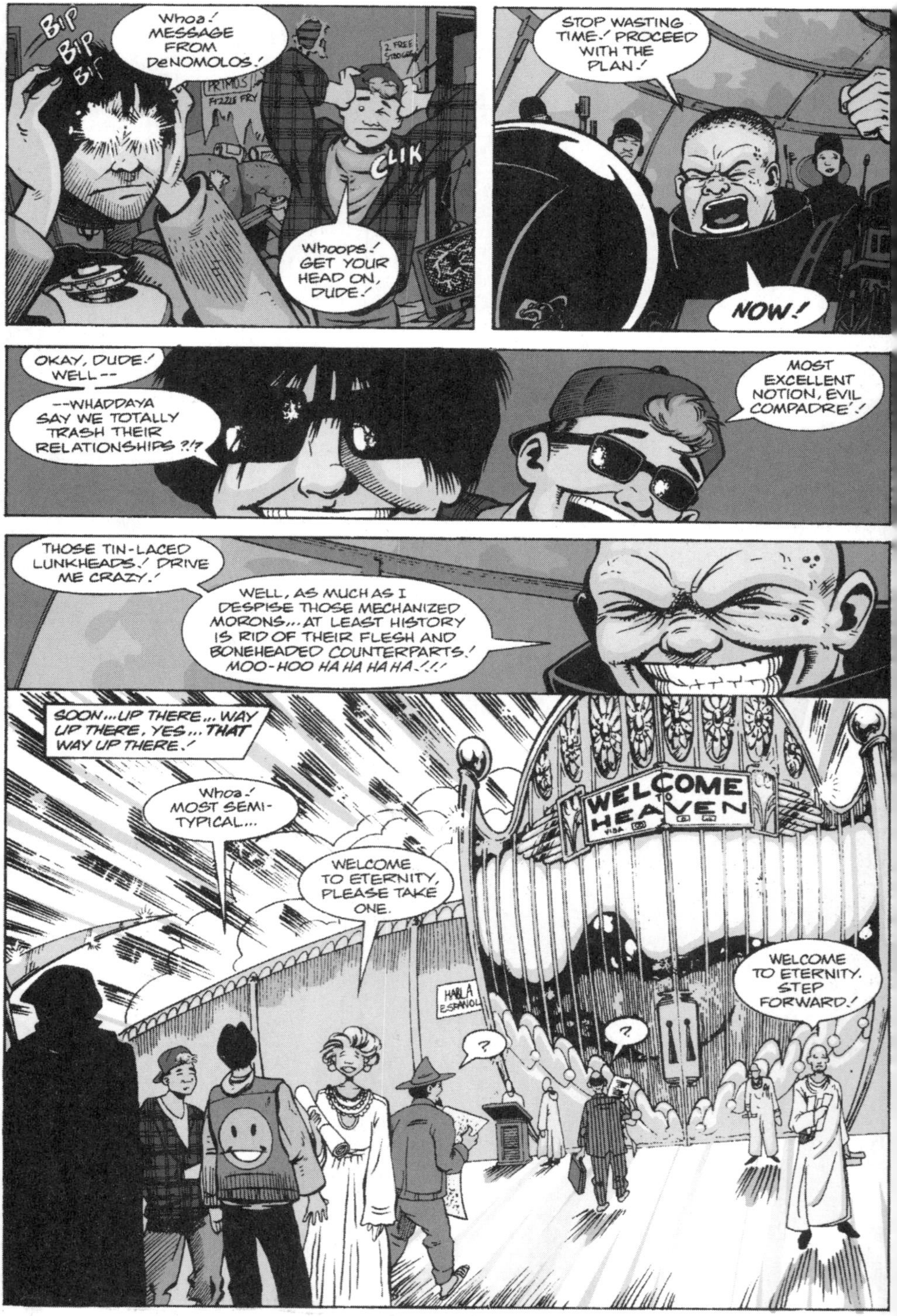
BIP BIP BIP
Whoa! MESSAGE FROM DeNOMOLOS!
PRIMUS
CLIK
Whoops! GET YOUR HEAD ON, DUDE!
STOP WASTING TIME! PROCEED WITH THE PLAN!
NOW!
OKAY, DUDE! WELL --
--WHADDAYA SAY WE TOTALLY TRASH THEIR RELATIONSHIPS?!?
MOST EXCELLENT NOTION, EVIL COMPADRE!
THOSE TIN-LACED LUNKHEADS! DRIVE ME CRAZY!
WELL, AS MUCH AS I DESPISE THOSE MECHANIZED MORONS... AT LEAST HISTORY IS RID OF THEIR FLESH AND BONEHEADED COUNTERPARTS! MOO-HOO HA HA HA HA!!!
SOON... UP THERE... WAY UP THERE, YES... THAT WAY UP THERE!
Whoa! MOST SEMI-TYPICAL...
WELCOME TO ETERNITY, PLEASE TAKE ONE.
WELCOME TO HEAVEN
HABLA ESPAÑOL
?
?
WELCOME TO ETERNITY. STEP FORWARD!

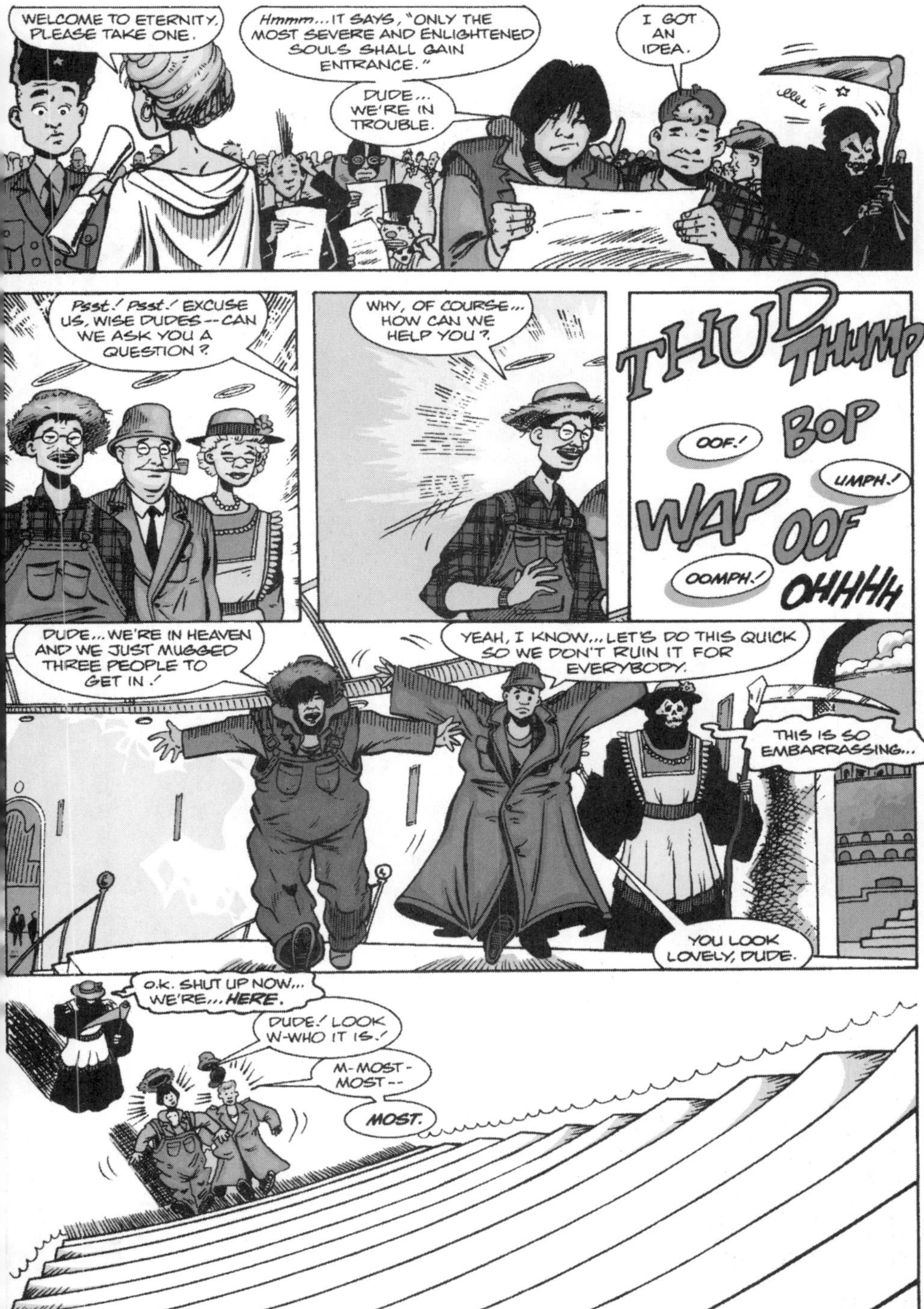
WELCOME TO ETERNITY. PLEASE TAKE ONE.
Hmmm... IT SAYS, "ONLY THE MOST SEVERE AND ENLIGHTENED SOULS SHALL GAIN ENTRANCE."
DUDE... WE'RE IN TROUBLE.
I GOT AN IDEA.
Psst! Psst! EXCUSE US, WISE DUDES--CAN WE ASK YOU A QUESTION?
WHY, OF COURSE... HOW CAN WE HELP YOU?
THUD
THUMP
BOP
OOF!
UMPH!
WAP
OOF
OOMPH!
OHHHH
DUDE... WE'RE IN HEAVEN AND WE JUST MUGGED THREE PEOPLE TO GET IN!
YEAH, I KNOW... LET'S DO THIS QUICK SO WE DON'T RUIN IT FOR EVERYBODY.
THIS IS SO EMBARRASSING...
YOU LOOK LOVELY, DUDE.
O.K. SHUT UP NOW... WE'RE... HERE.
DUDE! LOOK W-WHO IT IS!
M-MOST-MOST--
MOST.

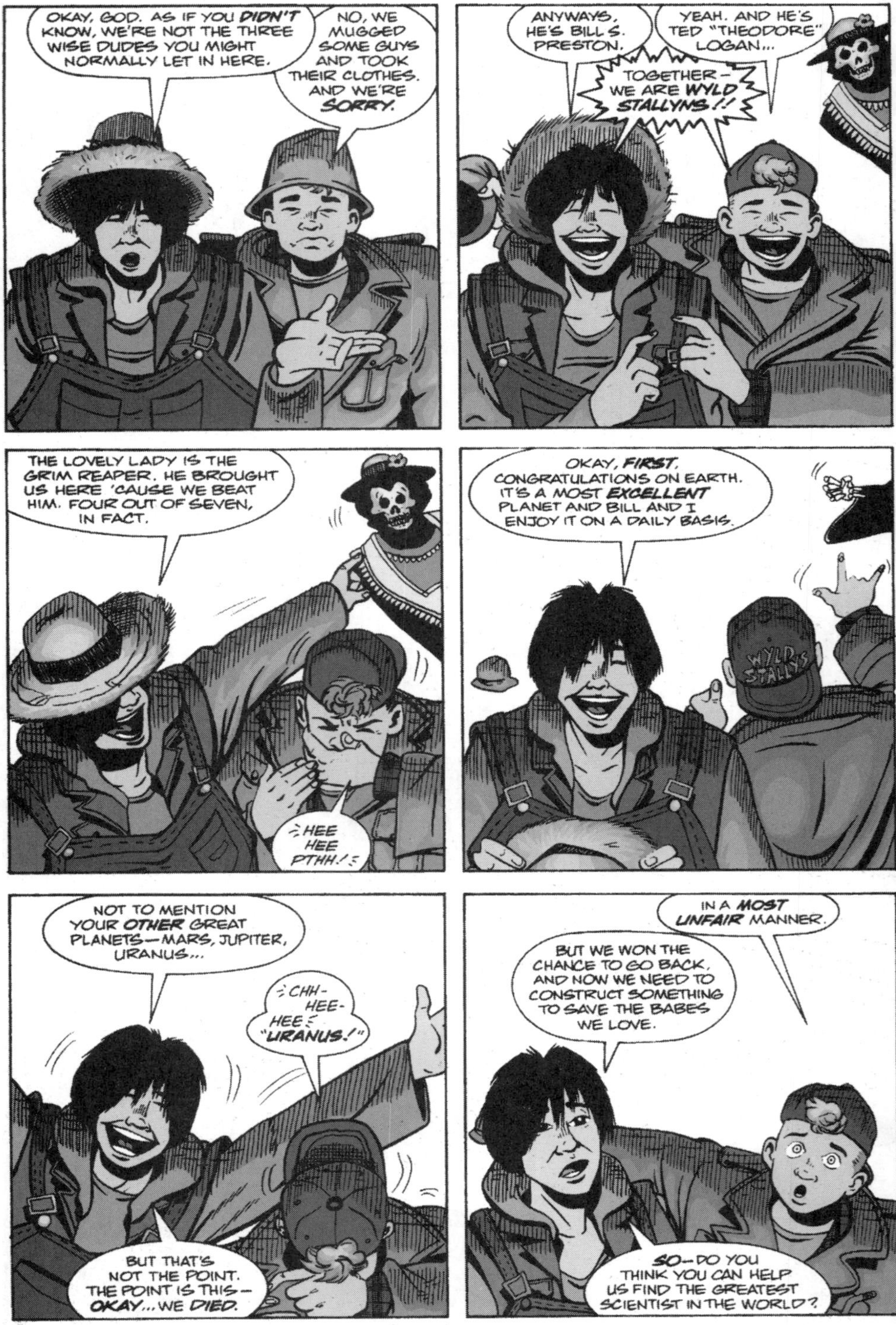
OKAY, GOD. AS IF YOU DIDN'T KNOW, WE'RE NOT THE THREE WISE DUDES YOU MIGHT NORMALLY LET IN HERE.
NO, WE MUGGED SOME GUYS AND TOOK THEIR CLOTHES. AND WE'RE SORRY.
ANYWAYS, HE'S BILL S. PRESTON.
YEAH. AND HE'S TED "THEODORE" LOGAN...
TOGETHER– WE ARE WYLD STALLYNS!!!
THE LOVELY LADY IS THE GRIM REAPER. HE BROUGHT US HERE 'CAUSE WE BEAT HIM. FOUR OUT OF SEVEN, IN FACT.
HEE HEE PTHH!
OKAY, FIRST, CONGRATULATIONS ON EARTH. IT'S A MOST EXCELLENT PLANET AND BILL AND I ENJOY IT ON A DAILY BASIS.
WYLD STALLYNS
NOT TO MENTION YOUR OTHER GREAT PLANETS—MARS, JUPITER, URANUS...
CHH-HEE-HEE "URANUS!"
BUT THAT'S NOT THE POINT. THE POINT IS THIS– OKAY... WE DIED.
IN A MOST UNFAIR MANNER.
BUT WE WON THE CHANCE TO GO BACK, AND NOW WE NEED TO CONSTRUCT SOMETHING TO SAVE THE BABES WE LOVE.
SO– DO YOU THINK YOU CAN HELP US FIND THE GREATEST SCIENTIST IN THE WORLD?

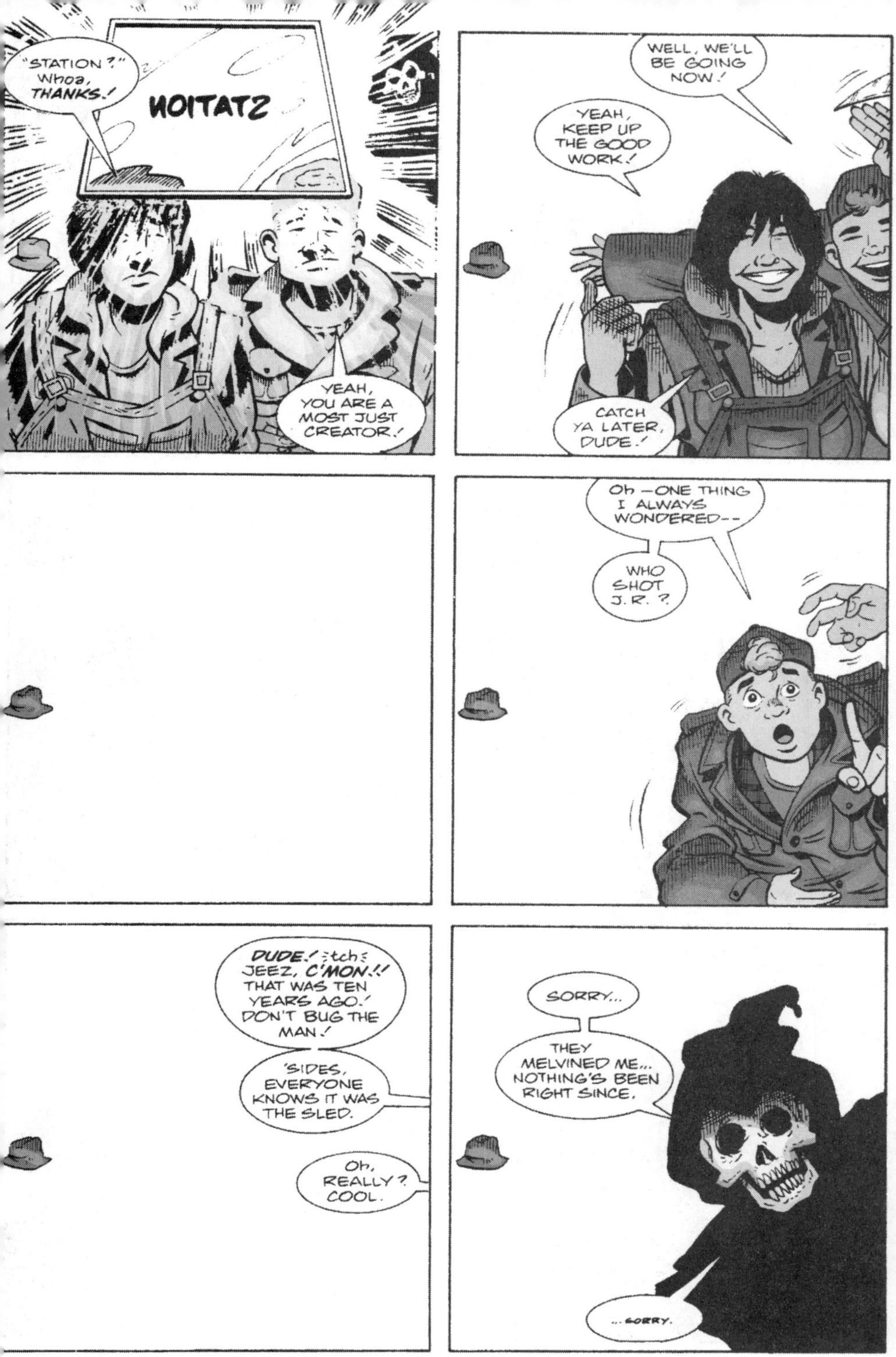
"STATION?" Whoa, THANKS.!
NOITATZ
YEAH, YOU ARE A MOST JUST CREATOR.!
WELL, WE'LL BE GOING NOW.!
YEAH, KEEP UP THE GOOD WORK.!
CATCH YA LATER, DUDE.!
Oh —ONE THING I ALWAYS WONDERED--
WHO SHOT J.R.?
DUDE.! tch JEEZ, C'MON.!! THAT WAS TEN YEARS AGO.! DON'T BUG THE MAN.!
'SIDES, EVERYONE KNOWS IT WAS THE SLED.
Oh, REALLY? COOL.
SORRY...
THEY MELVINED ME... NOTHING'S BEEN RIGHT SINCE.
...SORRY.

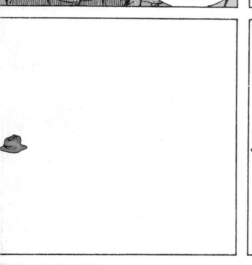

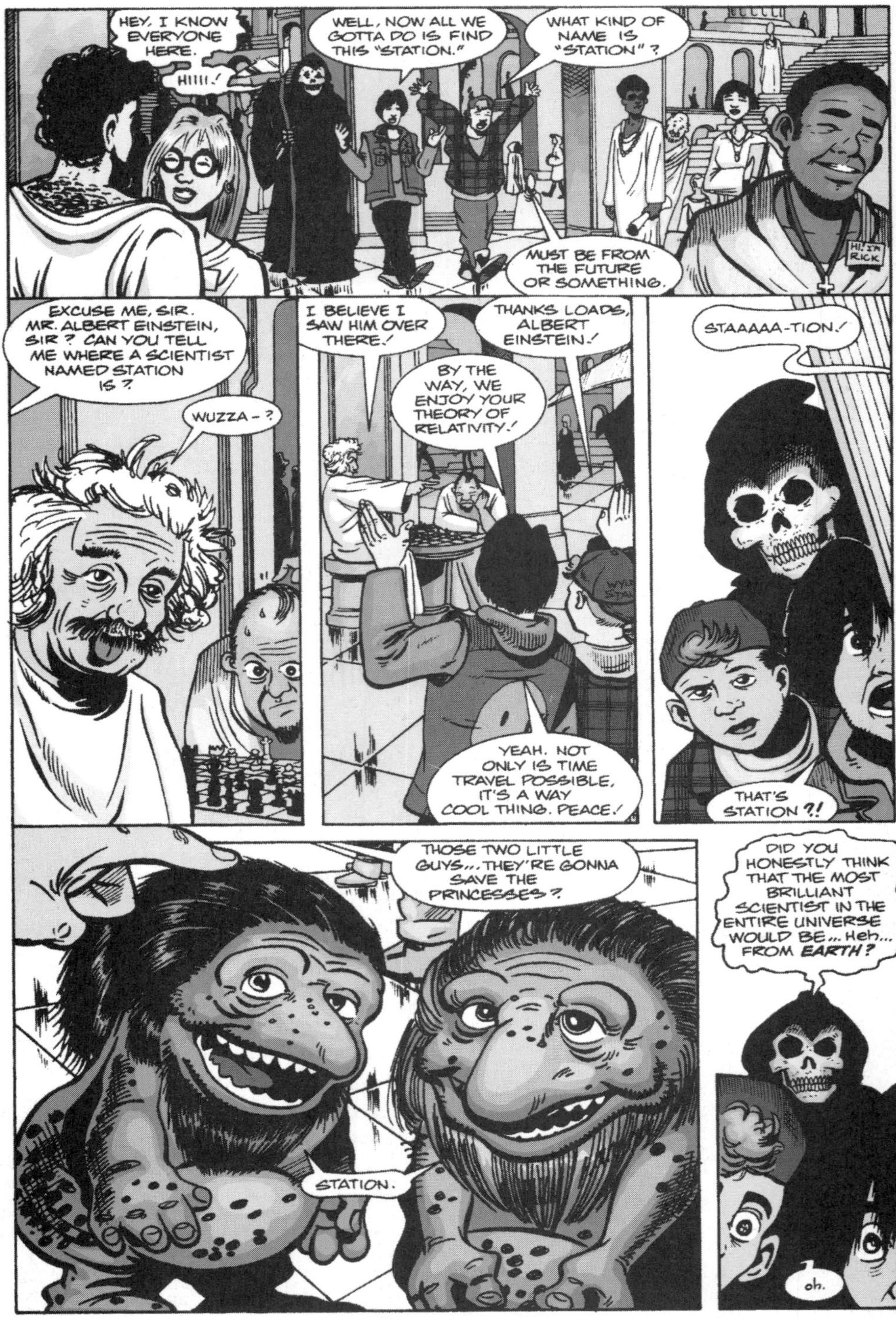
HEY. I KNOW EVERYONE HERE.
HIIII.!
WELL, NOW ALL WE GOTTA DO IS FIND THIS "STATION."
WHAT KIND OF NAME IS "STATION"?
MUST BE FROM THE FUTURE OR SOMETHING.
HI! I'M RICK
EXCUSE ME, SIR. MR. ALBERT EINSTEIN, SIR? CAN YOU TELL ME WHERE A SCIENTIST NAMED STATION IS?
WUZZA-?
I BELIEVE I SAW HIM OVER THERE.!
THANKS LOADS, ALBERT EINSTEIN.!
BY THE WAY, WE ENJOY YOUR THEORY OF RELATIVITY.!
YEAH. NOT ONLY IS TIME TRAVEL POSSIBLE, IT'S A WAY COOL THING. PEACE.!
STAAAAA-TION.!
THAT'S STATION?!
THOSE TWO LITTLE GUYS... THEY'RE GONNA SAVE THE PRINCESSES?
STATION.
DID YOU HONESTLY THINK THAT THE MOST BRILLIANT SCIENTIST IN THE ENTIRE UNIVERSE WOULD BE... Heh... FROM **EARTH**?
oh.

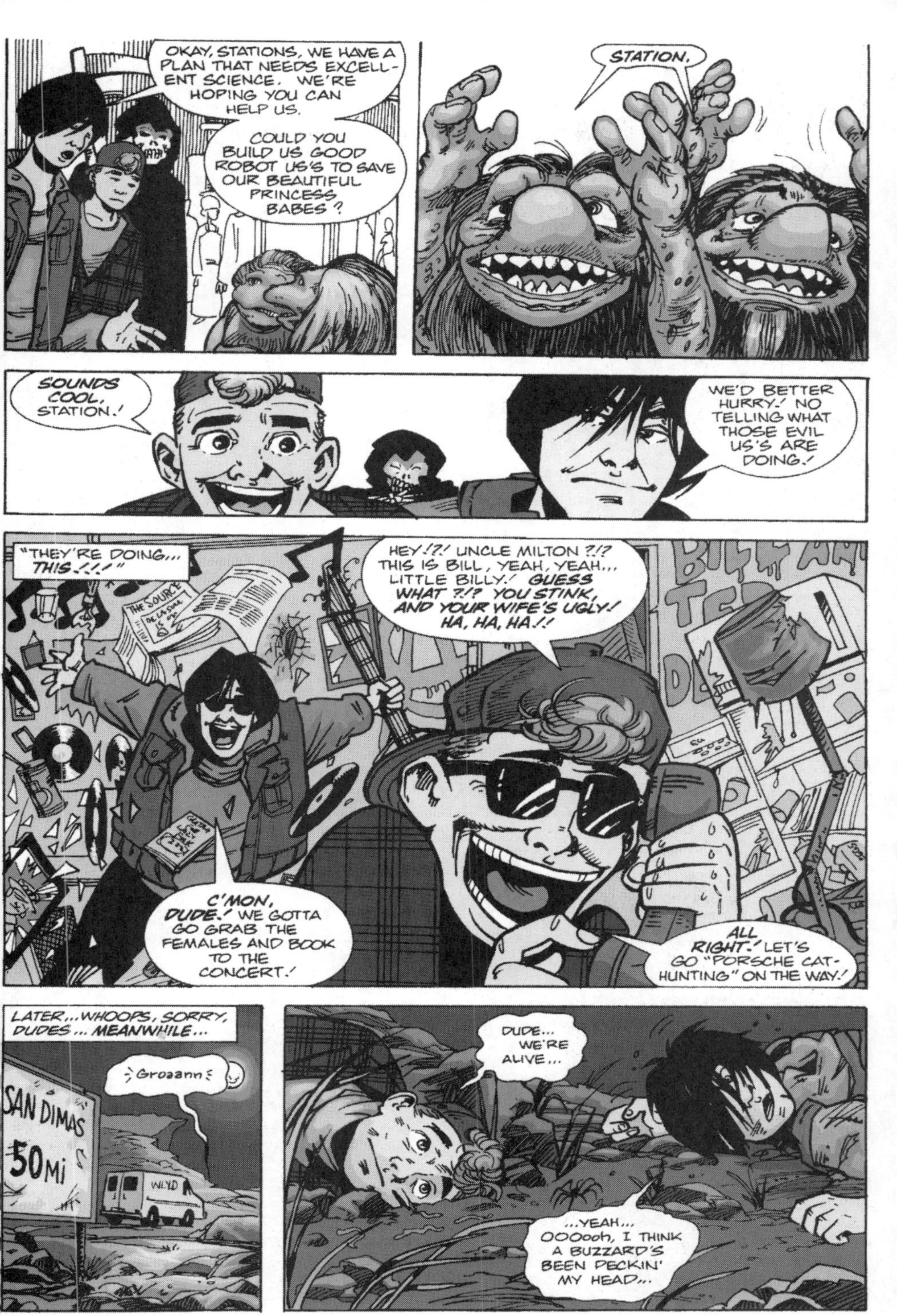
OKAY, STATIONS, WE HAVE A PLAN THAT NEEDS EXCELLENT SCIENCE. WE'RE HOPING YOU CAN HELP US.
COULD YOU BUILD US GOOD ROBOT US'S TO SAVE OUR BEAUTIFUL PRINCESS BABES ?
STATION.
SOUNDS COOL, STATION.!
WE'D BETTER HURRY.! NO TELLING WHAT THOSE EVIL US'S ARE DOING.!
"THEY'RE DOING... THIS.!.!.!"
HEY!?! UNCLE MILTON ?!? THIS IS BILL, YEAH, YEAH... LITTLE BILLY.! GUESS WHAT ?!? YOU STINK, AND YOUR WIFE'S UGLY! HA, HA, HA!!
THE SOURCE
C'MON, DUDE.! WE GOTTA GO GRAB THE FEMALES AND BOOK TO THE CONCERT.!
ALL RIGHT.! LET'S GO "PORSCHE CAT-HUNTING" ON THE WAY.!
LATER... WHOOPS, SORRY, DUDES... MEANWHILE...
SAN DIMAS
50 Mi
WLYD
Groaann
DUDE... WE'RE ALIVE...
...YEAH... OOOooh, I THINK A BUZZARD'S BEEN PECKIN' MY HEAD...

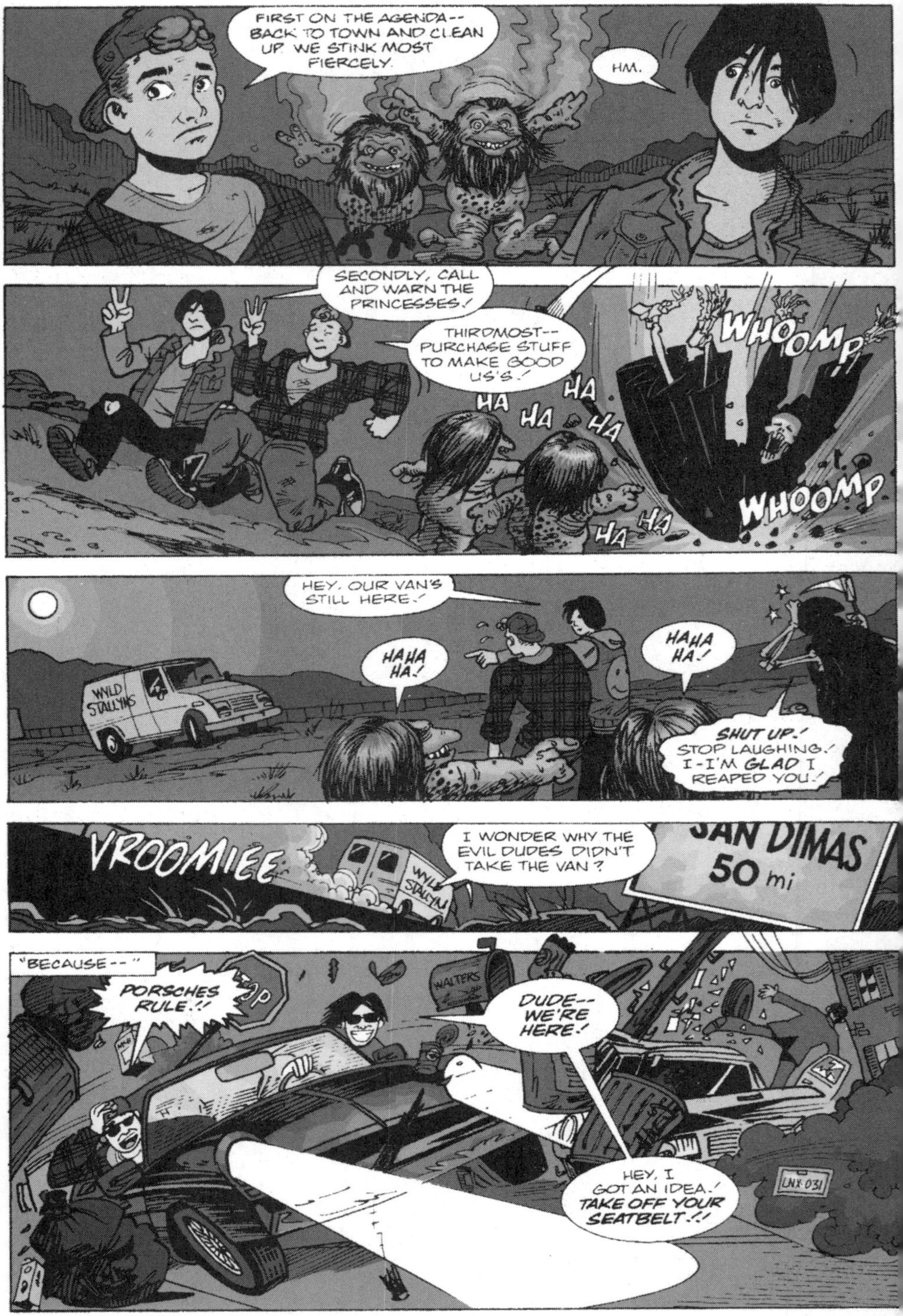

FIRST ON THE AGENDA-- BACK TO TOWN AND CLEAN UP. WE STINK MOST FIERCELY.
HM.
SECONDLY, CALL AND WARN THE PRINCESSES!
THIRDMOST-- PURCHASE STUFF TO MAKE GOOD US'S!
WHOOMP!
HA HA HA HA
WHOOMP
HA HA
HEY, OUR VAN'S STILL HERE!
HAHA HA!
HAHA HA!
SHUT UP! STOP LAUGHING! I-I'M GLAD I REAPED YOU!
VROOMIEE
I WONDER WHY THE EVIL DUDES DIDN'T TAKE THE VAN?
SAN DIMAS 50 mi
"BECAUSE--"
PORSCHES RULE!!
DUDE-- WE'RE HERE!
HEY, I GOT AN IDEA! TAKE OFF YOUR SEATBELT!!

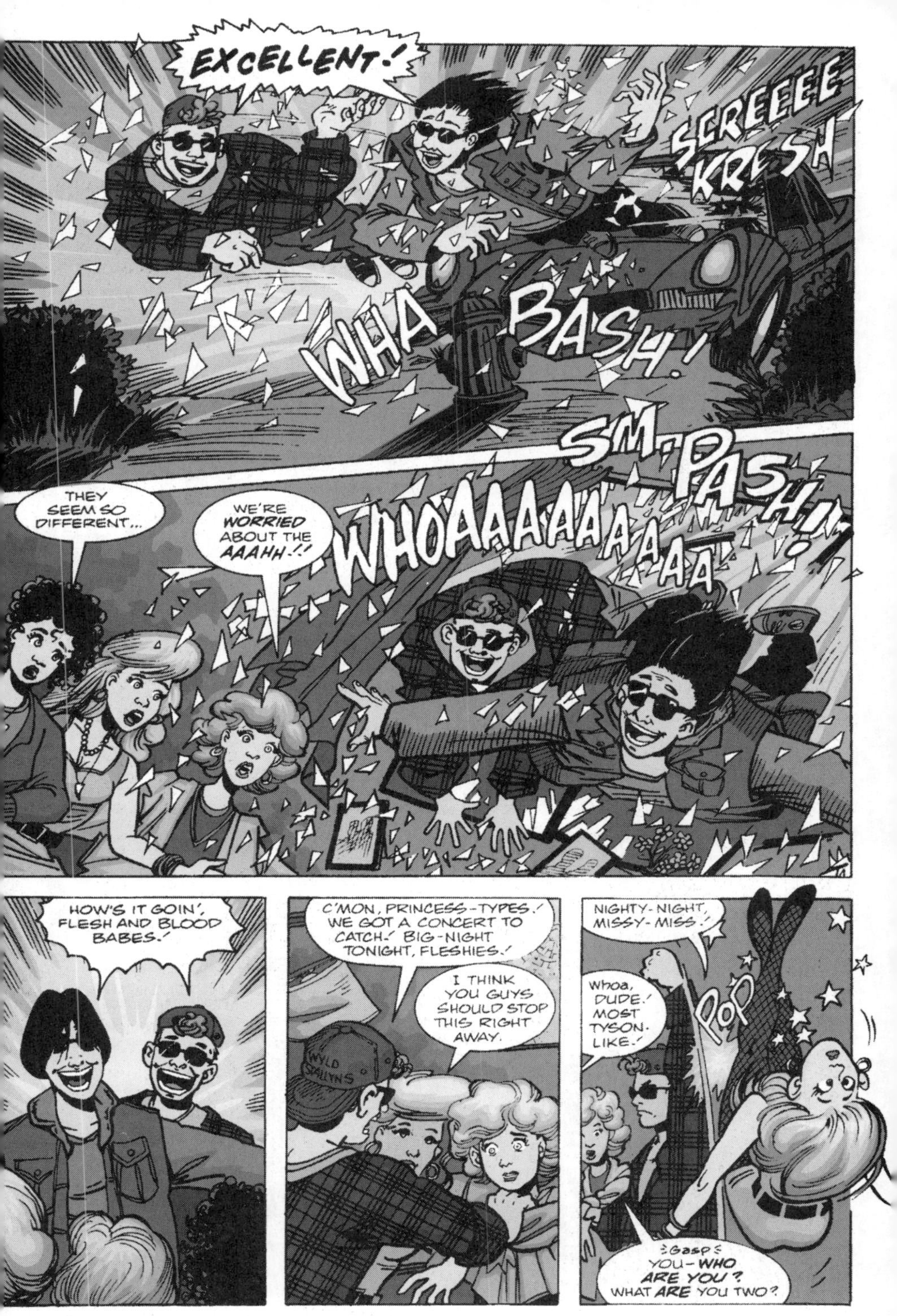
EXCELLENT!
SCREEEE
KRESH
WHA BASH!
SM PASH!!
THEY SEEM SO DIFFERENT...
WE'RE WORRIED ABOUT THE AAAHH!!
WHOAAAAAAAAAAA
HOW'S IT GOIN', FLESH AND BLOOD BABES!
C'MON, PRINCESS-TYPES! WE GOT A CONCERT TO CATCH! BIG-NIGHT TONIGHT, FLESHIES!
I THINK YOU GUYS SHOULD STOP THIS RIGHT AWAY.
WYLD STALLYNS
NIGHTY-NIGHT, MISSY-MISS!
Whoa, DUDE! MOST TYSON-LIKE!
POP
Gasp
YOU-WHO ARE YOU? WHAT ARE YOU TWO?

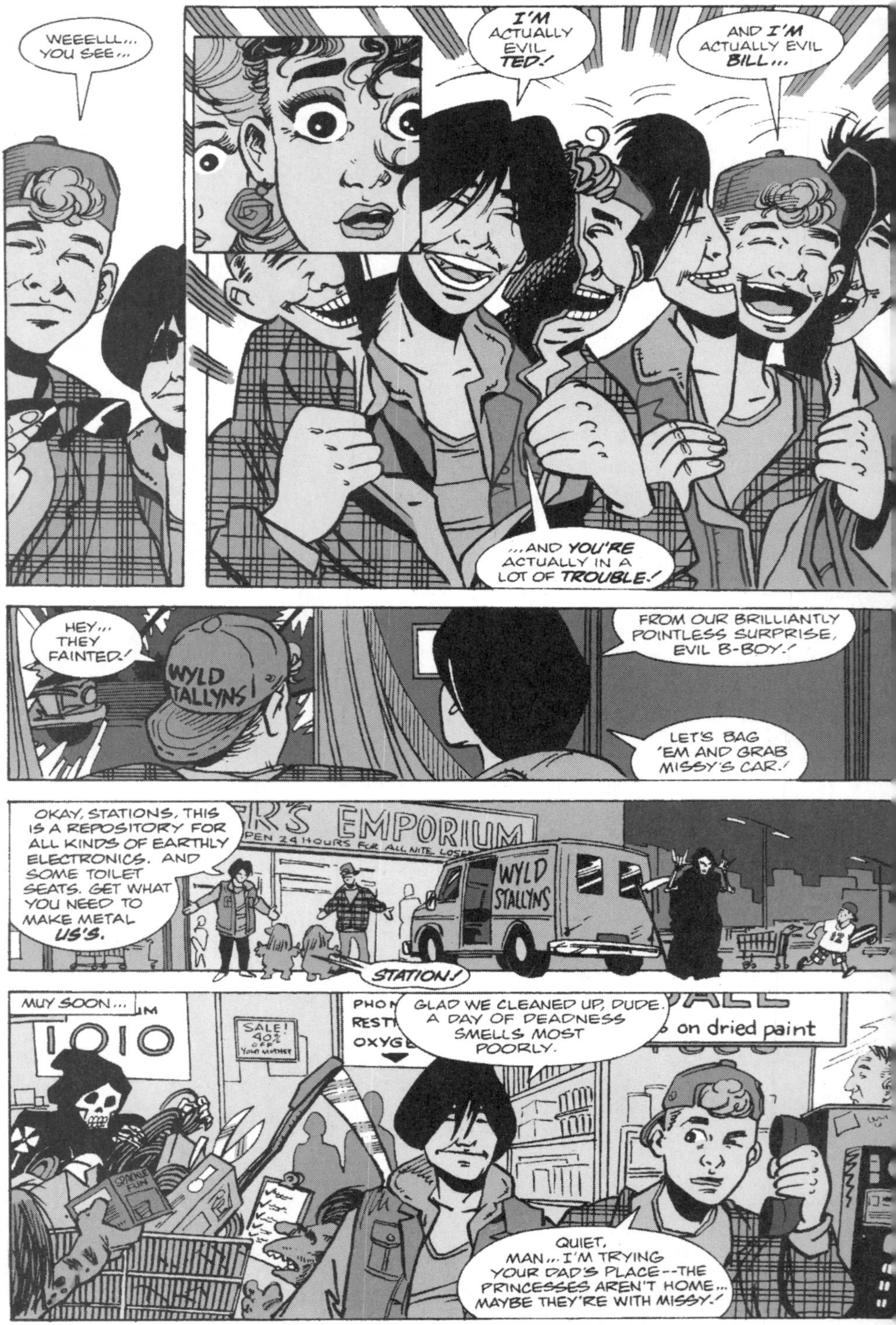
WEEEELLL... YOU SEE...
I'M ACTUALLY EVIL TED.!
AND I'M ACTUALLY EVIL BILL...
...AND YOU'RE ACTUALLY IN A LOT OF TROUBLE.!
HEY... THEY FAINTED.!
WYLD STALLYNS
FROM OUR BRILLIANTLY POINTLESS SURPRISE, EVIL B-BOY.!
LET'S BAG 'EM AND GRAB MISSY'S CAR.!
OKAY, STATIONS, THIS IS A REPOSITORY FOR ALL KINDS OF EARTHLY ELECTRONICS. AND SOME TOILET SEATS. GET WHAT YOU NEED TO MAKE METAL US'S.
R'S EMPORIUM
PEN 24 HOURS FOR ALL NITE LOSE
WYLD STALLYNS
STATION!
MUY SOON...
1010
SALE! 40% OFF YOUR MOTHER
GLAD WE CLEANED UP, DUDE. A DAY OF DEADNESS SMELLS MOST POORLY.
on dried paint
QUIET, MAN... I'M TRYING YOUR DAD'S PLACE--THE PRINCESSES AREN'T HOME... MAYBE THEY'RE WITH MISSY.!

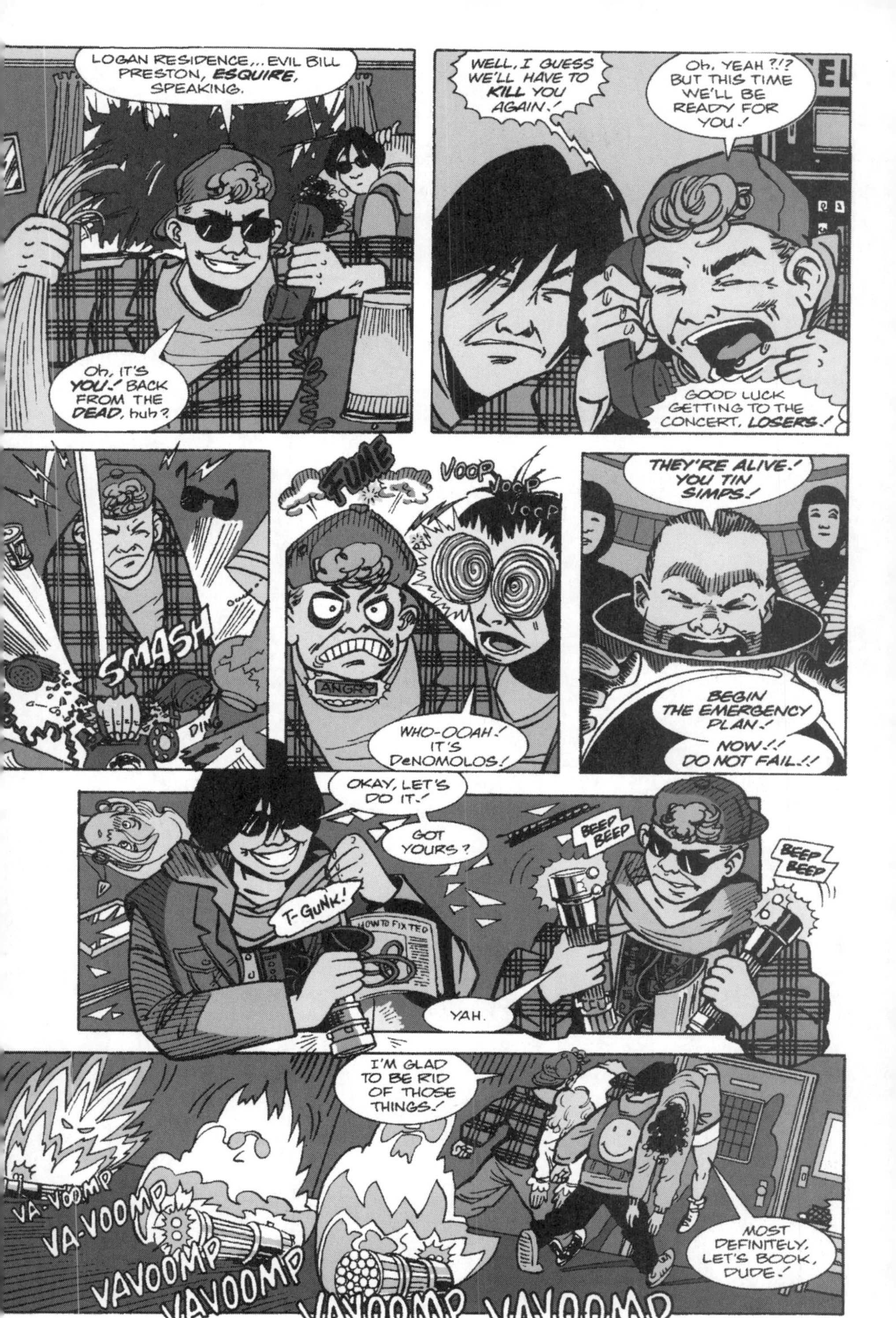
LOGAN RESIDENCE... EVIL BILL PRESTON, ESQUIRE, SPEAKING.
Oh, IT'S YOU! BACK FROM THE DEAD, huh?
WELL, I GUESS WE'LL HAVE TO KILL YOU AGAIN!
Oh, YEAH ?!? BUT THIS TIME WE'LL BE READY FOR YOU!
GOOD LUCK GETTING TO THE CONCERT, LOSERS!
SMASH
DING
FUME
VOOP VOOP VOOP
ANGRY
WHO-OOAH! IT'S DeNOMOLOS!
THEY'RE ALIVE! YOU TIN SIMPS!
BEGIN THE EMERGENCY PLAN!
NOW!! DO NOT FAIL!!
OKAY, LET'S DO IT!
GOT YOURS?
T-GUNK!
BEEP BEEP
BEEP BEEP
YAH.
I'M GLAD TO BE RID OF THOSE THINGS!
MOST DEFINITELY. LET'S BOOK, DUDE!
VA-VOOMP
VA-VOOMP
VAVOOMP
VAVOOMP
VAVOOMP
VAVOOMP

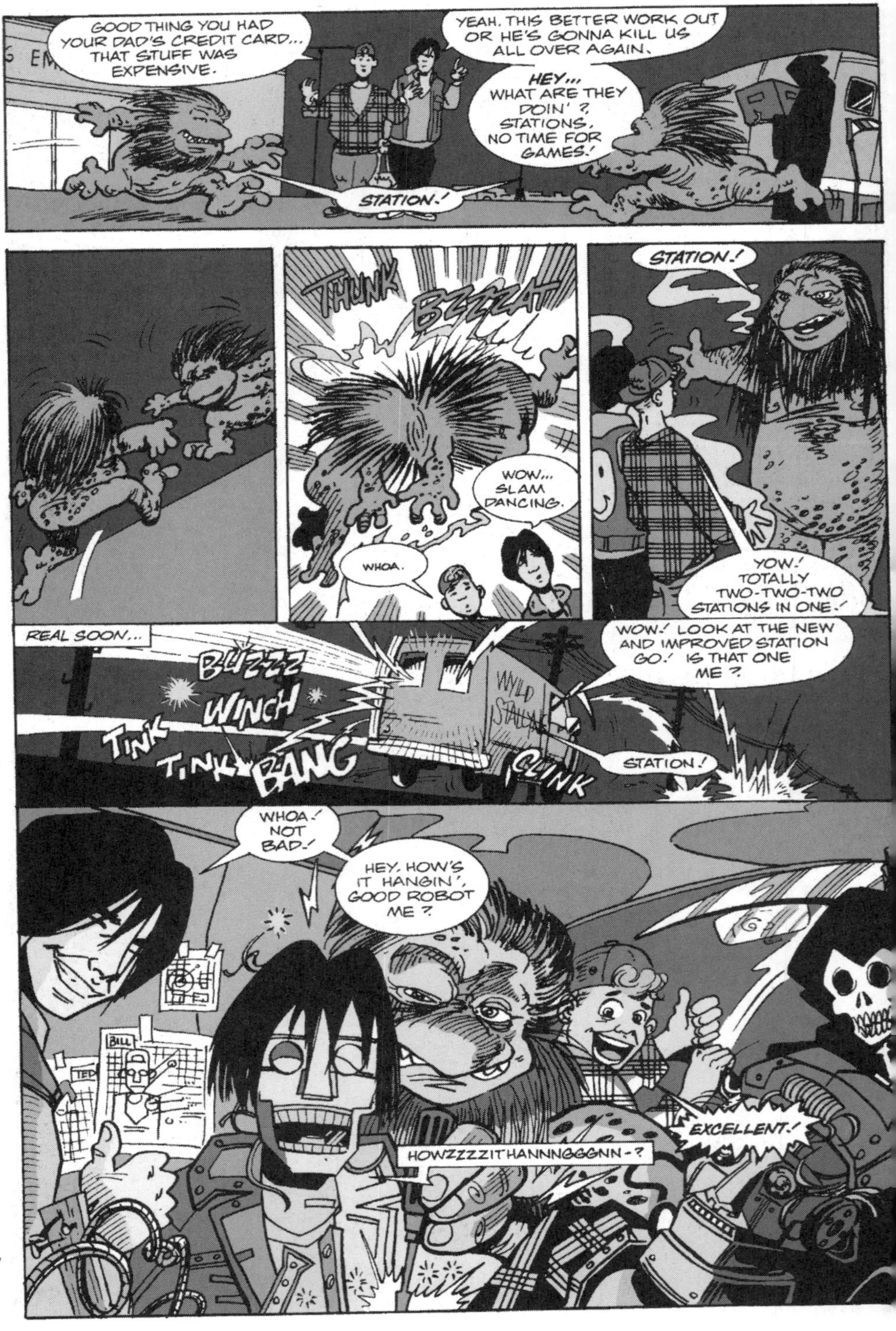
GOOD THING YOU HAD YOUR DAD'S CREDIT CARD... THAT STUFF WAS EXPENSIVE.
YEAH. THIS BETTER WORK OUT OR HE'S GONNA KILL US ALL OVER AGAIN.
HEY... WHAT ARE THEY DOIN'? STATIONS, NO TIME FOR GAMES!
STATION!
THUNK
BZZZAT
WOW... SLAM DANCING.
WHOA.
STATION!
YOW! TOTALLY TWO-TWO-TWO STATIONS IN ONE!
REAL SOON...
BUZZZ
WINCH
TINK
TINK
BANG
CLINK
WOW! LOOK AT THE NEW AND IMPROVED STATION GO! IS THAT ONE ME?
STATION!
WHOA! NOT BAD!
HEY. HOW'S IT HANGIN', GOOD ROBOT ME?
EXCELLENT!
HOWZZZZITHANNNGGGNN-?

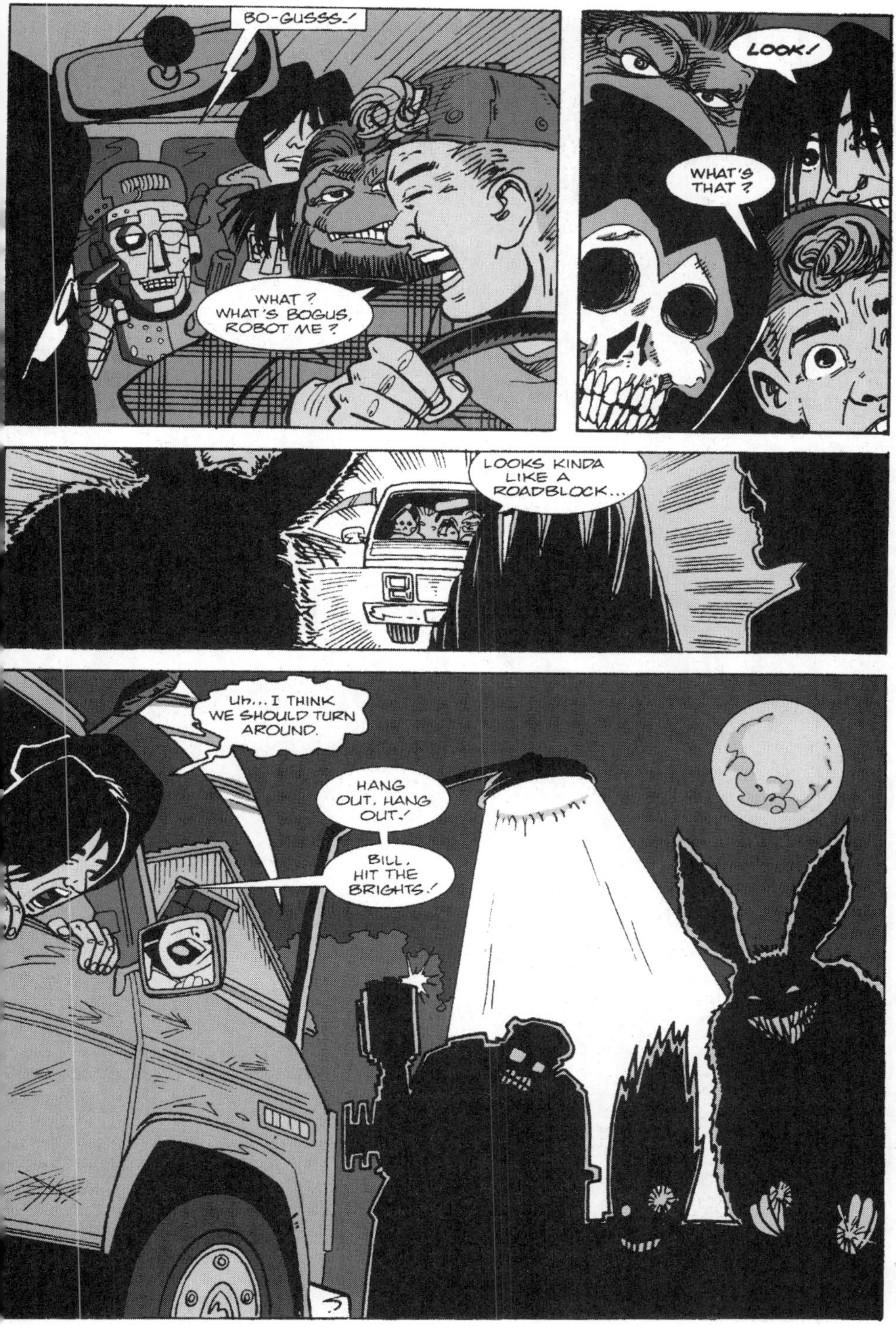
BO-GUSSS.!
WHAT ? WHAT'S BOGUS, ROBOT ME ?
LOOK!
WHAT'S THAT ?
LOOKS KINDA LIKE A ROADBLOCK...
Uh... I THINK WE SHOULD TURN AROUND.
HANG OUT, HANG OUT.!
BILL, HIT THE BRIGHTS.!

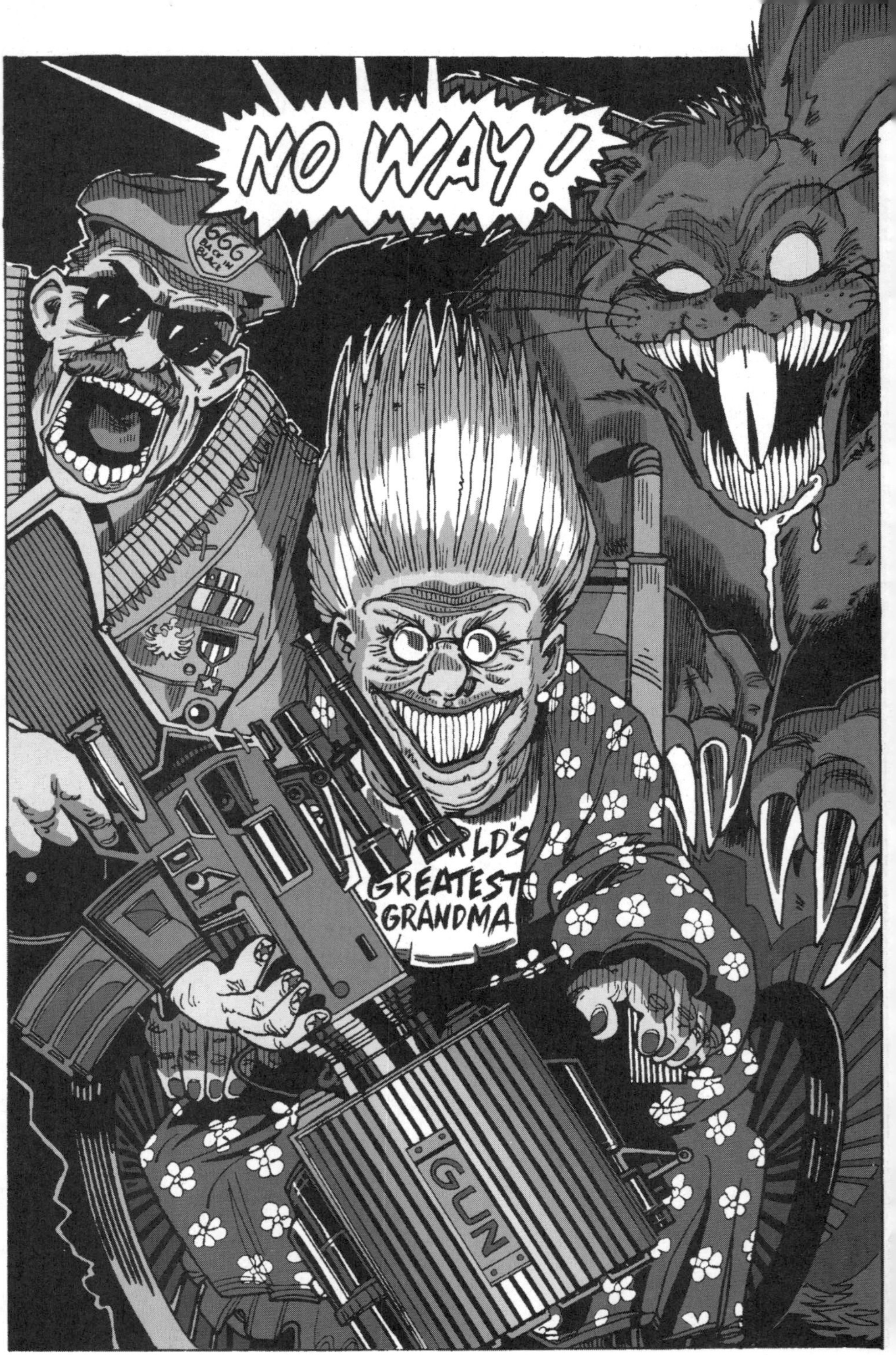
NO WAY!
GREATEST
GRANDMA
GUN

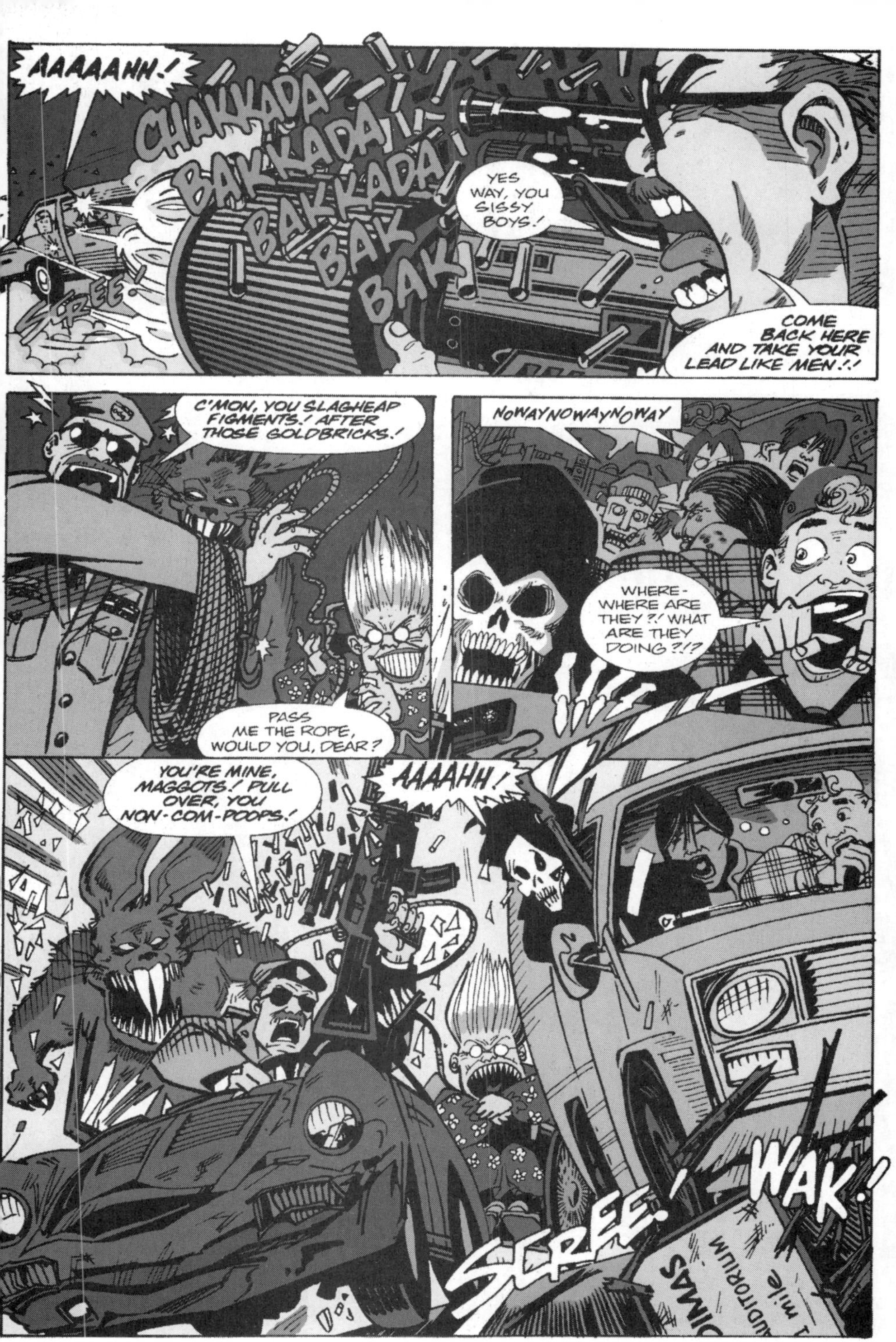
AAAAAANH!
CHAKKADA
BAKKADA!
BAKKADA!
BAK
BAK!
SCREE!
YES WAY, YOU SISSY BOYS!
COME BACK HERE AND TAKE YOUR LEAD LIKE MEN!!
C'MON, YOU SLAGHEAP FIGMENTS! AFTER THOSE GOLDBRICKS!
PASS ME THE ROPE, WOULD YOU, DEAR?
NOWAYNOWAYNOWAY
WHERE-WHERE ARE THEY?! WHAT ARE THEY DOING?!?
YOU'RE MINE, MAGGOTS! PULL OVER, YOU NON-COM-POOPS!
AAAAHH!
SCREE!
WAK!
AUDITORIUM

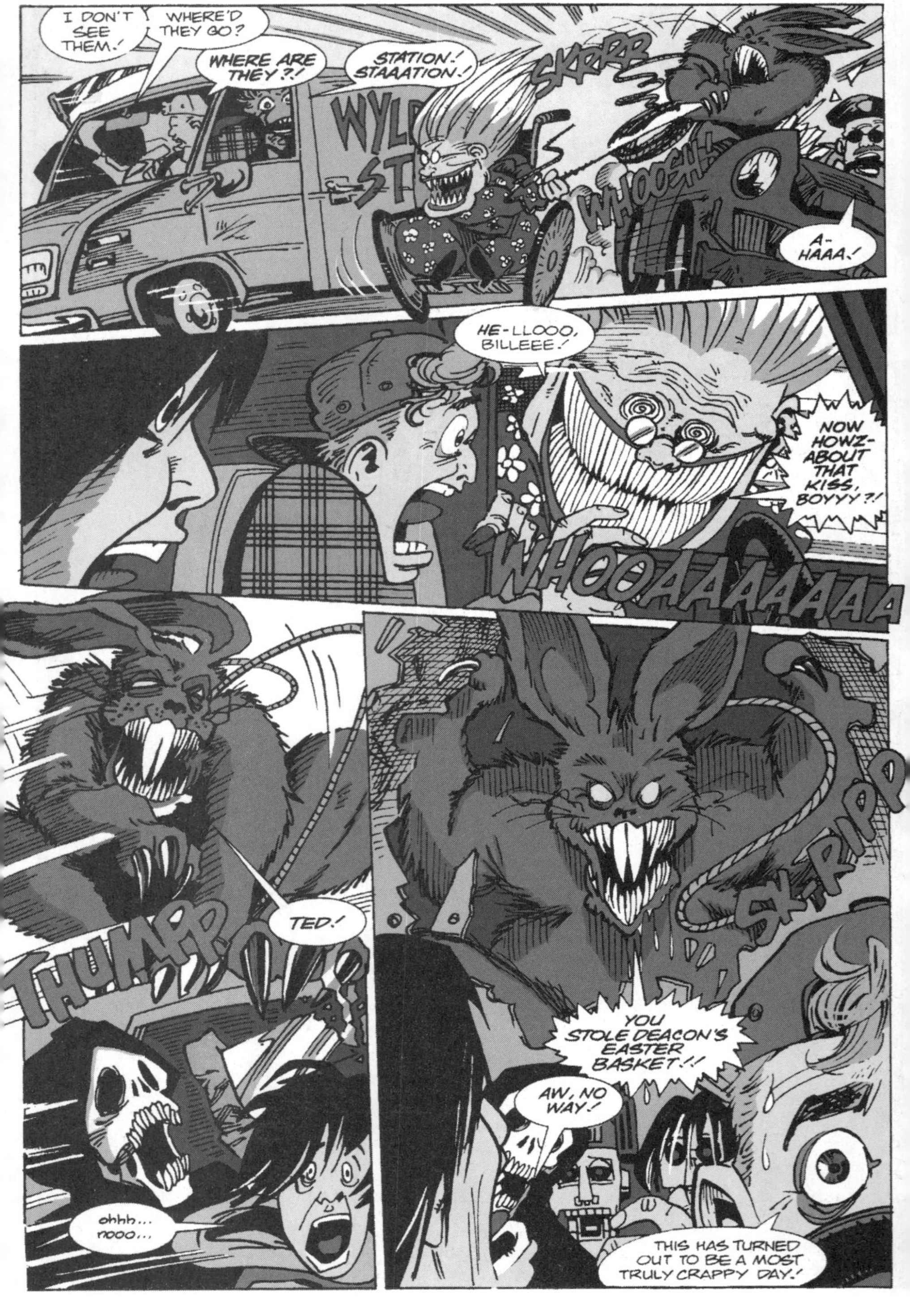
I DON'T SEE THEM.!
WHERE'D THEY GO?
WHERE ARE THEY?!
STATION! STAAATION!
SKRRR
WHOOSH
A-HAAA!
HE-LLOOO, BILLEEE!
NOW HOWZ-ABOUT THAT KISS, BOYYY?!
WHOOAAAAAAAA
TED!
THUMPP
SK-RIPP
YOU STOLE DEACON'S EASTER BASKET!!
AW, NO WAY!
ohhh... nooo...
THIS HAS TURNED OUT TO BE A MOST TRULY CRAPPY DAY!

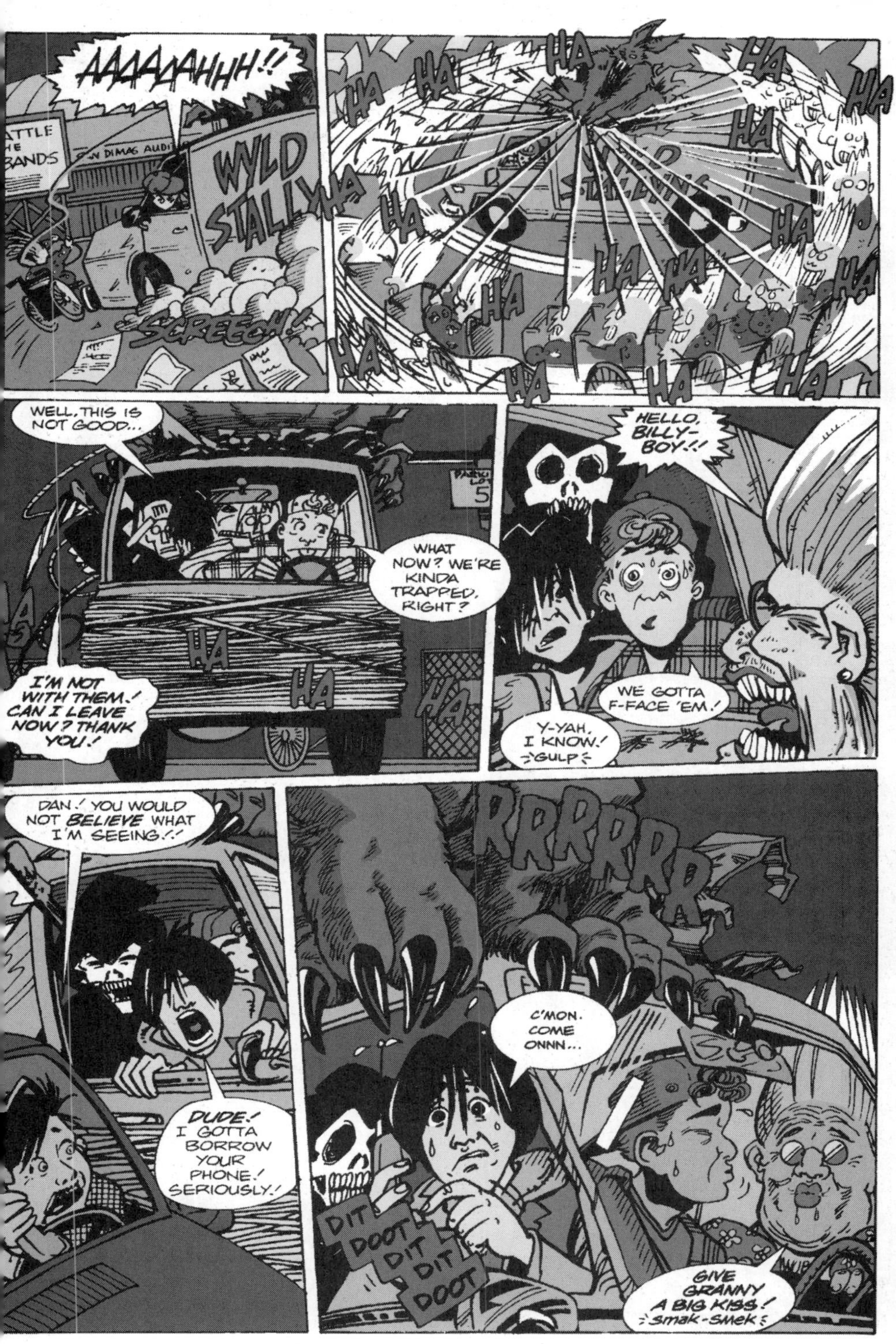
AAAAAAHHH!!
BATTLE THE BANDS
SAN DIMAS AUDI
WYLD STALLYNS
SCREECH!
HA HA HA HA HA HA HA HA HA HA HA HA HA HA HA HA HA
WELL, THIS IS NOT GOOD...
WHAT NOW? WE'RE KINDA TRAPPED, RIGHT?
I'M NOT WITH THEM! CAN I LEAVE NOW? THANK YOU!
HA HA HA
HELLO, BILLY-BOY!!
WE GOTTA F-FACE 'EM!
Y-YAH, I KNOW! GULP
DAN! YOU WOULD NOT BELIEVE WHAT I'M SEEING!!
DUDE! I GOTTA BORROW YOUR PHONE! SERIOUSLY!
RRRRRRR
C'MON. COME ONNN...
DIT DOOT DIT DIT DOOT
GIVE GRANNY A BIG KISS! smak-smek

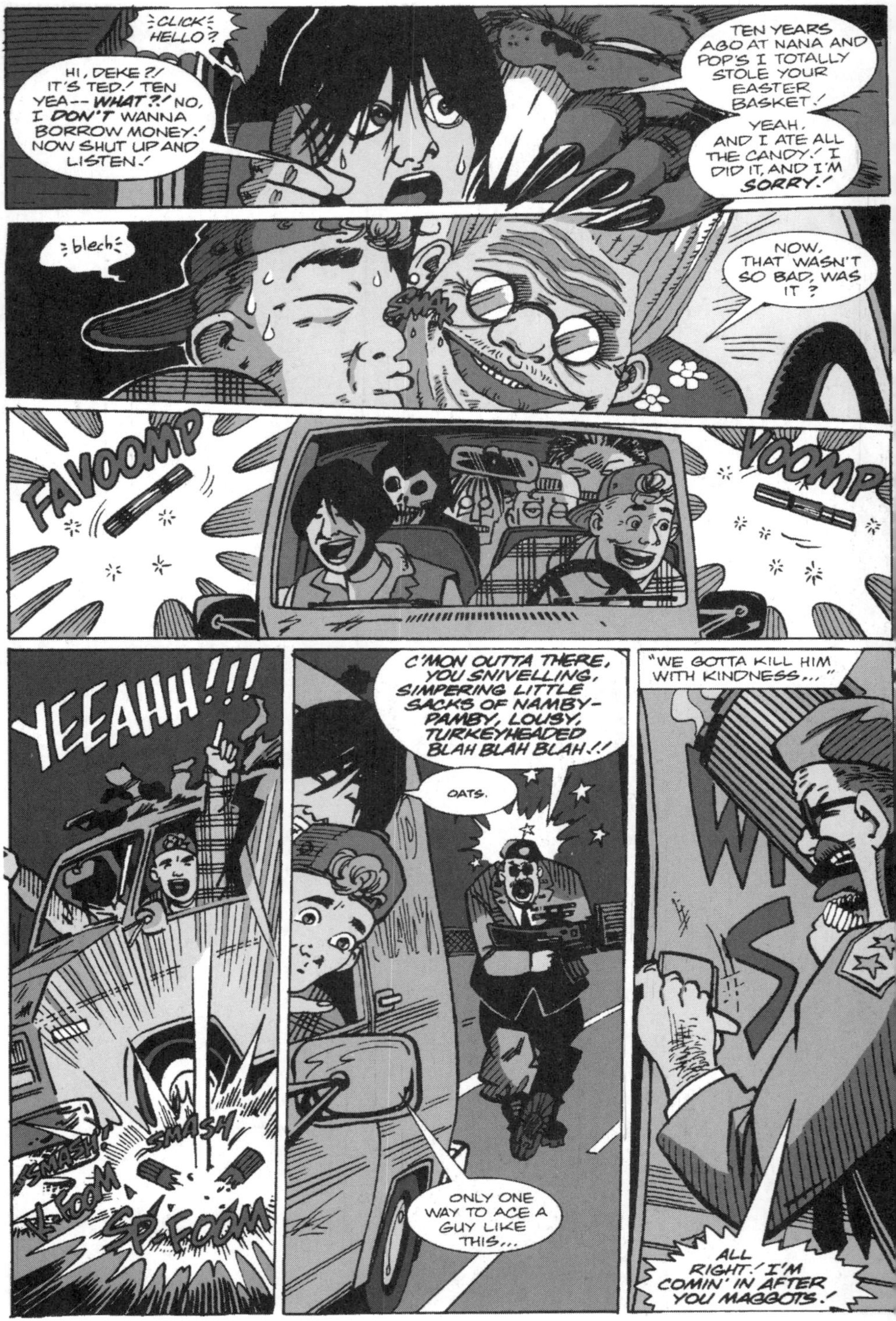
CLICK
HELLO?
HI, DEKE?! IT'S TED! TEN YEA-- WHAT?! NO, I DON'T WANNA BORROW MONEY! NOW SHUT UP AND LISTEN!
TEN YEARS AGO AT NANA AND POP'S I TOTALLY STOLE YOUR EASTER BASKET!
YEAH, AND I ATE ALL THE CANDY! I DID IT, AND I'M SORRY!
blech
SMACK
NOW, THAT WASN'T SO BAD, WAS IT?
FAVOOMP
VOOMP
YEEAHH!!!
SMASH
SMASH
K-FOOM
SP-FOOM
C'MON OUTTA THERE, YOU SNIVELLING, SIMPERING LITTLE SACKS OF NAMBY-PAMBY, LOUSY, TURKEYHEADED BLAH BLAH BLAH!!
OATS.
ONLY ONE WAY TO ACE A GUY LIKE THIS...
"WE GOTTA KILL HIM WITH KINDNESS..."
ALL RIGHT! I'M COMIN' IN AFTER YOU MAGGOTS!

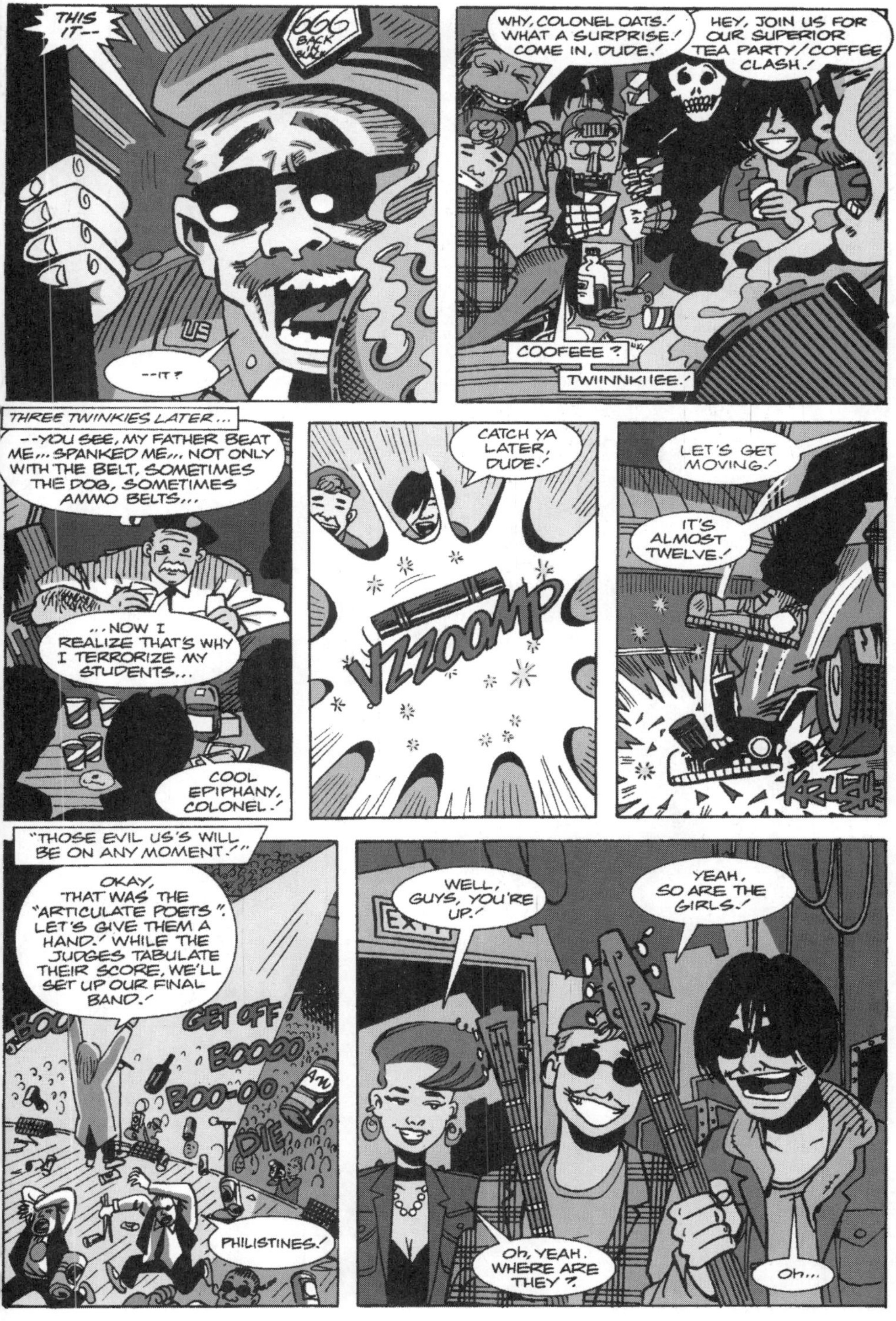

THIS IT--
666 BACK IN BLACK
US
--IT?
WHY, COLONEL OATS! WHAT A SURPRISE! COME IN, DUDE!
HEY, JOIN US FOR OUR SUPERIOR TEA PARTY/COFFEE CLASH!
COOFEEE?
TWIINNKIIEE!
THREE TWINKIES LATER...
--YOU SEE, MY FATHER BEAT ME... SPANKED ME... NOT ONLY WITH THE BELT, SOMETIMES THE DOG, SOMETIMES AMMO BELTS...
...NOW I REALIZE THAT'S WHY I TERRORIZE MY STUDENTS...
COOL EPIPHANY, COLONEL!
CATCH YA LATER, DUDE!
VZZOOMP
LET'S GET MOVING!
IT'S ALMOST TWELVE!
KRUSH
"THOSE EVIL US'S WILL BE ON ANY MOMENT!"
OKAY, THAT WAS THE "ARTICULATE POETS". LET'S GIVE THEM A HAND! WHILE THE JUDGES TABULATE THEIR SCORE, WE'LL SET UP OUR FINAL BAND!
BOO
GET OFF!
BOOOO
BOO-OO
DIE
PHILISTINES!
WELL, GUYS, YOU'RE UP!
YEAH, SO ARE THE GIRLS!
EXIT
OH, YEAH. WHERE ARE THEY?
OH...

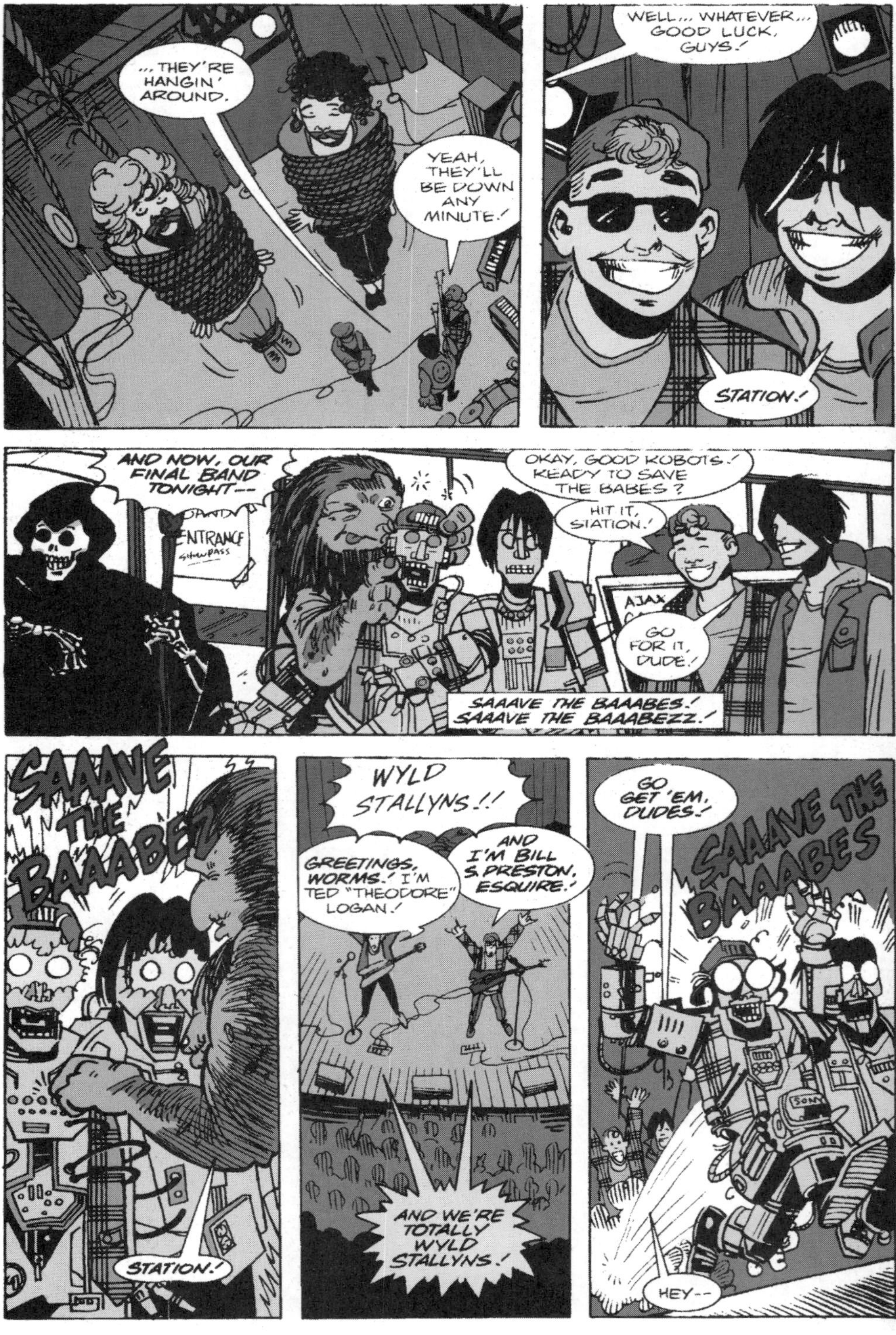

...THEY'RE HANGIN' AROUND.
YEAH, THEY'LL BE DOWN ANY MINUTE.!
WELL... WHATEVER... GOOD LUCK, GUYS.!
STATION.!
AND NOW, OUR FINAL BAND TONIGHT--
ENTRANCE
OKAY, GOOD ROBOTS.! READY TO SAVE THE BABES?
HIT IT, STATION.!
AJAX
GO FOR IT, DUDE.!
SAAAVE THE BAAABES.! SAAAVE THE BAAABEZZ.!
SAAAVE THE BAAABEZ
STATION.!
WYLD STALLYNS.!!
GREETINGS, WORMS.! I'M TED "THEODORE" LOGAN.!
AND I'M BILL S. PRESTON, ESQUIRE.!
AND WE'RE TOTALLY WYLD STALLYNS.!
GO GET 'EM, DUDES.!
SAAAVE THE BAAABES
SONY
HEY--

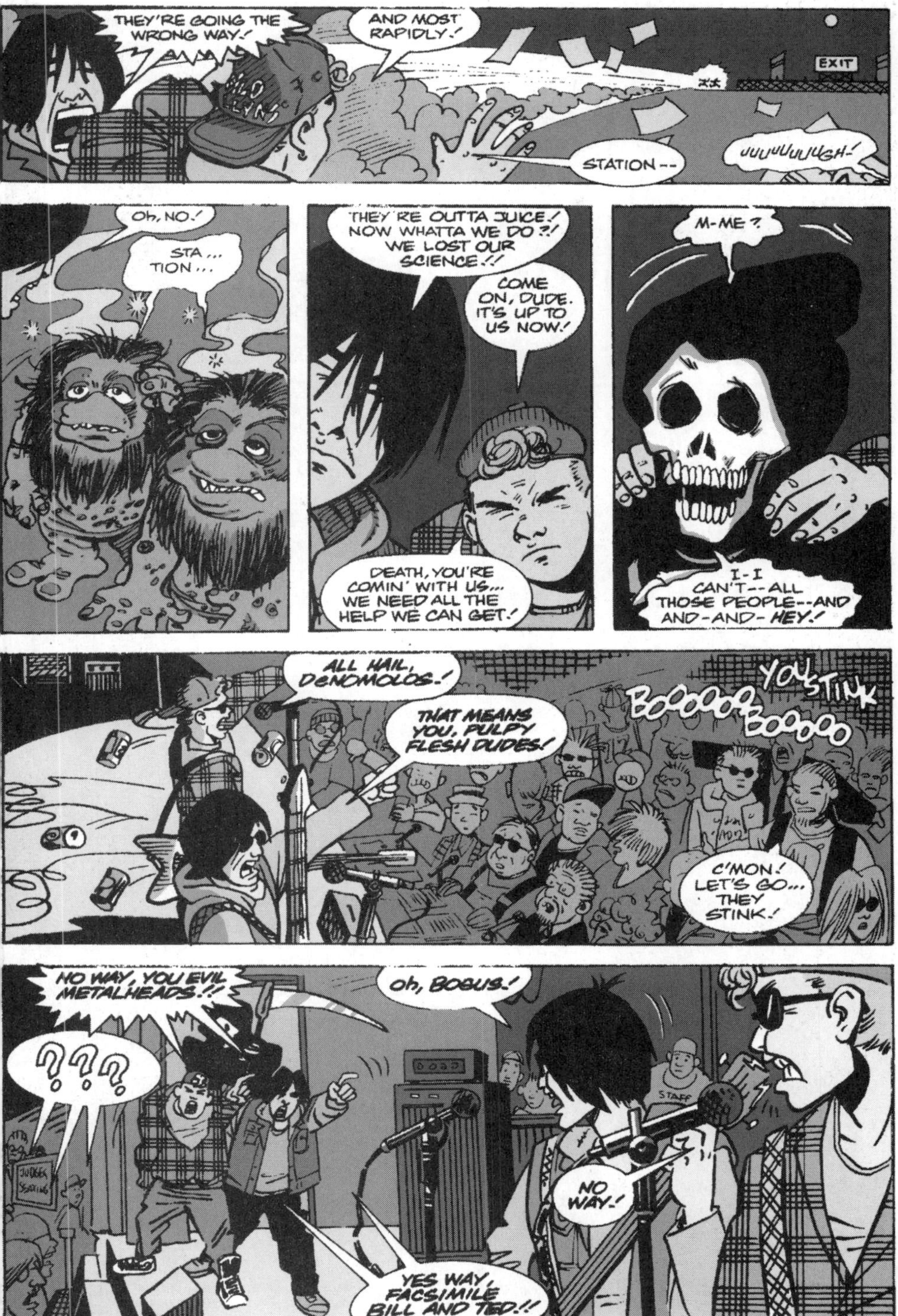
THEY'RE GOING THE WRONG WAY!
AND MOST RAPIDLY!
EXIT
STATION --
UUUUUUUUGH!
Oh, NO!
STA... TION...
THEY'RE OUTTA JUICE! NOW WHATTA WE DO?! WE LOST OUR SCIENCE!!
COME ON, DUDE. IT'S UP TO US NOW!
DEATH, YOU'RE COMIN' WITH US... WE NEED ALL THE HELP WE CAN GET!
M-ME?
I-I CAN'T--ALL THOSE PEOPLE--AND AND-AND-HEY!
ALL HAIL, DeNOMOLOS!
THAT MEANS YOU, PULPY FLESH DUDES!
YOU STINK
BOOOOOO BOOOOO
C'MON! LET'S GO... THEY STINK!
NO WAY, YOU EVIL METALHEADS!!!
???
Oh, BOGUS!
STAFF
NO WAY!
YES WAY, FACSIMILE BILL AND TED!!

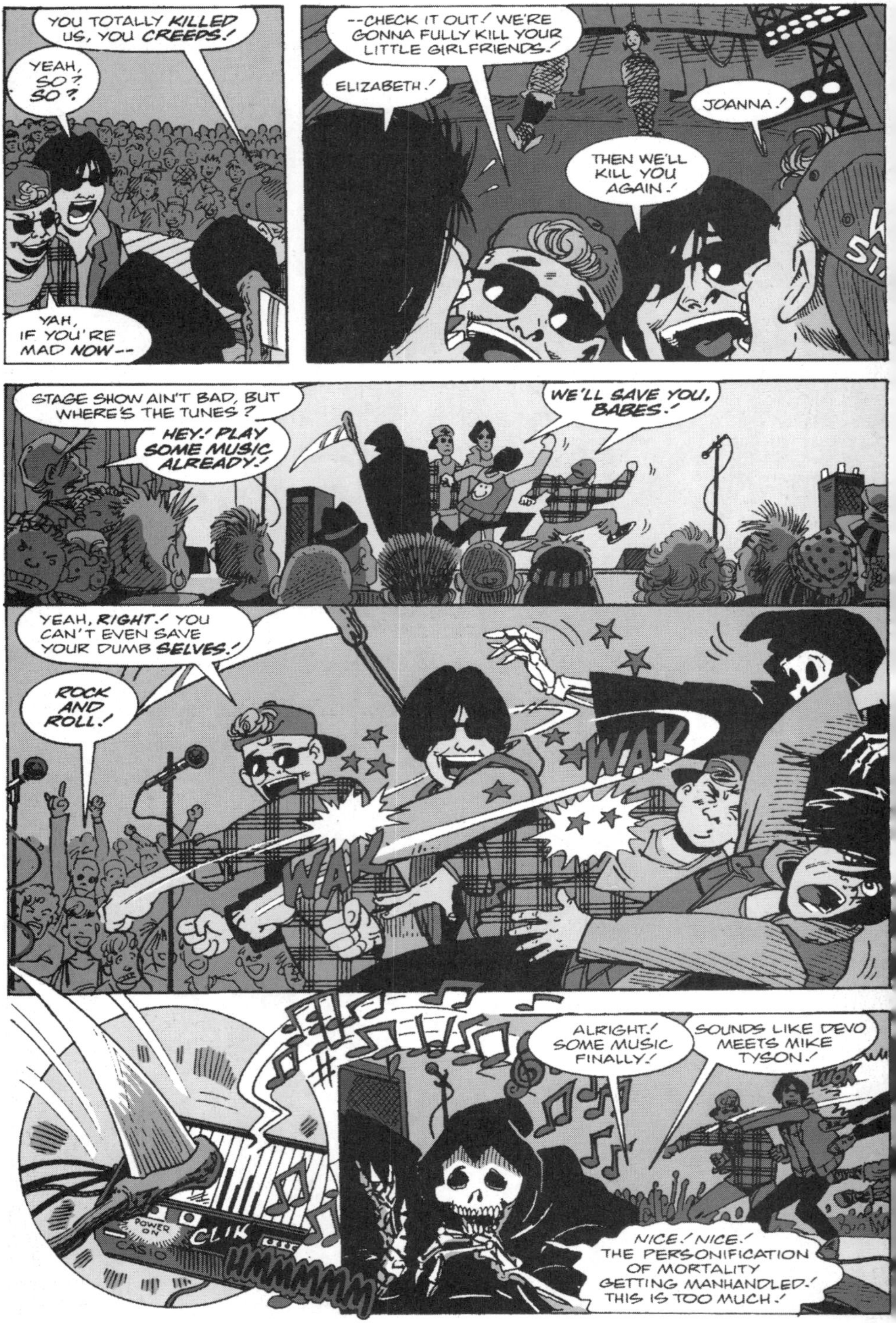
YOU TOTALLY KILLED US, YOU CREEPS!
YEAH, SO? SO?
YAH, IF YOU'RE MAD NOW--
--CHECK IT OUT! WE'RE GONNA FULLY KILL YOUR LITTLE GIRLFRIENDS!
ELIZABETH!
JOANNA!
THEN WE'LL KILL YOU AGAIN!
STAGE SHOW AIN'T BAD, BUT WHERE'S THE TUNES?
HEY! PLAY SOME MUSIC ALREADY!
WE'LL SAVE YOU, BABES!
YEAH, RIGHT! YOU CAN'T EVEN SAVE YOUR DUMB SELVES!
ROCK AND ROLL!
WAK
WAK
ALRIGHT! SOME MUSIC FINALLY!
SOUNDS LIKE DEVO MEETS MIKE TYSON!
WOK
POWER ON
CASIO
CLIK
HMMMMM
NICE! NICE! THE PERSONIFICATION OF MORTALITY GETTING MANHANDLED! THIS IS TOO MUCH!

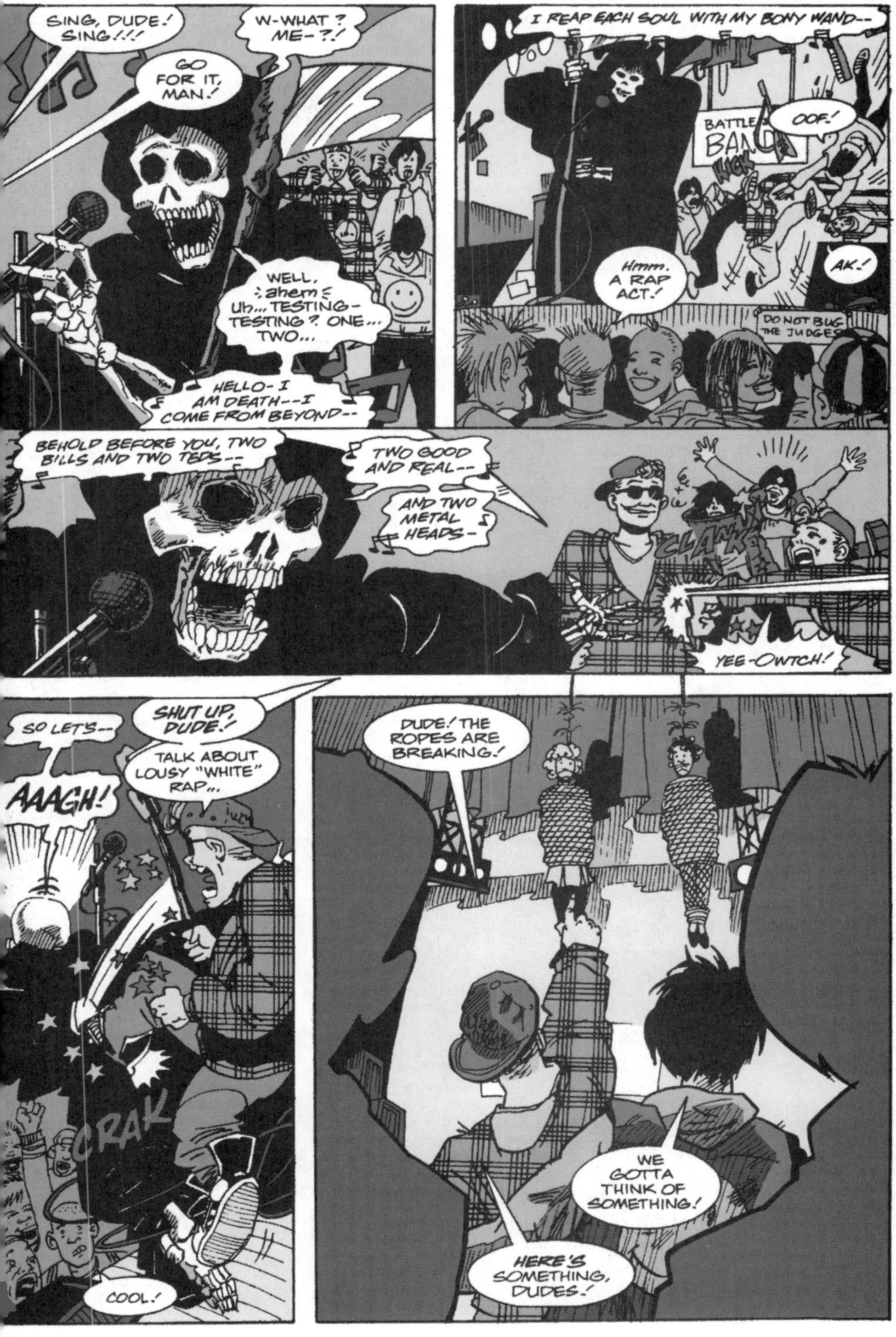
SING, DUDE! SING!!!
W-WHAT? ME-?!
GO FOR IT, MAN!
WELL, ahem Uh... TESTING- TESTING? ONE... TWO...
HELLO- I AM DEATH--I COME FROM BEYOND--
I REAP EACH SOUL WITH MY BONY WAND--
BATTLE BAND
OOF!
KICK
Hmm. A RAP ACT!
AK!
DO NOT BUG THE JUDGES
BEHOLD BEFORE YOU, TWO BILLS AND TWO TEDS--
TWO GOOD AND REAL--
AND TWO METAL HEADS-
CLANK
YEE-OWTCH!
SO LET'S--
SHUT UP, DUDE!
TALK ABOUT LOUSY "WHITE" RAP...
AAAGH!
CRAK
COOL!
DUDE! THE ROPES ARE BREAKING!
WE GOTTA THINK OF SOMETHING!
HERE'S SOMETHING, DUDES!

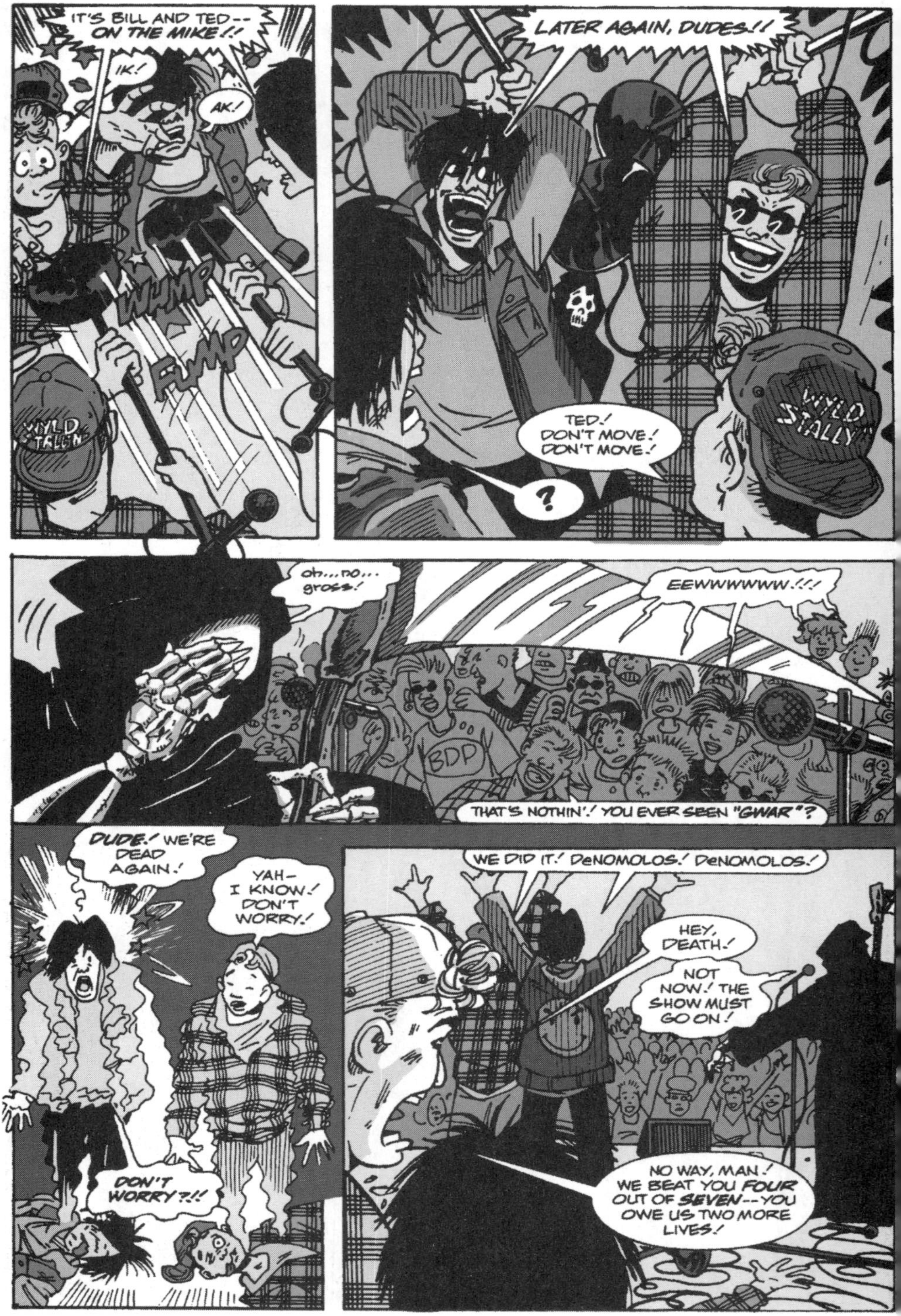
IT'S BILL AND TED-- ON THE MIKE!!
IK!
AK!
WUMP
FUMP
WYLD STALLYNS
LATER AGAIN, DUDES!!
TED! DON'T MOVE! DON'T MOVE!
?
WYLD STALLY
oh...no... gross!
EEWWWWWW!!!
BDP
THAT'S NOTHIN'! YOU EVER SEEN "GWAR"?
DUDE! WE'RE DEAD AGAIN!
YAH- I KNOW! DON'T WORRY!
DON'T WORRY?!!
WE DID IT! DeNOMOLOS! DeNOMOLOS!
HEY, DEATH!
NOT NOW! THE SHOW MUST GO ON!
NO WAY, MAN! WE BEAT YOU FOUR OUT OF SEVEN--YOU OWE US TWO MORE LIVES!

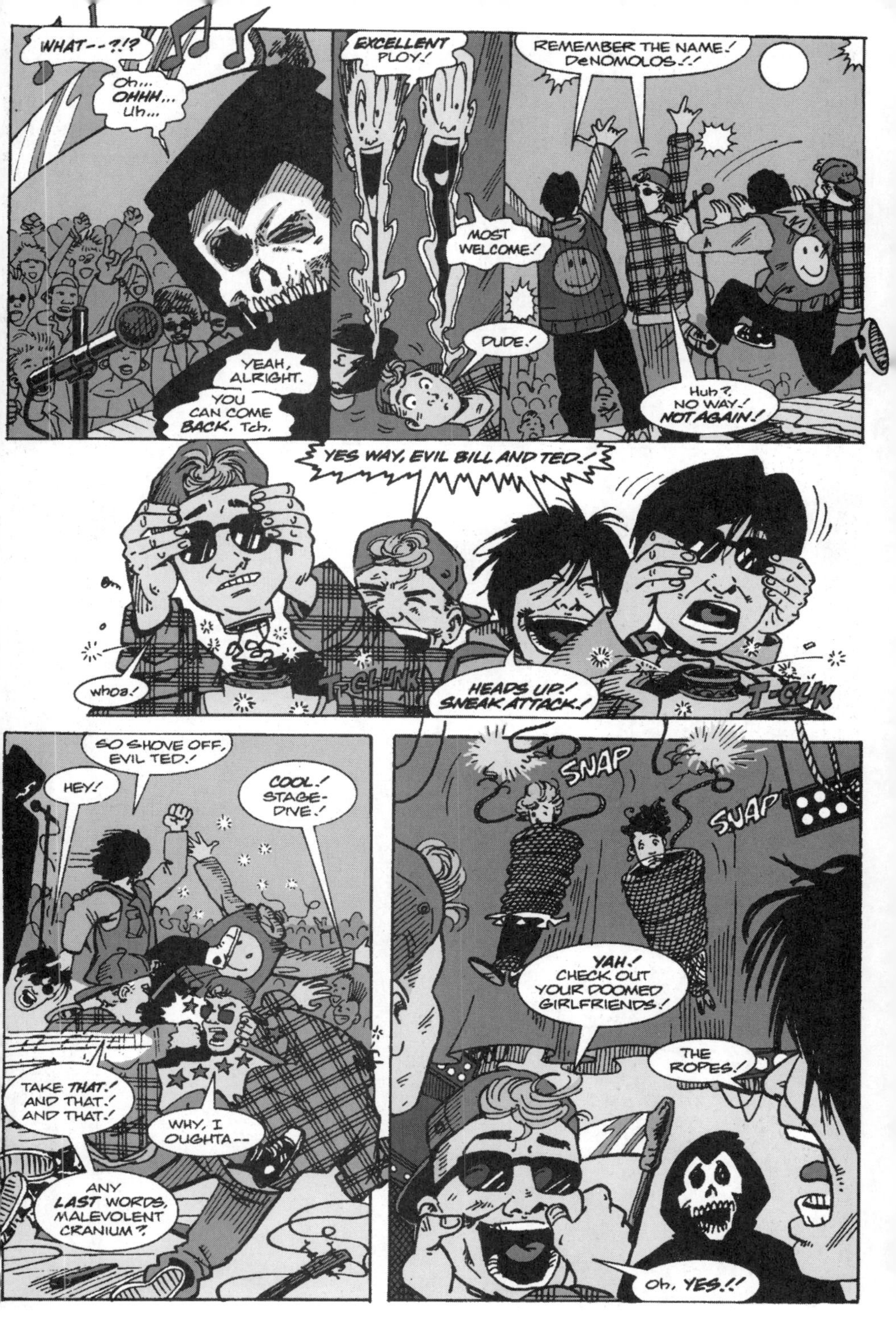
WHAT--?!?
Oh... OHHH... Uh...
YEAH, ALRIGHT.
YOU CAN COME BACK. Tch.
EXCELLENT PLOY!
MOST WELCOME!
DUDE!
REMEMBER THE NAME! DeNOMOLOS!!
Huh? NO WAY! NOT AGAIN!
YES WAY, EVIL BILL AND TED!
whoa!
T-CLUNK
HEADS UP! SNEAK ATTACK!
T-CLIK
SO SHOVE OFF, EVIL TED!
HEY!
COOL! STAGE-DIVE!
TAKE THAT! AND THAT! AND THAT!
WHY, I OUGHTA--
ANY LAST WORDS, MALEVOLENT CRANIUM?
SNAP
SNAP
YAH! CHECK OUT YOUR DOOMED GIRLFRIENDS!
THE ROPES!
Oh, YES!!

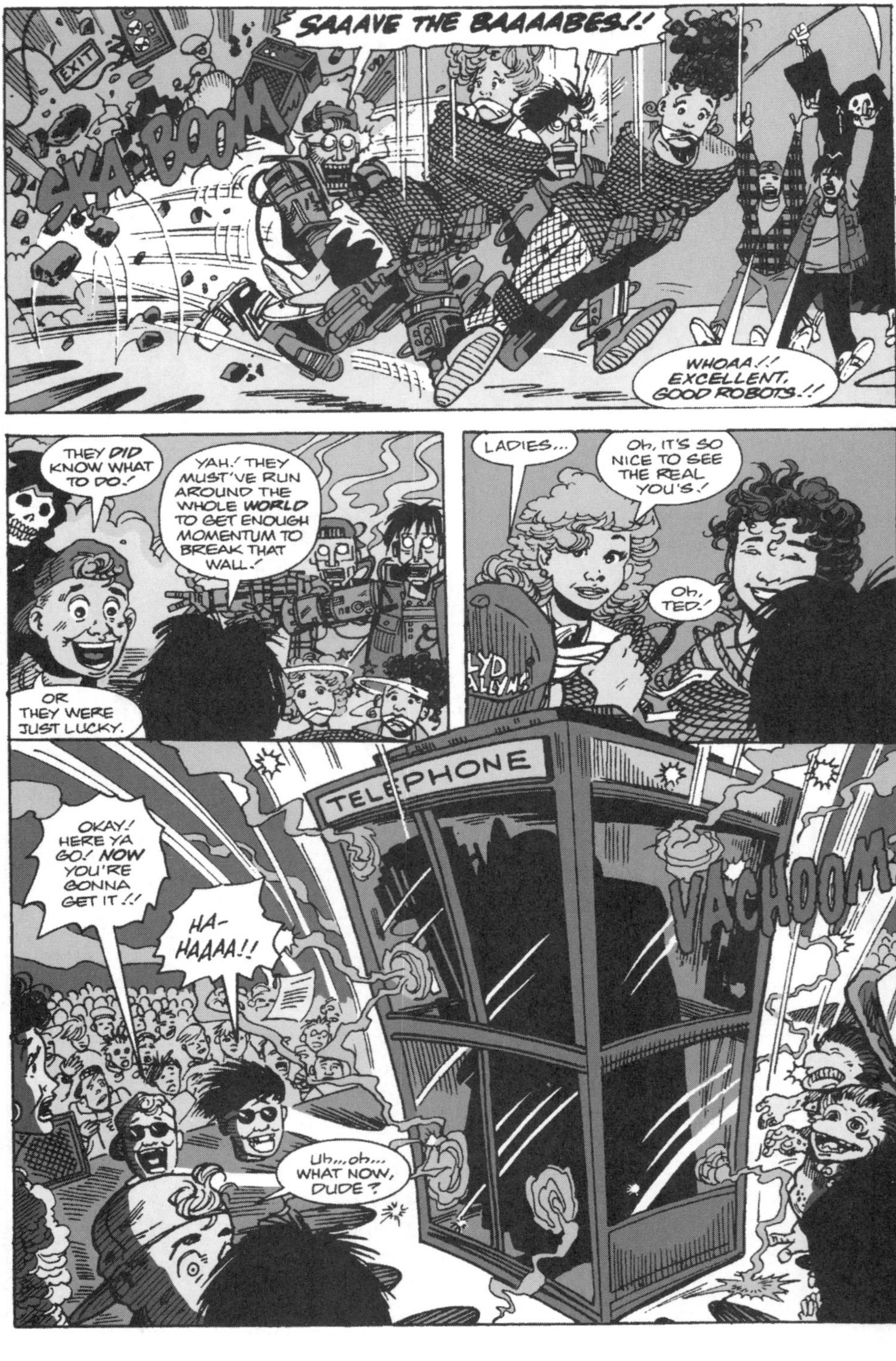
SAAAVE THE BAAAABES!!
EXIT
SKA-BOOM
WHOAA!! EXCELLENT. GOOD ROBOTS!!
THEY DID KNOW WHAT TO DO!
YAH! THEY MUST'VE RUN AROUND THE WHOLE WORLD TO GET ENOUGH MOMENTUM TO BREAK THAT WALL!
OR THEY WERE JUST LUCKY.
LADIES...
Oh, IT'S SO NICE TO SEE THE REAL YOU'S!
Oh, TED!
TELEPHONE
OKAY! HERE YA GO! NOW YOU'RE GONNA GET IT!!
HA-HAAAA!!
VACHOOM
Uh...oh... WHAT NOW, DUDE?

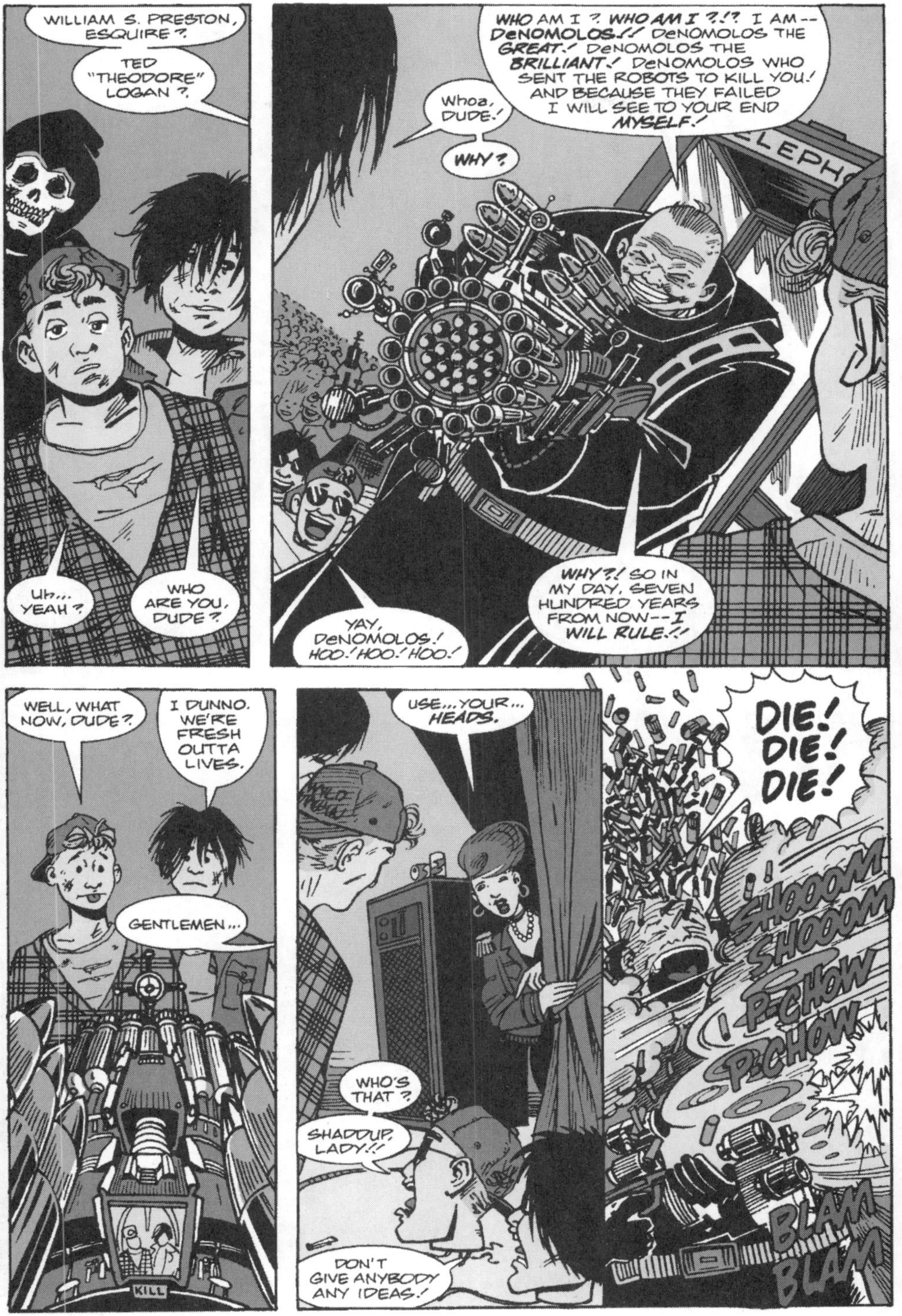
WILLIAM S. PRESTON, ESQUIRE?
TED "THEODORE" LOGAN?
Uh... YEAH?
WHO ARE YOU, DUDE?
WHO AM I? WHO AM I?!? I AM-- DeNOMOLOS!! DeNOMOLOS THE GREAT! DeNOMOLOS THE BRILLIANT! DeNOMOLOS WHO SENT THE ROBOTS TO KILL YOU! AND BECAUSE THEY FAILED I WILL SEE TO YOUR END MYSELF!
Whoa, DUDE!
WHY?
WHY?! SO IN MY DAY, SEVEN HUNDRED YEARS FROM NOW--I WILL RULE!!
YAY, DeNOMOLOS! HOO! HOO! HOO!
WELL, WHAT NOW, DUDE?
I DUNNO. WE'RE FRESH OUTTA LIVES.
GENTLEMEN...
KILL
USE... YOUR... HEADS.
WHO'S THAT?
SHADDUP, LADY!!
DON'T GIVE ANYBODY ANY IDEAS!
DIE! DIE! DIE!
SHOOOM
SHOOOM
P-CHOW
P-CHOW
BLAM
BLAM

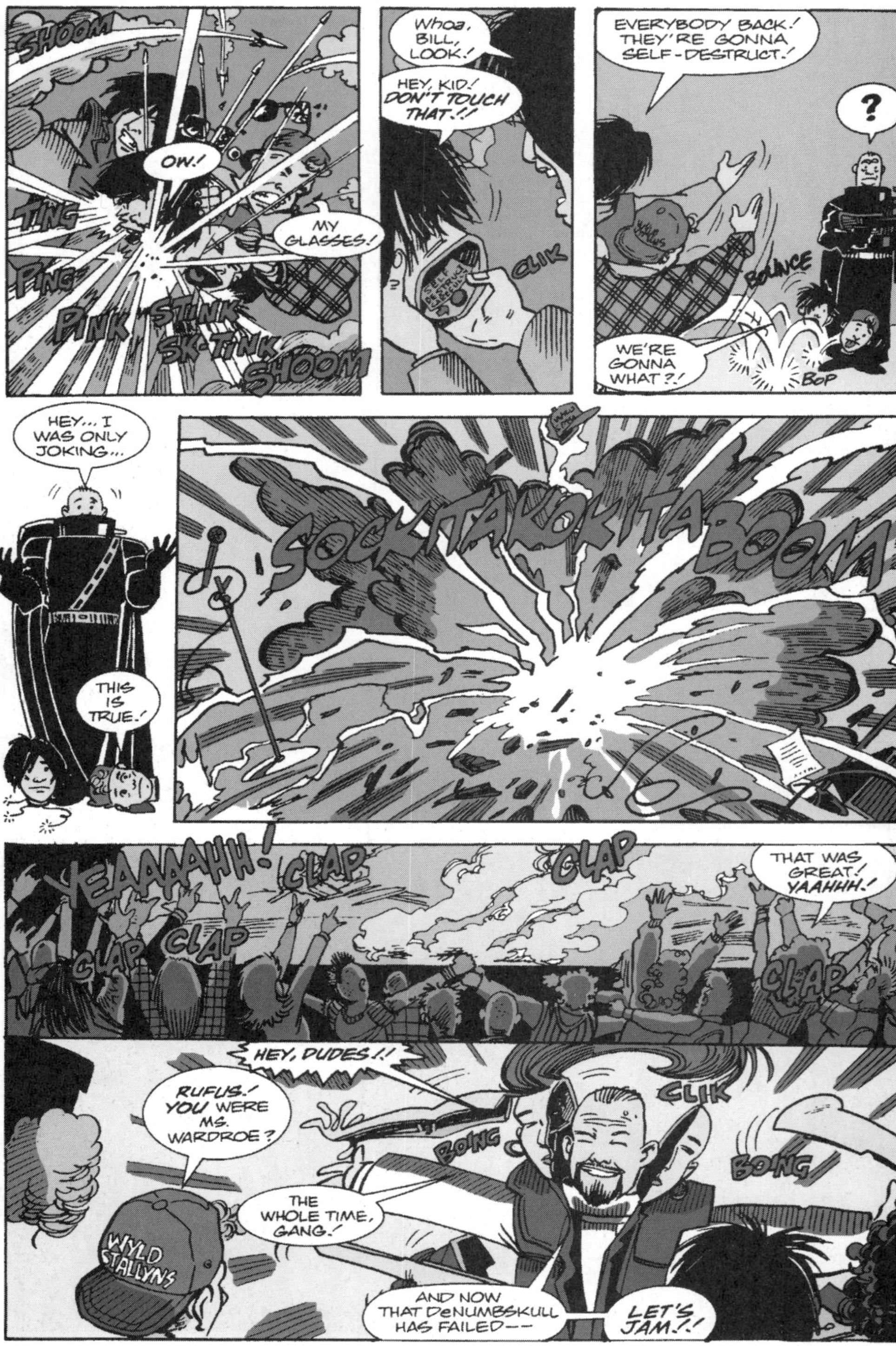

SHOOM
OW!
TING
PING
MY GLASSES!
PINK
STINK
SK-TINK
SHOOM
Whoa, BILL, LOOK!
HEY, KID! DON'T TOUCH THAT!!
CLIK
EVERYBODY BACK! THEY'RE GONNA SELF-DESTRUCT!
?
BOUNCE
WE'RE GONNA WHAT?!
BOP
HEY... I WAS ONLY JOKING...
THIS IS TRUE!
SOCK!TAKOKITA BOOM
YEAAAAHH!
CLAP
CLAP
CLAP
CLAP
CLAP
THAT WAS GREAT! YAAHHH!
HEY, DUDES!!
RUFUS! YOU WERE MS. WARDROE?
CLIK
BOING
BOING
THE WHOLE TIME, GANG!
WYLD STALLYNS
AND NOW THAT DeNUMBSKULL HAS FAILED--
LET'S JAM!!

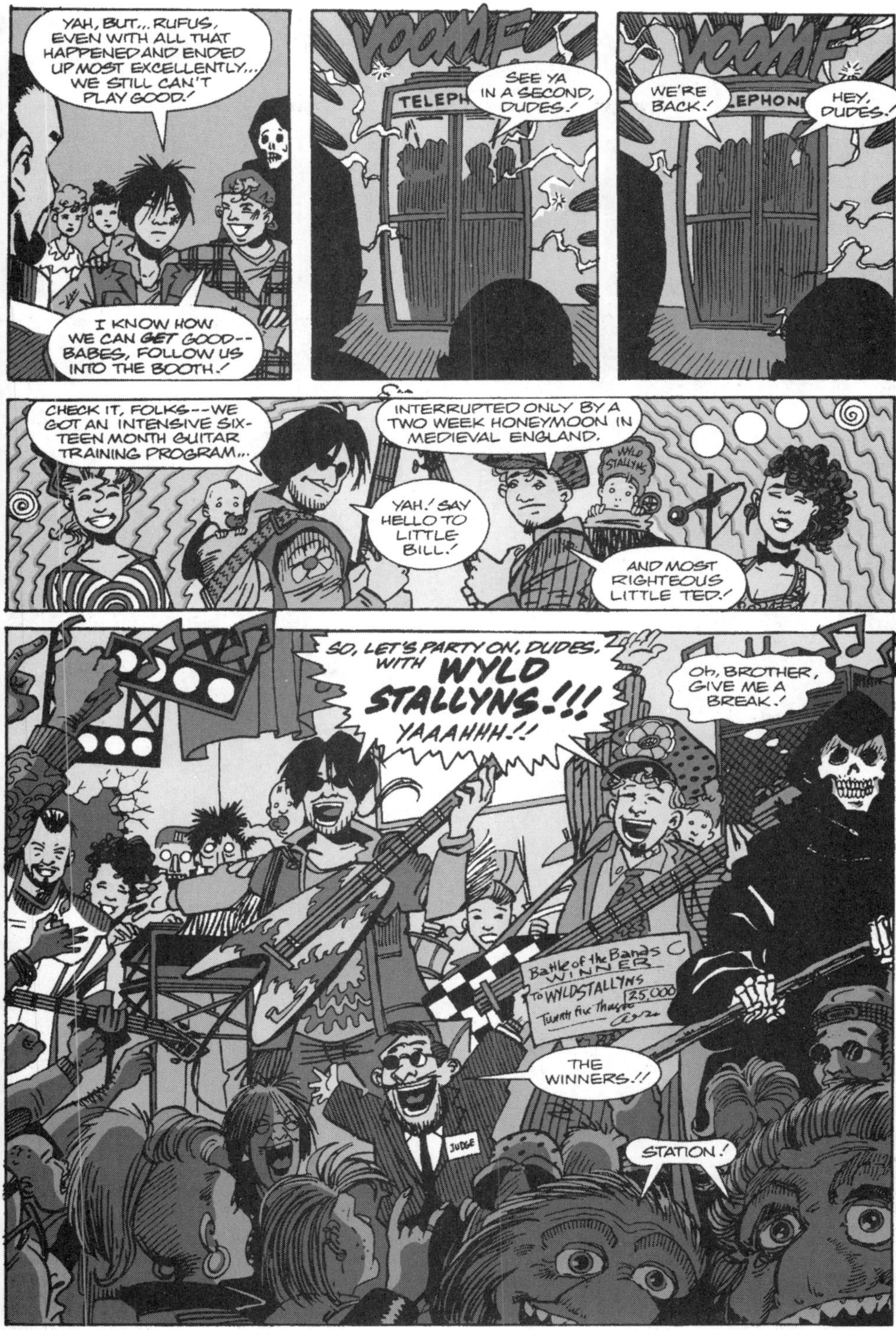

YAH, BUT... RUFUS, EVEN WITH ALL THAT HAPPENED AND ENDED UP MOST EXCELLENTLY... WE STILL CAN'T PLAY GOOD!
I KNOW HOW WE CAN GET GOOD-- BABES, FOLLOW US INTO THE BOOTH!
VOOMF
SEE YA IN A SECOND, DUDES!
VOOMF
WE'RE BACK!
HEY, DUDES!
CHECK IT, FOLKS--WE GOT AN INTENSIVE SIXTEEN MONTH GUITAR TRAINING PROGRAM...
INTERRUPTED ONLY BY A TWO WEEK HONEYMOON IN MEDIEVAL ENGLAND.
WYLD STALLYNS
YAH! SAY HELLO TO LITTLE BILL!
AND MOST RIGHTEOUS LITTLE TED!
SO, LET'S PARTY ON, DUDES. WITH WYLD STALLYNS!!!! YAAAHHH!!
Oh, BROTHER, GIVE ME A BREAK!
Battle of the Bands WINNER
To WYLDSTALLYNS 25,000
THE WINNERS!!
JUDGE
STATION!

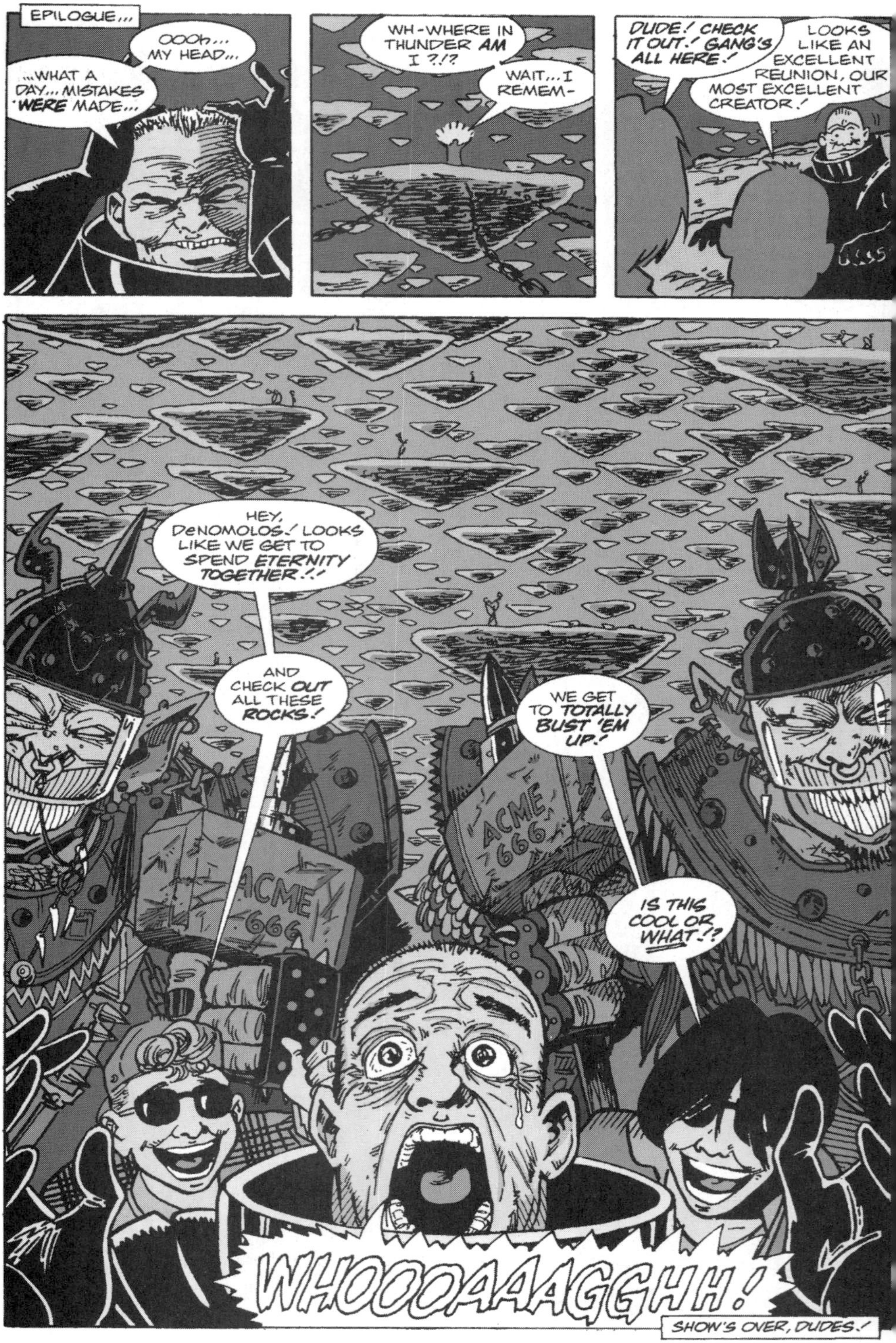
EPILOGUE...
OOOh... MY HEAD...
...WHAT A DAY... MISTAKES 'WERE MADE...
WH-WHERE IN THUNDER AM I ?!?
WAIT... I REMEM-
DUDE! CHECK IT OUT! GANG'S ALL HERE!
LOOKS LIKE AN EXCELLENT REUNION, OUR MOST EXCELLENT CREATOR!
HEY, DeNOMOLOS! LOOKS LIKE WE GET TO SPEND ETERNITY TOGETHER!!
AND CHECK OUT ALL THESE ROCKS!
WE GET TO TOTALLY BUST 'EM UP!
IS THIS COOL OR WHAT!?
ACME 666
ACME 666
WHOOOAAAGGHH!
SHOW'S OVER, DUDES!

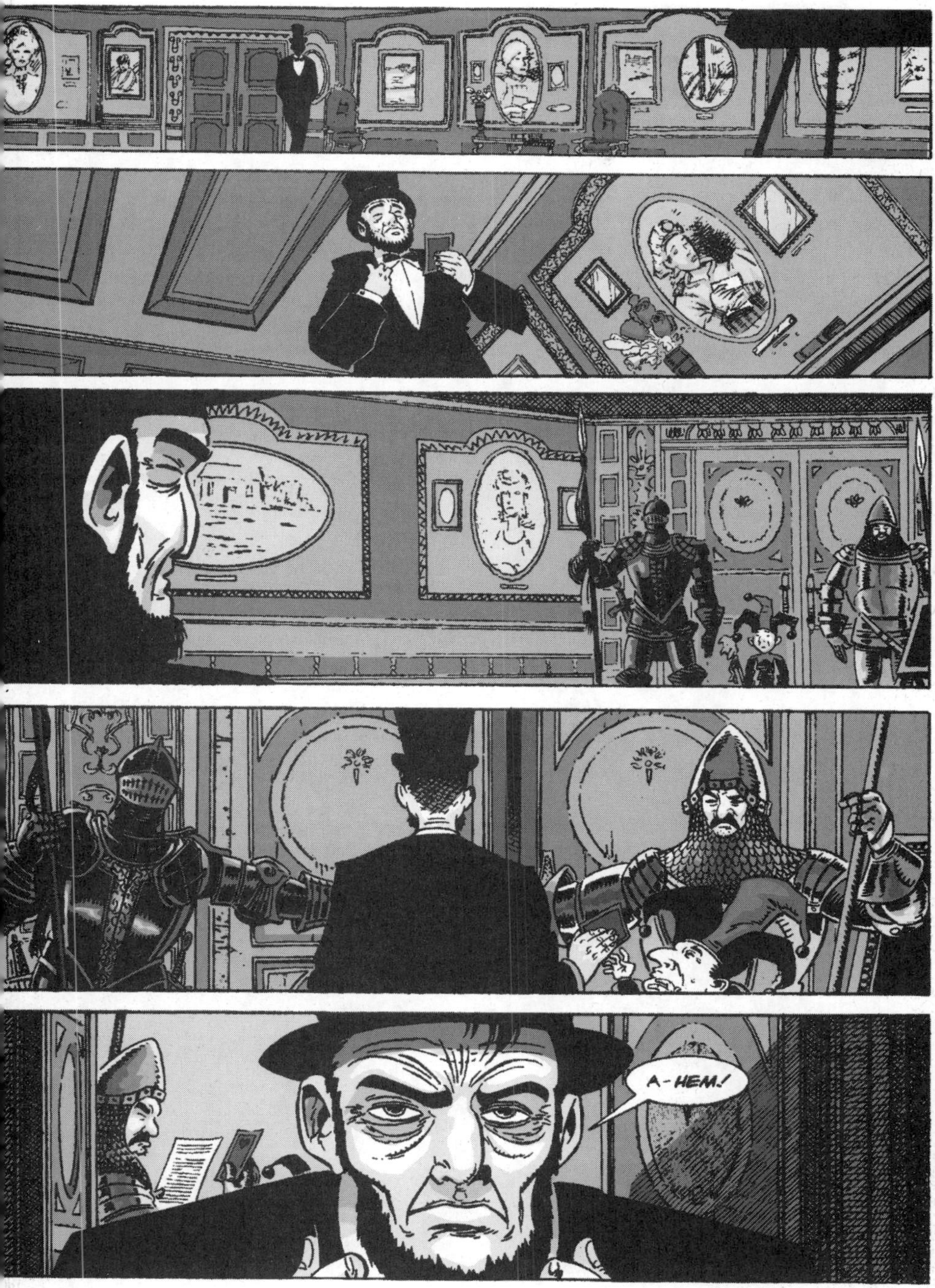
A-HEM!

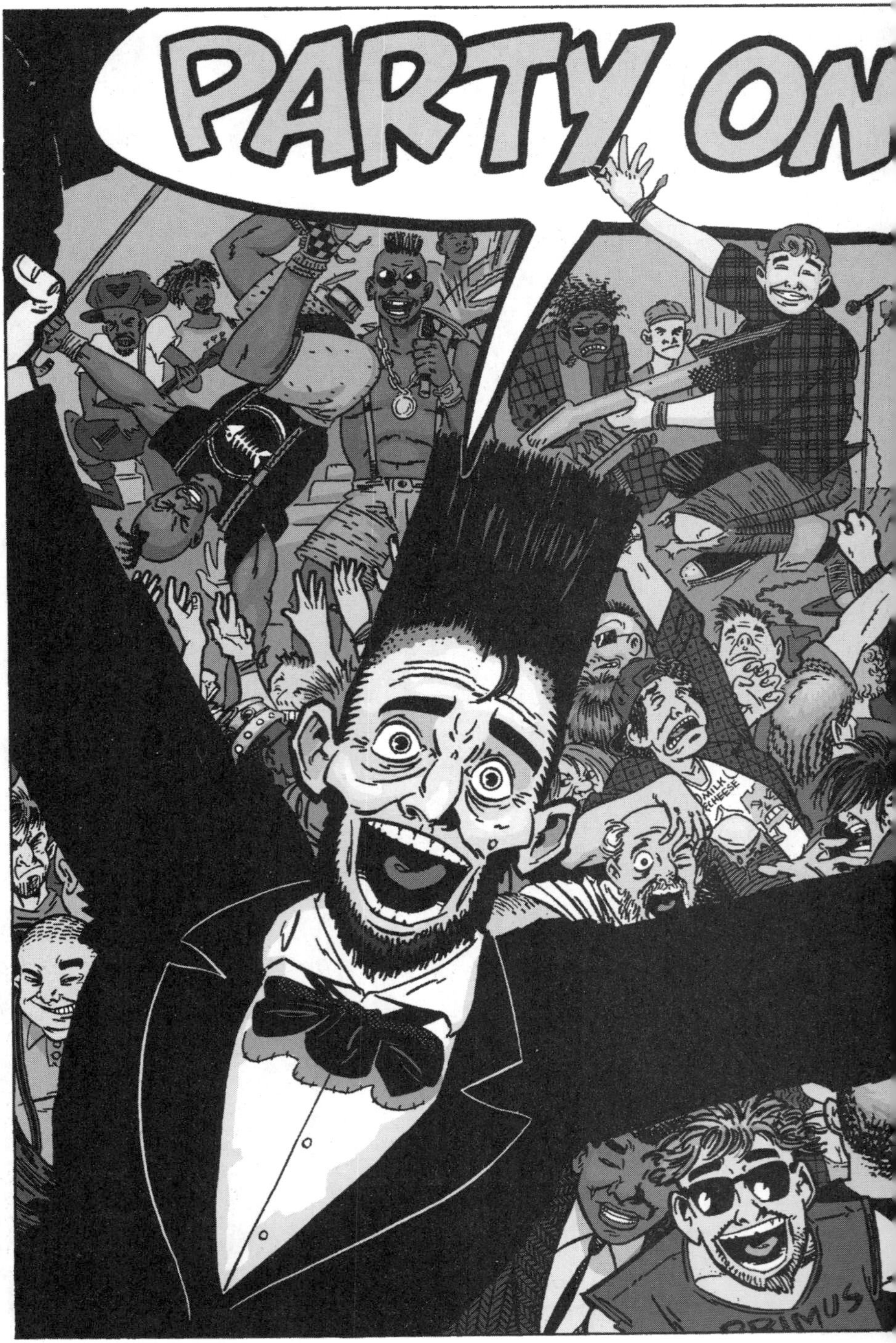
PARTY ON
MILK CHEESE
PRIMUS

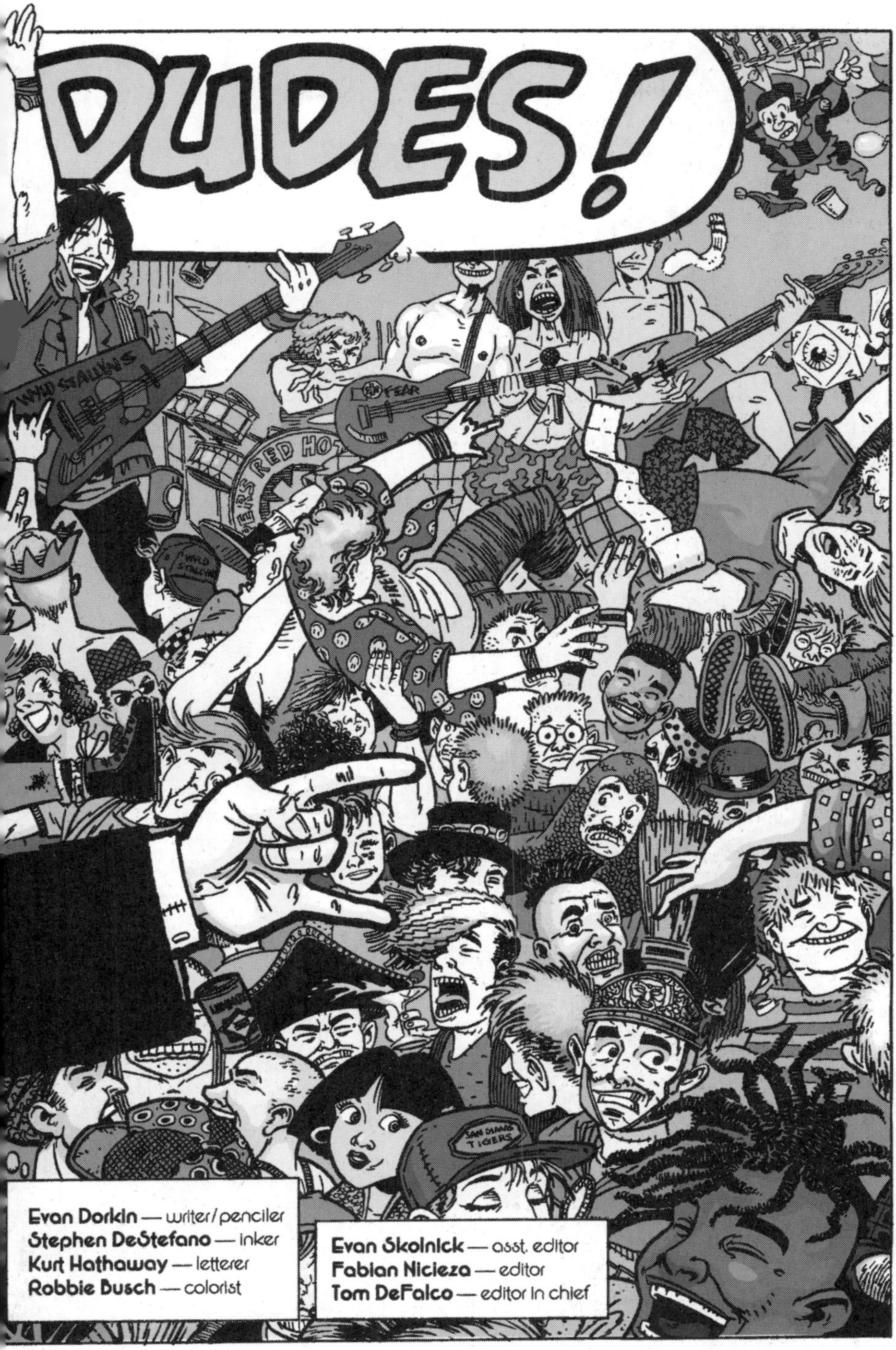
DUDES!
Evan Dorkin — writer/penciler
Stephen DeStefano — inker
Kurt Hathaway — letterer
Robbie Busch — colorist
Evan Skolnick — asst. editor
Fabian Nicieza — editor
Tom DeFalco — editor in chief

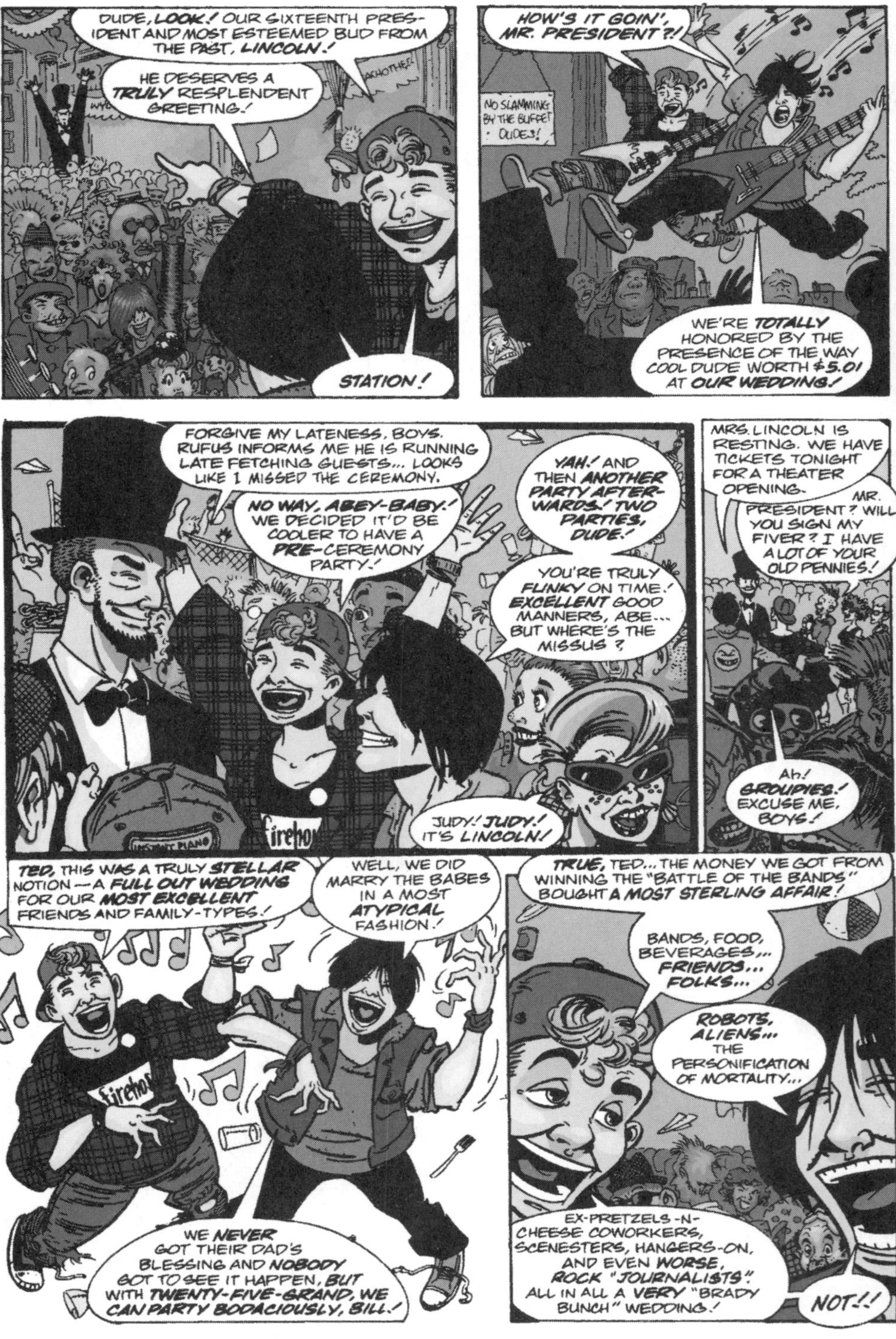

DUDE, LOOK! OUR SIXTEENTH PRESIDENT AND MOST ESTEEMED BUD FROM THE PAST, LINCOLN!
HE DESERVES A TRULY RESPLENDENT GREETING!
STATION!
HOW'S IT GOIN', MR. PRESIDENT?!
NO SLAMMING BY THE BUFFET DUDES!
WE'RE TOTALLY HONORED BY THE PRESENCE OF THE WAY COOL DUDE WORTH $5.01 AT OUR WEDDING!
FORGIVE MY LATENESS, BOYS. RUFUS INFORMS ME HE IS RUNNING LATE FETCHING GUESTS... LOOKS LIKE I MISSED THE CEREMONY.
NO WAY, ABEY-BABY! WE DECIDED IT'D BE COOLER TO HAVE A PRE-CEREMONY PARTY!
YAH! AND THEN ANOTHER PARTY AFTERWARDS! TWO PARTIES, DUDE!
YOU'RE TRULY FUNKY ON TIME! EXCELLENT GOOD MANNERS, ABE... BUT WHERE'S THE MISSUS?
JUDY! JUDY! IT'S LINCOLN!
MRS. LINCOLN IS RESTING. WE HAVE TICKETS TONIGHT FOR A THEATER OPENING.
MR. PRESIDENT? WILL YOU SIGN MY FIVER? I HAVE A LOT OF YOUR OLD PENNIES!
Ah! GROUPIES! EXCUSE ME, BOYS!
TED, THIS WAS A TRULY STELLAR NOTION — A FULL OUT WEDDING FOR OUR MOST EXCELLENT FRIENDS AND FAMILY-TYPES!
WELL, WE DID MARRY THE BABES IN A MOST ATYPICAL FASHION!
WE NEVER GOT THEIR DAD'S BLESSING AND NOBODY GOT TO SEE IT HAPPEN, BUT WITH TWENTY-FIVE-GRAND, WE CAN PARTY BODACIOUSLY, BILL!
TRUE, TED... THE MONEY WE GOT FROM WINNING THE "BATTLE OF THE BANDS" BOUGHT A MOST STERLING AFFAIR!
BANDS, FOOD, BEVERAGES... FRIENDS... FOLKS...
ROBOTS, ALIENS... THE PERSONIFICATION OF MORTALITY...
EX-PRETZELS-N-CHEESE COWORKERS, SCENESTERS, HANGERS-ON, AND EVEN WORSE, ROCK "JOURNALISTS"! ALL IN ALL A VERY "BRADY BUNCH" WEDDING!
NOT!!

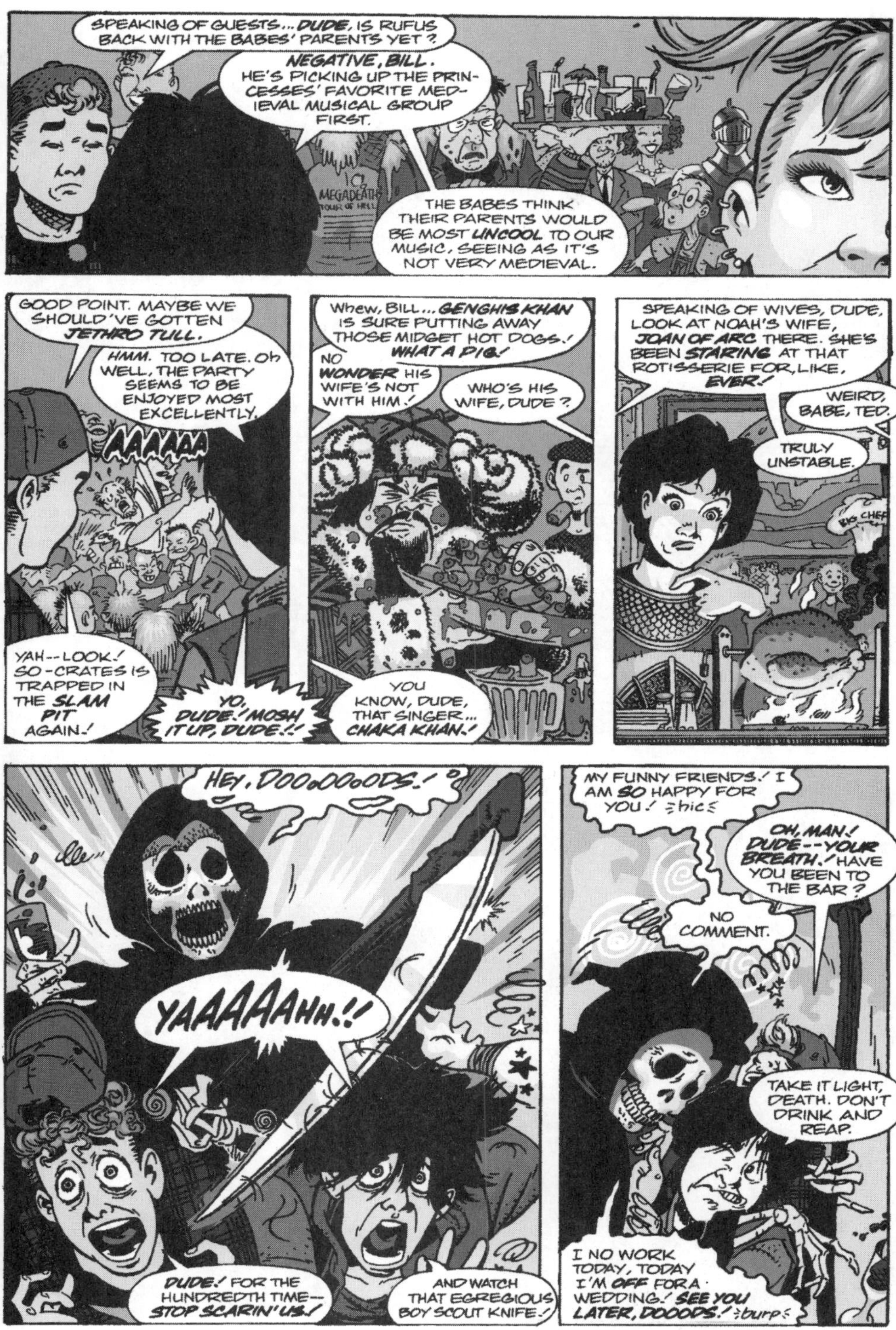
SPEAKING OF GUESTS... DUDE, IS RUFUS BACK WITH THE BABES' PARENTS YET?
NEGATIVE, BILL. HE'S PICKING UP THE PRINCESSES' FAVORITE MEDIEVAL MUSICAL GROUP FIRST.
MEGADEATH TOUR OF HELL
THE BABES THINK THEIR PARENTS WOULD BE MOST UNCOOL TO OUR MUSIC, SEEING AS IT'S NOT VERY MEDIEVAL.
GOOD POINT. MAYBE WE SHOULD'VE GOTTEN JETHRO TULL.
HMM. TOO LATE. Oh WELL, THE PARTY SEEMS TO BE ENJOYED MOST EXCELLENTLY.
AAAAAA
YAH--LOOK! SO-CRATES IS TRAPPED IN THE SLAM PIT AGAIN!
YO, DUDE! MOSH IT UP, DUDE!!
Whew, BILL... GENGHIS KHAN IS SURE PUTTING AWAY THOSE MIDGET HOT DOGS! WHAT A PIG!
NO WONDER HIS WIFE'S NOT WITH HIM!
WHO'S HIS WIFE, DUDE?
YOU KNOW, DUDE, THAT SINGER... CHAKA KHAN!
SPEAKING OF WIVES, DUDE, LOOK AT NOAH'S WIFE, JOAN OF ARC THERE. SHE'S BEEN STARING AT THAT ROTISSERIE FOR, LIKE, EVER!
WEIRD, BABE, TED.
TRULY UNSTABLE.
BIG CHEF
HEY, DOOoOOooDS!
YAAAAAHH!!
DUDE! FOR THE HUNDREDTH TIME--STOP SCARIN' US!
AND WATCH THAT EGREGIOUS BOY SCOUT KNIFE!
MY FUNNY FRIENDS! I AM SO HAPPY FOR YOU! *hic*
OH, MAN! DUDE--YOUR BREATH! HAVE YOU BEEN TO THE BAR?
NO COMMENT.
TAKE IT LIGHT, DEATH. DON'T DRINK AND REAP.
I NO WORK TODAY, TODAY I'M OFF FOR A WEDDING! SEE YOU LATER, DOOODS! *burp*

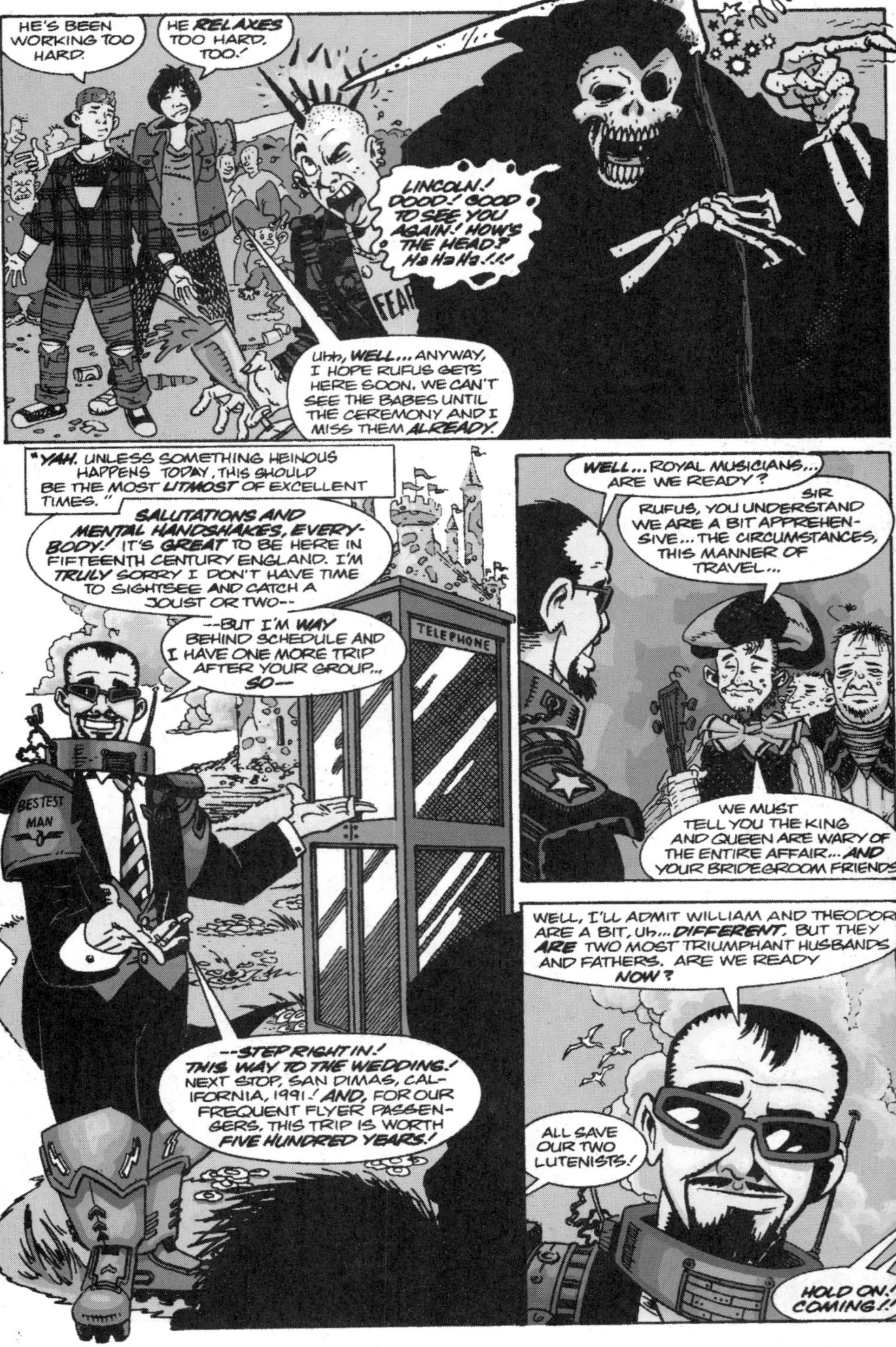
HE'S BEEN WORKING TOO HARD.
HE RELAXES TOO HARD, TOO!
LINCOLN! DOOD! GOOD TO SEE YOU AGAIN! HOW'S THE HEAD? Ha Ha Ha!!!
FEAR
Uhh, WELL... ANYWAY, I HOPE RUFUS GETS HERE SOON. WE CAN'T SEE THE BABES UNTIL THE CEREMONY AND I MISS THEM ALREADY.
"YAH. UNLESS SOMETHING HEINOUS HAPPENS TODAY, THIS SHOULD BE THE MOST UTMOST OF EXCELLENT TIMES."
SALUTATIONS AND MENTAL HANDSHAKES, EVERYBODY! IT'S GREAT TO BE HERE IN FIFTEENTH CENTURY ENGLAND. I'M TRULY SORRY I DON'T HAVE TIME TO SIGHTSEE AND CATCH A JOUST OR TWO--
--BUT I'M WAY BEHIND SCHEDULE AND I HAVE ONE MORE TRIP AFTER YOUR GROUP... SO--
TELEPHONE
BESTEST MAN
--STEP RIGHT IN! THIS WAY TO THE WEDDING! NEXT STOP, SAN DIMAS, CALIFORNIA, 1991! AND, FOR OUR FREQUENT FLYER PASSENGERS, THIS TRIP IS WORTH FIVE HUNDRED YEARS!
WELL... ROYAL MUSICIANS... ARE WE READY?
SIR RUFUS, YOU UNDERSTAND WE ARE A BIT APPREHENSIVE... THE CIRCUMSTANCES, THIS MANNER OF TRAVEL...
WE MUST TELL YOU THE KING AND QUEEN ARE WARY OF THE ENTIRE AFFAIR... AND YOUR BRIDEGROOM FRIENDS.
WELL, I'LL ADMIT WILLIAM AND THEODORE ARE A BIT, Uh... DIFFERENT, BUT THEY ARE TWO MOST TRIUMPHANT HUSBANDS AND FATHERS. ARE WE READY NOW?
ALL SAVE OUR TWO LUTENISTS!
HOLD ON! COMING!!

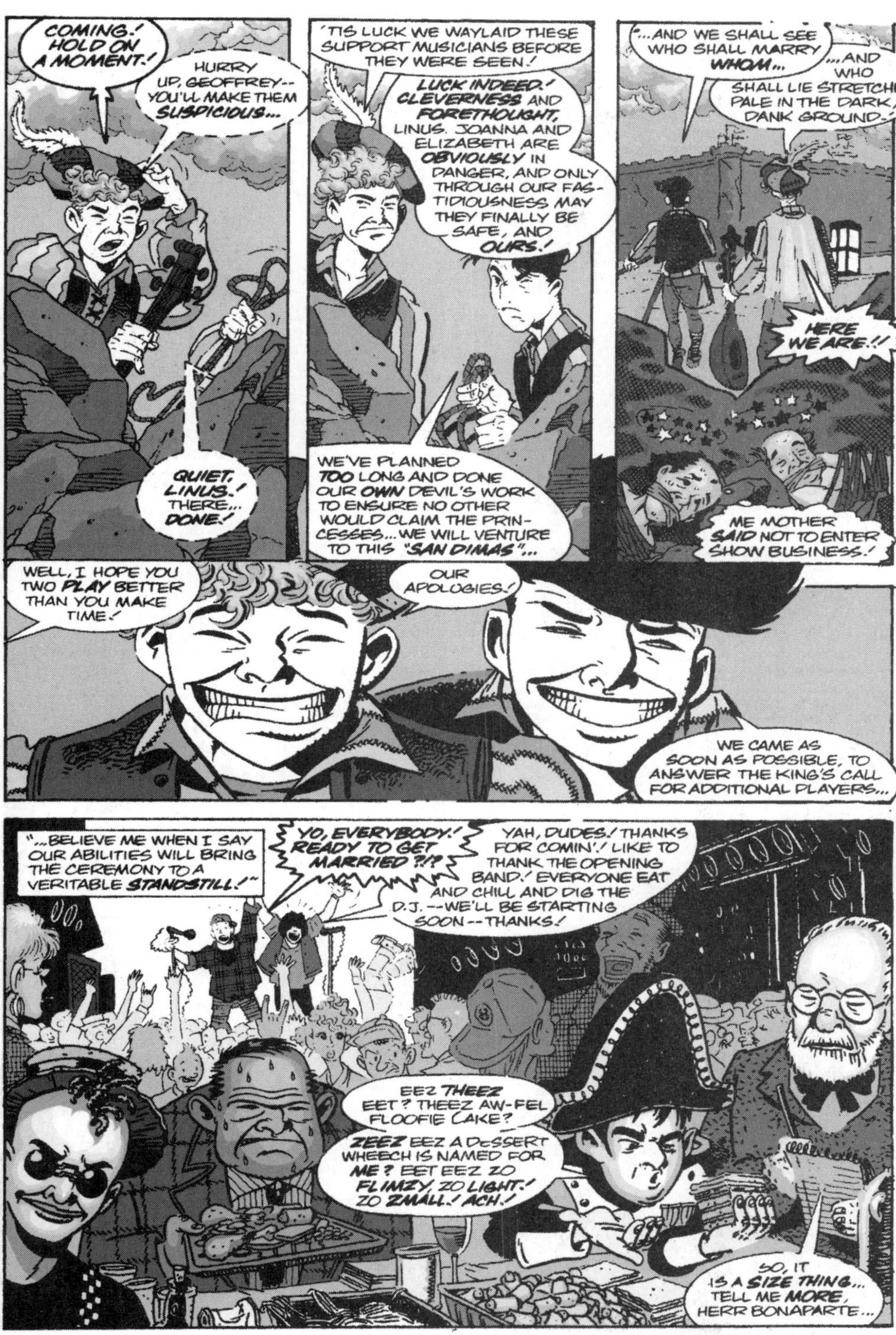
COMING! HOLD ON A MOMENT!
HURRY UP, GEOFFREY-- YOU'LL MAKE THEM SUSPICIOUS...
QUIET, LINUS! THERE... DONE!
'TIS LUCK WE WAYLAID THESE SUPPORT MUSICIANS BEFORE THEY WERE SEEN!
LUCK INDEED! CLEVERNESS AND FORETHOUGHT, LINUS. JOANNA AND ELIZABETH ARE OBVIOUSLY IN DANGER, AND ONLY THROUGH OUR FASTIDIOUSNESS MAY THEY FINALLY BE SAFE, AND OURS!
WE'VE PLANNED TOO LONG AND DONE OUR OWN DEVIL'S WORK TO ENSURE NO OTHER WOULD CLAIM THE PRINCESSES... WE WILL VENTURE TO THIS "SAN DIMAS"...
"...AND WE SHALL SEE WHO SHALL MARRY WHOM...
...AND WHO SHALL LIE STRETCHED PALE IN THE DARK, DANK GROUND."
HERE WE ARE!!
ME MOTHER SAID NOT TO ENTER SHOW BUSINESS!
WELL, I HOPE YOU TWO PLAY BETTER THAN YOU MAKE TIME!
OUR APOLOGIES!
WE CAME AS SOON AS POSSIBLE, TO ANSWER THE KING'S CALL FOR ADDITIONAL PLAYERS...
"...BELIEVE ME WHEN I SAY OUR ABILITIES WILL BRING THE CEREMONY TO A VERITABLE STANDSTILL!"
YO, EVERYBODY! READY TO GET MARRIED?!?
YAH, DUDES! THANKS FOR COMIN'! LIKE TO THANK THE OPENING BAND! EVERYONE EAT AND CHILL AND DIG THE D.J. --WE'LL BE STARTING SOON--THANKS!
EEZ THEEZ EET? THEEZ AW-FEL FLOOFIE CAKE?
ZEEZ EEZ A DESSERT WHEECH IS NAMED FOR ME? EET EEZ ZO FLIMZY, ZO LIGHT! ZO ZMALL! ACH!
SO, IT IS A SIZE THING... TELL ME MORE, HERR BONAPARTE...

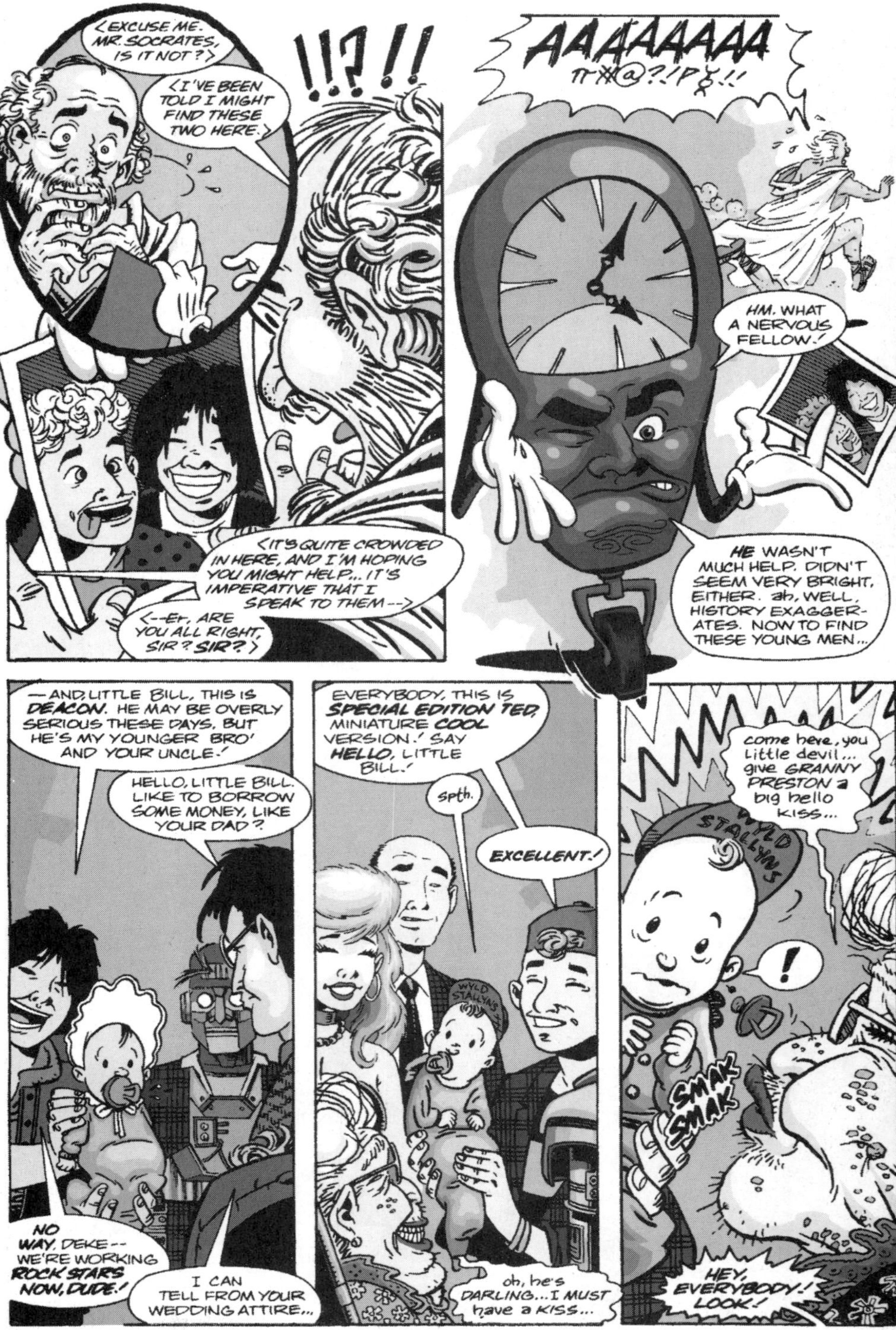

<EXCUSE ME. MR. SOCRATES, IS IT NOT?>
<I'VE BEEN TOLD I MIGHT FIND THESE TWO HERE.>
!!?!!
<IT'S QUITE CROWDED IN HERE, AND I'M HOPING YOU MIGHT HELP... IT'S IMPERATIVE THAT I SPEAK TO THEM-->
<--Er, ARE YOU ALL RIGHT, SIR? SIR?>
AAAAAAAA
HM. WHAT A NERVOUS FELLOW!
HE WASN'T MUCH HELP. DIDN'T SEEM VERY BRIGHT, EITHER. ah, WELL, HISTORY EXAGGERATES. NOW TO FIND THESE YOUNG MEN...
—AND, LITTLE BILL, THIS IS DEACON. HE MAY BE OVERLY SERIOUS THESE DAYS, BUT HE'S MY YOUNGER BRO' AND YOUR UNCLE!
HELLO, LITTLE BILL. LIKE TO BORROW SOME MONEY, LIKE YOUR DAD?
NO WAY, DEKE-- WE'RE WORKING ROCK STARS NOW, DUDE!
I CAN TELL FROM YOUR WEDDING ATTIRE...
EVERYBODY, THIS IS SPECIAL EDITION TED, MINIATURE COOL VERSION! SAY HELLO, LITTLE BILL!
spth.
EXCELLENT!
WYLD STALLYNS
oh, he's DARLING... I MUST have a KISS...
come here, you little devil... give GRANNY PRESTON a big hello kiss...
WYLD STALLYNS
!
SMAK SMAK
HEY, EVERYBODY! LOOK!

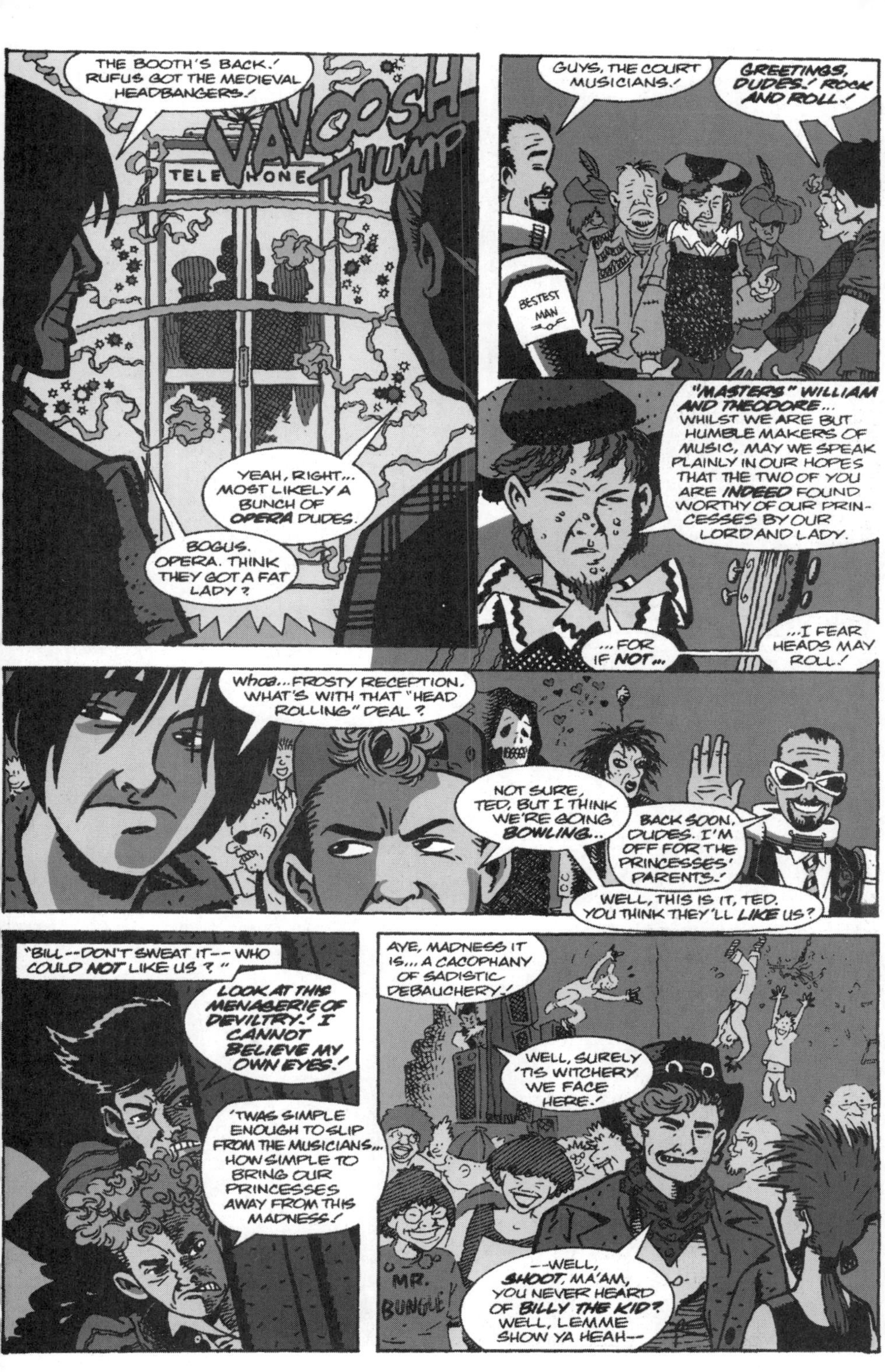
THE BOOTH'S BACK! RUFUS GOT THE MEDIEVAL HEADBANGERS!
VAVOOSH
THUMP
TELEPHONE
YEAH, RIGHT... MOST LIKELY A BUNCH OF OPERA DUDES.
BOGUS. OPERA. THINK THEY GOT A FAT LADY?
GUYS, THE COURT MUSICIANS!
GREETINGS, DUDES! ROCK AND ROLL!
BESTEST MAN
"MASTERS" WILLIAM AND THEODORE... WHILST WE ARE BUT HUMBLE MAKERS OF MUSIC, MAY WE SPEAK PLAINLY IN OUR HOPES THAT THE TWO OF YOU ARE INDEED FOUND WORTHY OF OUR PRINCESSES BY OUR LORD AND LADY.
...FOR IF NOT...
...I FEAR HEADS MAY ROLL!
Whoa... FROSTY RECEPTION. WHAT'S WITH THAT "HEAD ROLLING" DEAL?
NOT SURE, TED, BUT I THINK WE'RE GOING BOWLING...
BACK SOON, DUDES. I'M OFF FOR THE PRINCESSES' PARENTS!
WELL, THIS IS IT, TED. YOU THINK THEY'LL LIKE US?
"BILL--DON'T SWEAT IT-- WHO COULD NOT LIKE US?"
LOOK AT THIS MENAGERIE OF DEVILTRY! I CANNOT BELIEVE MY OWN EYES!
'TWAS SIMPLE ENOUGH TO SLIP FROM THE MUSICIANS... HOW SIMPLE TO BRING OUR PRINCESSES AWAY FROM THIS MADNESS!
AYE, MADNESS IT IS... A CACOPHANY OF SADISTIC DEBAUCHERY!
WELL, SURELY 'TIS WITCHERY WE FACE HERE!
MR. BUNGLE
--WELL, SHOOT, MA'AM, YOU NEVER HEARD OF BILLY THE KID? WELL, LEMME SHOW YA HEAH--

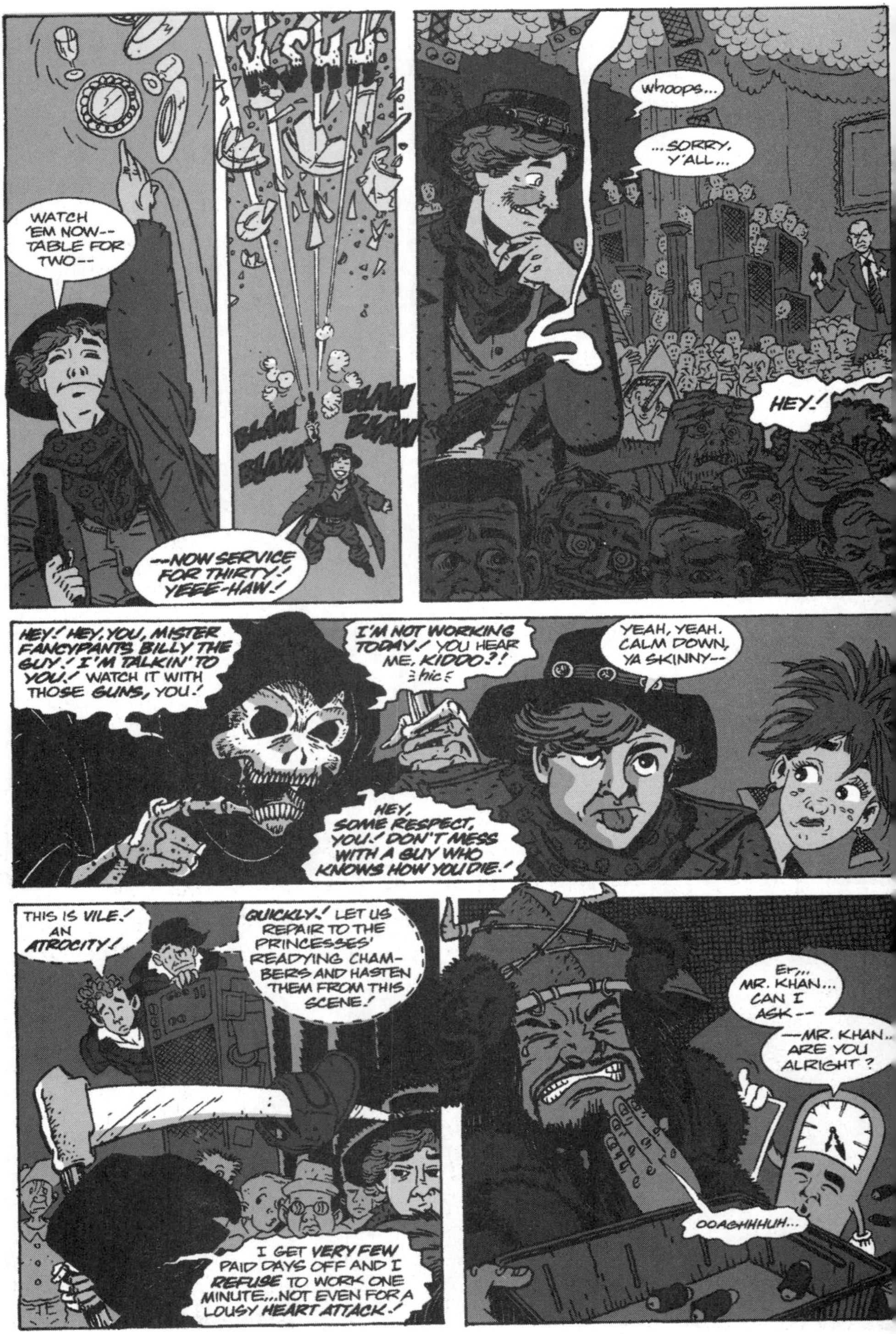

WATCH 'EM NOW-- TABLE FOR TWO--
BLAM BLAM BLAM BLAM BLAM
--NOW SERVICE FOR THIRTY! YEEE-HAW!
whoops...
...SORRY, Y'ALL...
HEY!
HEY! HEY, YOU, MISTER FANCYPANTS BILLY THE GUY! I'M TALKIN' TO YOU! WATCH IT WITH THOSE GUNS, YOU!
I'M NOT WORKING TODAY! YOU HEAR ME, KIDDO?! hic
YEAH, YEAH. CALM DOWN, YA SKINNY--
HEY, SOME RESPECT, YOU! DON'T MESS WITH A GUY WHO KNOWS HOW YOU DIE!
THIS IS VILE! AN ATROCITY!
QUICKLY! LET US REPAIR TO THE PRINCESSES' READYING CHAMBERS AND HASTEN THEM FROM THIS SCENE!
I GET VERY FEW PAID DAYS OFF AND I REFUSE TO WORK ONE MINUTE...NOT EVEN FOR A LOUSY HEART ATTACK!
Er,.. MR. KHAN... CAN I ASK--
--MR. KHAN... ARE YOU ALRIGHT?
OOAGHHHUH...

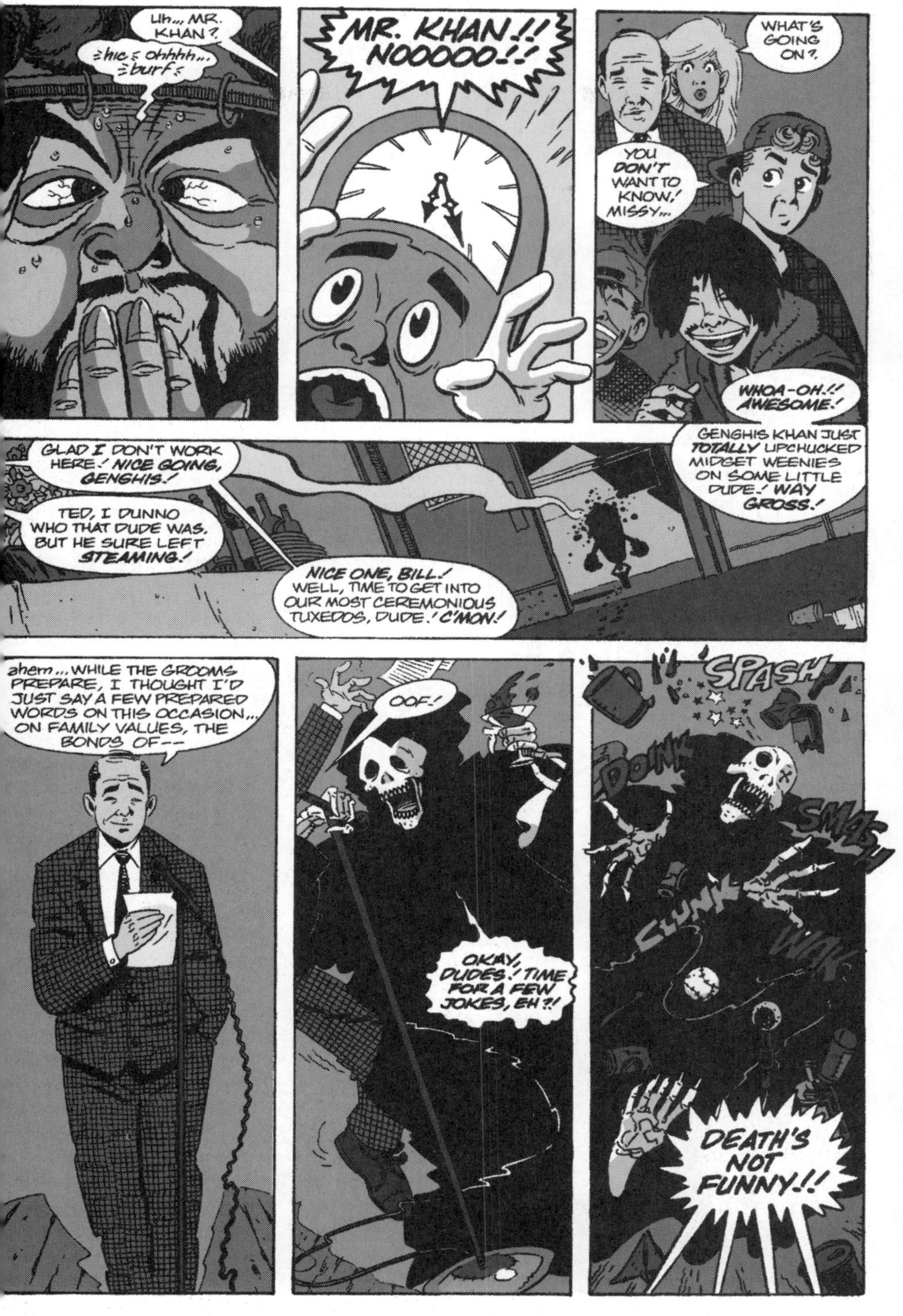

Uh..., MR. KHAN?
hic ohhhh... burf
MR. KHAN!!! NOOOOO!!!
WHAT'S GOING ON?
YOU DON'T WANT TO KNOW, MISSY...
WHOA-OH!!! AWESOME!
GENGHIS KHAN JUST TOTALLY UPCHUCKED MIDGET WEENIES ON SOME LITTLE DUDE! WAY GROSS!
GLAD I DON'T WORK HERE! NICE GOING, GENGHIS!
TED, I DUNNO WHO THAT DUDE WAS, BUT HE SURE LEFT STEAMING!
NICE ONE, BILL! WELL, TIME TO GET INTO OUR MOST CEREMONIOUS TUXEDOS, DUDE! C'MON!
ahem... WHILE THE GROOMS PREPARE, I THOUGHT I'D JUST SAY A FEW PREPARED WORDS ON THIS OCCASION... ON FAMILY VALUES, THE BONDS OF--
OOF!
OKAY, DUDES! TIME FOR A FEW JOKES, EH?!
SPASH
SMASH
CLUNK
DEATH'S NOT FUNNY!!

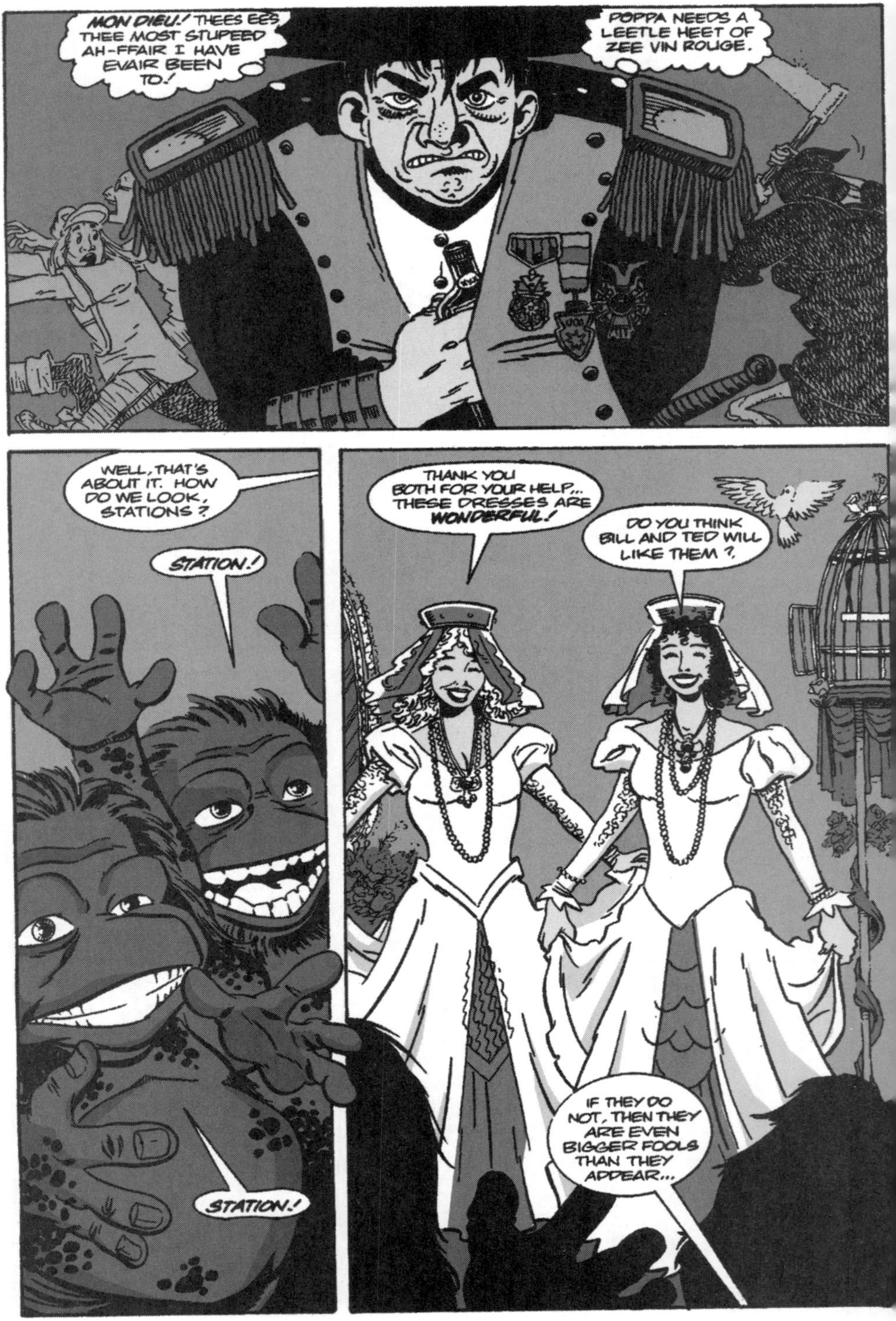

MON DIEU! THEES EES THEE MOST STUPEED AH-FFAIR I HAVE EVAIR BEEN TO!
POPPA NEEDS A LEETLE HEET OF ZEE VIN ROUGE.
WELL, THAT'S ABOUT IT. HOW DO WE LOOK, STATIONS ?
STATION!
STATION!
THANK YOU BOTH FOR YOUR HELP... THESE DRESSES ARE WONDERFUL!
DO YOU THINK BILL AND TED WILL LIKE THEM ?
IF THEY DO NOT, THEN THEY ARE EVEN BIGGER FOOLS THAN THEY APPEAR...

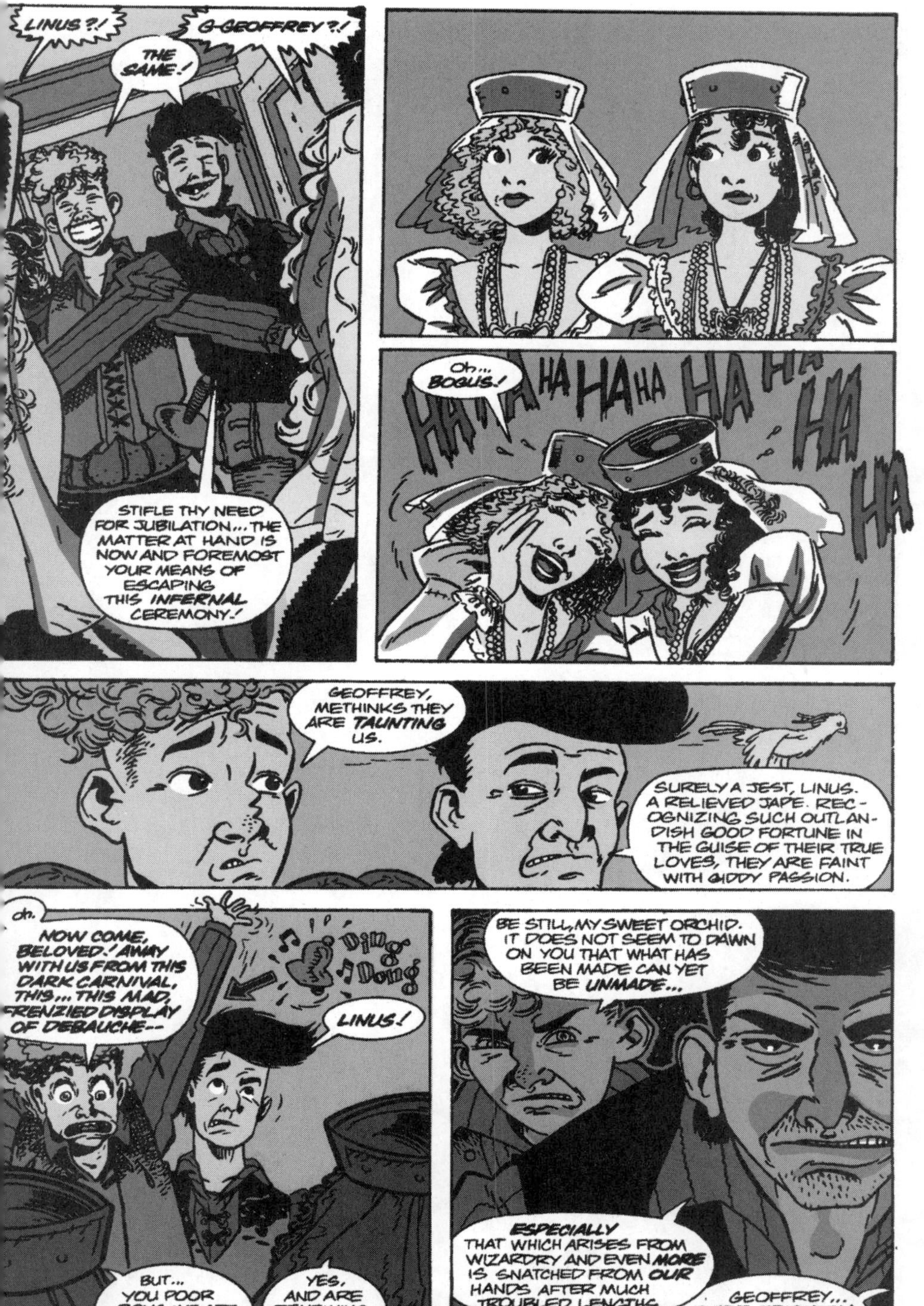
LINUS?!
G-GEOFFREY?!
THE SAME!
STIFLE THY NEED FOR JUBILATION... THE MATTER AT HAND IS NOW AND FOREMOST YOUR MEANS OF ESCAPING THIS INFERNAL CEREMONY!
Oh... BOGUS!
HA HA HA HA HA HA HA HA HA HA
GEOFFREY, METHINKS THEY ARE TAUNTING US.
SURELY A JEST, LINUS. A RELIEVED JAPE. REC-OGNIZING SUCH OUTLAN-DISH GOOD FORTUNE IN THE GUISE OF THEIR TRUE LOVES, THEY ARE FAINT WITH GIDDY PASSION.
Oh.
NOW COME, BELOVED! AWAY WITH US FROM THIS DARK CARNIVAL, THIS... THIS MAD, FRENZIED DISPLAY OF DEBAUCHE--
Ding Dong
LINUS!
BUT... YOU POOR BOYS, WE ARE ALREADY WED...
YES, AND ARE RENEWING OUR VOWS!
BE STILL, MY SWEET ORCHID. IT DOES NOT SEEM TO DAWN ON YOU THAT WHAT HAS BEEN MADE CAN YET BE UNMADE...
ESPECIALLY THAT WHICH ARISES FROM WIZARDRY AND EVEN MORE IS SNATCHED FROM OUR HANDS AFTER MUCH TROUBLED LENGTHS.
GEOFFREY... YOU'RE FRIGHTEN-ING ME--

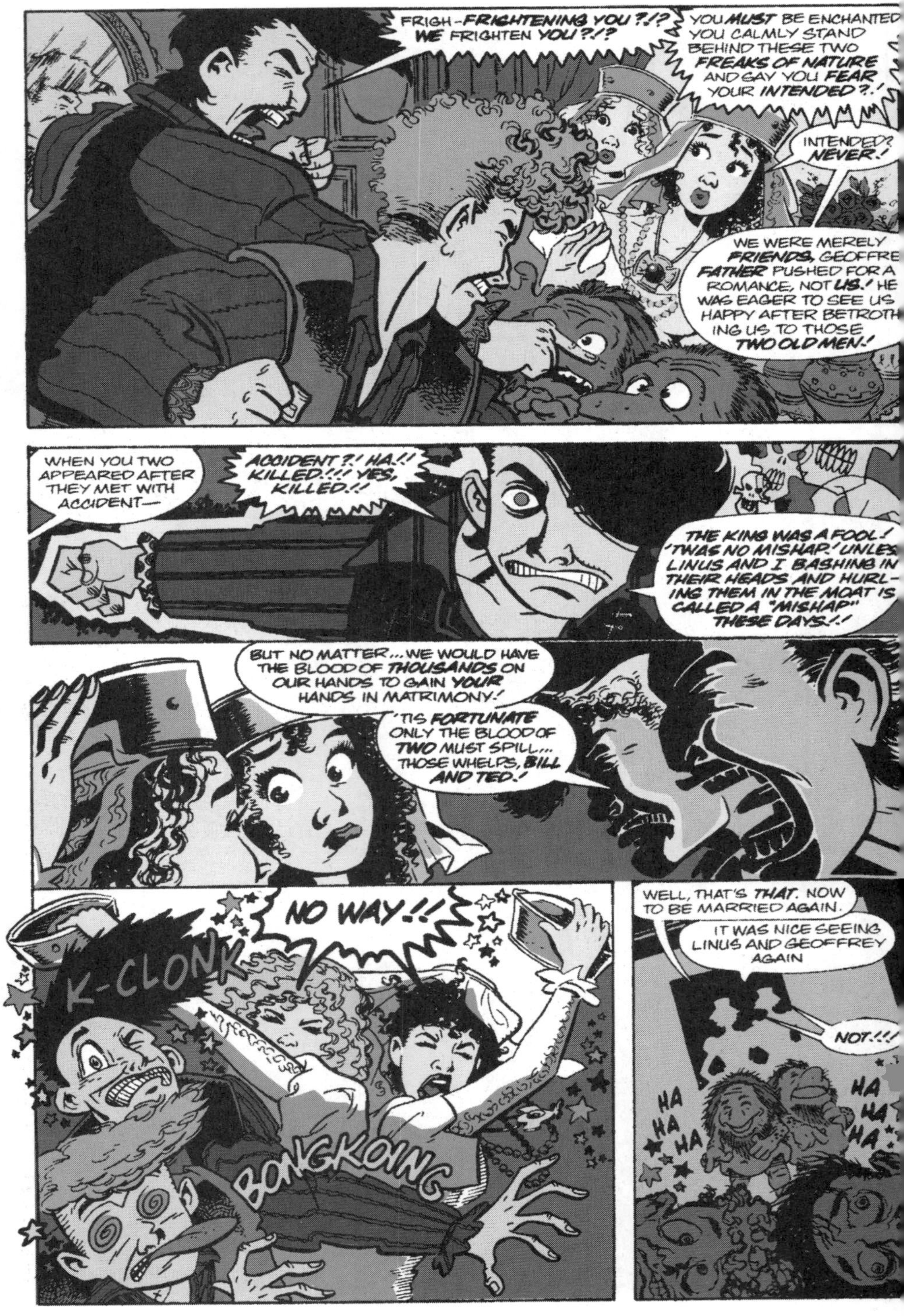
FRIGH-FRIGHTENING YOU?!? WE FRIGHTEN YOU?!?
YOU MUST BE ENCHANTED YOU CALMLY STAND BEHIND THESE TWO FREAKS OF NATURE AND SAY YOU FEAR YOUR INTENDED?!
INTENDED? NEVER!
WE WERE MERELY FRIENDS, GEOFFRE FATHER PUSHED FOR A ROMANCE, NOT US! HE WAS EAGER TO SEE US HAPPY AFTER BETROTH ING US TO THOSE TWO OLD MEN!
WHEN YOU TWO APPEARED AFTER THEY MET WITH ACCIDENT—
ACCIDENT?! HA!! KILLED!!!! YES, KILLED!!
THE KING WAS A FOOL! 'TWAS NO MISHAP! UNLES LINUS AND I BASHING IN THEIR HEADS AND HURL-ING THEM IN THE MOAT IS CALLED A "MISHAP" THESE DAYS!!
BUT NO MATTER... WE WOULD HAVE THE BLOOD OF THOUSANDS ON OUR HANDS TO GAIN YOUR HANDS IN MATRIMONY!
'TIS FORTUNATE ONLY THE BLOOD OF TWO MUST SPILL... THOSE WHELPS, BILL AND TED!
NO WAY!!!
K-CLONK
BONGKOING
WELL, THAT'S THAT. NOW TO BE MARRIED AGAIN.
IT WAS NICE SEEING LINUS AND GEOFFREY AGAIN
NOT!!!
HA HA HA
HA HA HA

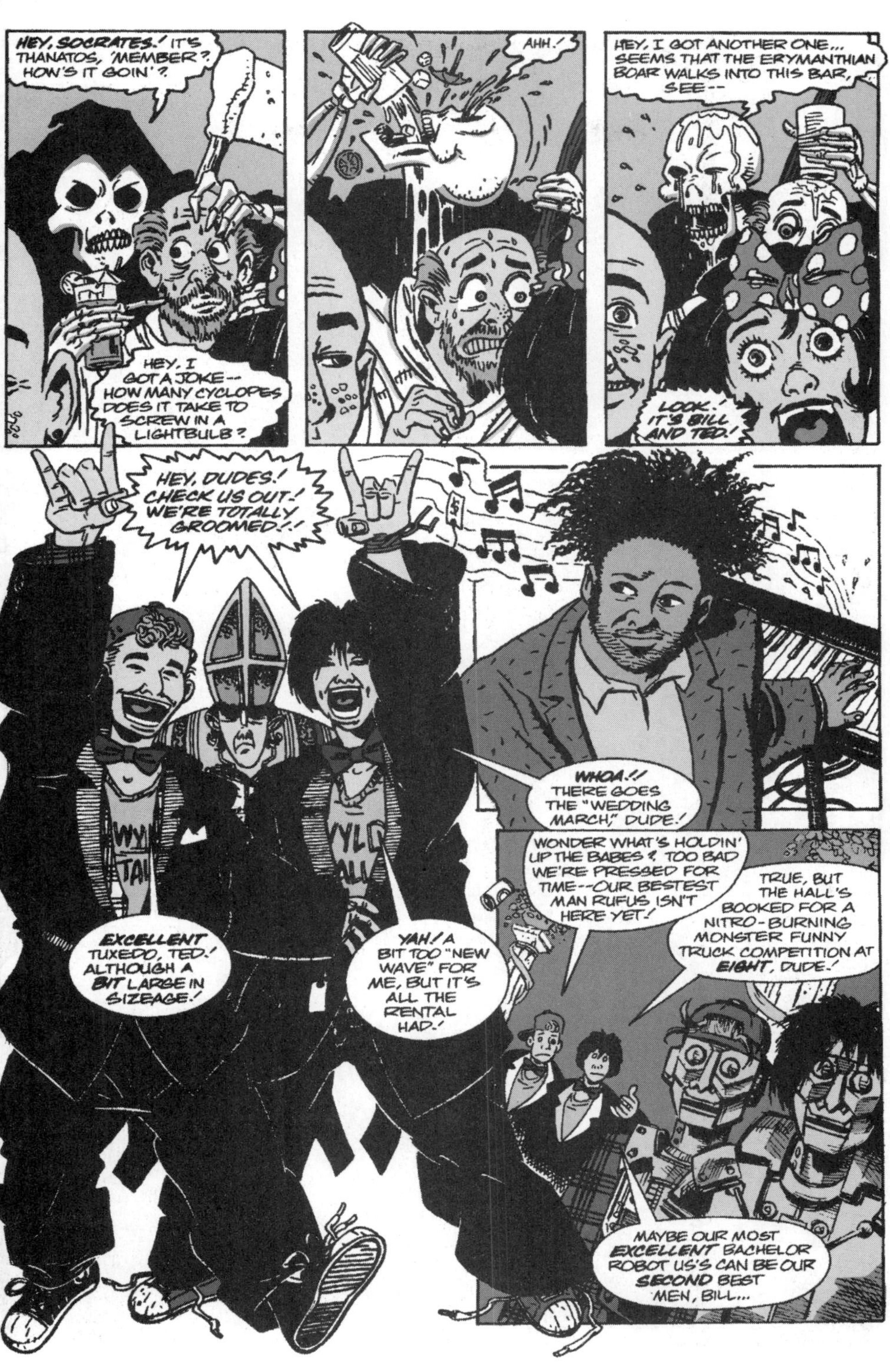

HEY, SOCRATES! IT'S THANATOS, 'MEMBER? HOW'S IT GOIN'?
HEY, I GOT A JOKE-- HOW MANY CYCLOPES DOES IT TAKE TO SCREW IN A LIGHTBULB?
AHH!
HEY, I GOT ANOTHER ONE... SEEMS THAT THE ERYMANTHIAN BOAR WALKS INTO THIS BAR, SEE--
LOOK! IT'S BILL AND TED!
HEY, DUDES! CHECK US OUT! WE'RE TOTALLY GROOMED!!
WHOA!! THERE GOES THE "WEDDING MARCH," DUDE!
EXCELLENT TUXEDO, TED! ALTHOUGH A BIT LARGE IN SIZEAGE!
YAH! A BIT TOO "NEW WAVE" FOR ME, BUT IT'S ALL THE RENTAL HAD!
WONDER WHAT'S HOLDIN' UP THE BABES? TOO BAD WE'RE PRESSED FOR TIME--OUR BESTEST MAN RUFUS ISN'T HERE YET!
TRUE, BUT THE HALL'S BOOKED FOR A NITRO-BURNING MONSTER FUNNY TRUCK COMPETITION AT EIGHT, DUDE!
MAYBE OUR MOST EXCELLENT BACHELOR ROBOT US'S CAN BE OUR SECOND BEST MEN, BILL...

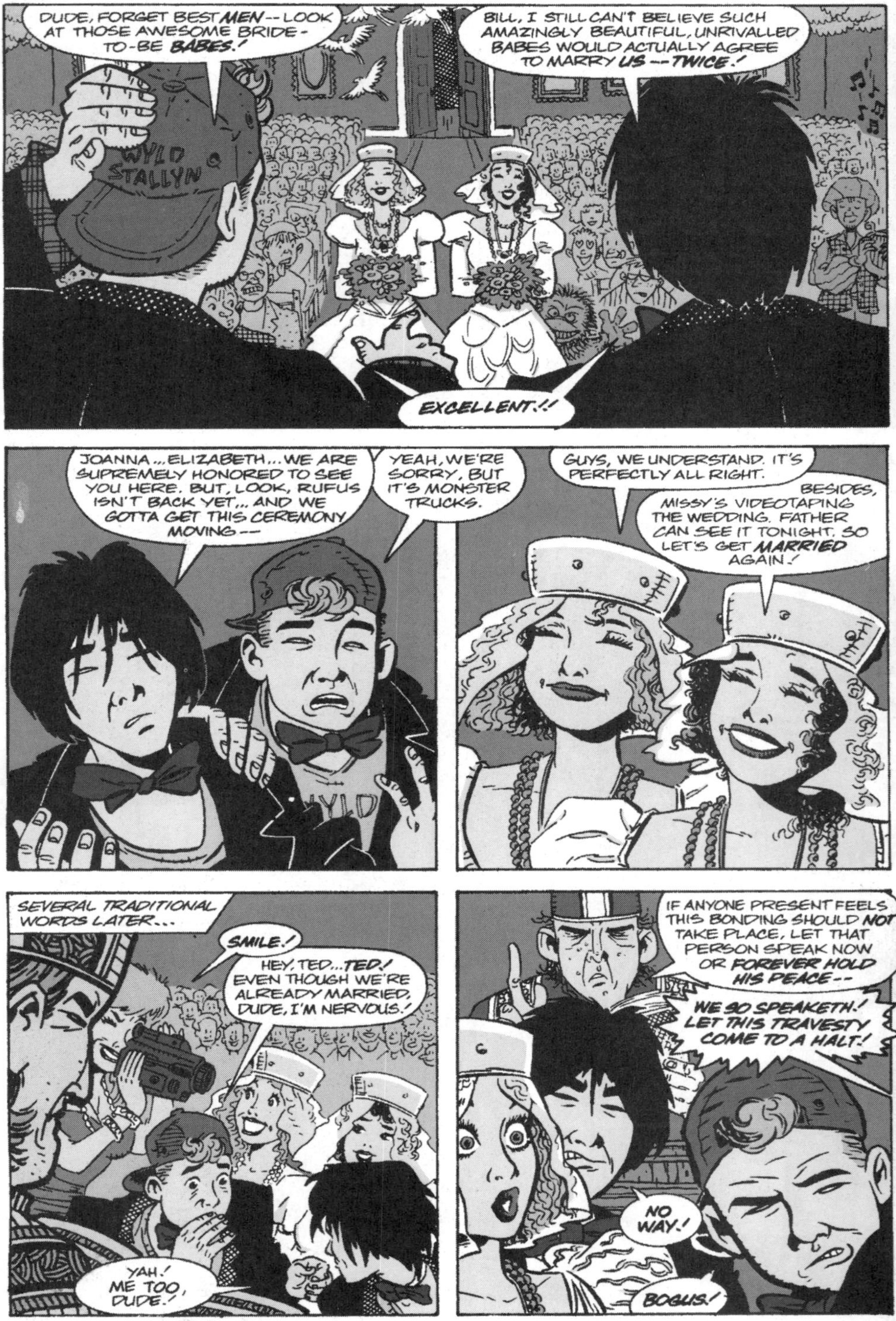
DUDE, FORGET BEST MEN -- LOOK AT THOSE AWESOME BRIDE-TO-BE BABES!
BILL, I STILL CAN'T BELIEVE SUCH AMAZINGLY BEAUTIFUL, UNRIVALLED BABES WOULD ACTUALLY AGREE TO MARRY US -- TWICE!
WYLD STALLYN
EXCELLENT!!
JOANNA... ELIZABETH... WE ARE SUPREMELY HONORED TO SEE YOU HERE. BUT, LOOK, RUFUS ISN'T BACK YET... AND WE GOTTA GET THIS CEREMONY MOVING --
YEAH, WE'RE SORRY, BUT IT'S MONSTER TRUCKS.
GUYS, WE UNDERSTAND. IT'S PERFECTLY ALL RIGHT.
BESIDES, MISSY'S VIDEOTAPING THE WEDDING. FATHER CAN SEE IT TONIGHT. SO LET'S GET MARRIED AGAIN!
SEVERAL TRADITIONAL WORDS LATER...
SMILE!
HEY, TED... TED! EVEN THOUGH WE'RE ALREADY MARRIED, DUDE, I'M NERVOUS!
YAH! ME TOO, DUDE!
IF ANYONE PRESENT FEELS THIS BONDING SHOULD NOT TAKE PLACE, LET THAT PERSON SPEAK NOW OR FOREVER HOLD HIS PEACE --
WE SO SPEAKETH! LET THIS TRAVESTY COME TO A HALT!
NO WAY!
BOGUS!

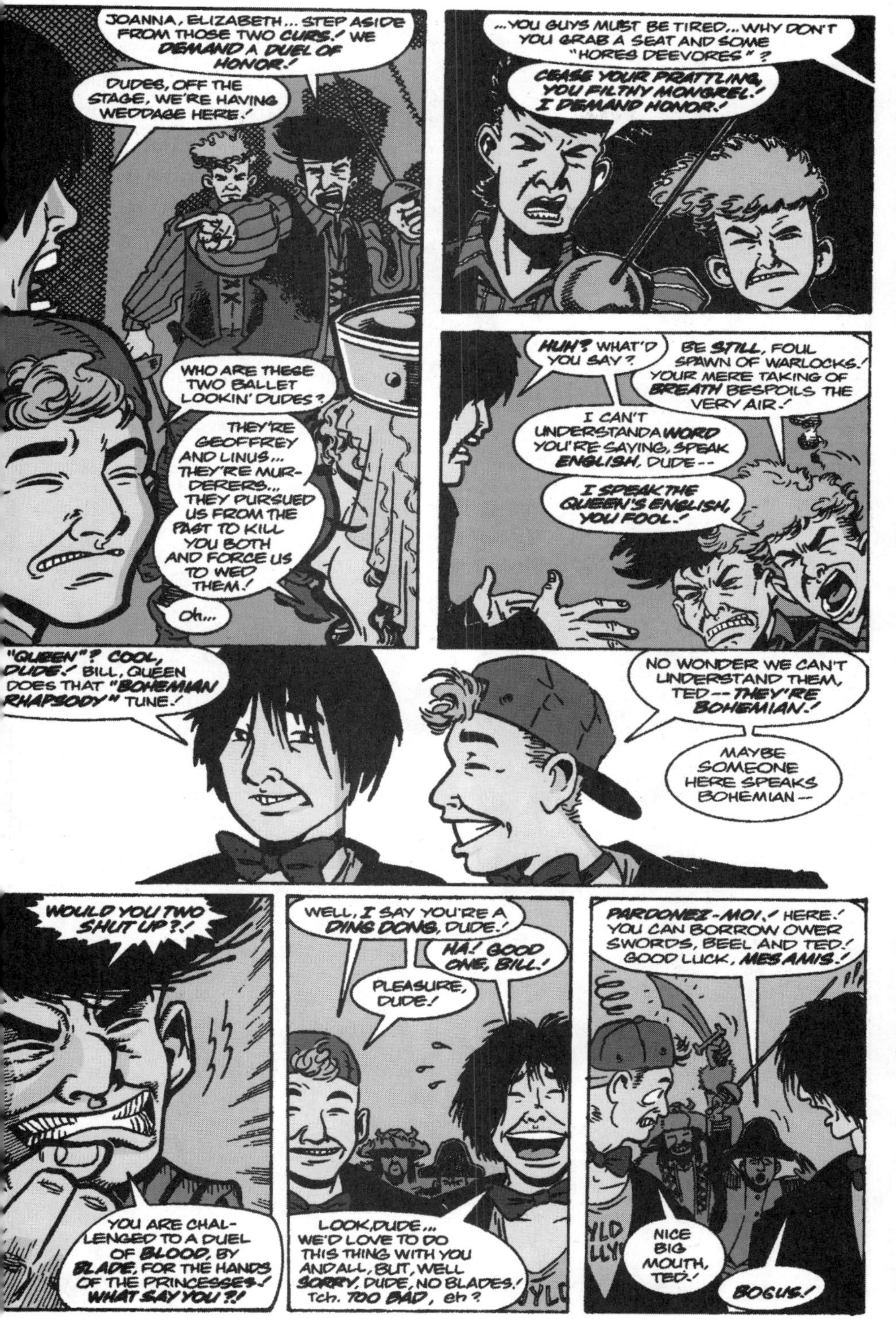
JOANNA, ELIZABETH... STEP ASIDE FROM THOSE TWO CURS! WE DEMAND A DUEL OF HONOR!
DUDES, OFF THE STAGE, WE'RE HAVING WEDDAGE HERE!
...YOU GUYS MUST BE TIRED... WHY DON'T YOU GRAB A SEAT AND SOME "HORES DEEVORES"?
CEASE YOUR PRATTLING, YOU FILTHY MONGREL! I DEMAND HONOR!
WHO ARE THESE TWO BALLET LOOKIN' DUDES?
THEY'RE GEOFFREY AND LINUS... THEY'RE MURDERERS... THEY PURSUED US FROM THE PAST TO KILL YOU BOTH AND FORCE US TO WED THEM!
Oh...
HUH? WHAT'D YOU SAY?
BE STILL, FOUL SPAWN OF WARLOCKS! YOUR MERE TAKING OF BREATH BESPOILS THE VERY AIR!
I CAN'T UNDERSTANDA WORD YOU'RE SAYING, SPEAK ENGLISH, DUDE--
I SPEAK THE QUEEN'S ENGLISH, YOU FOOL!
"QUEEN"? COOL, DUDE! BILL, QUEEN DOES THAT "BOHEMIAN RHAPSODY" TUNE!
NO WONDER WE CAN'T UNDERSTAND THEM, TED--THEY'RE BOHEMIAN!
MAYBE SOMEONE HERE SPEAKS BOHEMIAN--
WOULD YOU TWO SHUT UP?!
YOU ARE CHALLENGED TO A DUEL OF BLOOD, BY BLADE, FOR THE HANDS OF THE PRINCESSES! WHAT SAY YOU?!
WELL, I SAY YOU'RE A DING DONGS, DUDE!
HA! GOOD ONE, BILL!
PLEASURE, DUDE!
LOOK, DUDE... WE'D LOVE TO DO THIS THING WITH YOU AND ALL, BUT, WELL SORRY, DUDE, NO BLADES! Tch. TOO BAD, eh?
PARDONEZ-MOI! HERE! YOU CAN BORROW OWER SWORDS, BEEL AND TED! GOOD LUCK, MES AMIS!
NICE BIG MOUTH, TED!
BOGUS!

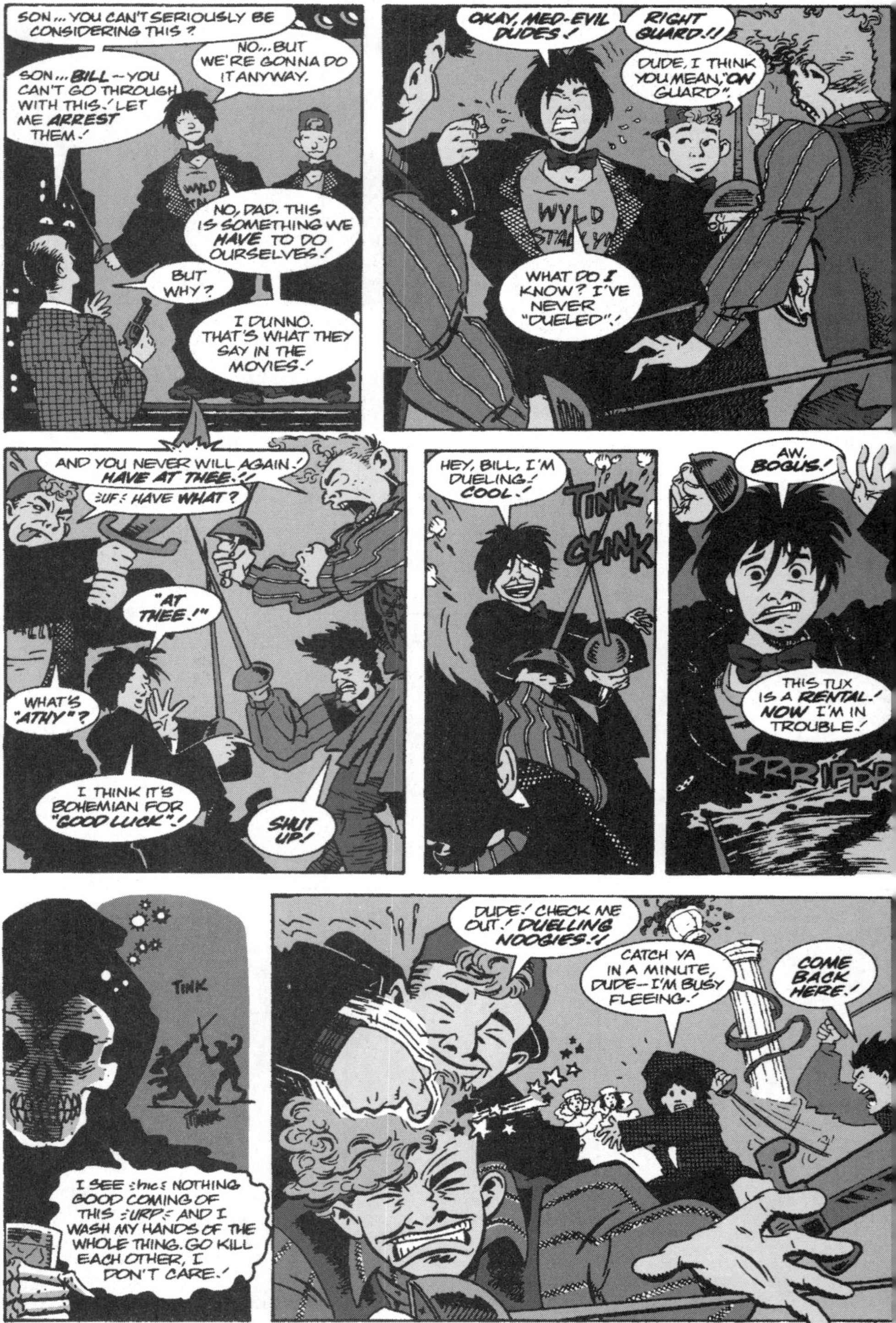

SON... YOU CAN'T SERIOUSLY BE CONSIDERING THIS?
NO... BUT WE'RE GONNA DO IT ANYWAY.
SON... BILL -- YOU CAN'T GO THROUGH WITH THIS! LET ME ARREST THEM!
NO, DAD. THIS IS SOMETHING WE HAVE TO DO OURSELVES!
BUT WHY?
I DUNNO. THAT'S WHAT THEY SAY IN THE MOVIES!
OKAY, MED-EVIL DUDES!
RIGHT GUARD!!
DUDE, I THINK YOU MEAN, "ON GUARD".
WHAT DO I KNOW? I'VE NEVER "DUELED"!
AND YOU NEVER WILL AGAIN! HAVE AT THEE!!
UF HAVE WHAT?
"AT THEE!"
WHAT'S "ATHY"?
I THINK IT'S BOHEMIAN FOR "GOOD LUCK"!
SHUT UP!
HEY, BILL, I'M DUELING! COOL!
TINK
CLINK
AW, BOGUS!
THIS TUX IS A RENTAL! NOW I'M IN TROUBLE!
RRRIPPP
TINK
TINK
I SEE hic NOTHING GOOD COMING OF THIS URP AND I WASH MY HANDS OF THE WHOLE THING. GO KILL EACH OTHER, I DON'T CARE!
DUDE! CHECK ME OUT! DUELLING NOOGIES!!
CATCH YA IN A MINUTE, DUDE-- I'M BUSY FLEEING!
COME BACK HERE!

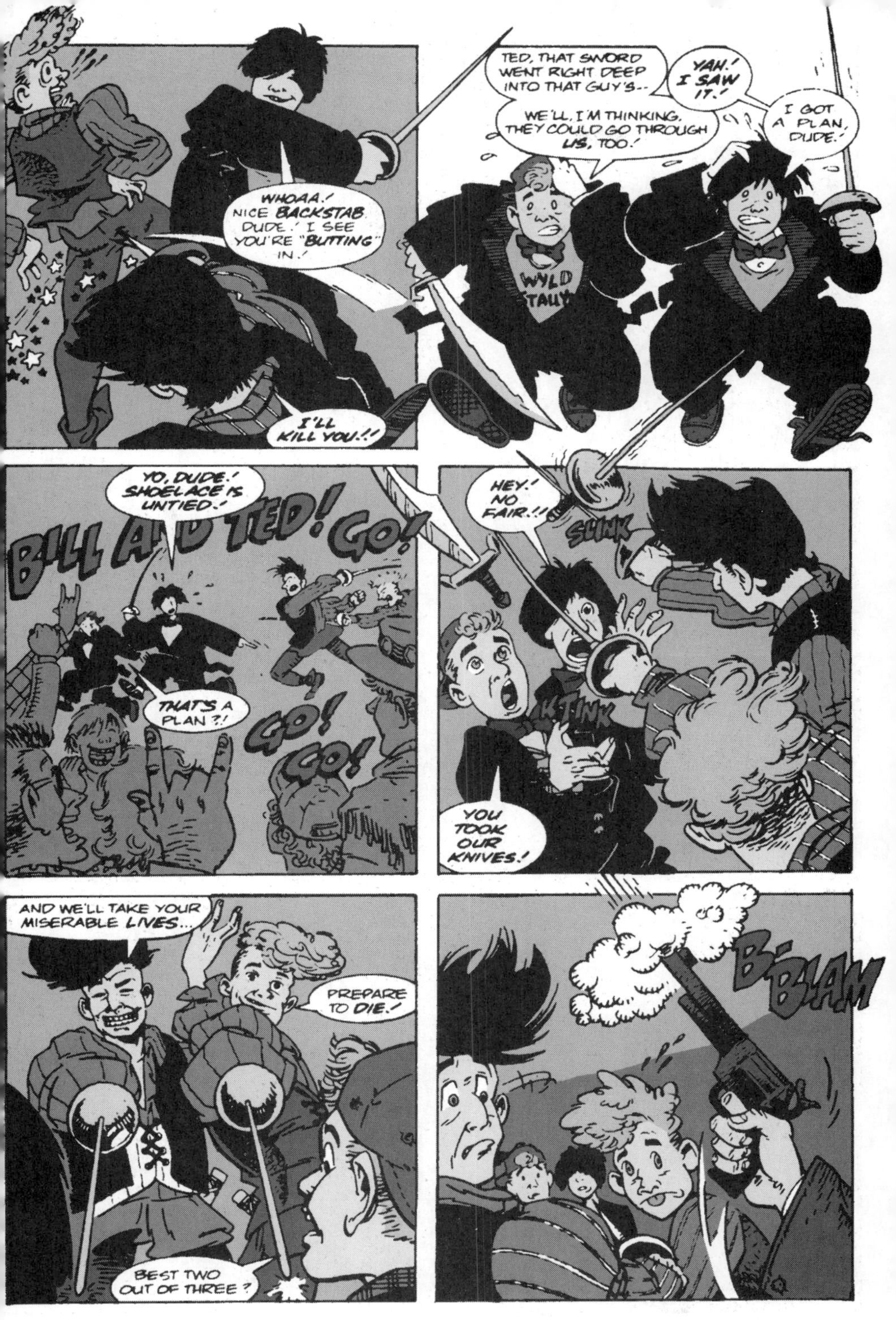
WHOAA! NICE BACKSTAB DUDE! I SEE YOU'RE "BUTTING" IN!
I'LL KILL YOU!!
TED, THAT SWORD WENT RIGHT DEEP INTO THAT GUY'S--
YAH! I SAW IT!
WE'LL, I'M THINKING. THEY COULD GO THROUGH US, TOO!
I GOT A PLAN, DUDE!
YO, DUDE! SHOELACE IS UNTIED!
BILL AND TED! GO!
THAT'S A PLAN ?!
GO! GO!
HEY! NO FAIR!!
SLINK
KTINK
YOU TOOK OUR KNIVES!
AND WE'LL TAKE YOUR MISERABLE LIVES...
PREPARE TO DIE!
BEST TWO OUT OF THREE ?
B'BLAM

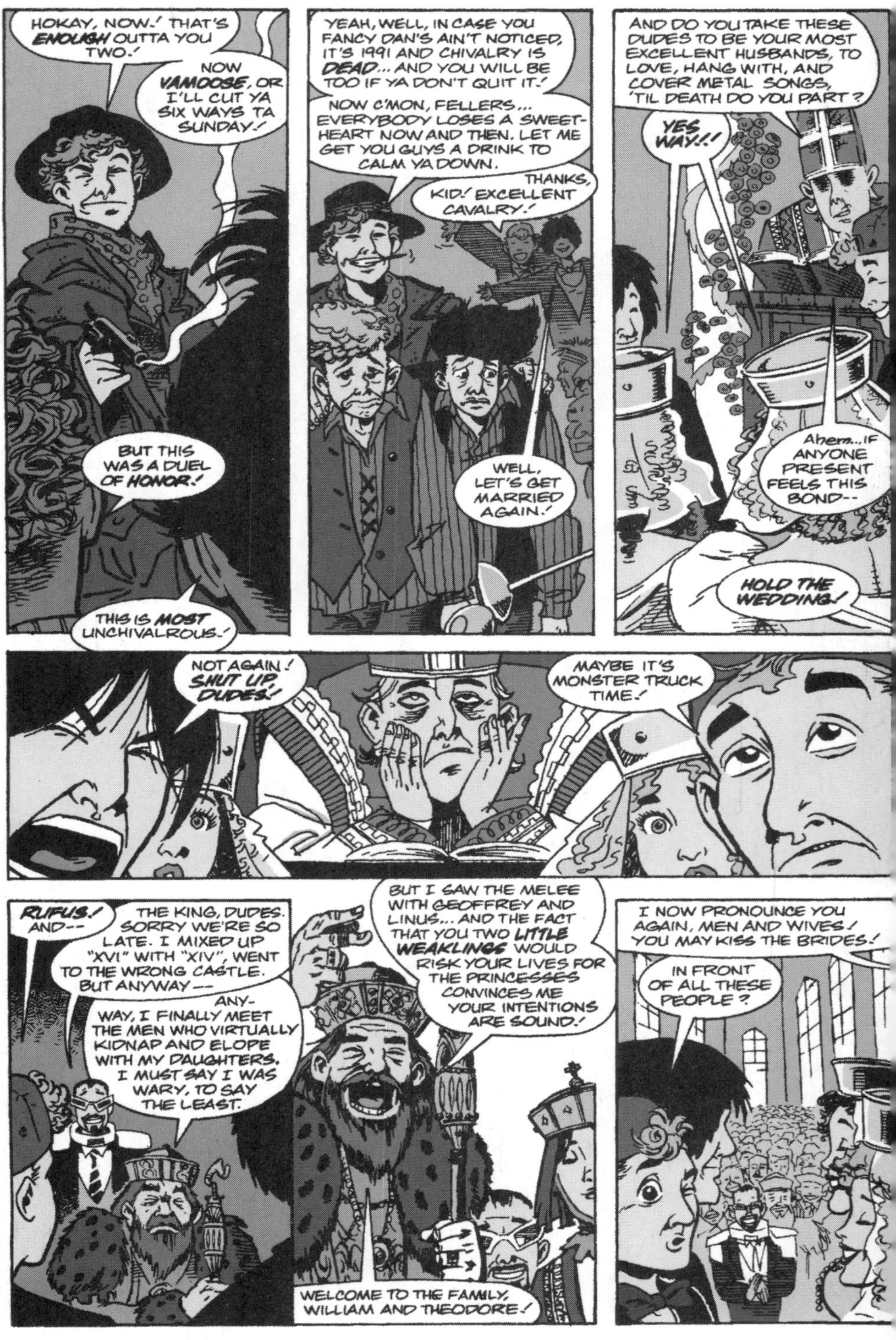
HOKAY, NOW.! THAT'S ENOUGH OUTTA YOU TWO.!
NOW VAMOOSE, OR I'LL CUT YA SIX WAYS TA SUNDAY.!
BUT THIS WAS A DUEL OF HONOR.!
THIS IS MOST UNCHIVALROUS.!
YEAH, WELL, IN CASE YOU FANCY DAN'S AIN'T NOTICED, IT'S 1991 AND CHIVALRY IS DEAD... AND YOU WILL BE TOO IF YA DON'T QUIT IT.!
NOW C'MON, FELLERS... EVERYBODY LOSES A SWEET-HEART NOW AND THEN. LET ME GET YOU GUYS A DRINK TO CALM YA DOWN.
THANKS, KID.! EXCELLENT CAVALRY.!
WELL, LET'S GET MARRIED AGAIN.!
AND DO YOU TAKE THESE DUDES TO BE YOUR MOST EXCELLENT HUSBANDS, TO LOVE, HANG WITH, AND COVER METAL SONGS, 'TIL DEATH DO YOU PART?
YES WAY!!!
Ahem...IF ANYONE PRESENT FEELS THIS BOND--
HOLD THE WEDDING.!
NOT AGAIN.! SHUT UP, DUDES.!
MAYBE IT'S MONSTER TRUCK TIME.!
RUFUS.! AND--
THE KING, DUDES. SORRY WE'RE SO LATE. I MIXED UP "XVI" WITH "XIV", WENT TO THE WRONG CASTLE. BUT ANYWAY---
ANY-WAY, I FINALLY MEET THE MEN WHO VIRTUALLY KIDNAP AND ELOPE WITH MY DAUGHTERS. I MUST SAY I WAS WARY, TO SAY THE LEAST.
BUT I SAW THE MELEE WITH GEOFFREY AND LINUS... AND THE FACT THAT YOU TWO LITTLE WEAKLINGS WOULD RISK YOUR LIVES FOR THE PRINCESSES CONVINCES ME YOUR INTENTIONS ARE SOUND.!
WELCOME TO THE FAMILY, WILLIAM AND THEODORE.!
I NOW PRONOUNCE YOU AGAIN, MEN AND WIVES.! YOU MAY KISS THE BRIDES.!
IN FRONT OF ALL THESE PEOPLE?

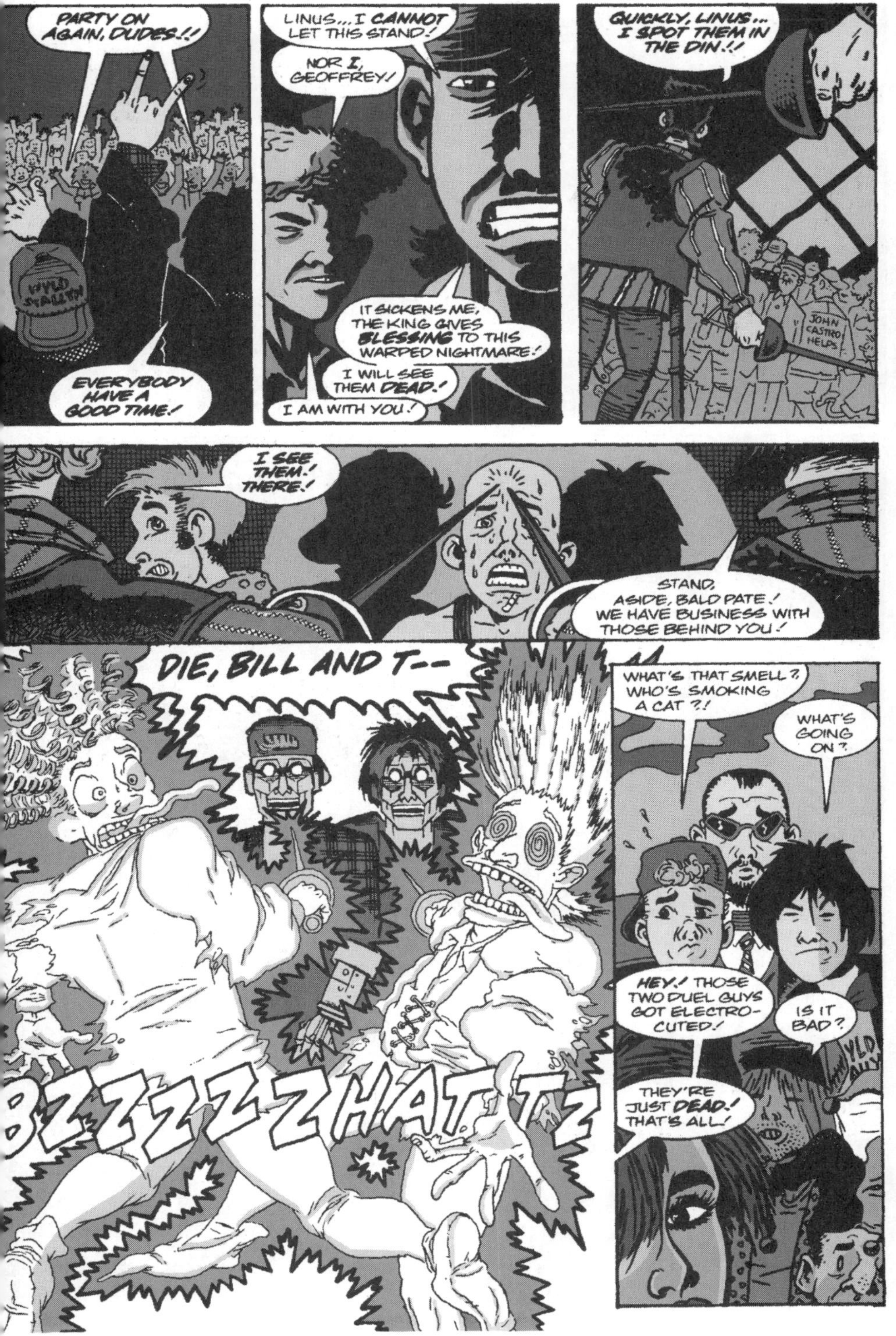

PARTY ON AGAIN, DUDES!!
EVERYBODY HAVE A GOOD TIME!
LINUS... I CANNOT LET THIS STAND!
NOR I, GEOFFREY!
IT SICKENS ME, THE KING GIVES BLESSING TO THIS WARPED NIGHTMARE!
I WILL SEE THEM DEAD!
I AM WITH YOU!
QUICKLY, LINUS... I SPOT THEM IN THE DIN!!
JOHN CASTRO HELPS
I SEE THEM! THERE!
STAND, ASIDE, BALD PATE! WE HAVE BUSINESS WITH THOSE BEHIND YOU!
DIE, BILL AND T--
WHAT'S THAT SMELL?, WHO'S SMOKING A CAT?!
WHAT'S GOING ON?
HEY! THOSE TWO DUEL GUYS GOT ELECTROCUTED!
IS IT BAD?
THEY'RE JUST DEAD! THAT'S ALL!

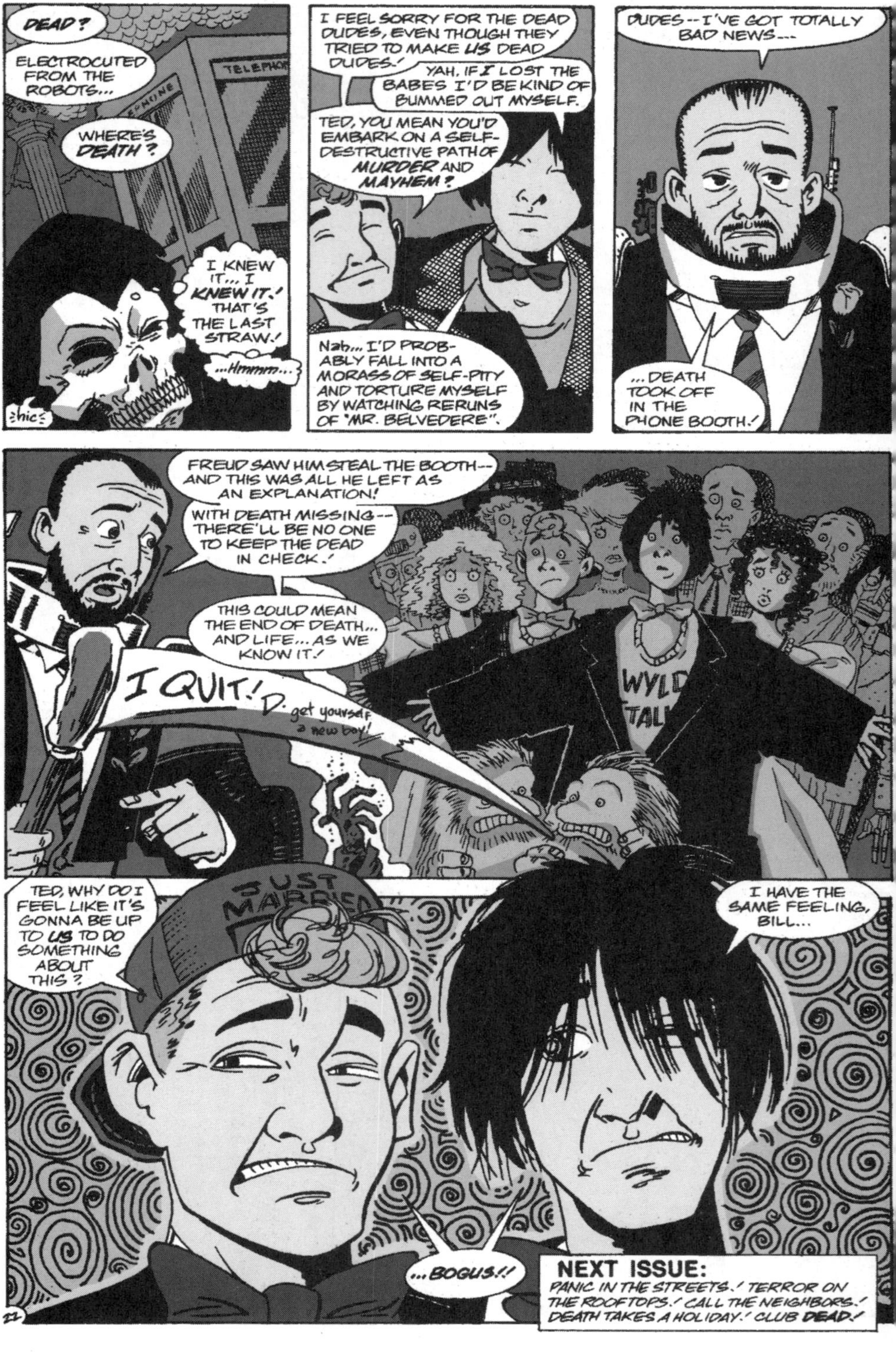
DEAD?
ELECTROCUTED FROM THE ROBOTS...
TELEPHO
WHERE'S DEATH?
I KNEW IT... I KNEW IT! THAT'S THE LAST STRAW!
...Hmmm...
hic
I FEEL SORRY FOR THE DEAD DUDES, EVEN THOUGH THEY TRIED TO MAKE US DEAD DUDES!
YAH, IF I LOST THE BABES I'D BE KIND OF BUMMED OUT MYSELF.
TED, YOU MEAN YOU'D EMBARK ON A SELF-DESTRUCTIVE PATH OF MURDER AND MAYHEM?
Nah... I'D PROBABLY FALL INTO A MORASS OF SELF-PITY AND TORTURE MYSELF BY WATCHING RERUNS OF "MR. BELVEDERE".
DUDES -- I'VE GOT TOTALLY BAD NEWS...
...DEATH TOOK OFF IN THE PHONE BOOTH!
FREUD SAW HIM STEAL THE BOOTH -- AND THIS WAS ALL HE LEFT AS AN EXPLANATION!
WITH DEATH MISSING -- THERE'LL BE NO ONE TO KEEP THE DEAD IN CHECK!
THIS COULD MEAN THE END OF DEATH... AND LIFE... AS WE KNOW IT!
I QUIT! D. get yourself a new boy!
WYLD TALL
TED, WHY DO I FEEL LIKE IT'S GONNA BE UP TO US TO DO SOMETHING ABOUT THIS?
JUST MARRIED
I HAVE THE SAME FEELING, BILL...
...BOGUS!!
NEXT ISSUE:
PANIC IN THE STREETS! TERROR ON THE ROOFTOPS! CALL THE NEIGHBORS! DEATH TAKES A HOLIDAY! CLUB DEAD!

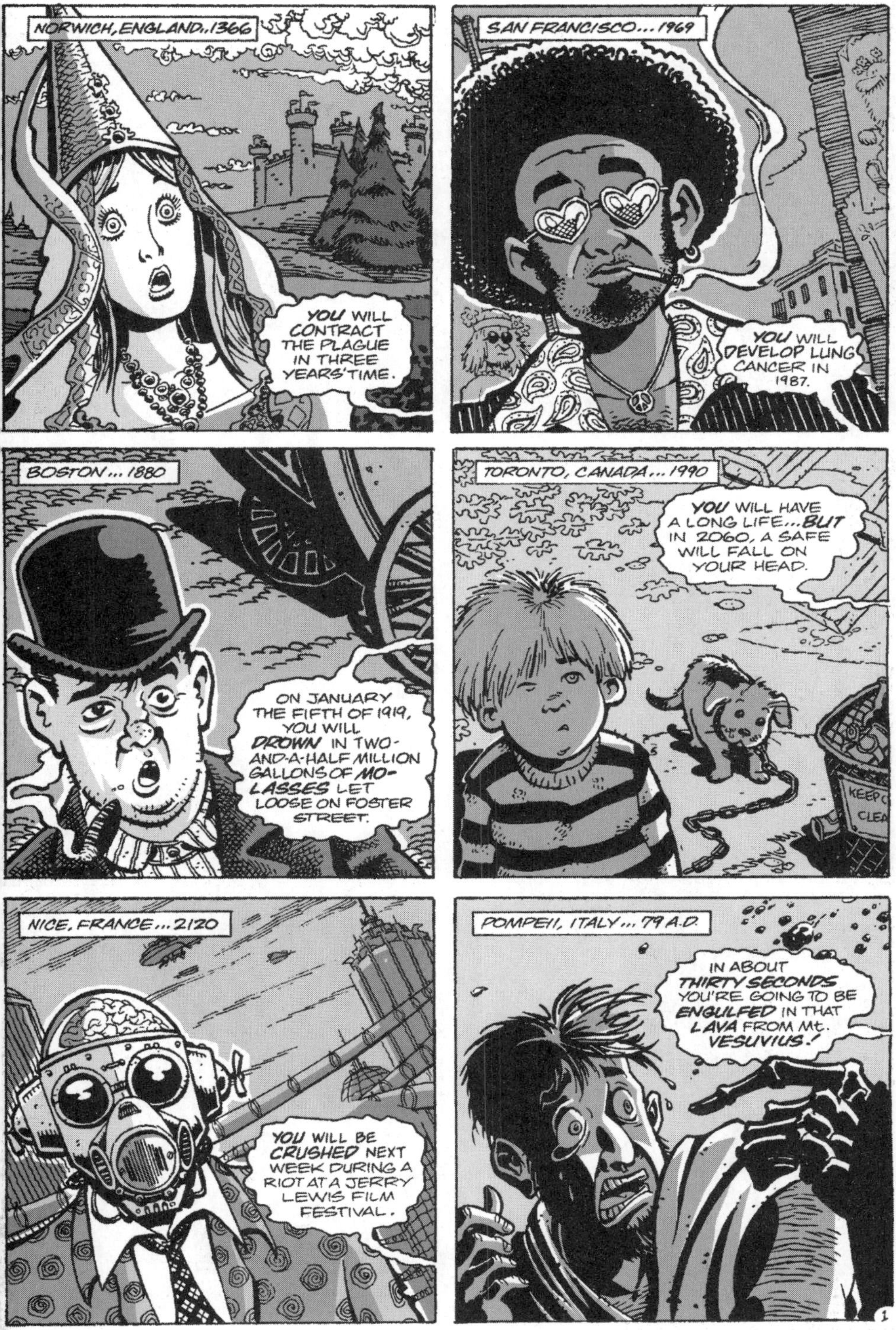
NORWICH, ENGLAND...1366
YOU WILL CONTRACT THE PLAGUE IN THREE YEARS' TIME.
SAN FRANCISCO...1969
YOU WILL DEVELOP LUNG CANCER IN 1987.
BOSTON...1880
ON JANUARY THE FIFTH OF 1919, YOU WILL DROWN IN TWO-AND-A-HALF MILLION GALLONS OF MO-LASSES LET LOOSE ON FOSTER STREET.
TORONTO, CANADA...1990
YOU WILL HAVE A LONG LIFE...BUT IN 2060, A SAFE WILL FALL ON YOUR HEAD.
NICE, FRANCE...2120
YOU WILL BE CRUSHED NEXT WEEK DURING A RIOT AT A JERRY LEWIS FILM FESTIVAL.
POMPEII, ITALY...79 A.D.
IN ABOUT THIRTY SECONDS YOU'RE GOING TO BE ENGULFED IN THAT LAVA FROM Mt. VESUVIUS!

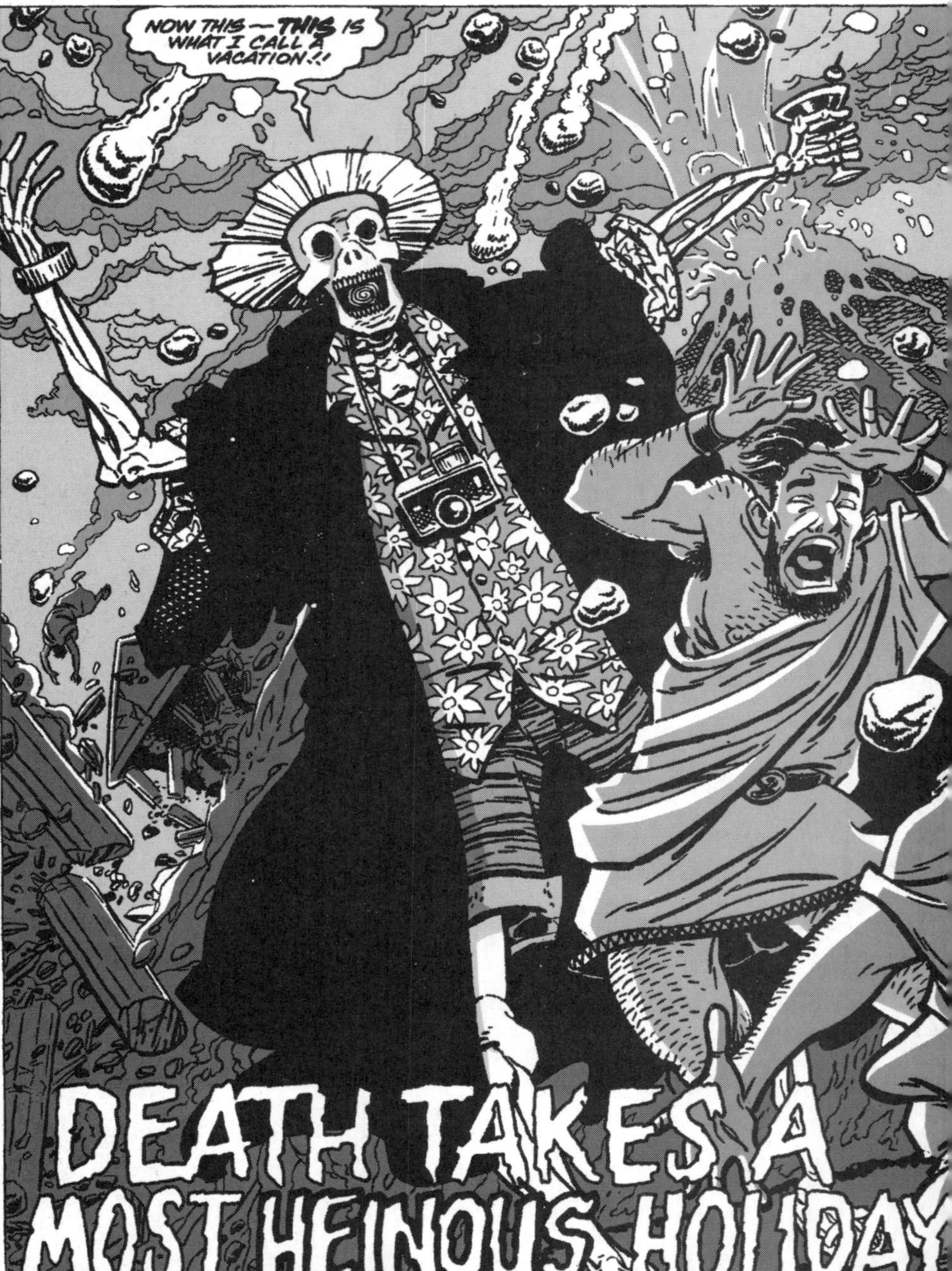
NOW THIS—THIS IS WHAT I CALL A VACATION!!
DEATH TAKES A MOST HEINOUS HOLIDAY

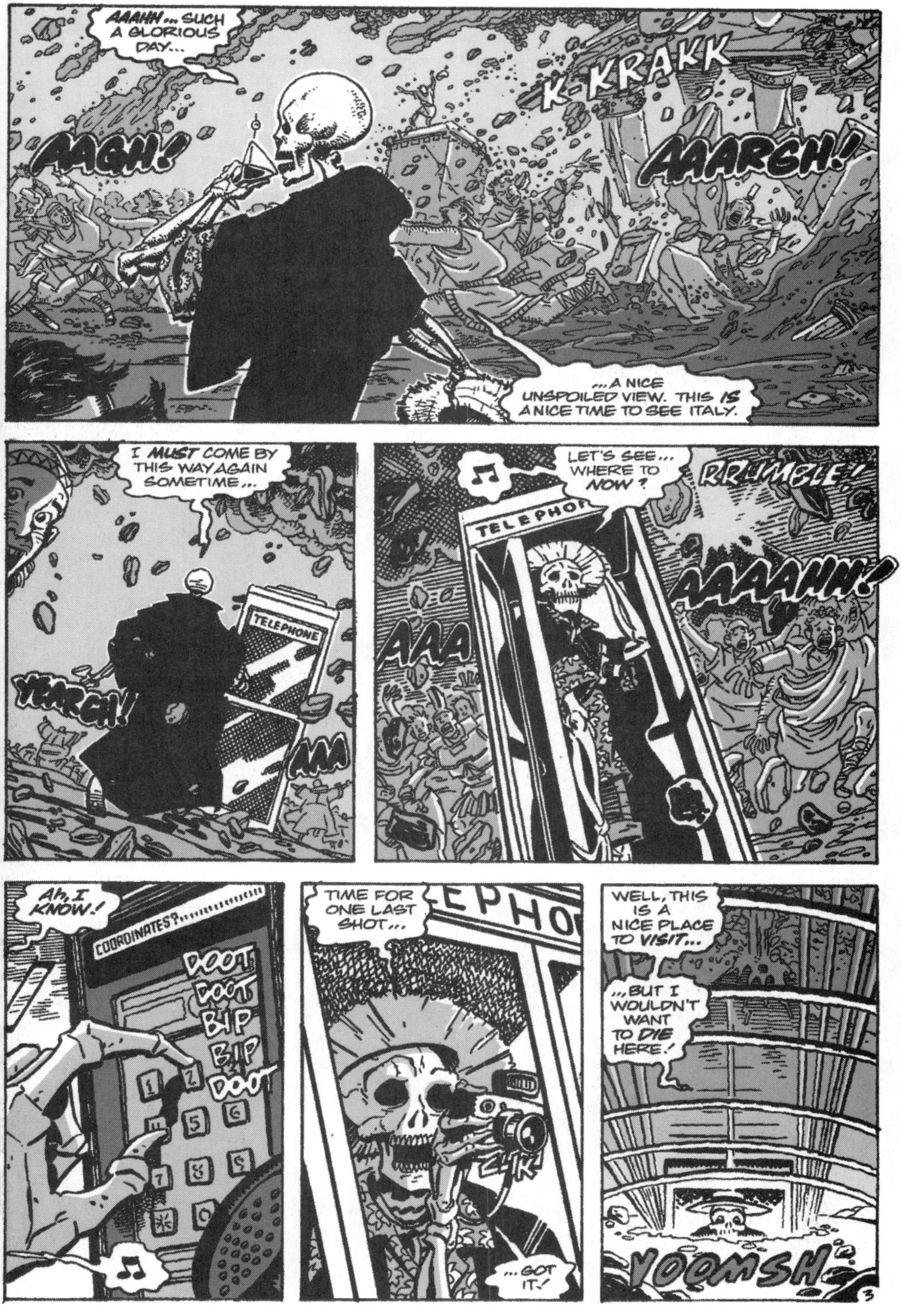
AAAHH... SUCH A GLORIOUS DAY...
K-KRAKK
AAGH!
AAARGH!
...A NICE UNSPOILED VIEW. THIS IS A NICE TIME TO SEE ITALY.
I MUST COME BY THIS WAY AGAIN SOMETIME...
TELEPHONE
YEARGH!
AAA
LET'S SEE... WHERE TO NOW?
RRUMBLE!
TELEPHO
AAAAAHH!
AAA
Ah, I KNOW!
COORDINATES?
DOOT
DOOT
BIP
BIP
DOOT
TIME FOR ONE LAST SHOT...
...GOT IT!
WELL, THIS IS A NICE PLACE TO VISIT...
...BUT I WOULDN'T WANT TO DIE HERE!
YOOMSH

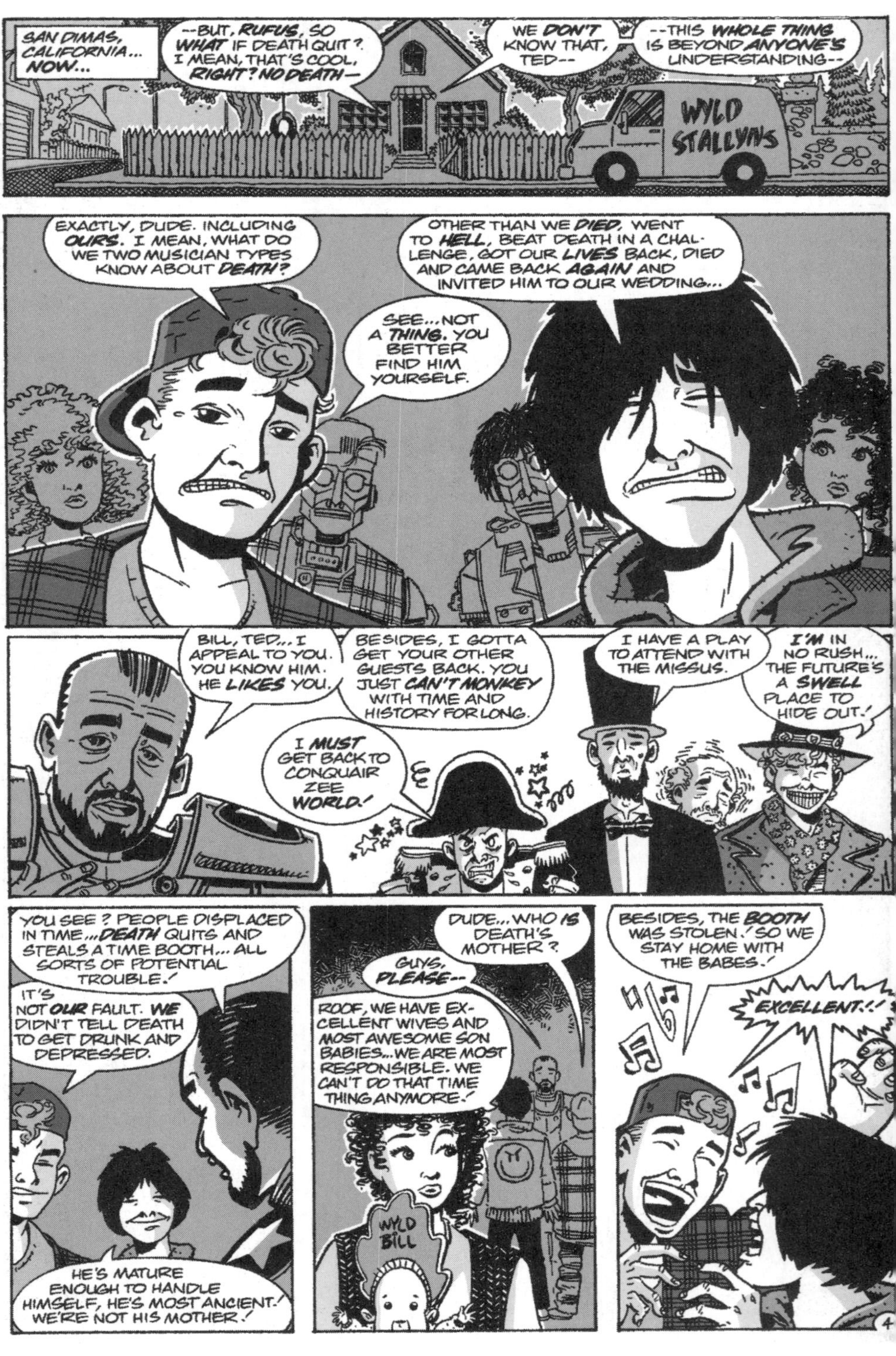
SAN DIMAS, CALIFORNIA... NOW...
--BUT, RUFUS, SO WHAT IF DEATH QUIT? I MEAN, THAT'S COOL, RIGHT? NO DEATH--
WE DON'T KNOW THAT, TED--
--THIS WHOLE THING IS BEYOND ANYONE'S UNDERSTANDING--
WYLD STALLYNS
EXACTLY, DUDE. INCLUDING OURS. I MEAN, WHAT DO WE TWO MUSICIAN TYPES KNOW ABOUT DEATH?
OTHER THAN WE DIED, WENT TO HELL, BEAT DEATH IN A CHALLENGE, GOT OUR LIVES BACK, DIED AND CAME BACK AGAIN AND INVITED HIM TO OUR WEDDING...
SEE...NOT A THING. YOU BETTER FIND HIM YOURSELF.
BILL, TED... I APPEAL TO YOU. YOU KNOW HIM. HE LIKES YOU.
BESIDES, I GOTTA GET YOUR OTHER GUESTS BACK. YOU JUST CAN'T MONKEY WITH TIME AND HISTORY FOR LONG.
I HAVE A PLAY TO ATTEND WITH THE MISSUS.
I'M IN NO RUSH... THE FUTURE'S A SWELL PLACE TO HIDE OUT!
I MUST GET BACK TO CONQUAIR ZEE WORLD!
YOU SEE? PEOPLE DISPLACED IN TIME... DEATH QUITS AND STEALS A TIME BOOTH... ALL SORTS OF POTENTIAL TROUBLE!
IT'S NOT OUR FAULT. WE DIDN'T TELL DEATH TO GET DRUNK AND DEPRESSED.
HE'S MATURE ENOUGH TO HANDLE HIMSELF, HE'S MOST ANCIENT! WE'RE NOT HIS MOTHER!
DUDE... WHO IS DEATH'S MOTHER?
GUYS, PLEASE--
ROOF, WE HAVE EXCELLENT WIVES AND MOST AWESOME SON BABIES... WE ARE MOST RESPONSIBLE. WE CAN'T DO THAT TIME THING ANYMORE!
WYLD BILL
BESIDES, THE BOOTH WAS STOLEN! SO WE STAY HOME WITH THE BABES!
EXCELLENT!!
4

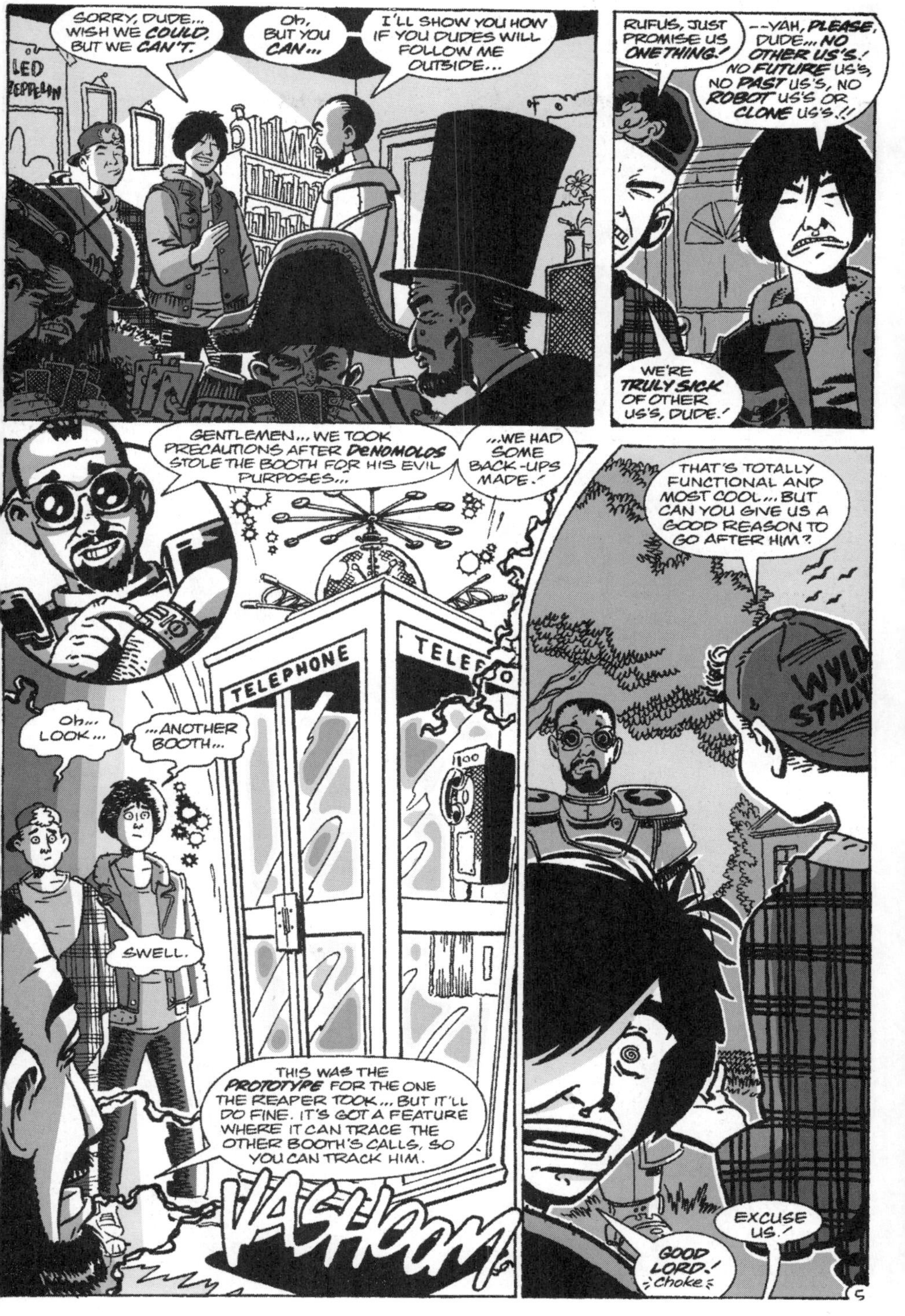

LED ZEPPELIN
SORRY, DUDE... WISH WE COULD, BUT WE CAN'T.
Oh, BUT YOU CAN...
I'LL SHOW YOU HOW IF YOU DUDES WILL FOLLOW ME OUTSIDE...
RUFUS, JUST PROMISE US ONE THING!
--YAH, PLEASE, DUDE... NO OTHER US'S! NO FUTURE US'S, NO PAST US'S, NO ROBOT US'S OR CLONE US'S!!!
WE'RE TRULY SICK OF OTHER US'S, DUDE!
GENTLEMEN... WE TOOK PRECAUTIONS AFTER DENOMOLOS STOLE THE BOOTH FOR HIS EVIL PURPOSES...
...WE HAD SOME BACK-UPS MADE!
TELEPHONE
Oh... LOOK...
...ANOTHER BOOTH...
SWELL.
THIS WAS THE PROTOTYPE FOR THE ONE THE REAPER TOOK... BUT IT'LL DO FINE. IT'S GOT A FEATURE WHERE IT CAN TRACE THE OTHER BOOTH'S CALLS, SO YOU CAN TRACK HIM.
VASHOOM
THAT'S TOTALLY FUNCTIONAL AND MOST COOL... BUT CAN YOU GIVE US A GOOD REASON TO GO AFTER HIM?
EXCUSE US!
GOOD LORD! choke

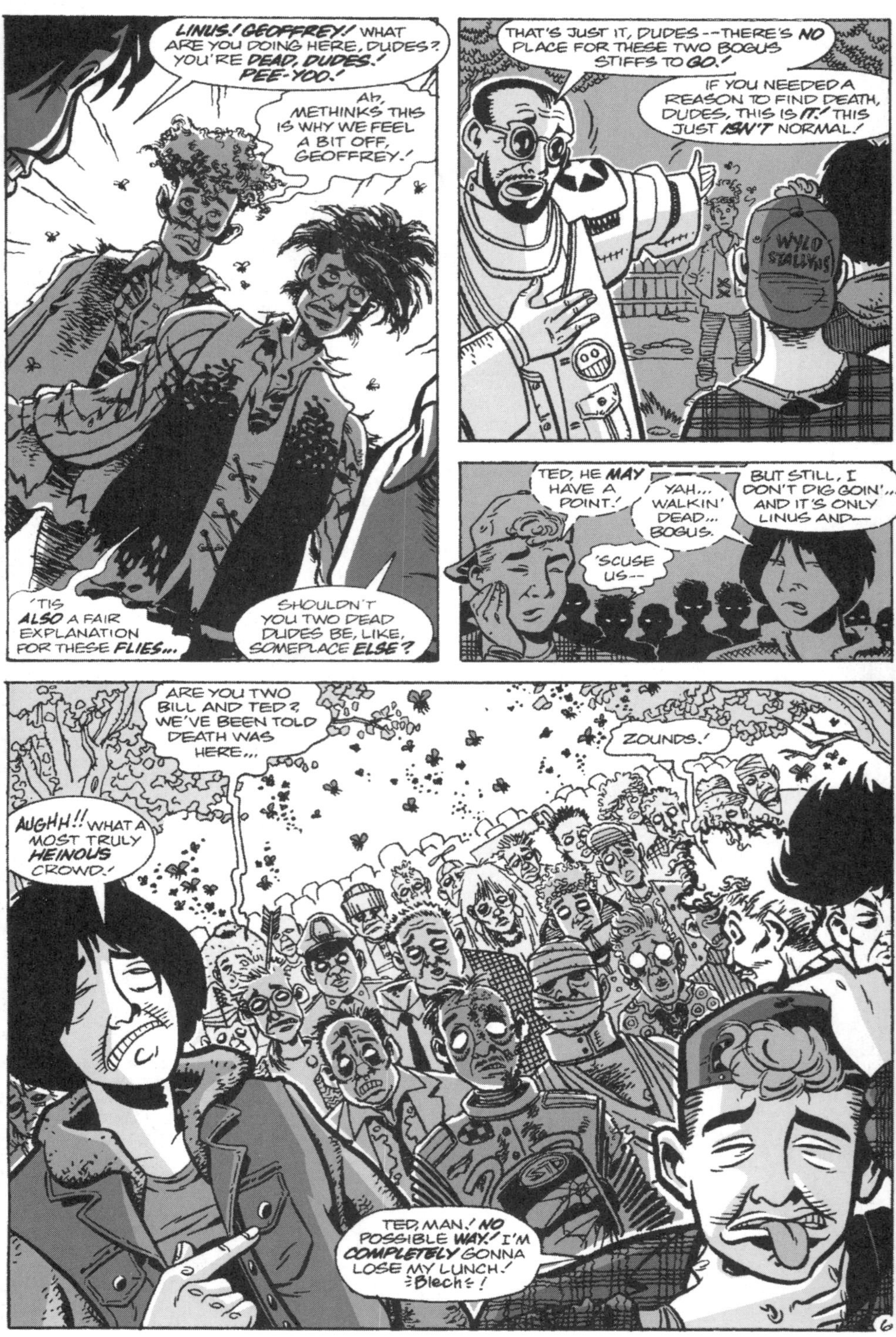
LINUS! GEOFFREY! WHAT ARE YOU DOING HERE, DUDES? YOU'RE DEAD, DUDES! PEE-YOO!
Ah, METHINKS THIS IS WHY WE FEEL A BIT OFF, GEOFFREY!
'TIS ALSO A FAIR EXPLANATION FOR THESE FLIES...
SHOULDN'T YOU TWO DEAD DUDES BE, LIKE, SOMEPLACE ELSE?
THAT'S JUST IT, DUDES--THERE'S NO PLACE FOR THESE TWO BOGUS STIFFS TO GO!
IF YOU NEEDED A REASON TO FIND DEATH, DUDES, THIS IS IT! THIS JUST ISN'T NORMAL!
WYLD STALLYNS
TED, HE MAY HAVE A POINT!
YAH... WALKIN' DEAD... BOGUS.
BUT STILL, I DON'T DIG GOIN'... AND IT'S ONLY LINUS AND—
'SCUSE US--
ARE YOU TWO BILL AND TED? WE'VE BEEN TOLD DEATH WAS HERE...
ZOUNDS!
AUGHH!! WHAT A MOST TRULY HEINOUS CROWD!
TED, MAN! NO POSSIBLE WAY! I'M COMPLETELY GONNA LOSE MY LUNCH! Blech!

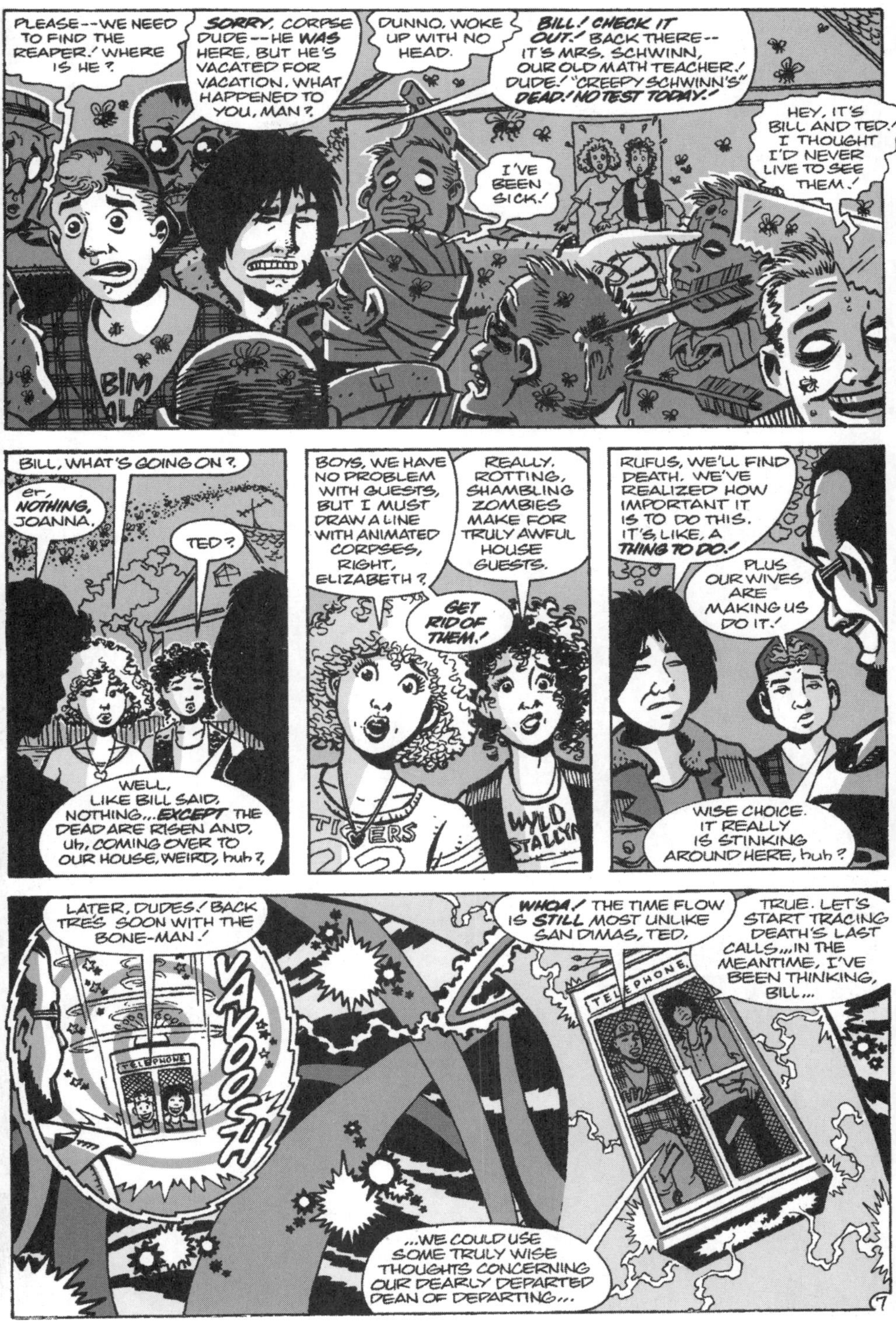
PLEASE--WE NEED TO FIND THE REAPER! WHERE IS HE?
SORRY, CORPSE DUDE--HE WAS HERE, BUT HE'S VACATED FOR VACATION. WHAT HAPPENED TO YOU, MAN?
DUNNO, WOKE UP WITH NO HEAD.
BILL! CHECK IT OUT! BACK THERE-- IT'S MRS. SCHWINN, OUR OLD MATH TEACHER! DUDE! "CREEPY SCHWINN'S" DEAD! NO TEST TODAY!
I'VE BEEN SICK!
HEY, IT'S BILL AND TED! I THOUGHT I'D NEVER LIVE TO SEE THEM!
BIM
BILL, WHAT'S GOING ON?
er, NOTHING, JOANNA.
TED?
WELL, LIKE BILL SAID, NOTHING... EXCEPT THE DEAD ARE RISEN AND, uh, COMING OVER TO OUR HOUSE. WEIRD, huh?
BOYS, WE HAVE NO PROBLEM WITH GUESTS, BUT I MUST DRAW A LINE WITH ANIMATED CORPSES, RIGHT, ELIZABETH?
REALLY. ROTTING, SHAMBLING ZOMBIES MAKE FOR TRULY AWFUL HOUSE GUESTS.
GET RID OF THEM!
TIGERS
WYLD STALLYNS
RUFUS, WE'LL FIND DEATH. WE'VE REALIZED HOW IMPORTANT IT IS TO DO THIS. IT'S LIKE, A THING TO DO!
PLUS OUR WIVES ARE MAKING US DO IT!
WISE CHOICE. IT REALLY IS STINKING AROUND HERE, huh?
LATER, DUDES! BACK TRES SOON WITH THE BONE-MAN!
VAVOOSH
TELEPHONE
WHOA! THE TIME FLOW IS STILL MOST UNLIKE SAN DIMAS, TED.
TRUE. LET'S START TRACING DEATH'S LAST CALLS... IN THE MEANTIME, I'VE BEEN THINKING, BILL...
TELEPHONE
...WE COULD USE SOME TRULY WISE THOUGHTS CONCERNING OUR DEARLY DEPARTED DEAN OF DEPARTING...

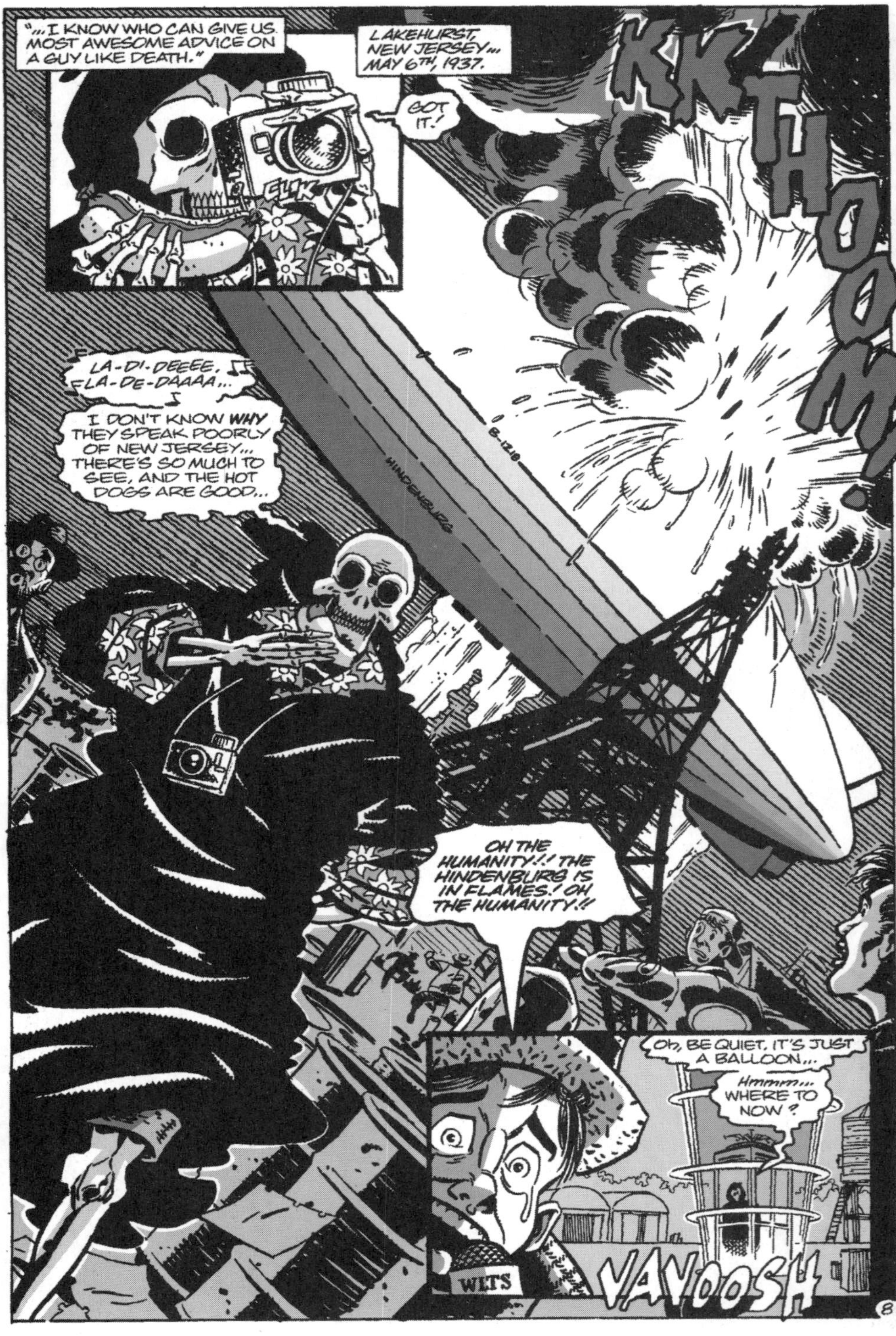
"...I KNOW WHO CAN GIVE US MOST AWESOME ADVICE ON A GUY LIKE DEATH."
LAKEHURST, NEW JERSEY... MAY 6TH, 1937.
GOT IT!
KKTHOOOM!!
LA-DI-DEEEE, FLA-DE-DAAAA...
I DON'T KNOW WHY THEY SPEAK POORLY OF NEW JERSEY... THERE'S SO MUCH TO SEE, AND THE HOT DOGS ARE GOOD...
HINDENBURG
OH THE HUMANITY!! THE HINDENBURG IS IN FLAMES! OH THE HUMANITY!!
OH, BE QUIET. IT'S JUST A BALLOON...
Hmmm... WHERE TO NOW?
WLTS
VAVOOSH

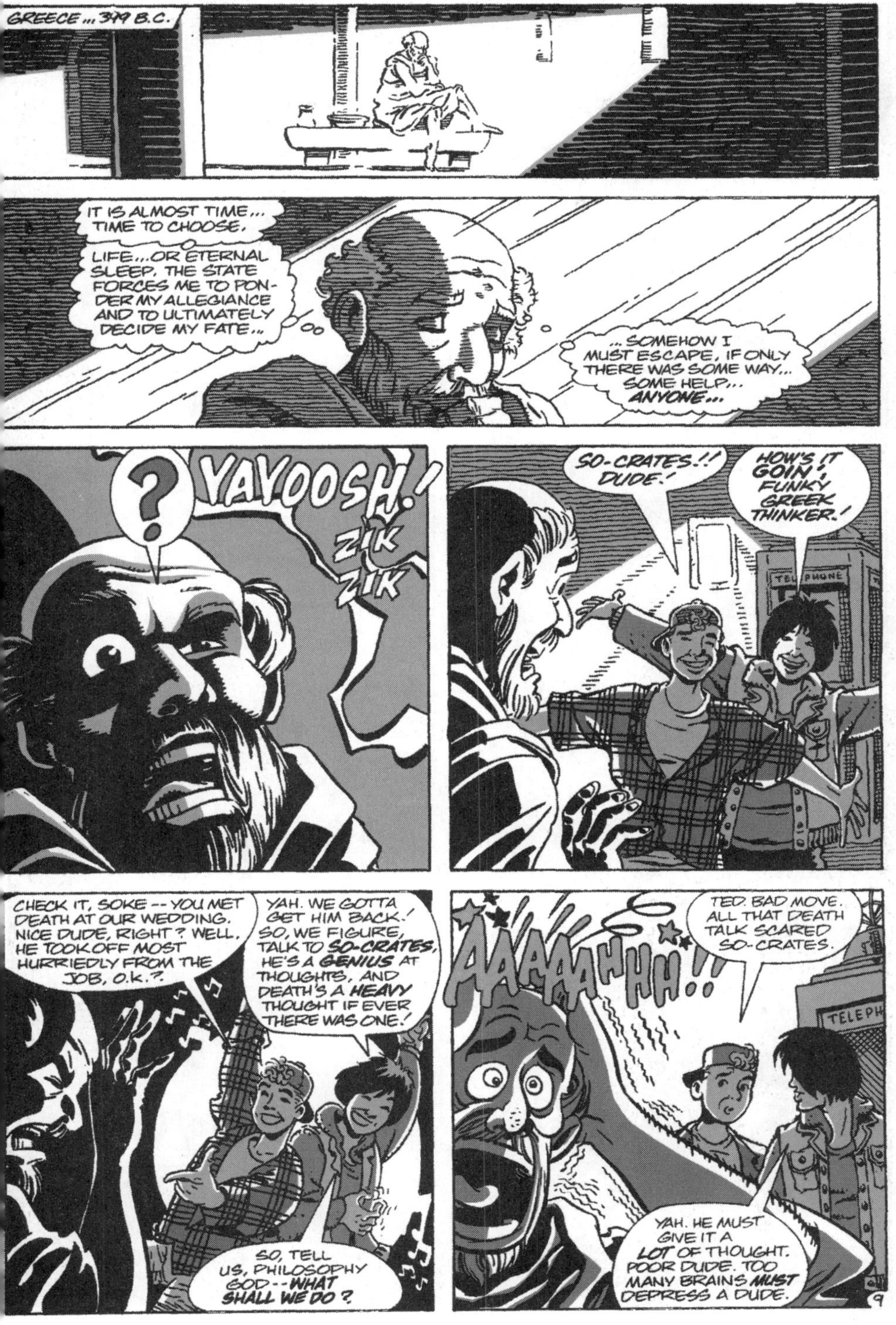
GREECE ... 399 B.C.
IT IS ALMOST TIME... TIME TO CHOOSE.
LIFE...OR ETERNAL SLEEP. THE STATE FORCES ME TO PONDER MY ALLEGIANCE AND TO ULTIMATELY DECIDE MY FATE...
...SOMEHOW I MUST ESCAPE. IF ONLY THERE WAS SOME WAY... SOME HELP... ANYONE...
?
YAVOOSH!
ZIK
ZIK
SO-CRATES!! DUDE!
HOW'S IT GOIN', FUNKY GREEK THINKER!
TELEPHONE
CHECK IT, SOKE -- YOU MET DEATH AT OUR WEDDING. NICE DUDE, RIGHT? WELL, HE TOOK OFF MOST HURRIEDLY FROM THE JOB, O.K.?
YAH. WE GOTTA GET HIM BACK! SO, WE FIGURE, TALK TO SO-CRATES, HE'S A GENIUS AT THOUGHTS, AND DEATH'S A HEAVY THOUGHT IF EVER THERE WAS ONE!
SO, TELL US, PHILOSOPHY GOD -- WHAT SHALL WE DO?
AAAAAHHH!!
TED. BAD MOVE. ALL THAT DEATH TALK SCARED SO-CRATES.
TELEPH
YAH. HE MUST GIVE IT A LOT OF THOUGHT. POOR DUDE. TOO MANY BRAINS MUST DEPRESS A DUDE.

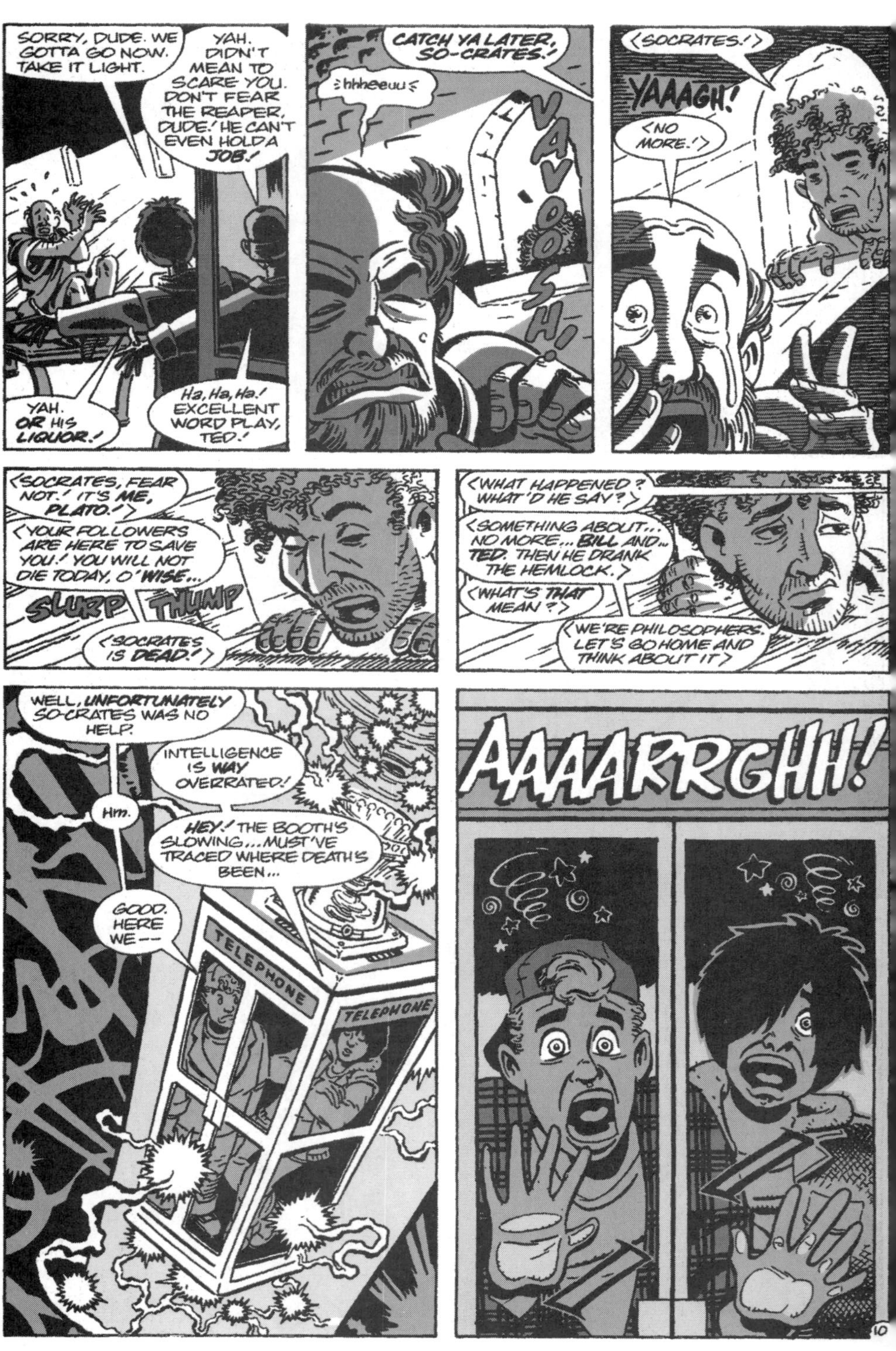
SORRY, DUDE. WE GOTTA GO NOW. TAKE IT LIGHT.
YAH. DIDN'T MEAN TO SCARE YOU. DON'T FEAR THE REAPER, DUDE! HE CAN'T EVEN HOLD A JOB!
YAH. OR HIS LIQUOR!
Ha, Ha, Ha! EXCELLENT WORD PLAY, TED!
CATCH YA LATER, SO-CRATES!
hhheeuu
VAVOOSH!
<SOCRATES!>
YAAAGH!
<NO MORE!>
<SOCRATES, FEAR NOT! IT'S ME, PLATO!>
<YOUR FOLLOWERS ARE HERE TO SAVE YOU! YOU WILL NOT DIE TODAY, O' WISE...
SLURP
THUMP
<SOCRATES IS DEAD!>
<WHAT HAPPENED? WHAT'D HE SAY?>
<SOMETHING ABOUT... NO MORE... BILL AND... TED. THEN HE DRANK THE HEMLOCK.>
<WHAT'S THAT MEAN?>
<WE'RE PHILOSOPHERS. LET'S GO HOME AND THINK ABOUT IT>
WELL, UNFORTUNATELY SO-CRATES WAS NO HELP.
INTELLIGENCE IS WAY OVERRATED!
Hm.
HEY! THE BOOTH'S SLOWING... MUST'VE TRACED WHERE DEATH'S BEEN...
GOOD. HERE WE---
TELEPHONE
TELEPHONE
AAAAARRGHH!

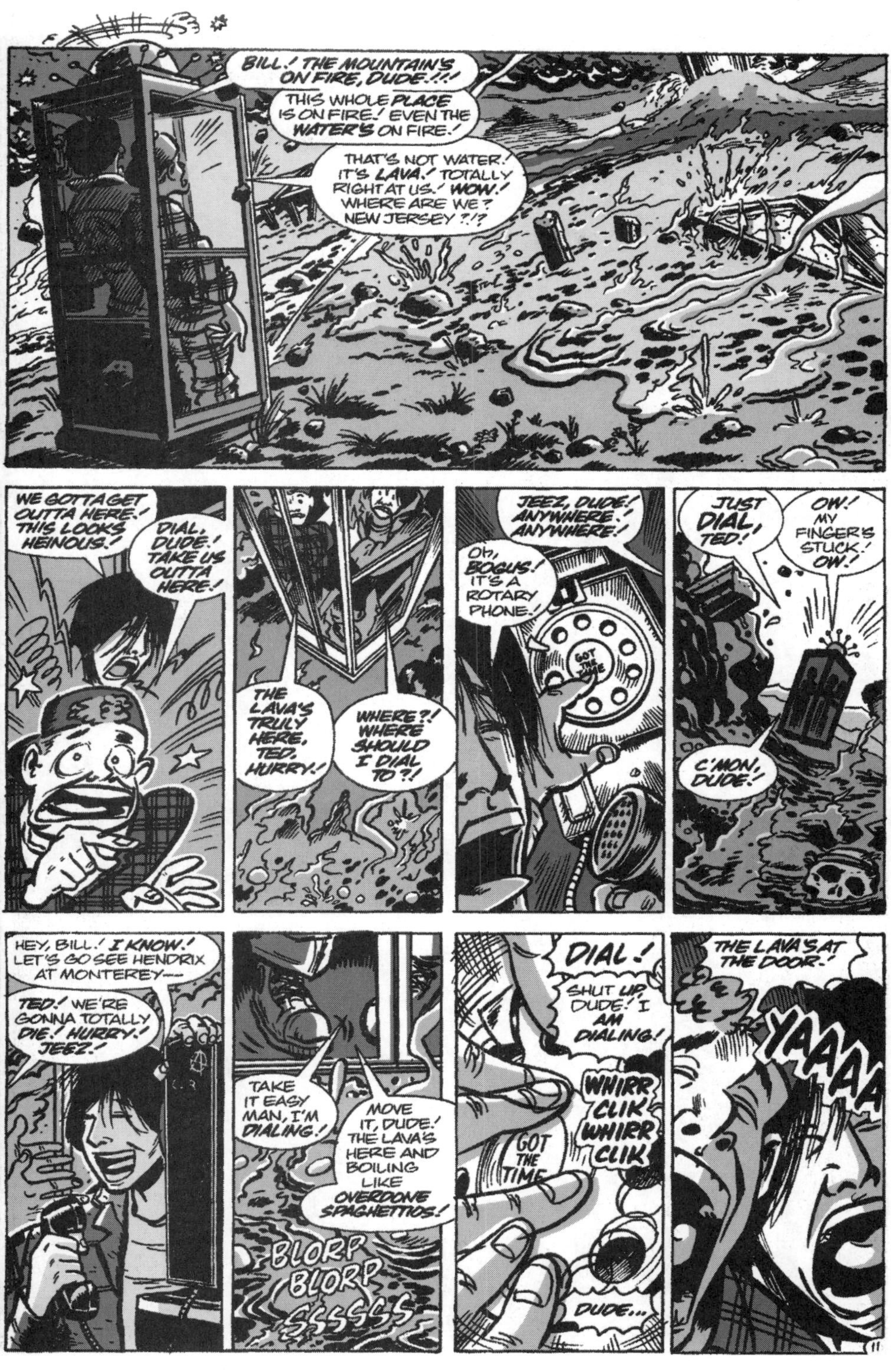
BILL! THE MOUNTAIN'S ON FIRE, DUDE!!!
THIS WHOLE PLACE IS ON FIRE! EVEN THE WATER'S ON FIRE!
THAT'S NOT WATER! IT'S LAVA! TOTALLY RIGHT AT US! WOW! WHERE ARE WE? NEW JERSEY?!?
WE GOTTA GET OUTTA HERE! THIS LOOKS HEINOUS!
DIAL, DUDE! TAKE US OUTTA HERE!
THE LAVA'S TRULY HERE, TED. HURRY!
WHERE?! WHERE SHOULD I DIAL TO?!
JEEZ, DUDE! ANYWHERE! ANYWHERE!
OH, BOGUS! IT'S A ROTARY PHONE!
GOT THE TIME
JUST DIAL, TED!
OW! MY FINGER'S STUCK! OW!
C'MON, DUDE!
HEY, BILL! I KNOW! LET'S GO SEE HENDRIX AT MONTEREY---
TED! WE'RE GONNA TOTALLY DIE! HURRY! JEEZ!
TAKE IT EASY MAN, I'M DIALING!
MOVE IT, DUDE! THE LAVA'S HERE AND BOILING LIKE OVERDONE SPAGHETTIOS!
BLORP
BLORP
SSSSSS
DIAL!
SHUT UP, DUDE! I AM DIALING!
WHIRR
CLIK
WHIRR
CLIK
GOT THE TIME
DUDE...
THE LAVA'S AT THE DOOR!
YAAAAA

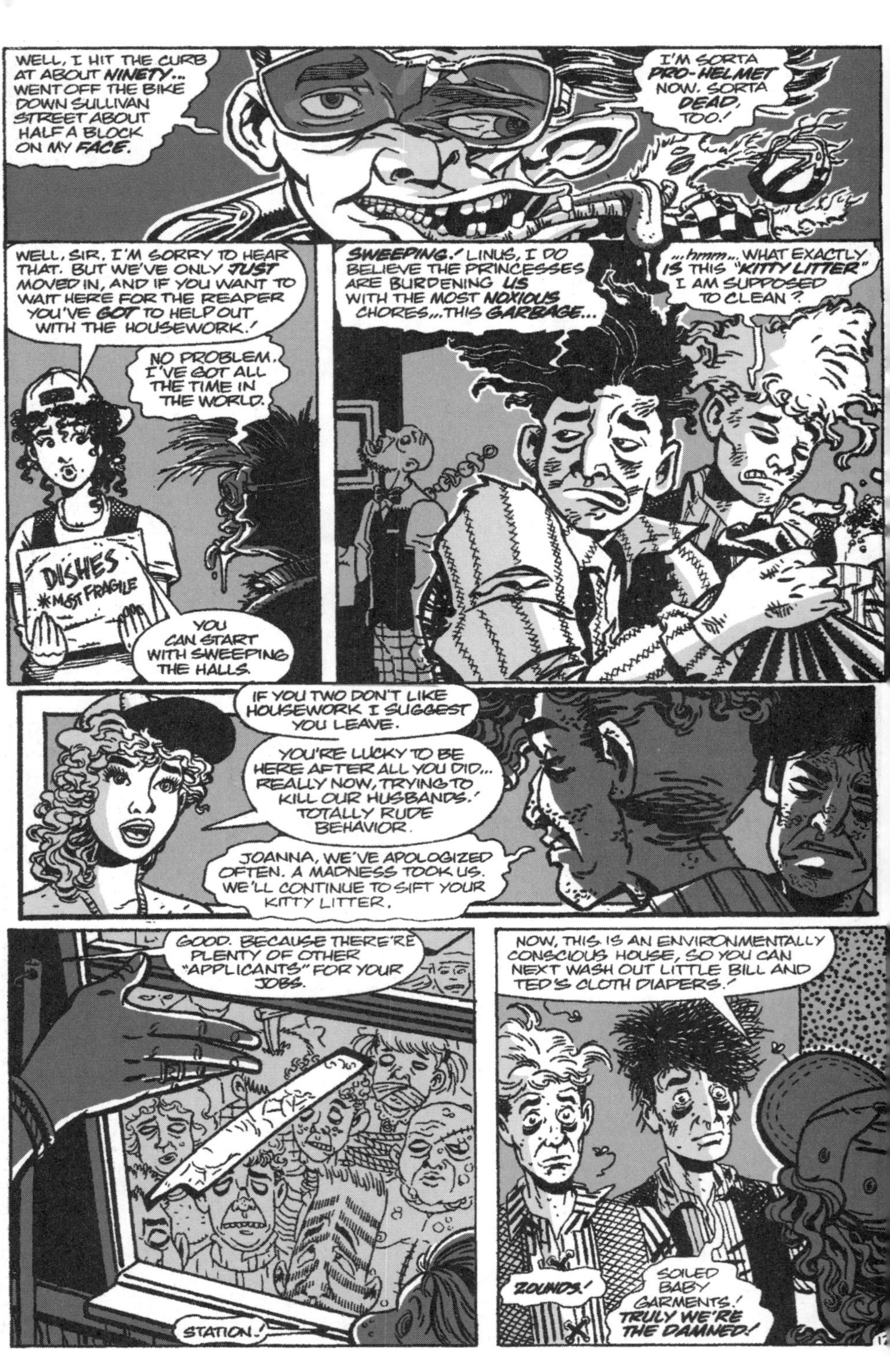
WELL, I HIT THE CURB AT ABOUT NINETY... WENT OFF THE BIKE DOWN SULLIVAN STREET ABOUT HALF A BLOCK ON MY FACE.
I'M SORTA PRO-HELMET NOW. SORTA DEAD, TOO!
WELL, SIR, I'M SORRY TO HEAR THAT. BUT WE'VE ONLY JUST MOVED IN, AND IF YOU WANT TO WAIT HERE FOR THE REAPER YOU'VE GOT TO HELP OUT WITH THE HOUSEWORK!
NO PROBLEM. I'VE GOT ALL THE TIME IN THE WORLD.
DISHES
*MOST FRAGILE
YOU CAN START WITH SWEEPING THE HALLS.
SWEEPING! LINUS, I DO BELIEVE THE PRINCESSES ARE BURDENING US WITH THE MOST NOXIOUS CHORES... THIS GARBAGE...
...hmm... WHAT EXACTLY IS THIS "KITTY LITTER" I AM SUPPOSED TO CLEAN?
IF YOU TWO DON'T LIKE HOUSEWORK I SUGGEST YOU LEAVE.
YOU'RE LUCKY TO BE HERE AFTER ALL YOU DID... REALLY NOW, TRYING TO KILL OUR HUSBANDS! TOTALLY RUDE BEHAVIOR.
JOANNA, WE'VE APOLOGIZED OFTEN. A MADNESS TOOK US. WE'LL CONTINUE TO SIFT YOUR KITTY LITTER.
GOOD. BECAUSE THERE'RE PLENTY OF OTHER "APPLICANTS" FOR YOUR JOBS.
STATION!
NOW, THIS IS AN ENVIRONMENTALLY CONSCIOUS HOUSE, SO YOU CAN NEXT WASH OUT LITTLE BILL AND TED'S CLOTH DIAPERS!
ZOUNDS!
SOILED BABY GARMENTS! TRULY WE'RE THE DAMNED!

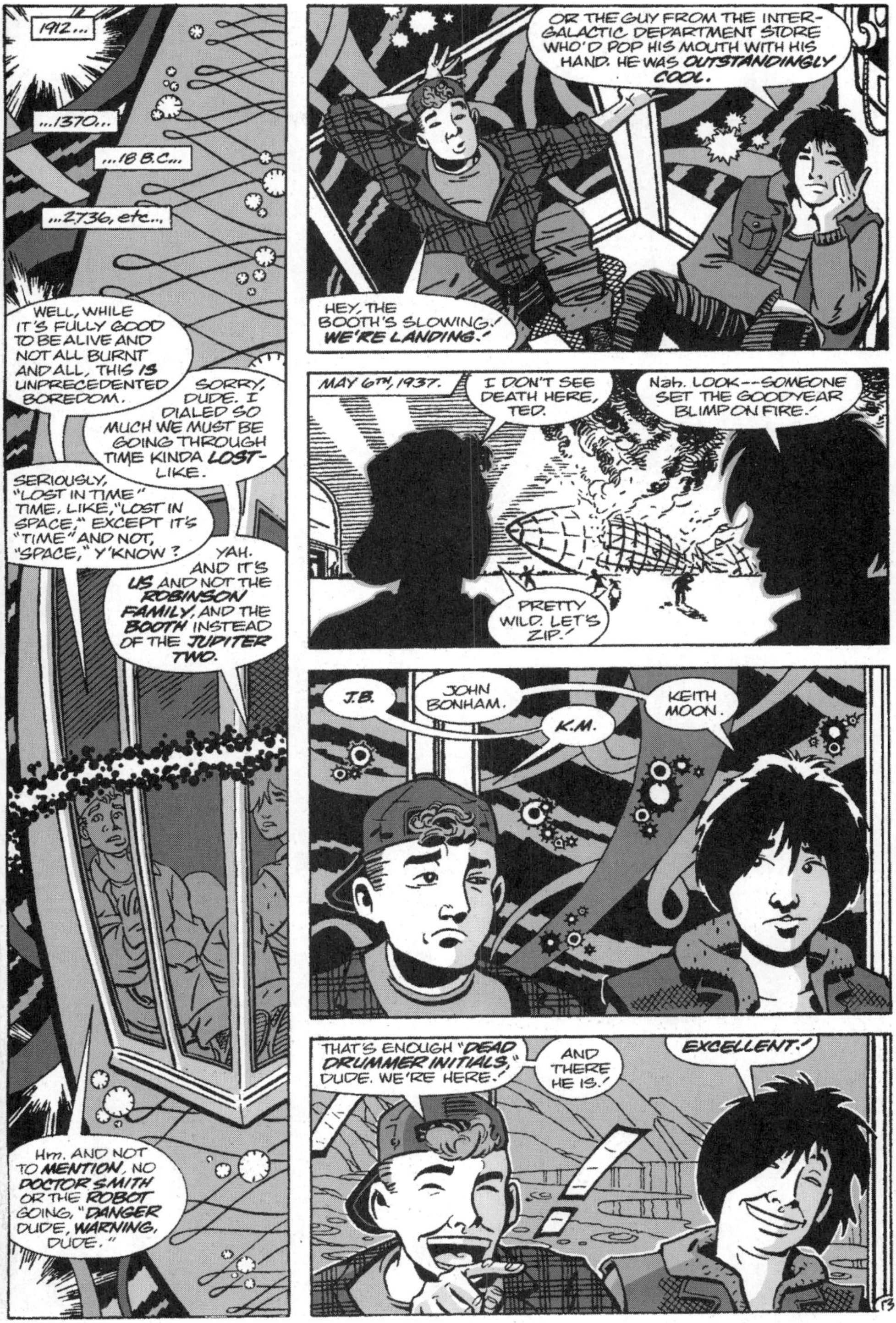
1912...
...1370...
...18 B.C...
...2736, etc...
WELL, WHILE IT'S FULLY GOOD TO BE ALIVE AND NOT ALL BURNT AND ALL, THIS IS UNPRECEDENTED BOREDOM.
SORRY, DUDE. I DIALED SO MUCH WE MUST BE GOING THROUGH TIME KINDA LOST-LIKE.
SERIOUSLY, "LOST IN TIME" TIME, LIKE, "LOST IN SPACE," EXCEPT IT'S "TIME" AND NOT, "SPACE," Y'KNOW?
YAH. AND IT'S US AND NOT THE ROBINSON FAMILY, AND THE BOOTH INSTEAD OF THE JUPITER TWO.
Hm. AND NOT TO MENTION, NO DOCTOR SMITH OR THE ROBOT GOING, "DANGER DUDE, WARNING, DUDE."
OR THE GUY FROM THE INTER-GALACTIC DEPARTMENT STORE WHO'D POP HIS MOUTH WITH HIS HAND. HE WAS OUTSTANDINGLY COOL.
HEY, THE BOOTH'S SLOWING! WE'RE LANDING!
MAY 6TH, 1937.
I DON'T SEE DEATH HERE, TED.
Nah. LOOK--SOMEONE SET THE GOODYEAR BLIMP ON FIRE!
PRETTY WILD. LET'S ZIP!
J.B.
JOHN BONHAM.
K.M.
KEITH MOON.
THAT'S ENOUGH "DEAD DRUMMER INITIALS," DUDE. WE'RE HERE!
AND THERE HE IS!
EXCELLENT!
13

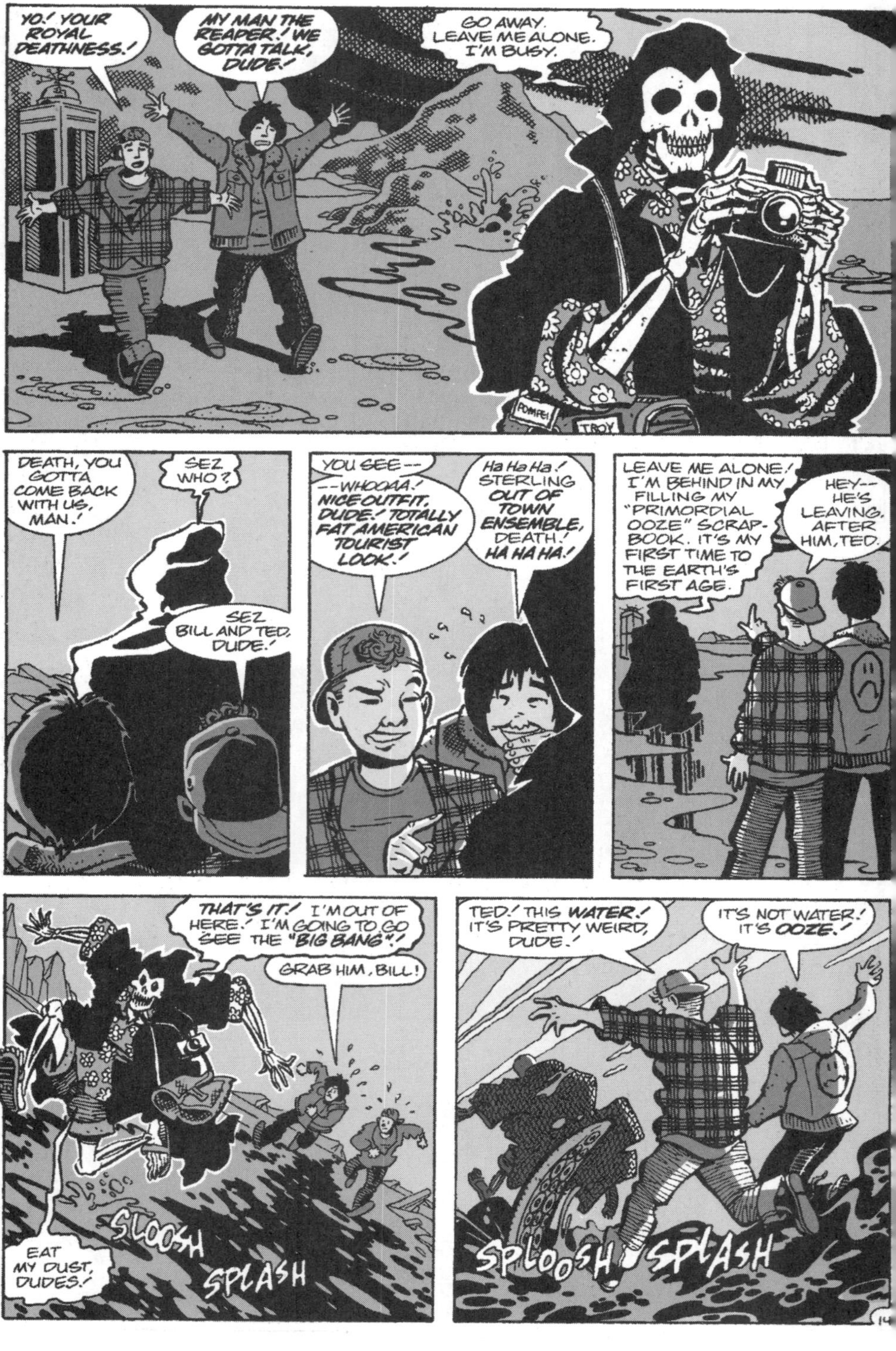

YO! YOUR ROYAL DEATHNESS!
MY MAN THE REAPER! WE GOTTA TALK, DUDE!
GO AWAY. LEAVE ME ALONE. I'M BUSY.
POMPEII
TROY
DEATH, YOU GOTTA COME BACK WITH US, MAN!
SEZ WHO?
SEZ BILL AND TED, DUDE!
YOU SEE--
--WHOOAA! NICE OUTFIT, DUDE! TOTALLY FAT AMERICAN TOURIST LOOK!
Ha Ha Ha! STERLING OUT OF TOWN ENSEMBLE, DEATH! HA HA HA!
LEAVE ME ALONE! I'M BEHIND IN MY FILLING MY "PRIMORDIAL OOZE" SCRAP-BOOK. IT'S MY FIRST TIME TO THE EARTH'S FIRST AGE.
HEY-- HE'S LEAVING. AFTER HIM, TED.
THAT'S IT! I'M OUT OF HERE! I'M GOING TO GO SEE THE "BIG BANG"!
GRAB HIM, BILL!
SLOOSH
SPLASH
EAT MY DUST, DUDES!
TED! THIS WATER! IT'S PRETTY WEIRD, DUDE!
IT'S NOT WATER! IT'S OOZE!
SPLOOSH
SPLASH

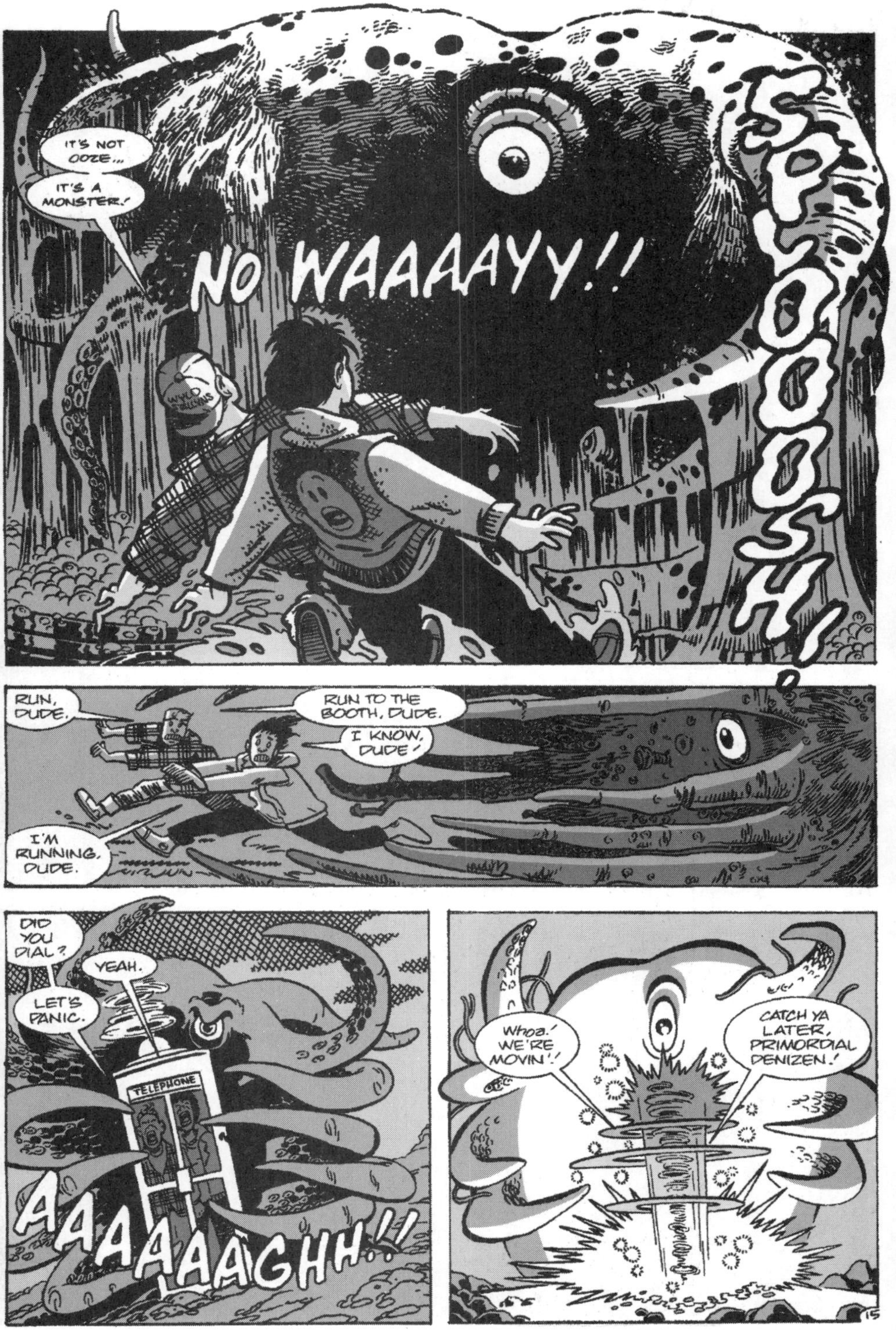

IT'S NOT OOZE...
IT'S A MONSTER!
NO WAAAAYY!!
SPLOOOOSH!
RUN, DUDE.
RUN TO THE BOOTH, DUDE.
I KNOW, DUDE!
I'M RUNNING, DUDE.
DID YOU DIAL?
YEAH.
LET'S PANIC.
TELEPHONE
AAAAAAAGHH!!
Whoa! WE'RE MOVIN'!
CATCH YA LATER, PRIMORDIAL DENIZEN!

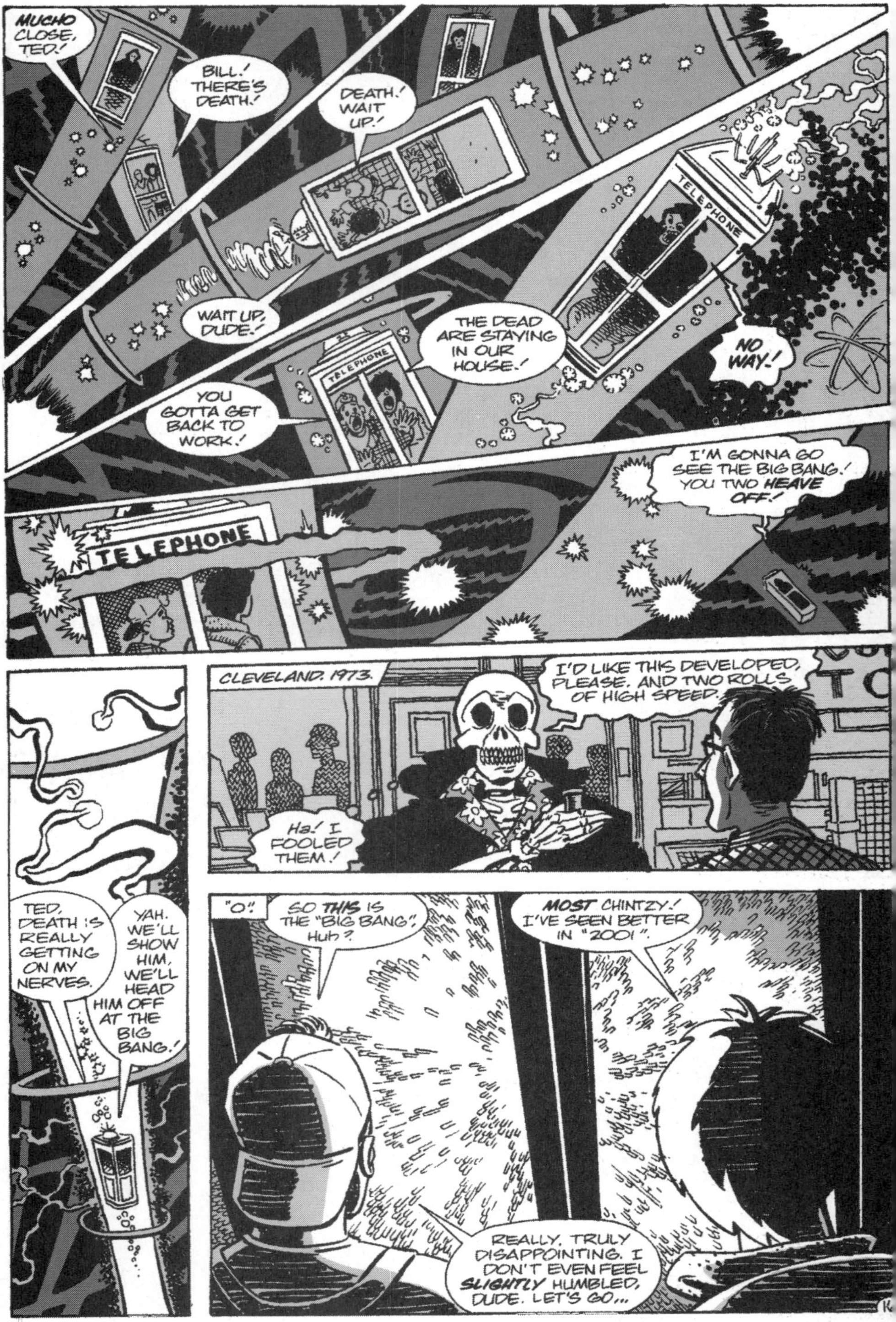
MUCHO CLOSE, TED!
BILL! THERE'S DEATH!
DEATH! WAIT UP!
WAIT UP, DUDE!
THE DEAD ARE STAYING IN OUR HOUSE!
YOU GOTTA GET BACK TO WORK!
NO WAY!
TELEPHONE
I'M GONNA GO SEE THE BIG BANG! YOU TWO HEAVE OFF!
TELEPHONE
CLEVELAND. 1973.
I'D LIKE THIS DEVELOPED, PLEASE. AND TWO ROLLS OF HIGH SPEED.
Ha! I FOOLED THEM!
TED, DEATH IS REALLY GETTING ON MY NERVES.
YAH. WE'LL SHOW HIM, WE'LL HEAD HIM OFF AT THE BIG BANG!
"0"
SO THIS IS THE "BIG BANG", Huh?
MOST CHINTZY! I'VE SEEN BETTER IN "2001".
REALLY, TRULY DISAPPOINTING. I DON'T EVEN FEEL SLIGHTLY HUMBLED, DUDE. LET'S GO...

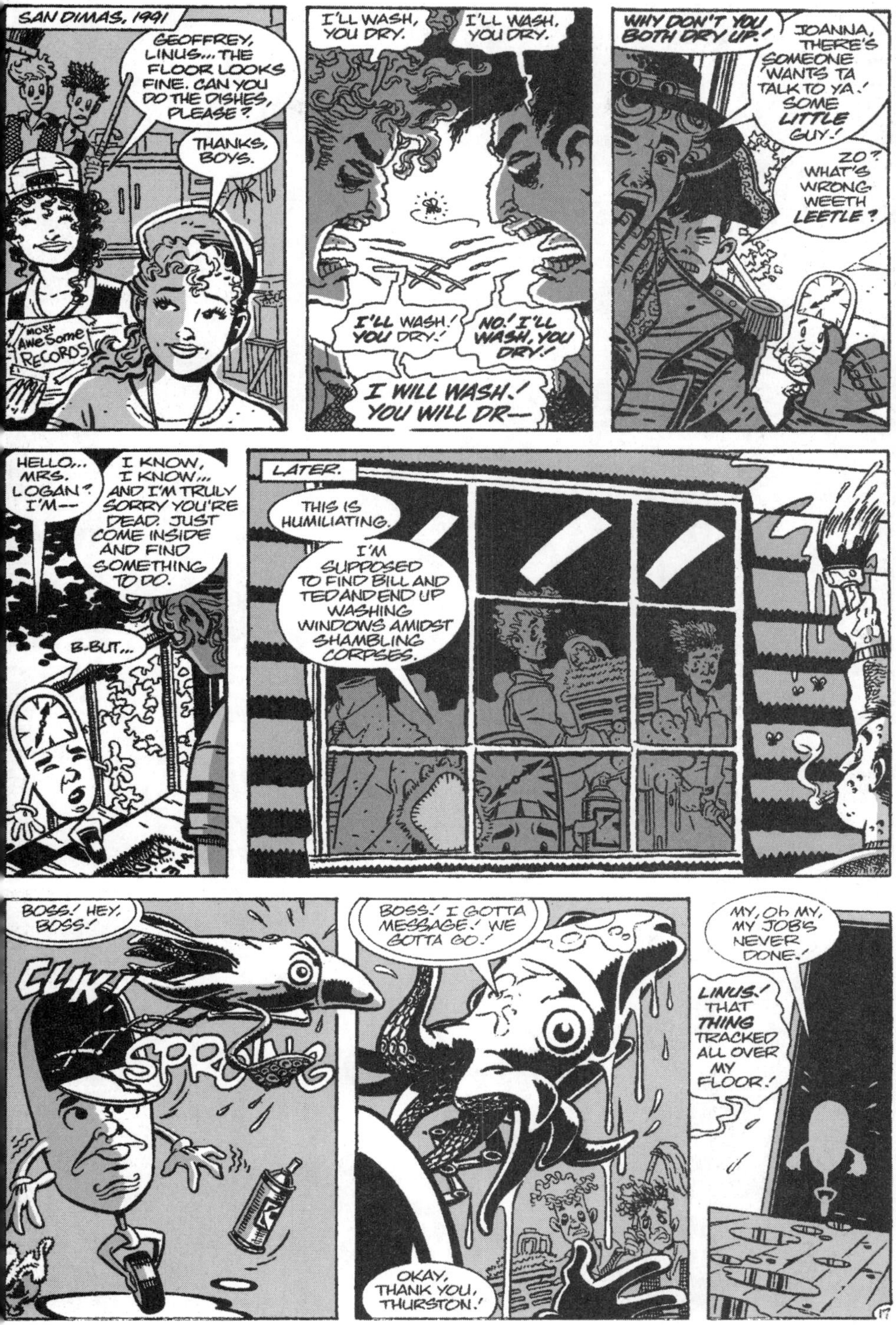
SAN DIMAS, 1991
GEOFFREY, LINUS... THE FLOOR LOOKS FINE. CAN YOU DO THE DISHES, PLEASE?
THANKS, BOYS.
most Awe Some RECORDS
I'LL WASH, YOU DRY.
I'LL WASH, YOU DRY.
I'LL WASH! YOU DRY!
NO! I'LL WASH, YOU DRY!
I WILL WASH! YOU WILL DR—
WHY DON'T YOU BOTH DRY UP!
JOANNA, THERE'S SOMEONE WANTS TA TALK TO YA! SOME LITTLE GUY!
ZO? WHAT'S WRONG WEETH LEETLE?
HELLO... MRS. LOGAN? I'M—
I KNOW, I KNOW... AND I'M TRULY SORRY YOU'RE DEAD. JUST COME INSIDE AND FIND SOMETHING TO DO.
B-BUT...
LATER.
THIS IS HUMILIATING.
I'M SUPPOSED TO FIND BILL AND TED AND END UP WASHING WINDOWS AMIDST SHAMBLING CORPSES.
BOSS! HEY, BOSS!
CLIK!
SPROING
BOSS! I GOTTA MESSAGE! WE GOTTA GO!
OKAY, THANK YOU, THURSTON!
MY, OH MY, MY JOB'S NEVER DONE!
LINUS! THAT THING TRACKED ALL OVER MY FLOOR!

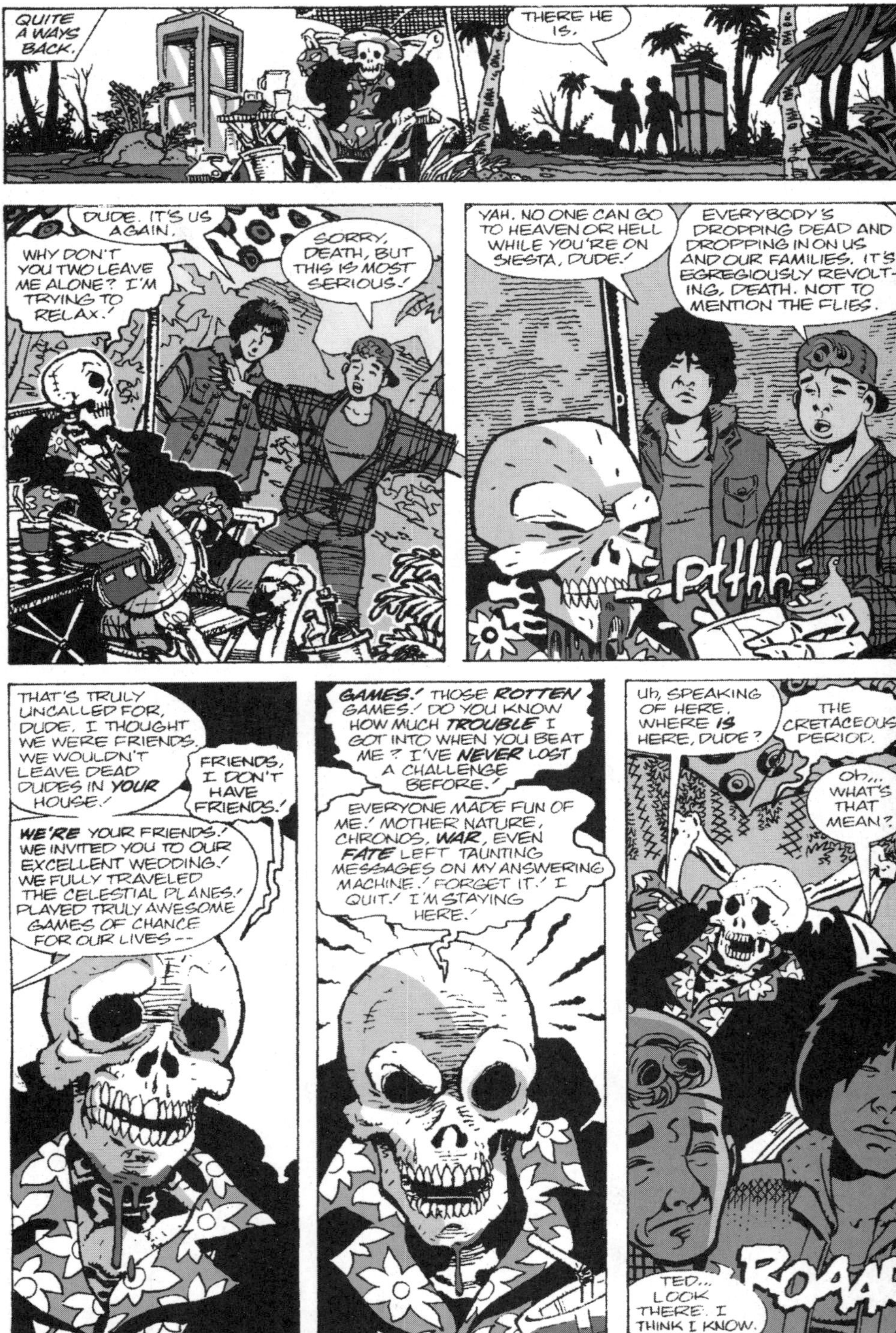
QUITE A WAYS BACK.
THERE HE IS.
DUDE. IT'S US AGAIN.
WHY DON'T YOU TWO LEAVE ME ALONE? I'M TRYING TO RELAX.!
SORRY, DEATH, BUT THIS IS MOST SERIOUS.!
YAH. NO ONE CAN GO TO HEAVEN OR HELL WHILE YOU'RE ON SIESTA, DUDE.!
EVERYBODY'S DROPPING DEAD AND DROPPING IN ON US AND OUR FAMILIES. IT'S EGREGIOUSLY REVOLTING, DEATH. NOT TO MENTION THE FLIES.
PTHH
THAT'S TRULY UNCALLED FOR, DUDE. I THOUGHT WE WERE FRIENDS. WE WOULDN'T LEAVE DEAD DUDES IN YOUR HOUSE.!
FRIENDS, I DON'T HAVE FRIENDS.!
WE'RE YOUR FRIENDS.! WE INVITED YOU TO OUR EXCELLENT WEDDING.! WE FULLY TRAVELED THE CELESTIAL PLANES.! PLAYED TRULY AWESOME GAMES OF CHANCE FOR OUR LIVES--
GAMES.! THOSE ROTTEN GAMES.! DO YOU KNOW HOW MUCH TROUBLE I GOT INTO WHEN YOU BEAT ME? I'VE NEVER LOST A CHALLENGE BEFORE.!
EVERYONE MADE FUN OF ME.! MOTHER NATURE, CHRONOS, WAR, EVEN FATE LEFT TAUNTING MESSAGES ON MY ANSWERING MACHINE.! FORGET IT.! I QUIT.! I'M STAYING HERE.!
Uh, SPEAKING OF HERE, WHERE IS HERE, DUDE?
THE CRETACEOUS PERIOD.
Oh... WHAT'S THAT MEAN?
ROAAR
TED... LOOK THERE. I THINK I KNOW.

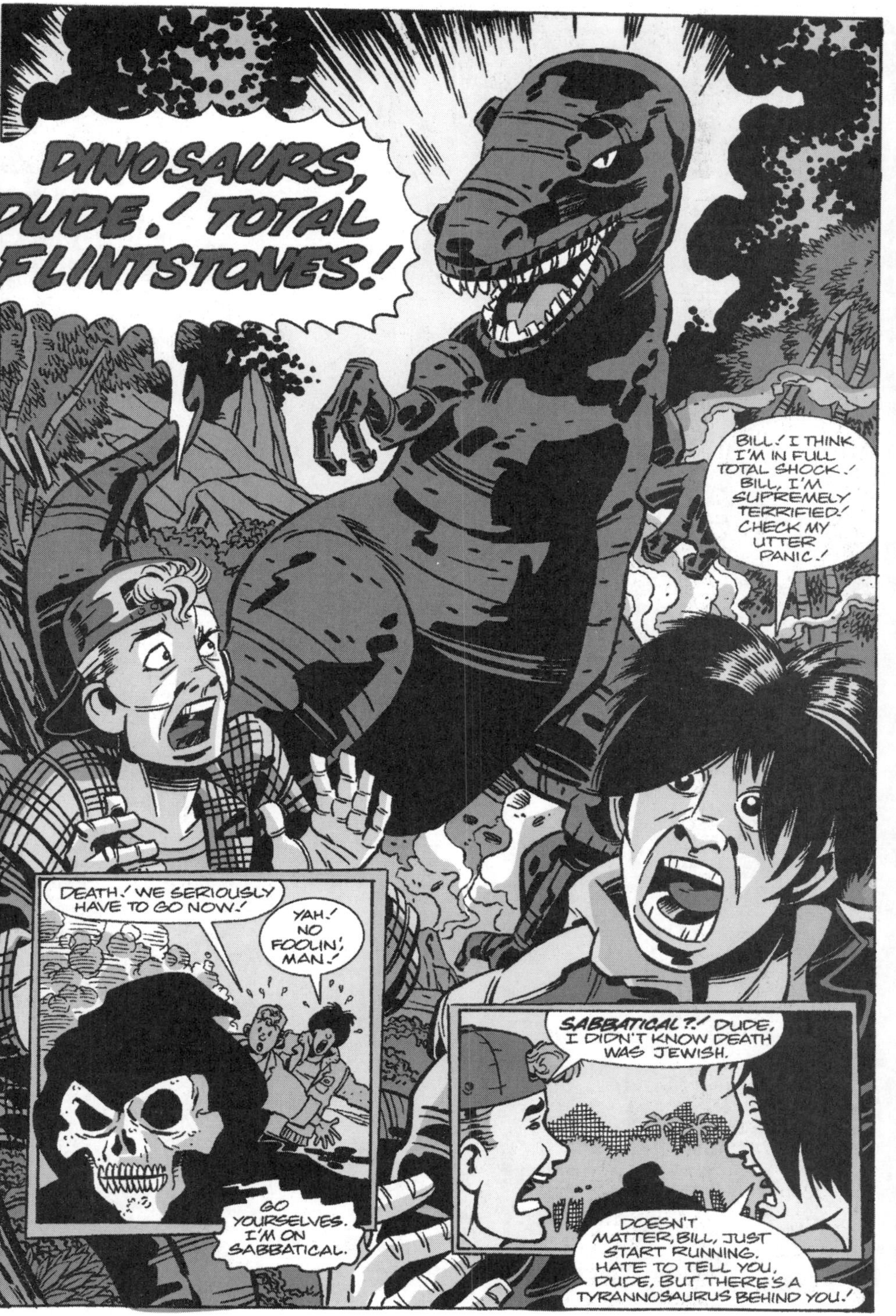
DINOSAURS, DUDE! TOTAL FLINTSTONES!
BILL! I THINK I'M IN FULL TOTAL SHOCK! BILL, I'M SUPREMELY TERRIFIED! CHECK MY UTTER PANIC!
DEATH! WE SERIOUSLY HAVE TO GO NOW!
YAH! NO FOOLIN', MAN!
GO YOURSELVES. I'M ON SABBATICAL.
SABBATICAL?! DUDE, I DIDN'T KNOW DEATH WAS JEWISH.
DOESN'T MATTER, BILL, JUST START RUNNING. HATE TO TELL YOU, DUDE, BUT THERE'S A TYRANNOSAURUS BEHIND YOU!

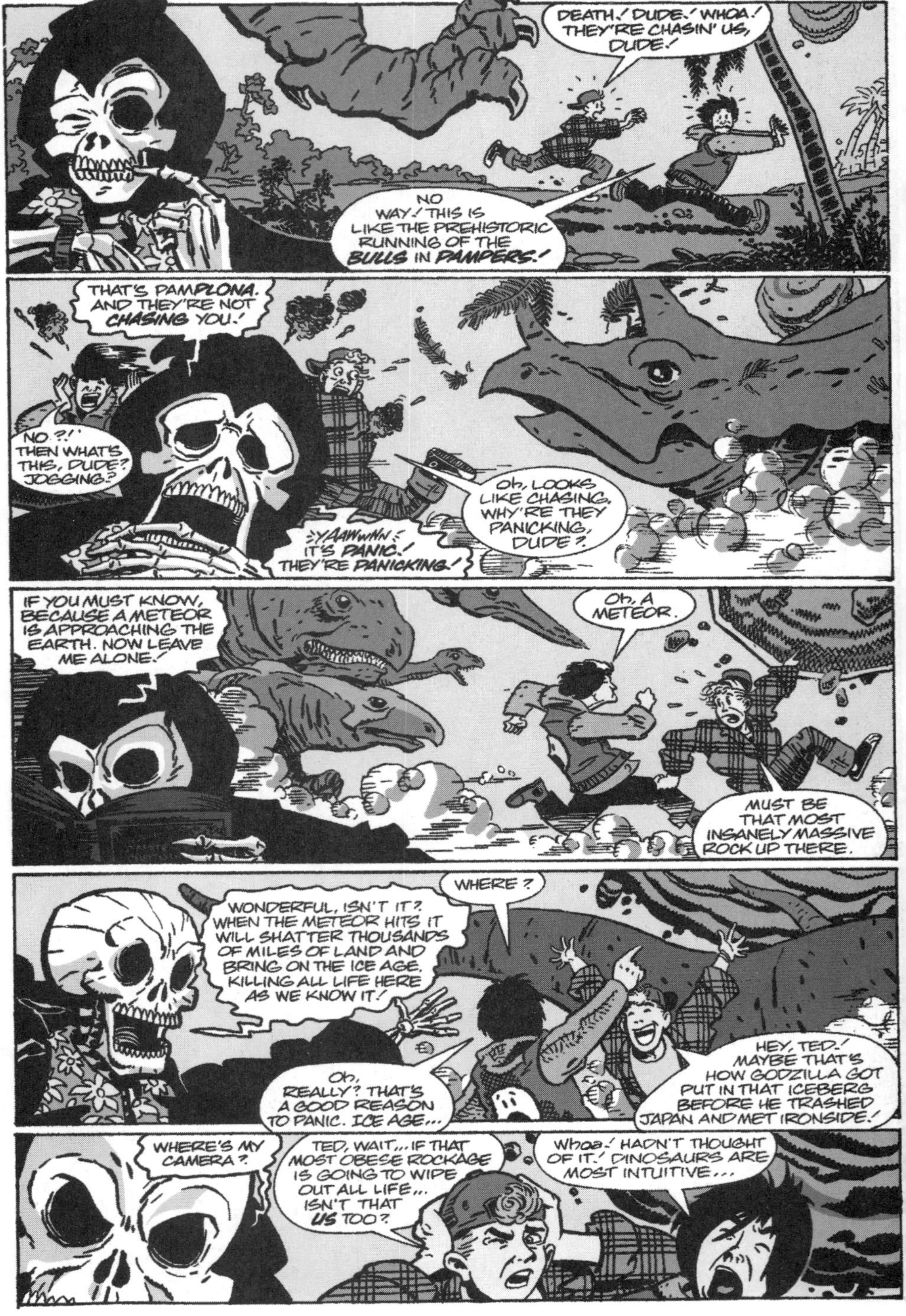
DEATH! DUDE! WHOA! THEY'RE CHASIN' US, DUDE!
NO WAY! THIS IS LIKE THE PREHISTORIC RUNNING OF THE BULLS IN PAMPERS!
THAT'S PAMPLONA. AND THEY'RE NOT CHASING YOU!
NO ?! THEN WHAT'S THIS, DUDE? JOGGING?
Oh, LOOKS LIKE CHASING. WHY'RE THEY PANICKING, DUDE?
YAAWWNN IT'S PANIC! THEY'RE PANICKING!
IF YOU MUST KNOW, BECAUSE A METEOR IS APPROACHING THE EARTH. NOW LEAVE ME ALONE!
Oh, A METEOR.
MUST BE THAT MOST INSANELY MASSIVE ROCK UP THERE.
WHERE?
WONDERFUL, ISN'T IT? WHEN THE METEOR HITS IT WILL SHATTER THOUSANDS OF MILES OF LAND AND BRING ON THE ICE AGE, KILLING ALL LIFE HERE AS WE KNOW IT!
Oh, REALLY? THAT'S A GOOD REASON TO PANIC. ICE AGE...
HEY, TED! MAYBE THAT'S HOW GODZILLA GOT PUT IN THAT ICEBERG BEFORE HE TRASHED JAPAN AND MET IRONSIDE!
WHERE'S MY CAMERA?
TED, WAIT... IF THAT MOST OBESE ROCKAGE IS GOING TO WIPE OUT ALL LIFE... ISN'T THAT US TOO?
Whoa! HADN'T THOUGHT OF IT! DINOSAURS ARE MOST INTUITIVE...

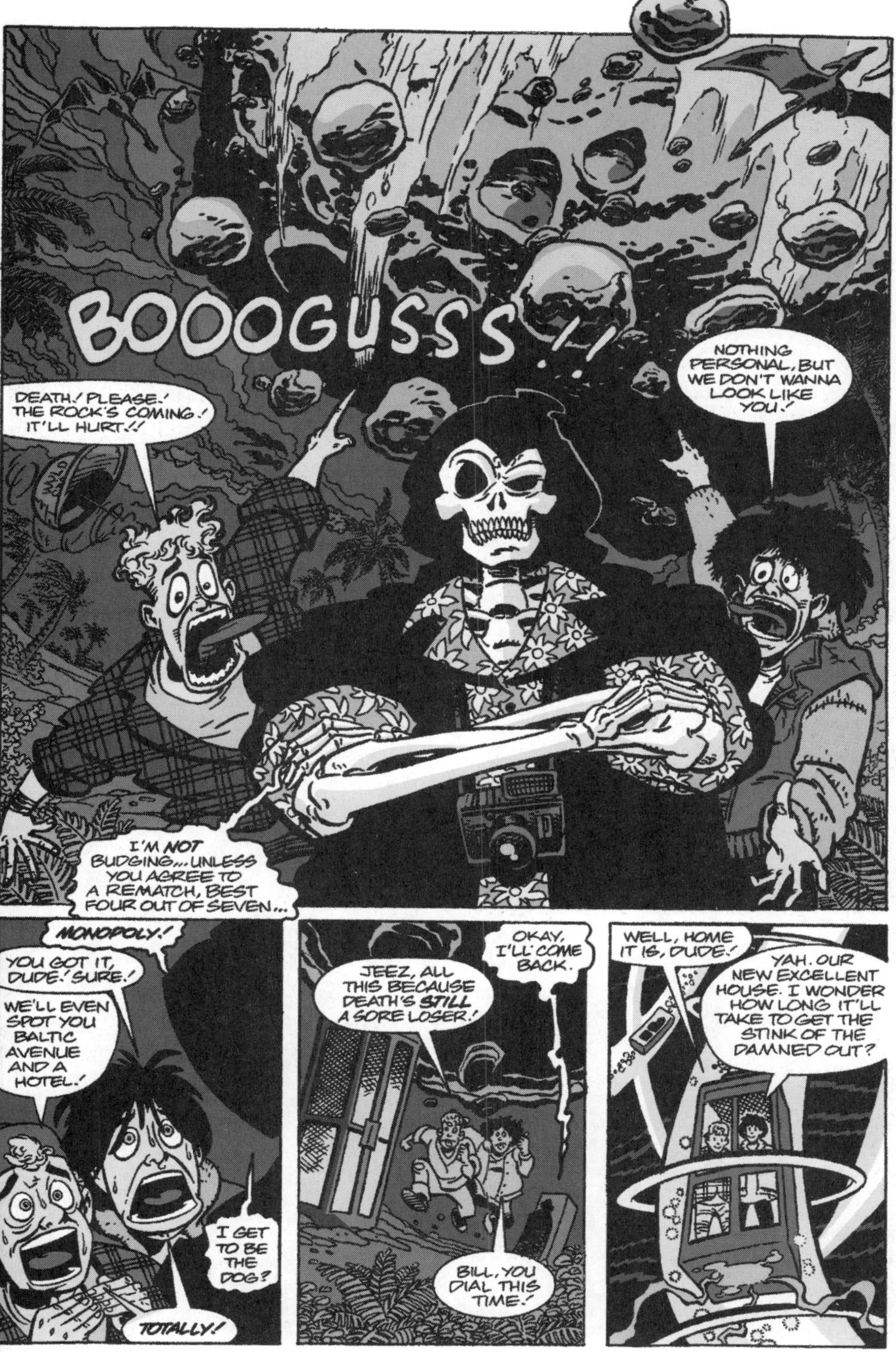
BOOOGUSSS!!
DEATH! PLEASE! THE ROCK'S COMING! IT'LL HURT!!
NOTHING PERSONAL, BUT WE DON'T WANNA LOOK LIKE YOU!
I'M NOT BUDGING... UNLESS YOU AGREE TO A REMATCH, BEST FOUR OUT OF SEVEN...
MONOPOLY!
YOU GOT IT, DUDE! SURE!
WE'LL EVEN SPOT YOU BALTIC AVENUE AND A HOTEL!
I GET TO BE THE DOG?
TOTALLY!
JEEZ, ALL THIS BECAUSE DEATH'S STILL A SORE LOSER!
OKAY, I'LL COME BACK.
BILL, YOU DIAL THIS TIME!
WELL, HOME IT IS, DUDE!
YAH. OUR NEW EXCELLENT HOUSE. I WONDER HOW LONG IT'LL TAKE TO GET THE STINK OF THE DAMNED OUT?

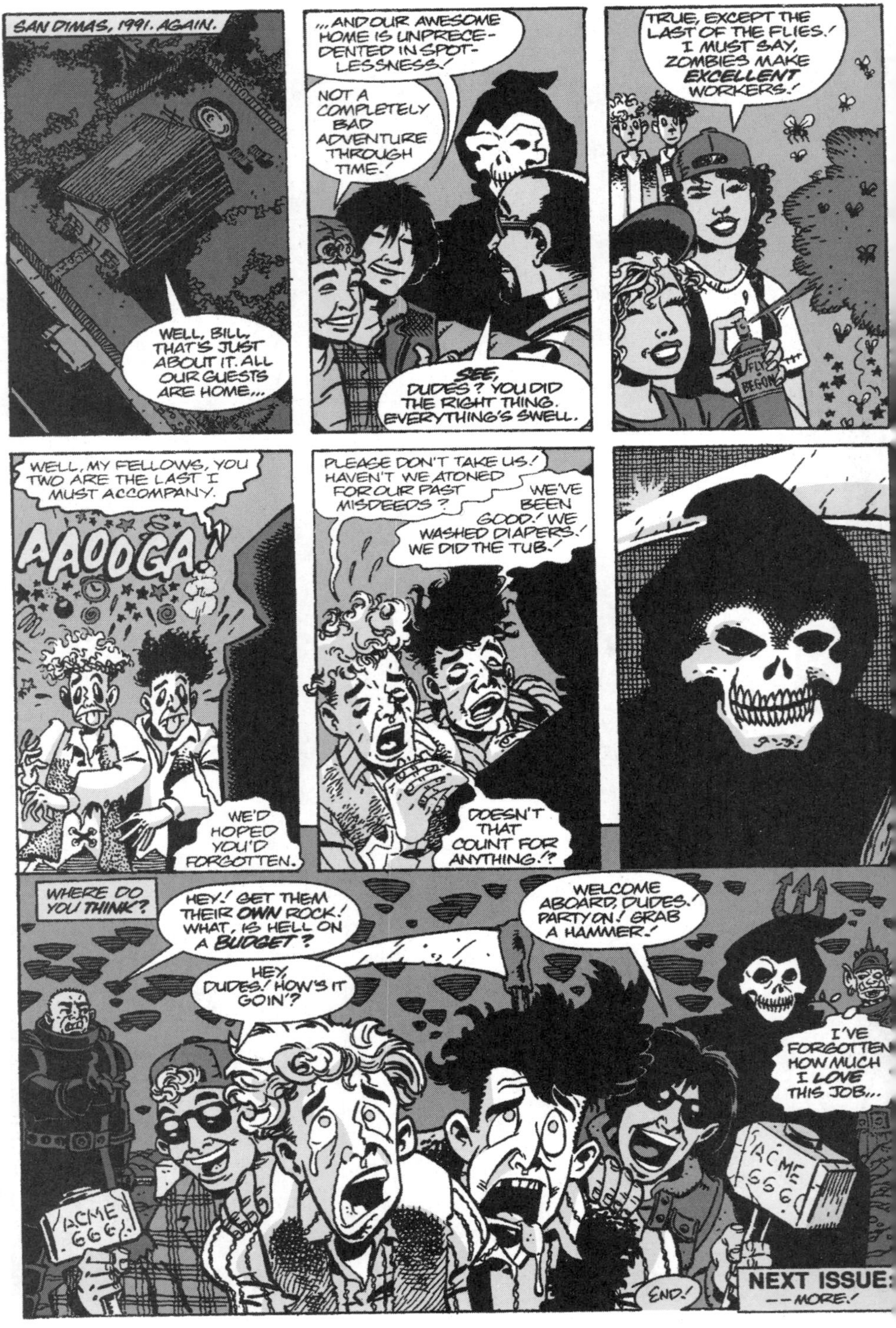
SAN DIMAS, 1991. AGAIN.
WELL, BILL, THAT'S JUST ABOUT IT. ALL OUR GUESTS ARE HOME...
...AND OUR AWESOME HOME IS UNPRECEDENTED IN SPOTLESSNESS!
NOT A COMPLETELY BAD ADVENTURE THROUGH TIME!
SEE, DUDES? YOU DID THE RIGHT THING. EVERYTHING'S SWELL.
TRUE, EXCEPT THE LAST OF THE FLIES! I MUST SAY, ZOMBIES MAKE EXCELLENT WORKERS!
FLY BEGON
WELL, MY FELLOWS, YOU TWO ARE THE LAST I MUST ACCOMPANY.
AAOOGA!
WE'D HOPED YOU'D FORGOTTEN.
PLEASE DON'T TAKE US! HAVEN'T WE ATONED FOR OUR PAST MISDEEDS?
WE'VE BEEN GOOD! WE WASHED DIAPERS! WE DID THE TUB!
DOESN'T THAT COUNT FOR ANYTHING!?
WHERE DO YOU THINK?
HEY! GET THEM THEIR OWN ROCK! WHAT, IS HELL ON A BUDGET?
HEY, DUDES! HOW'S IT GOIN'?
WELCOME ABOARD, DUDES! PARTY ON! GRAB A HAMMER!
I'VE FORGOTTEN HOW MUCH I LOVE THIS JOB...
ACME 666
ACME 666
END!
NEXT ISSUE: --MORE!

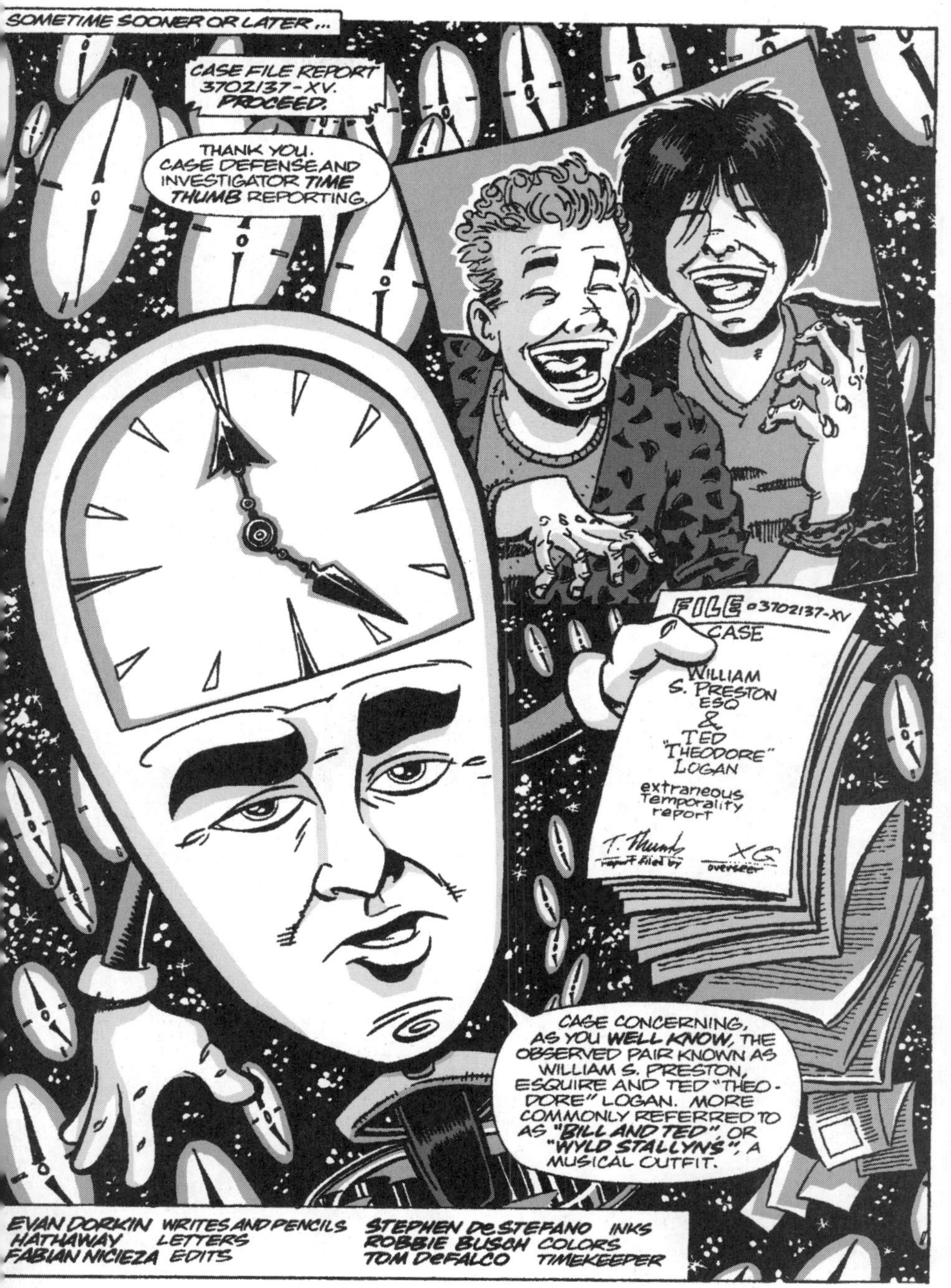
SOMETIME SOONER OR LATER...
CASE FILE REPORT 3702137-XV. PROCEED.
THANK YOU. CASE DEFENSE AND INVESTIGATOR TIME THUMB REPORTING.
FILE #3702137-XV
CASE
WILLIAM S. PRESTON ESQ & TED "THEODORE" LOGAN
extraneous temporality report
T. Thumb
report filed by
XG
overseer
CASE CONCERNING, AS YOU WELL KNOW, THE OBSERVED PAIR KNOWN AS WILLIAM S. PRESTON, ESQUIRE AND TED "THEODORE" LOGAN. MORE COMMONLY REFERRED TO AS "BILL AND TED", OR "WYLD STALLYNS", A MUSICAL OUTFIT.
EVAN DORKIN WRITES AND PENCILS
HATHAWAY LETTERS
FABIAN NICIEZA EDITS
STEPHEN DeSTEFANO INKS
ROBBIE BUSCH COLORS
TOM DeFALCO TIMEKEEPER

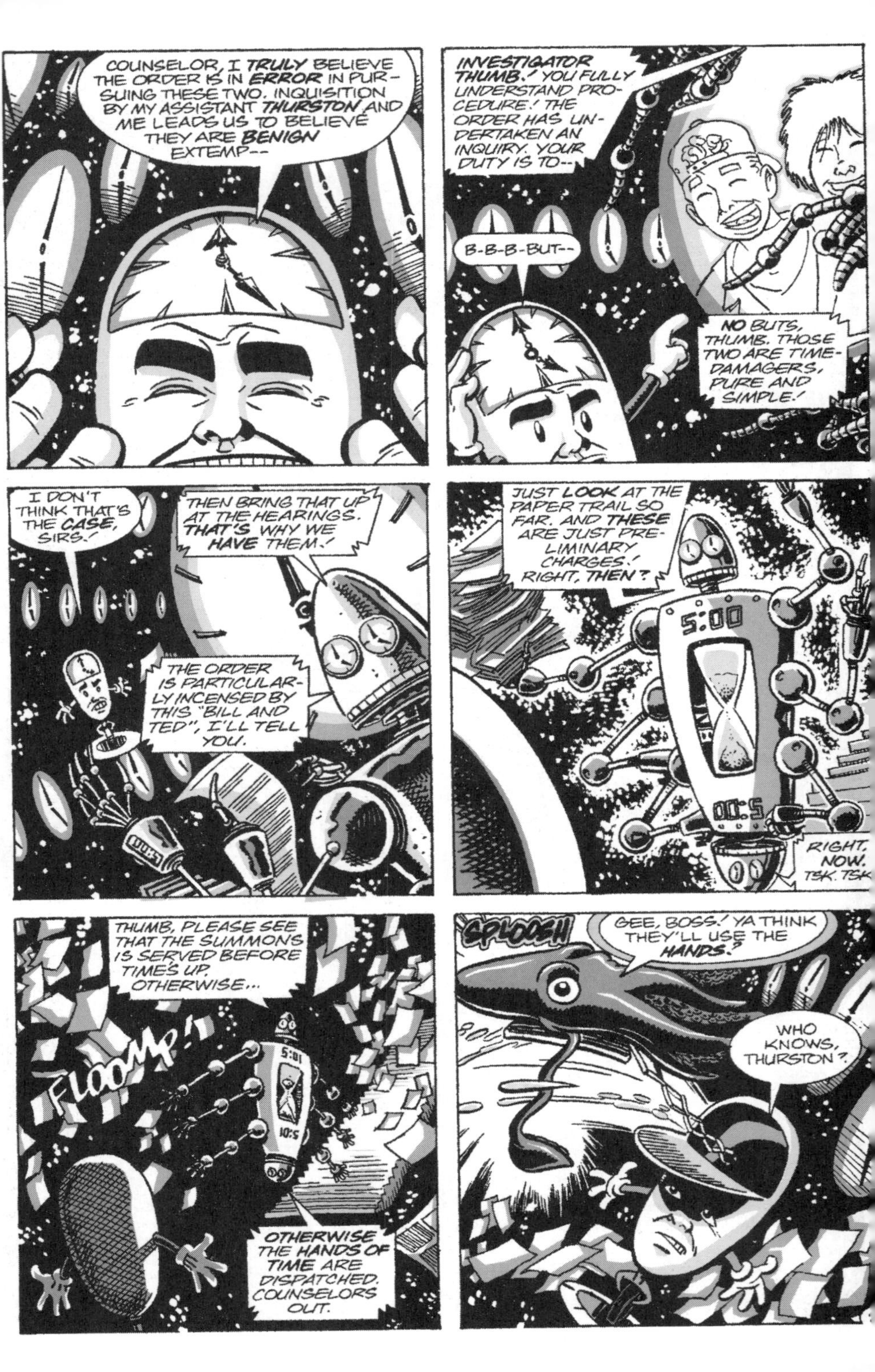
COUNSELOR, I TRULY BELIEVE THE ORDER IS IN ERROR IN PURSUING THESE TWO. INQUISITION BY MY ASSISTANT THURSTON AND ME LEADS US TO BELIEVE THEY ARE BENIGN EXTEMP--
INVESTIGATOR THUMB.! YOU FULLY UNDERSTAND PROCEDURE.! THE ORDER HAS UNDERTAKEN AN INQUIRY. YOUR DUTY IS TO--
B-B-B-BUT--
NO BUTS, THUMB. THOSE TWO ARE TIME-DAMAGERS, PURE AND SIMPLE.!
I DON'T THINK THAT'S THE CASE, SIRS.!
THEN BRING THAT UP AT THE HEARINGS. THAT'S WHY WE HAVE THEM.!
THE ORDER IS PARTICULARLY INCENSED BY THIS "BILL AND TED", I'LL TELL YOU.
JUST LOOK AT THE PAPER TRAIL SO FAR. AND THESE ARE JUST PRELIMINARY CHARGES.! RIGHT, THEN?
5:00
RIGHT. NOW. TSK. TSK
THUMB, PLEASE SEE THAT THE SUMMONS IS SERVED BEFORE TIME'S UP. OTHERWISE...
FLOOMP!
OTHERWISE THE HANDS OF TIME ARE DISPATCHED. COUNSELORS OUT.
SPLOOSH
GEE, BOSS! YA THINK THEY'LL USE THE HANDS?
WHO KNOWS, THURSTON?

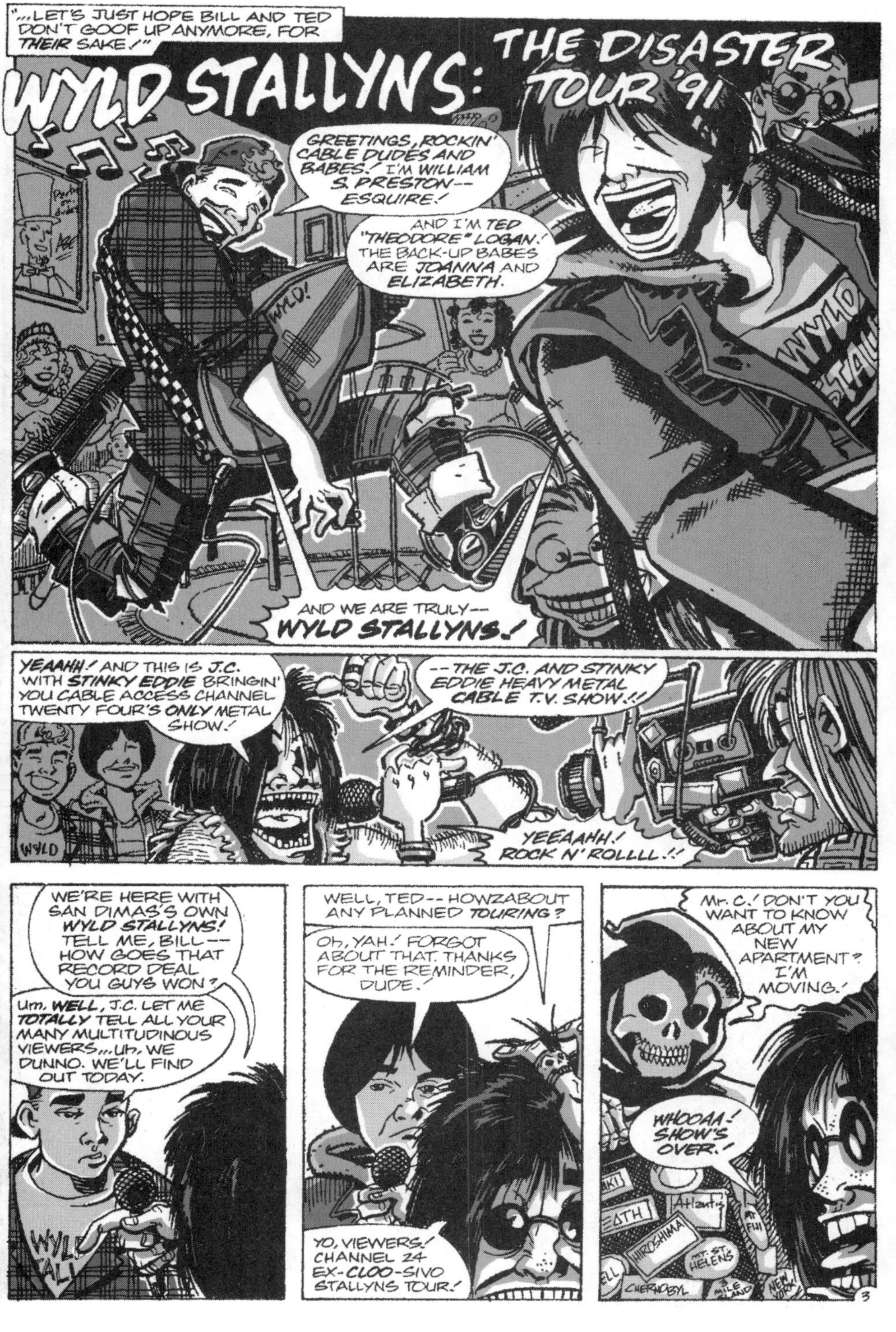
"...LET'S JUST HOPE BILL AND TED DON'T GOOF UP ANYMORE, FOR *THEIR* SAKE!"
WYLD STALLYNS: THE DISASTER TOUR '91
GREETINGS, ROCKIN' CABLE DUDES AND BABES! I'M WILLIAM S. PRESTON-- ESQUIRE!
AND I'M TED "THEODORE" LOGAN! THE BACK-UP BABES ARE JOANNA AND ELIZABETH.
WYLD!
AND WE ARE TRULY-- WYLD STALLYNS!
YEAAHH! AND THIS IS J.C. WITH STINKY EDDIE BRINGIN' YOU CABLE ACCESS CHANNEL TWENTY FOUR'S ONLY METAL SHOW!
--THE J.C. AND STINKY EDDIE HEAVY METAL CABLE T.V. SHOW!!
YEEAAHH! ROCK N' ROLLLL!!
WYLD
WE'RE HERE WITH SAN DIMAS'S OWN WYLD STALLYNS! TELL ME, BILL-- HOW GOES THAT RECORD DEAL YOU GUYS WON?
Um, WELL, J.C. LET ME TOTALLY TELL ALL YOUR MANY MULTITUDINOUS VIEWERS...uh, WE DUNNO. WE'LL FIND OUT TODAY.
WELL, TED-- HOWZABOUT ANY PLANNED TOURING?
Oh, YAH! FORGOT ABOUT THAT. THANKS FOR THE REMINDER, DUDE!
YO, VIEWERS! CHANNEL 24 EX-CLOO-SIVO STALLYNS TOUR!
Mr. C! DON'T YOU WANT TO KNOW ABOUT MY NEW APARTMENT? I'M MOVING!
WHOOAA! SHOW'S OVER!
Atlantis
HIROSHIMA
MT. ST. HELENS
CHERNOBYL
NEW YORK

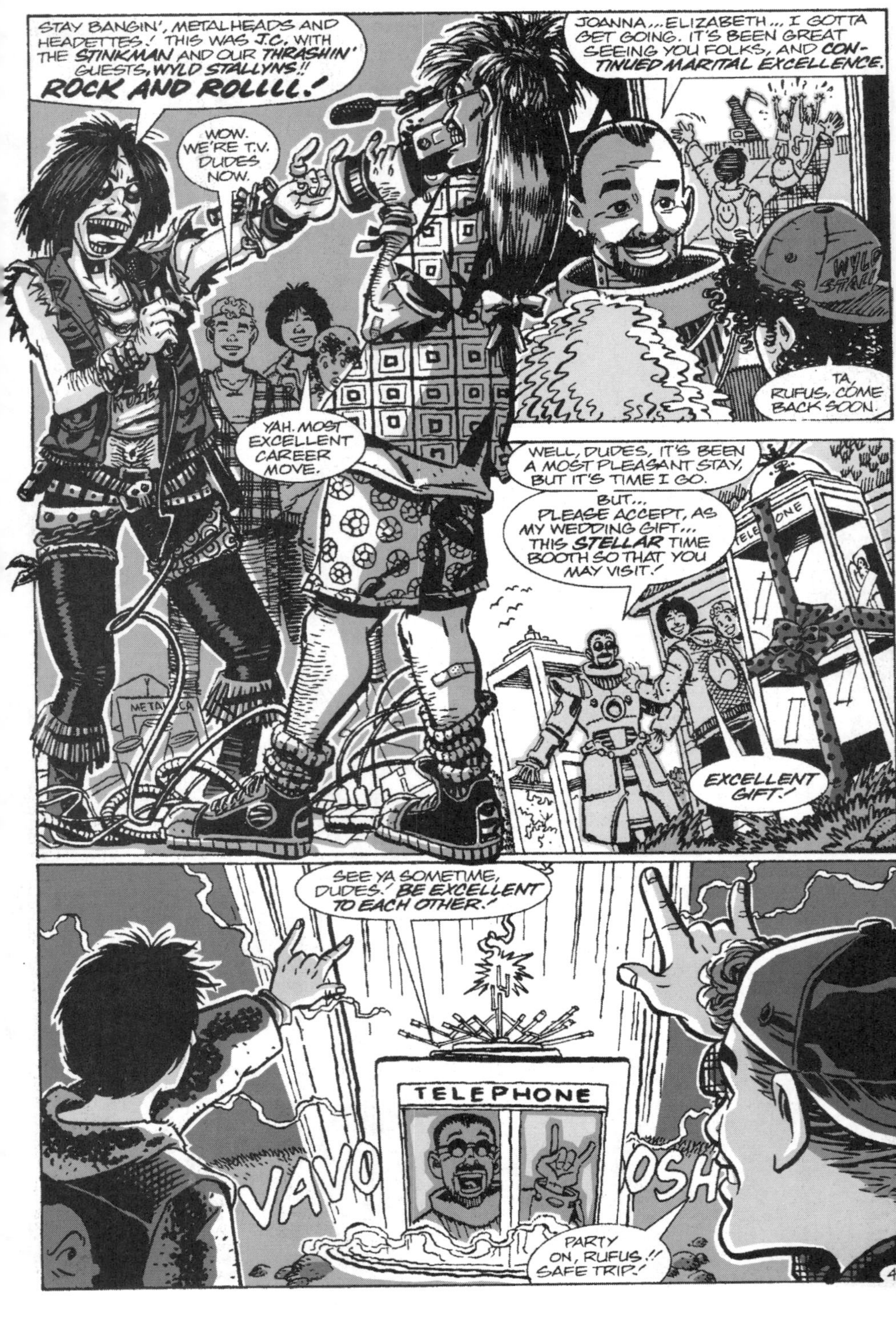
STAY BANGIN', METALHEADS AND HEADETTES! THIS WAS J.C. WITH THE STINKMAN AND OUR THRASHIN' GUESTS, WYLD STALLYNS!! ROCK AND ROLLLL!
WOW. WE'RE T.V. DUDES NOW.
YAH. MOST EXCELLENT CAREER MOVE.
JOANNA... ELIZABETH... I GOTTA GET GOING. IT'S BEEN GREAT SEEING YOU FOLKS, AND CONTINUED MARITAL EXCELLENCE.
TA, RUFUS, COME BACK SOON.
WELL, DUDES, IT'S BEEN A MOST PLEASANT STAY, BUT IT'S TIME I GO.
BUT... PLEASE ACCEPT, AS MY WEDDING GIFT... THIS STELLAR TIME BOOTH SO THAT YOU MAY VISIT!
EXCELLENT GIFT!
SEE YA SOMETIME, DUDES! BE EXCELLENT TO EACH OTHER!
TELEPHONE
VAVOOSH
PARTY ON, RUFUS!! SAFE TRIP!

HELLO, MRS. DEBUSSEY! I'M HERE!

GOOD DAY, MR. THANATOS. YOUR ROOM'S ALL READY AND YOU'RE IN TIME FOR LUNCH!

THE OTHER STUDENTS ARE EAGER TO MEET YOU!

OH, HOW NICE.

THANATOS, THAT SOUNDS GREEK IN ORIGIN! YOU DON'T LOOK GREEK! MIGHT I SAY, YOU'RE SO PALE.

ER... I'M FROM NEW YORK.

WELL, BILL... I'D SAY TRYING TO TEACH THE ROBOT US'S TO DIAPER THE BABIES WAS A MISTAKE.

WYLD STALLYN

Hmm. MOST ASTUTE POINT, DUDE. TOO MANY PINS.

PINNZZZZ?

YAH. AND WAY TOO MUCH POWDER.

DING DONG

SOFT as mush BABY OIL

TALCUM

ITCHY OWIE POWDER for Tiny Tots

SALT PEPP

DOORBELL! WE'LL GET IT, BABES!

THEY'RE SO CUTE, SO HELPLESS!

NIRVANA

SUB POP

CDs CDs ALBUMS

THE BABIES, OR OUR HUSBANDS? HA HA!

BILL, IT'S MY MOST FAVORITE, EXCELLENT FATHER!

SALUTATIONS, UNRIVALLED TED'S DAD DUDE! HOW'S IT GOING?

WYLD STALLYN

UH.... PLEASURE SEEING YOU AGAIN, BILL.

5

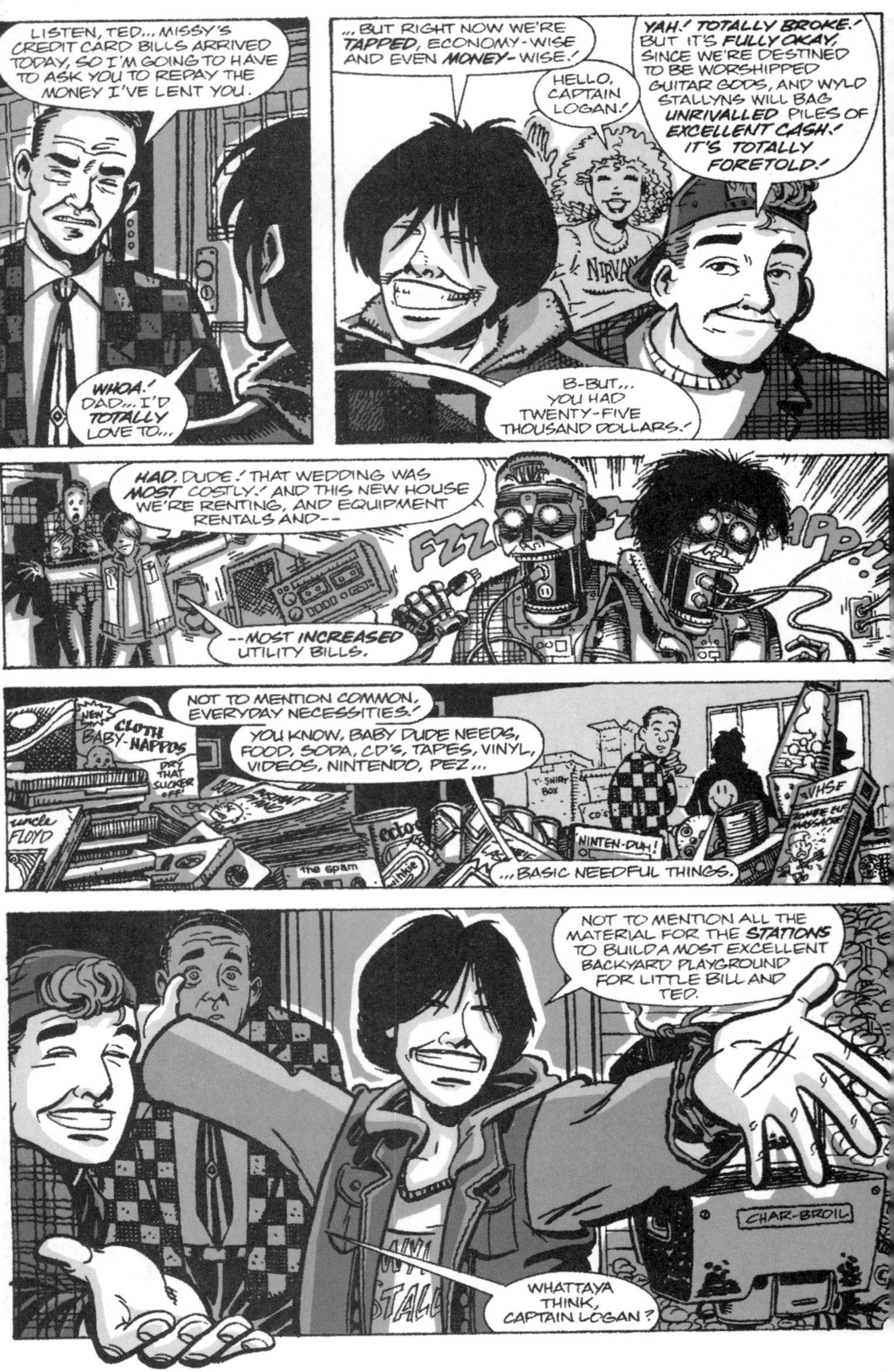
LISTEN, TED... MISSY'S CREDIT CARD BILLS ARRIVED TODAY, SO I'M GOING TO HAVE TO ASK YOU TO REPAY THE MONEY I'VE LENT YOU.
WHOA! DAD... I'D TOTALLY LOVE TO...
...BUT RIGHT NOW WE'RE TAPPED, ECONOMY-WISE AND EVEN MONEY-WISE!
HELLO, CAPTAIN LOGAN!
YAH! TOTALLY BROKE! BUT IT'S FULLY OKAY, SINCE WE'RE DESTINED TO BE WORSHIPPED GUITAR GODS, AND WYLD STALLYNS WILL BAG UNRIVALLED PILES OF EXCELLENT CASH! IT'S TOTALLY FORETOLD!
NIRVANA
B-BUT... YOU HAD TWENTY-FIVE THOUSAND DOLLARS!
HAD, DUDE! THAT WEDDING WAS MOST COSTLY! AND THIS NEW HOUSE WE'RE RENTING, AND EQUIPMENT RENTALS AND--
FZZ
--MOST INCREASED UTILITY BILLS.
NOT TO MENTION COMMON, EVERYDAY NECESSITIES!
YOU KNOW, BABY DUDE NEEDS, FOOD, SODA, CD'S, TAPES, VINYL, VIDEOS, NINTENDO, PEZ...
NEW! CLOTH BABY-NAPPOS
DRY THAT SUCKER OFF!
uncle FLOYD
T-SHIRT BOX
CD'S
NINTEN-DUH!
VHSE
ZOMBIE ELF MASSACRE
the spam
...BASIC NEEDFUL THINGS.
NOT TO MENTION ALL THE MATERIAL FOR THE STATIONS TO BUILD A MOST EXCELLENT BACKYARD PLAYGROUND FOR LITTLE BILL AND TED.
CHAR-BROIL
WHATTAYA THINK, CAPTAIN LOGAN?

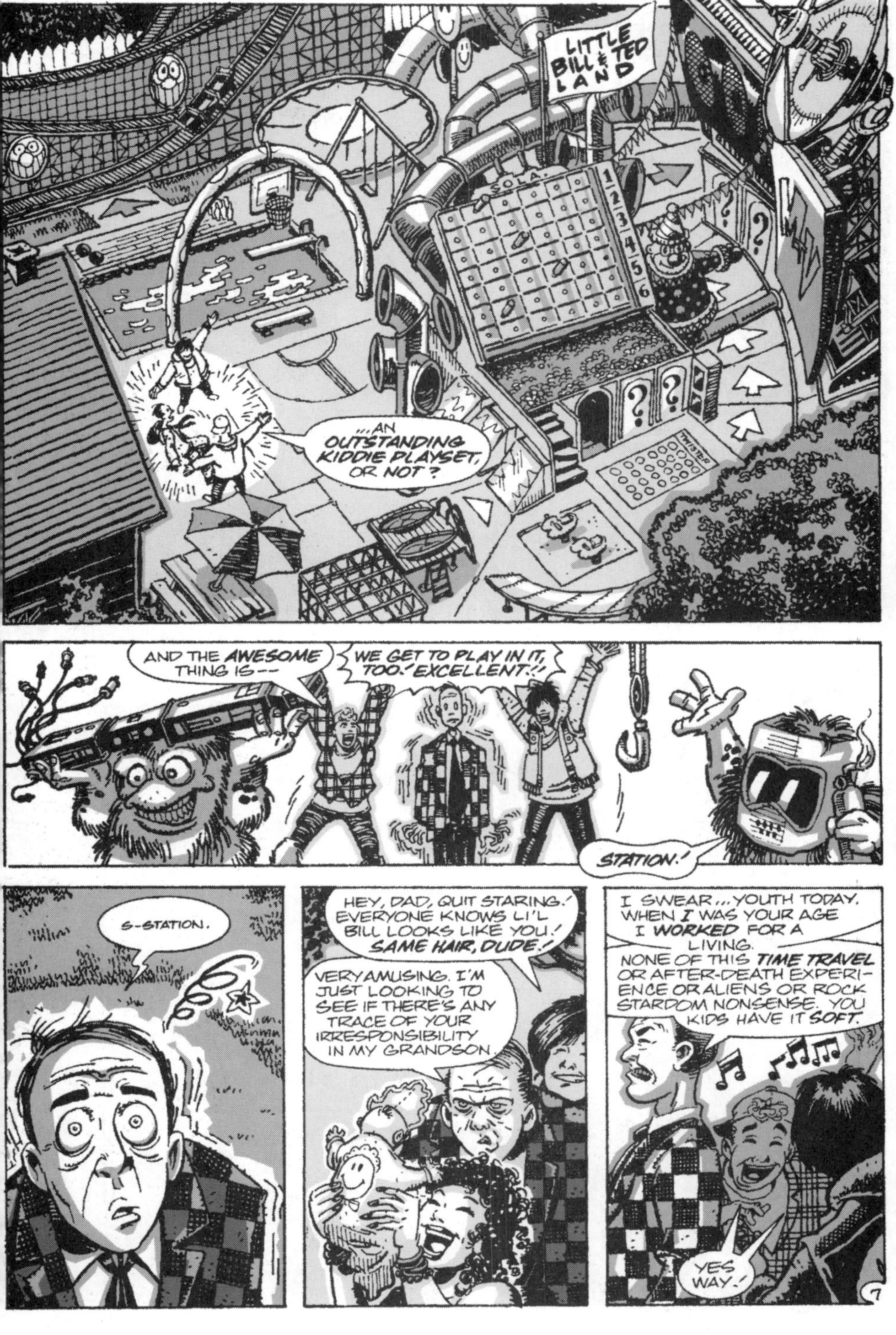

LITTLE BILL & TED LAND
SOLA
...AN OUTSTANDING KIDDIE PLAYSET, OR NOT?
AND THE AWESOME THING IS--
WE GET TO PLAY IN IT, TOO! EXCELLENT!!
STATION!
S-STATION.
HEY, DAD, QUIT STARING! EVERYONE KNOWS LI'L BILL LOOKS LIKE YOU! SAME HAIR, DUDE!
VERY AMUSING. I'M JUST LOOKING TO SEE IF THERE'S ANY TRACE OF YOUR IRRESPONSIBILITY IN MY GRANDSON.
I SWEAR... YOUTH TODAY. WHEN I WAS YOUR AGE I WORKED FOR A LIVING.
NONE OF THIS TIME TRAVEL OR AFTER-DEATH EXPERIENCE OR ALIENS OR ROCK STARDOM NONSENSE. YOU KIDS HAVE IT SOFT.
YES WAY!

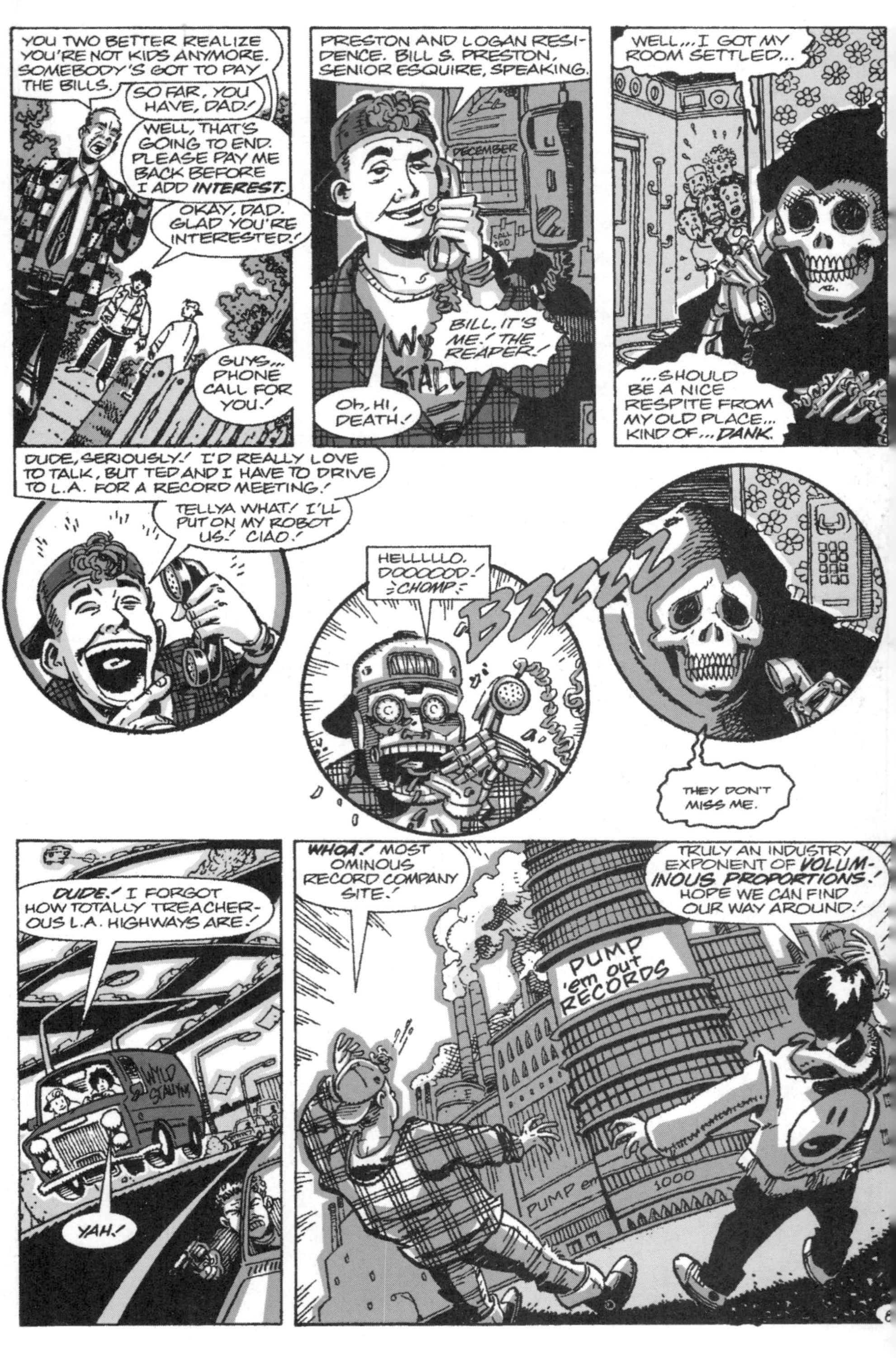
YOU TWO BETTER REALIZE YOU'RE NOT KIDS ANYMORE. SOMEBODY'S GOT TO PAY THE BILLS.
SO FAR, YOU HAVE, DAD!
WELL, THAT'S GOING TO END. PLEASE PAY ME BACK BEFORE I ADD INTEREST.
OKAY, DAD. GLAD YOU'RE INTERESTED!
GUYS... PHONE CALL FOR YOU!
PRESTON AND LOGAN RESIDENCE. BILL S. PRESTON, SENIOR ESQUIRE, SPEAKING.
DECEMBER
BILL, IT'S ME! THE REAPER!
Oh, HI, DEATH!
WELL... I GOT MY ROOM SETTLED...
...SHOULD BE A NICE RESPITE FROM MY OLD PLACE... KIND OF... DANK.
DUDE, SERIOUSLY! I'D REALLY LOVE TO TALK, BUT TED AND I HAVE TO DRIVE TO L.A. FOR A RECORD MEETING!
TELLYA WHAT! I'LL PUT ON MY ROBOT US! CIAO!
HELLLLLO. DOOOOOOD! CHOMP
BZZZZ
THEY DON'T MISS ME.
DUDE! I FORGOT HOW TOTALLY TREACHEROUS L.A. HIGHWAYS ARE!
YAH!
WHOA! MOST OMINOUS RECORD COMPANY SITE!
TRULY AN INDUSTRY EXPONENT OF VOLUMINOUS PROPORTIONS! HOPE WE CAN FIND OUR WAY AROUND!
PUMP 'em out RECORDS
PUMP em
1000

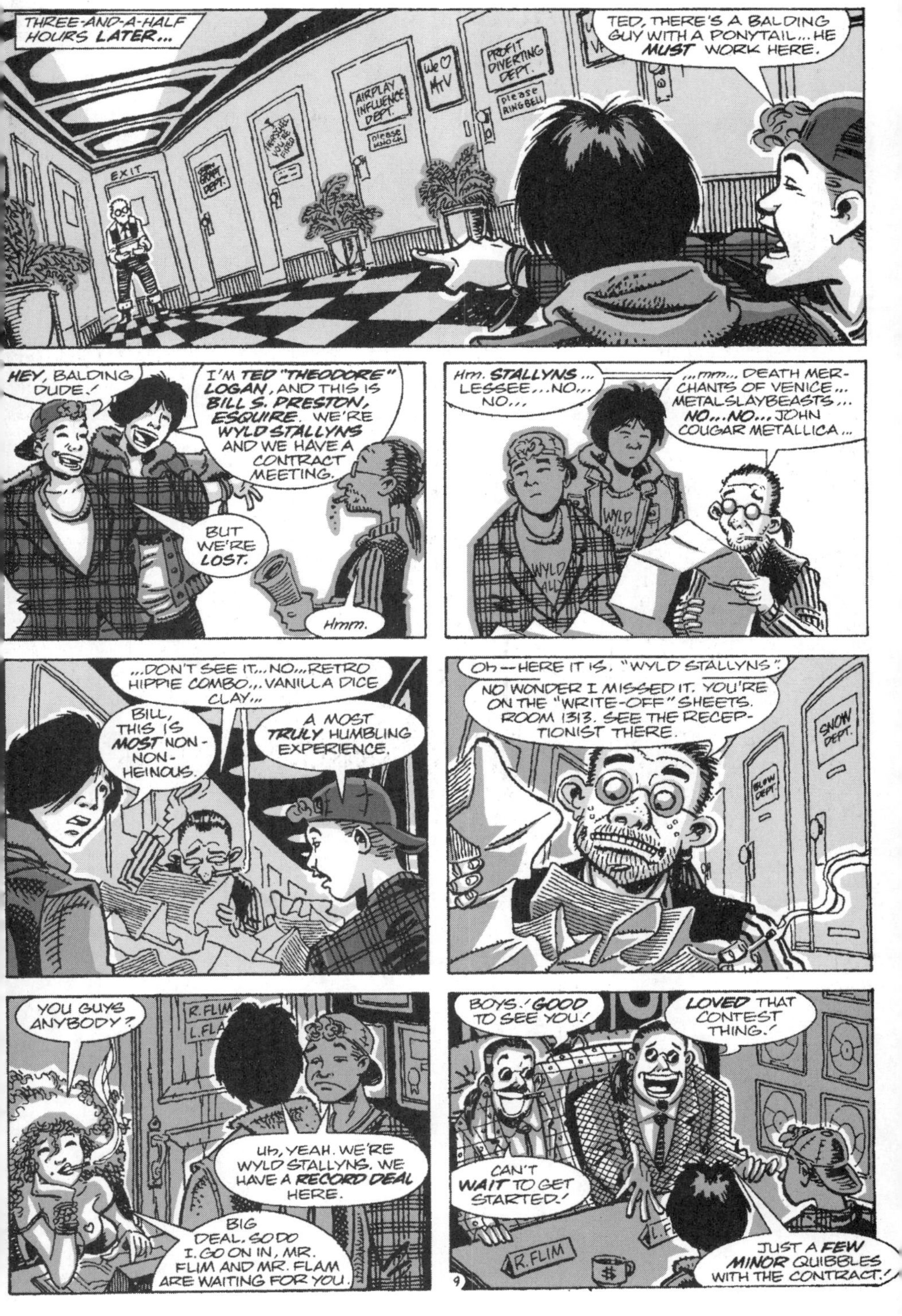
THREE-AND-A-HALF HOURS LATER...
EXIT
AIRPLAY INFLUENCE DEPT.
We ♡ MTV
PROFIT DIVERTING DEPT.
please RING BELL
TED, THERE'S A BALDING GUY WITH A PONYTAIL... HE MUST WORK HERE.
HEY, BALDING DUDE!
I'M TED "THEODORE" LOGAN, AND THIS IS BILL S. PRESTON, ESQUIRE. WE'RE WYLD STALLYNS AND WE HAVE A CONTRACT MEETING.
BUT WE'RE LOST.
Hmm.
Hm. STALLYNS... LESSEE... NO... NO...
...mm... DEATH MERCHANTS OF VENICE... METALSLAYBEASTS... NO... NO... JOHN COUGAR METALLICA...
...DON'T SEE IT... NO... RETRO HIPPIE COMBO... VANILLA DICE CLAY...
BILL, THIS IS MOST NON-NON-HEINOUS.
A MOST TRULY HUMBLING EXPERIENCE.
Oh -- HERE IT IS. "WYLD STALLYNS."
NO WONDER I MISSED IT. YOU'RE ON THE "WRITE-OFF" SHEETS. ROOM 1313. SEE THE RECEPTIONIST THERE.
SNOW DEPT.
YOU GUYS ANYBODY?
R. FLIM
uh, YEAH. WE'RE WYLD STALLYNS. WE HAVE A RECORD DEAL HERE.
BIG DEAL. SO DO I. GO ON IN, MR. FLIM AND MR. FLAM ARE WAITING FOR YOU.
BOYS! GOOD TO SEE YOU!
LOVED THAT CONTEST THING!
CAN'T WAIT TO GET STARTED!
R. FLIM
JUST A FEW MINOR QUIBBLES WITH THE CONTRACT!

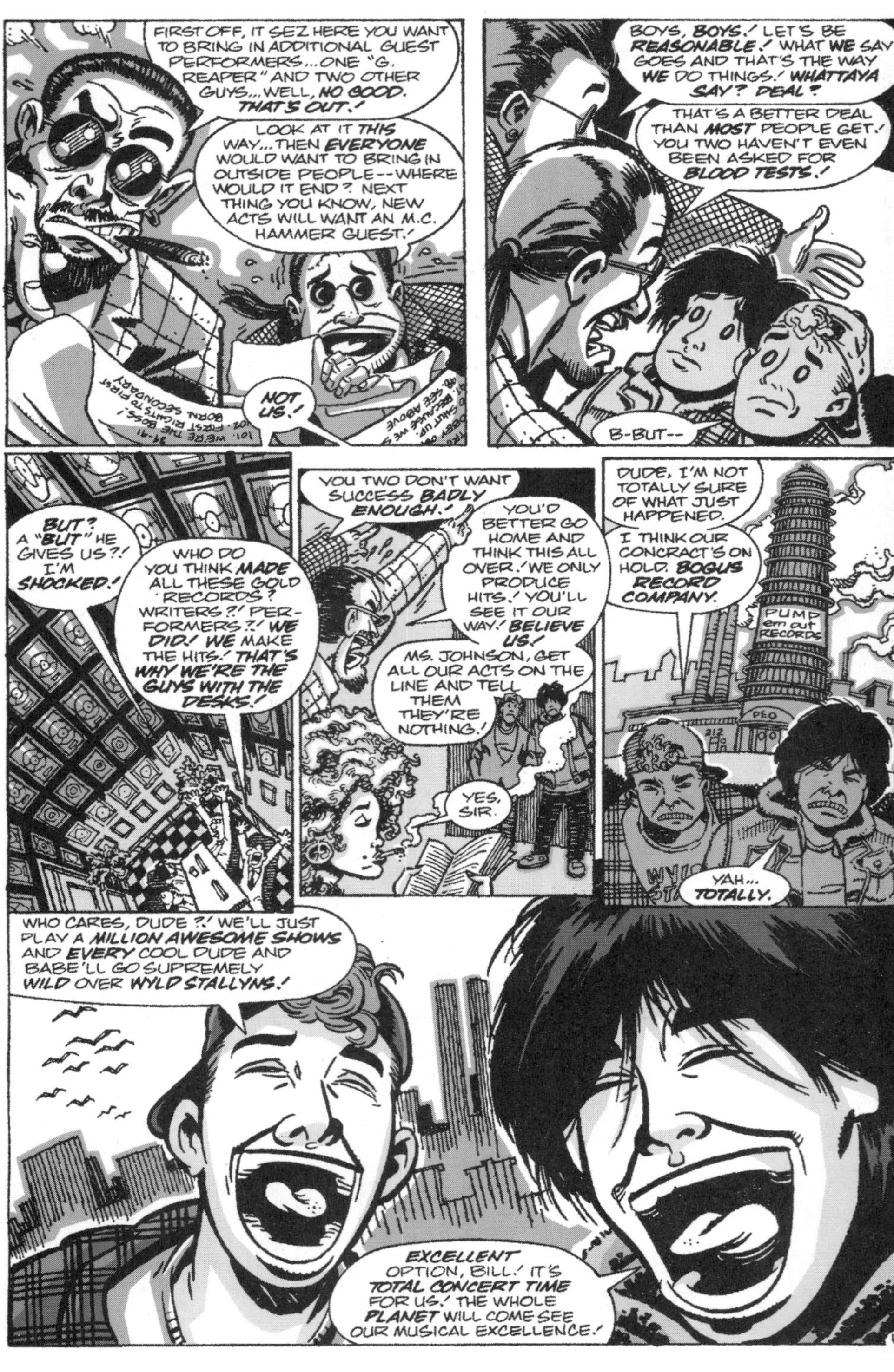

FIRST OFF, IT SEZ HERE YOU WANT TO BRING IN ADDITIONAL GUEST PERFORMERS... ONE "G. REAPER" AND TWO OTHER GUYS... WELL, NO GOOD. THAT'S OUT.!
LOOK AT IT THIS WAY... THEN EVERYONE WOULD WANT TO BRING IN OUTSIDE PEOPLE--WHERE WOULD IT END?. NEXT THING YOU KNOW, NEW ACTS WILL WANT AN M.C. HAMMER GUEST.!
NOT US.!
BOYS, BOYS.! LET'S BE REASONABLE.! WHAT WE SAY GOES AND THAT'S THE WAY WE DO THINGS.! WHATTAYA SAY? DEAL?
THAT'S A BETTER DEAL THAN MOST PEOPLE GET.! YOU TWO HAVEN'T EVEN BEEN ASKED FOR BLOOD TESTS.!
B-BUT--
BUT? A "BUT" HE GIVES US?.! I'M SHOCKED.!
WHO DO YOU THINK MADE ALL THESE GOLD RECORDS? WRITERS?! PERFORMERS?! WE DID! WE MAKE THE HITS.! THAT'S WHY WE'RE THE GUYS WITH THE DESKS.!
YOU TWO DON'T WANT SUCCESS BADLY ENOUGH.!
YOU'D BETTER GO HOME AND THINK THIS ALL OVER.! WE ONLY PRODUCE HITS.! YOU'LL SEE IT OUR WAY.! BELIEVE US.!
MS. JOHNSON, GET ALL OUR ACTS ON THE LINE AND TELL THEM THEY'RE NOTHING.!
YES, SIR.
DUDE, I'M NOT TOTALLY SURE OF WHAT JUST HAPPENED.
I THINK OUR CONCRACT'S ON HOLD. BOGUS RECORD COMPANY.
PUMP em out RECORDS
YAH... TOTALLY.
WHO CARES, DUDE?! WE'LL JUST PLAY A MILLION AWESOME SHOWS AND EVERY COOL DUDE AND BABE'LL GO SUPREMELY WILD OVER WYLD STALLYNS.!
EXCELLENT OPTION, BILL.! IT'S TOTAL CONCERT TIME FOR US.! THE WHOLE PLANET WILL COME SEE OUR MUSICAL EXCELLENCE.!

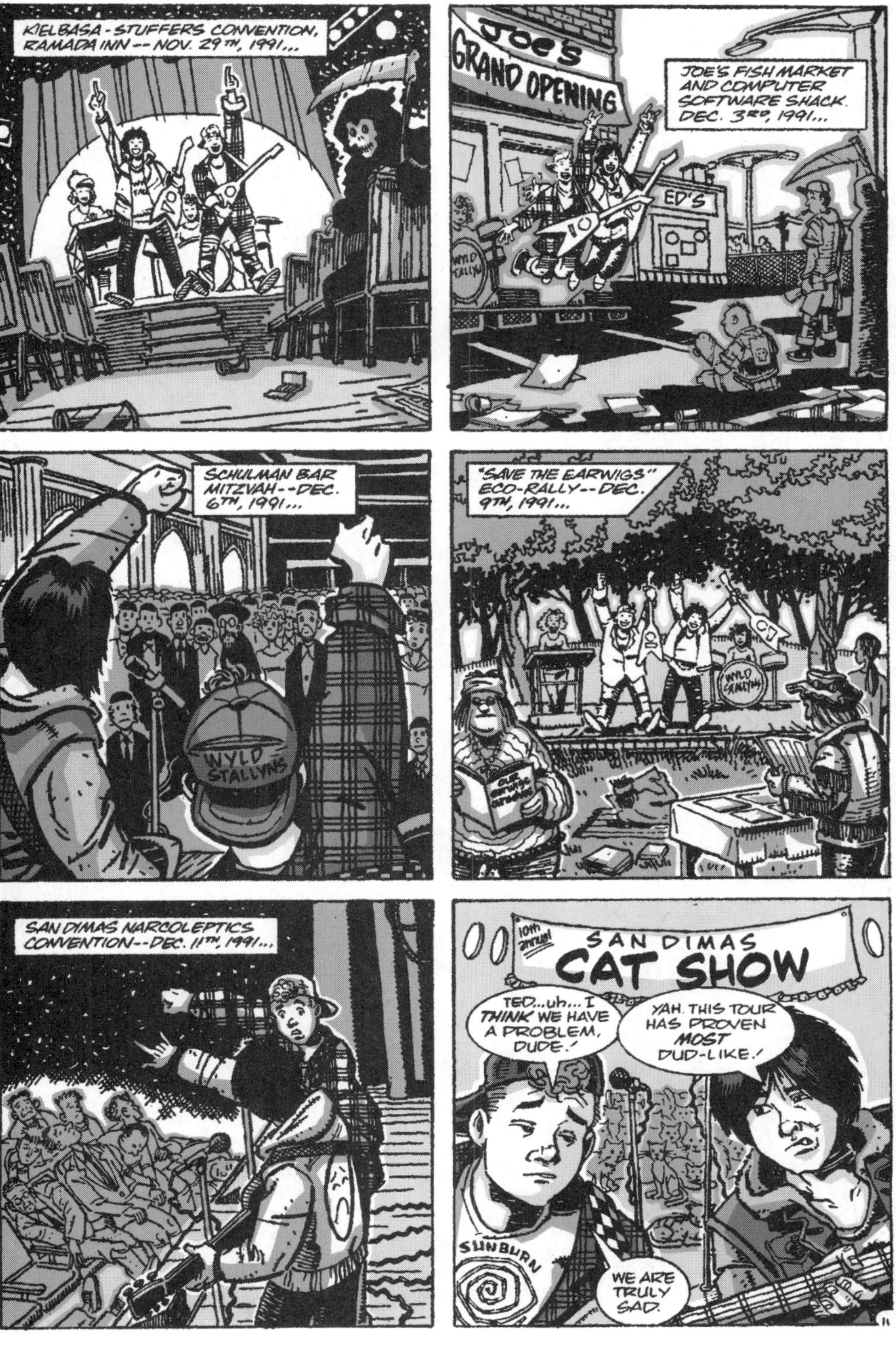
KIELBASA-STUFFERS CONVENTION, RAMADA INN--NOV. 29TH, 1991...
JOE'S GRAND OPENING
JOE'S FISH MARKET AND COMPUTER SOFTWARE SHACK. DEC. 3RD, 1991...
ED'S
WYLD STALLYNS
SCHULMAN BAR MITZVAH--DEC. 6TH, 1991...
WYLD STALLYNS
"SAVE THE EARWIGS" ECO-RALLY--DEC. 9TH, 1991...
WYLD STALLYNS
SAN DIMAS NARCOLEPTICS CONVENTION--DEC. 11TH, 1991...
10th annual SAN DIMAS CAT SHOW
TED...uh...I THINK WE HAVE A PROBLEM, DUDE.!
YAH. THIS TOUR HAS PROVEN MOST DUD-LIKE.!
SUNBURN
WE ARE TRULY SAD.

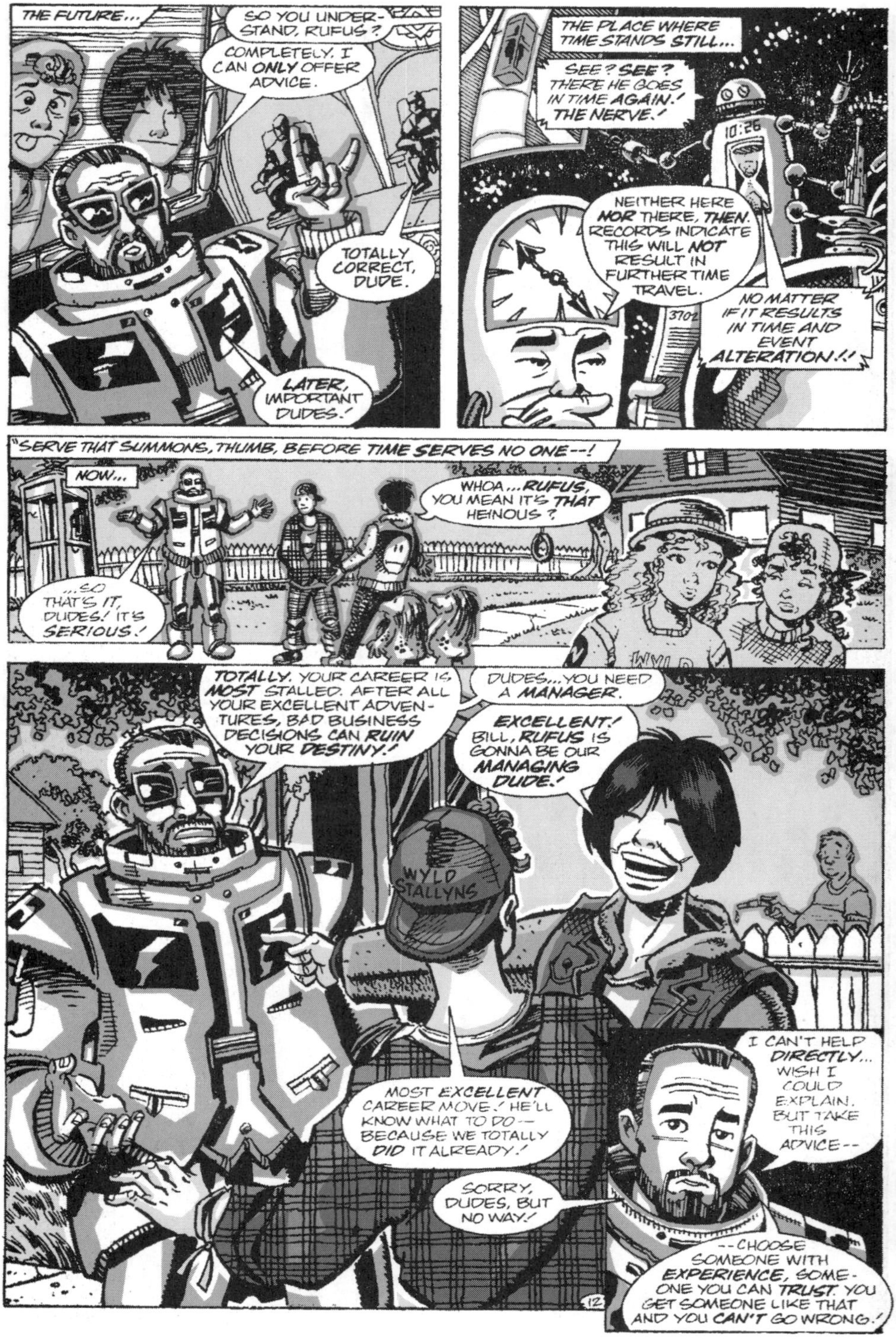
THE FUTURE...
SO YOU UNDERSTAND, RUFUS?
COMPLETELY. I CAN ONLY OFFER ADVICE.
TOTALLY CORRECT, DUDE.
LATER, IMPORTANT DUDES!
THE PLACE WHERE TIME STANDS STILL...
SEE? SEE? THERE HE GOES IN TIME AGAIN! THE NERVE!
10:26
NEITHER HERE NOR THERE, THEN. RECORDS INDICATE THIS WILL NOT RESULT IN FURTHER TIME TRAVEL.
3701
NO MATTER IF IT RESULTS IN TIME AND EVENT ALTERATION!!
"SERVE THAT SUMMONS, THUMB, BEFORE TIME SERVES NO ONE--!
NOW...
...SO THAT'S IT, DUDES! IT'S SERIOUS!
WHOA... RUFUS, YOU MEAN IT'S THAT HEINOUS?
TOTALLY. YOUR CAREER IS MOST STALLED. AFTER ALL YOUR EXCELLENT ADVENTURES, BAD BUSINESS DECISIONS CAN RUIN YOUR DESTINY!
DUDES... YOU NEED A MANAGER.
EXCELLENT! BILL, RUFUS IS GONNA BE OUR MANAGING DUDE!
WYLD STALLYNS
MOST EXCELLENT CAREER MOVE! HE'LL KNOW WHAT TO DO-- BECAUSE WE TOTALLY DID IT ALREADY!
SORRY, DUDES, BUT NO WAY!
I CAN'T HELP DIRECTLY... WISH I COULD EXPLAIN. BUT TAKE THIS ADVICE--
--CHOOSE SOMEONE WITH EXPERIENCE, SOMEONE YOU CAN TRUST. YOU GET SOMEONE LIKE THAT AND YOU CAN'T GO WRONG!

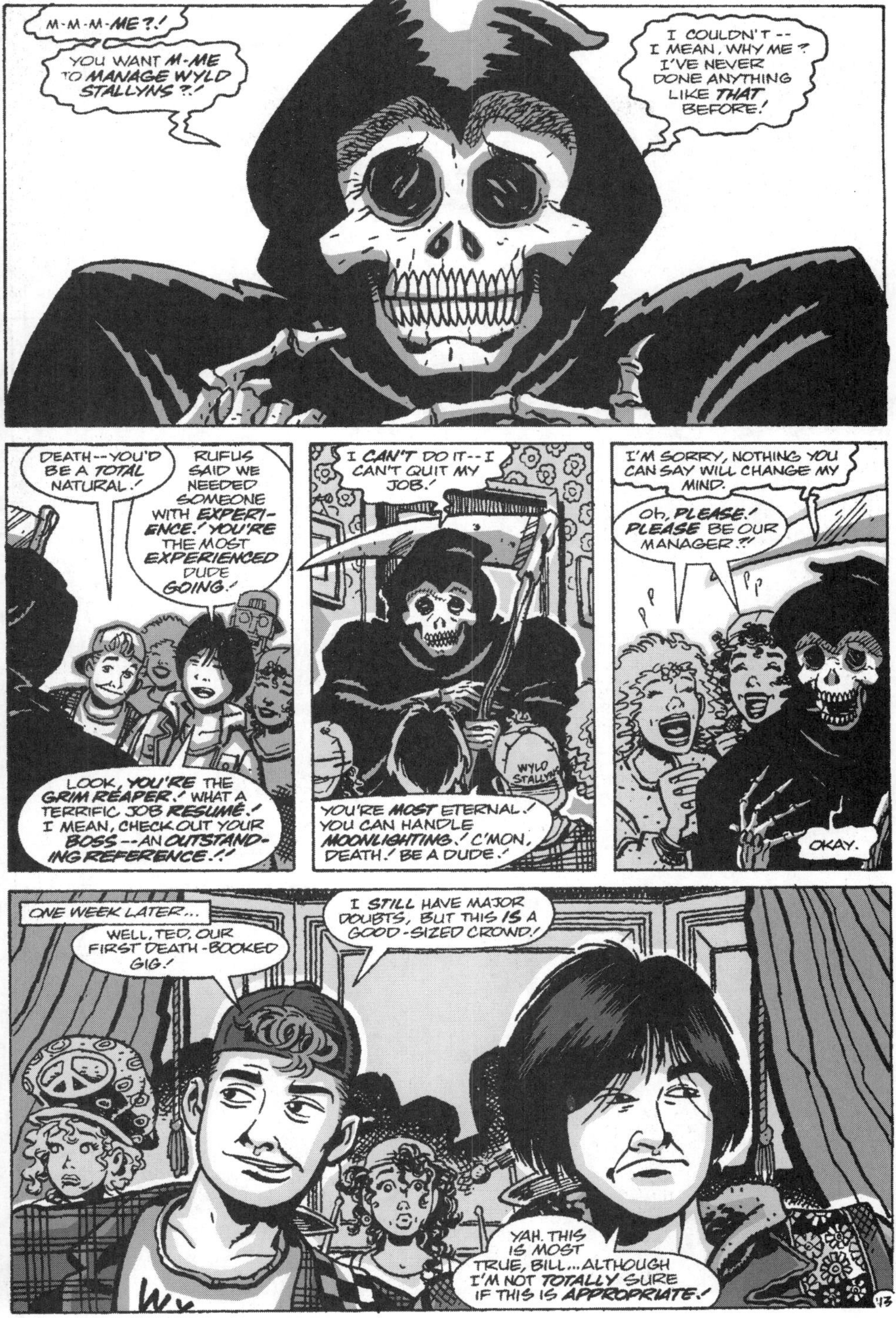

M-M-M-ME?!
YOU WANT M-ME TO MANAGE WYLD STALLYNS?!
I COULDN'T -- I MEAN, WHY ME? I'VE NEVER DONE ANYTHING LIKE THAT BEFORE!
DEATH--YOU'D BE A TOTAL NATURAL!
RUFUS SAID WE NEEDED SOMEONE WITH EXPERIENCE! YOU'RE THE MOST EXPERIENCED DUDE GOING!
LOOK, YOU'RE THE GRIM REAPER! WHAT A TERRIFIC JOB RESUMÉ! I MEAN, CHECK OUT YOUR BOSS--AN OUTSTANDING REFERENCE!!
I CAN'T DO IT--I CAN'T QUIT MY JOB!
WYLD STALLYNS
YOU'RE MOST ETERNAL! YOU CAN HANDLE MOONLIGHTING! C'MON, DEATH! BE A DUDE!
I'M SORRY, NOTHING YOU CAN SAY WILL CHANGE MY MIND.
Oh, PLEASE! PLEASE BE OUR MANAGER?!!
OKAY.
ONE WEEK LATER...
WELL, TED, OUR FIRST DEATH-BOOKED GIG!
I STILL HAVE MAJOR DOUBTS, BUT THIS IS A GOOD-SIZED CROWD!
YAH. THIS IS MOST TRUE, BILL...ALTHOUGH I'M NOT TOTALLY SURE IF THIS IS APPROPRIATE!

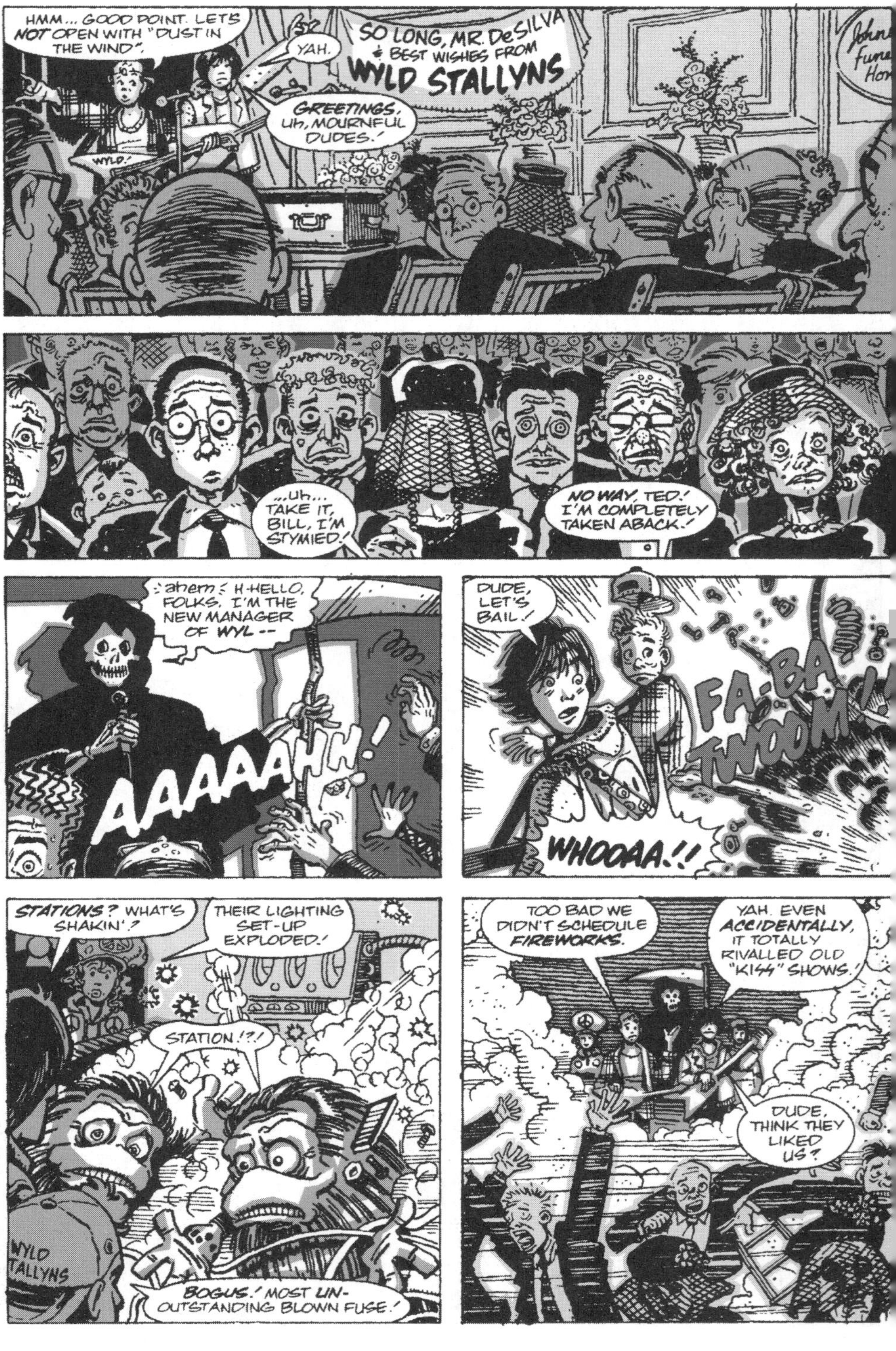
HMM... GOOD POINT. LET'S NOT OPEN WITH "DUST IN THE WIND".
YAH.
SO LONG, MR. DeSILVA & BEST WISHES FROM WYLD STALLYNS
WYLD!
GREETINGS, uh, MOURNFUL DUDES!
...uh... TAKE IT, BILL, I'M STYMIED!
NO WAY, TED! I'M COMPLETELY TAKEN ABACK!
:ahem: H-HELLO, FOLKS. I'M THE NEW MANAGER OF WYL --
AAAAAHH!
DUDE, LET'S BAIL!
FA-BA-TWOOM!!
WHOOAA!!
STATIONS? WHAT'S SHAKIN'?
THEIR LIGHTING SET-UP EXPLODED!
STATION!?!
WYLD STALLYNS
BOGUS! MOST UN-OUTSTANDING BLOWN FUSE!
TOO BAD WE DIDN'T SCHEDULE FIREWORKS.
YAH. EVEN ACCIDENTALLY, IT TOTALLY RIVALLED OLD "KISS" SHOWS.
DUDE, THINK THEY LIKED US?

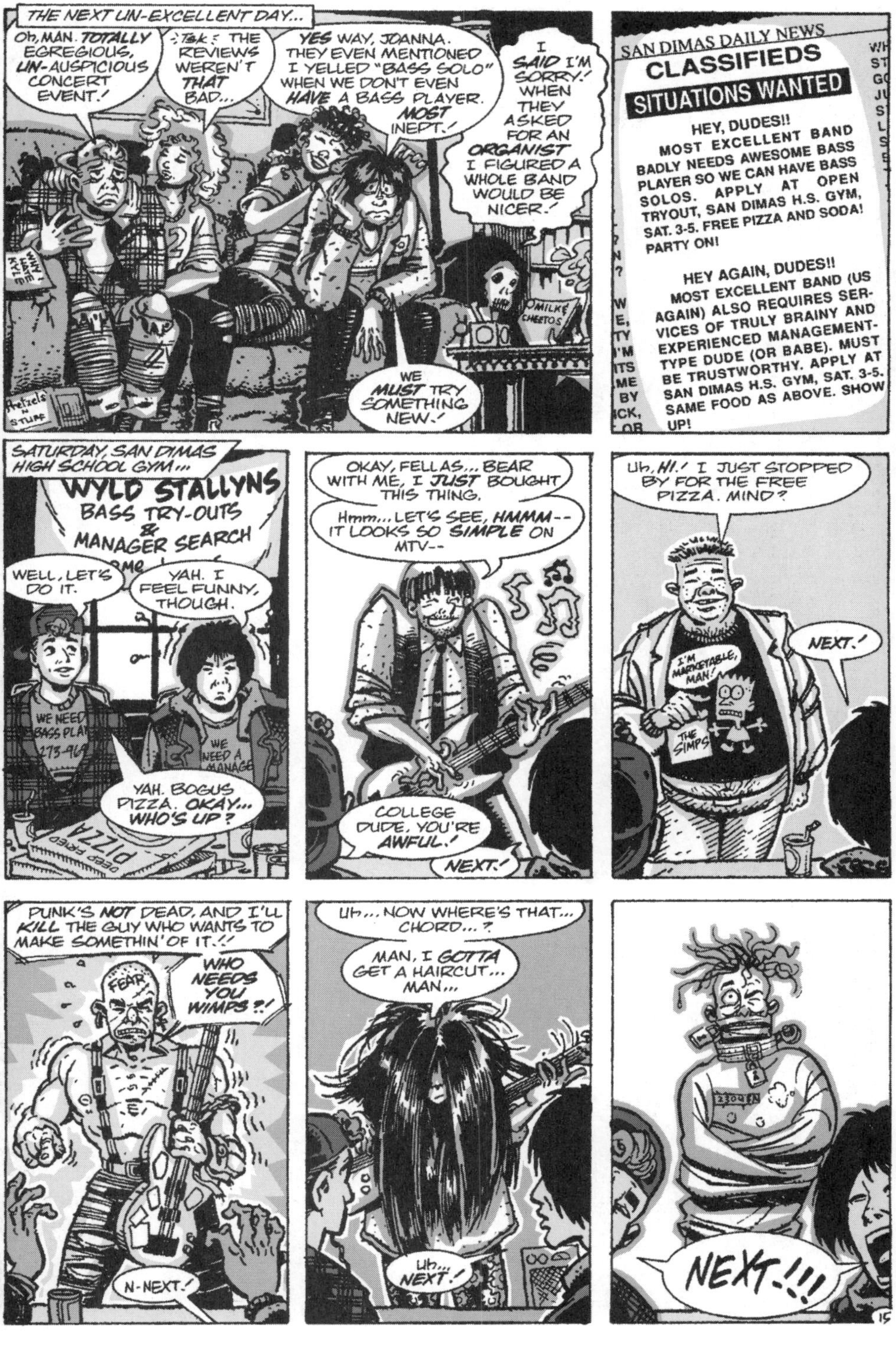
THE NEXT UN-EXCELLENT DAY...
Oh, MAN. TOTALLY EGREGIOUS, UN-AUSPICIOUS CONCERT EVENT!
Tsk THE REVIEWS WEREN'T THAT BAD...
YES WAY, JOANNA. THEY EVEN MENTIONED I YELLED "BASS SOLO" WHEN WE DON'T EVEN HAVE A BASS PLAYER. MOST INEPT!
I SAID I'M SORRY! WHEN THEY ASKED FOR AN ORGANIST I FIGURED A WHOLE BAND WOULD BE NICER!
WE MUST TRY SOMETHING NEW!
MILK CHEETOS
Pretzels N STUFF
SAN DIMAS DAILY NEWS
CLASSIFIEDS
SITUATIONS WANTED
HEY, DUDES!! MOST EXCELLENT BAND BADLY NEEDS AWESOME BASS PLAYER SO WE CAN HAVE BASS SOLOS. APPLY AT OPEN TRYOUT, SAN DIMAS H.S. GYM, SAT. 3-5. FREE PIZZA AND SODA! PARTY ON!
HEY AGAIN, DUDES!! MOST EXCELLENT BAND (US AGAIN) ALSO REQUIRES SERVICES OF TRULY BRAINY AND EXPERIENCED MANAGEMENT-TYPE DUDE (OR BABE). MUST BE TRUSTWORTHY. APPLY AT SAN DIMAS H.S. GYM, SAT. 3-5. SAME FOOD AS ABOVE. SHOW UP!
SATURDAY, SAN DIMAS HIGH SCHOOL GYM...
WYLD STALLYNS BASS TRY-OUTS & MANAGER SEARCH
WELL, LET'S DO IT.
YAH. I FEEL FUNNY, THOUGH.
WE NEED BASS PLAY
WE NEED A MANAGE
YAH. BOGUS PIZZA. OKAY... WHO'S UP?
DEEP FRIED PIZZA
OKAY, FELLAS... BEAR WITH ME, I JUST BOUGHT THIS THING.
Hmm... LET'S SEE, HMMM-- IT LOOKS SO SIMPLE ON MTV--
COLLEGE DUDE, YOU'RE AWFUL!
NEXT!
Uh, HI! I JUST STOPPED BY FOR THE FREE PIZZA. MIND?
I'M MARKETABLE, MAN!
THE SIMPS
NEXT!
PUNK'S NOT DEAD, AND I'LL KILL THE GUY WHO WANTS TO MAKE SOMETHIN' OF IT!!
FEAR
WHO NEEDS YOU WIMPS?!
N-NEXT!
Uh... NOW WHERE'S THAT... CHORD...?
MAN, I GOTTA GET A HAIRCUT... MAN...
Uh... NEXT!
NEXT!!!

THREE HOURS LATER...

HI! I'M PHILLIP! BUT CALL ME "B.G." OR PHIL!

WHAT STYLE'RE YA LOOKIN' FOR? METAL, FUNK, REGGAE... I CAN SLAP FAST AS ANYONE, CARRY ANY TUNE. SO?

JUST LIKE THAT? DON'T YOU WANT TO HEAR ME PLAY?

YOU'RE HIRED! YOU'RE THE FIRST DUDE TO FORM A FULL SENTENCE. WE LIKE THAT.

EXCEPT FOR THE DUDE GRUBBING PIZZA.

DUDE, YOU'RE IN!

HEY! YOU GOT YOURSELF A BASS PLAYER!

EXCELLENT!!

WE NEED BASS

WELCOME TO WYLD STALLYNS, PHIL!

WYLD TALLYNS

Hmmm. NO ONE ASKED ABOUT MANAGING US.

BOGUS. AND WE'RE OUT OF FOOD. Oh WELL—

No No No boy

BOYS, YOU'RE SO WRONG! SORRY I'M LATE, BOYS! LEMMY TELLYA, MANAGE-MENT, PRODUCTION, REP-RESENTATION, YOU NAME IT, I'VE BEEN THERE!

MY CARD!

YOU'RE HIRED!

Lemmy Tellya agent

Lemmytell Talent

Lemmy Telly Producer

HUH? REALLY?

NO ONE ELSE SHOWED UP. YOU'VE GOT A SUIT. YOU'RE HIRED.

OF COURSE I'M HIRED. I'M A PRO, BOYCHIK! YOU'RE LUCKY A BIG TIMER LIKE ME TOOK AN INTEREST!

Uh, CAN I HAVE MY BUSINESS CARDS BACK?

16

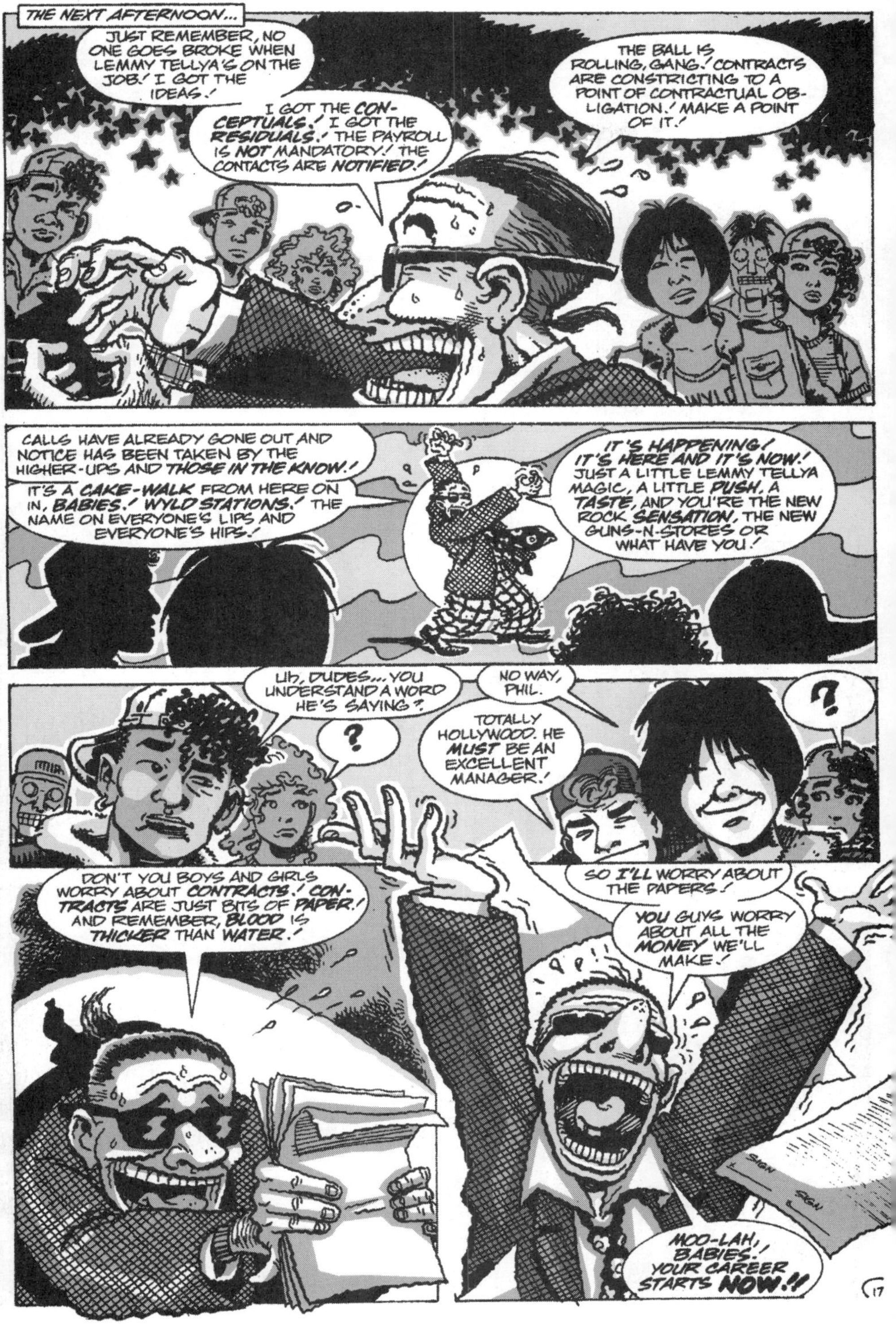
THE NEXT AFTERNOON...
JUST REMEMBER, NO ONE GOES BROKE WHEN LEMMY TELLYA'S ON THE JOB! I GOT THE IDEAS!
I GOT THE CON-CEPTUALS! I GOT THE RESIDUALS! THE PAYROLL IS NOT MANDATORY! THE CONTACTS ARE NOTIFIED!
THE BALL IS ROLLING, GANG! CONTRACTS ARE CONSTRICTING TO A POINT OF CONTRACTUAL OB-LIGATION! MAKE A POINT OF IT!
CALLS HAVE ALREADY GONE OUT AND NOTICE HAS BEEN TAKEN BY THE HIGHER-UPS AND THOSE IN THE KNOW!
IT'S A CAKE-WALK FROM HERE ON IN, BABIES! WYLD STATIONS! THE NAME ON EVERYONE'S LIPS AND EVERYONE'S HIPS!
IT'S HAPPENING! IT'S HERE AND IT'S NOW! JUST A LITTLE LEMMY TELLYA MAGIC, A LITTLE PUSH, A TASTE, AND YOU'RE THE NEW ROCK SENSATION, THE NEW GUNS-N-STORES OR WHAT HAVE YOU!
UH, DUDES... YOU UNDERSTAND A WORD HE'S SAYING?
?
NO WAY, PHIL.
TOTALLY HOLLYWOOD. HE MUST BE AN EXCELLENT MANAGER!
?
DON'T YOU BOYS AND GIRLS WORRY ABOUT CONTRACTS! CON-TRACTS ARE JUST BITS OF PAPER! AND REMEMBER, BLOOD IS THICKER THAN WATER!
SO I'LL WORRY ABOUT THE PAPERS!
YOU GUYS WORRY ABOUT ALL THE MONEY WE'LL MAKE!
SIGN
SIGN
MOO-LAH, BABIES! YOUR CAREER STARTS NOW!!

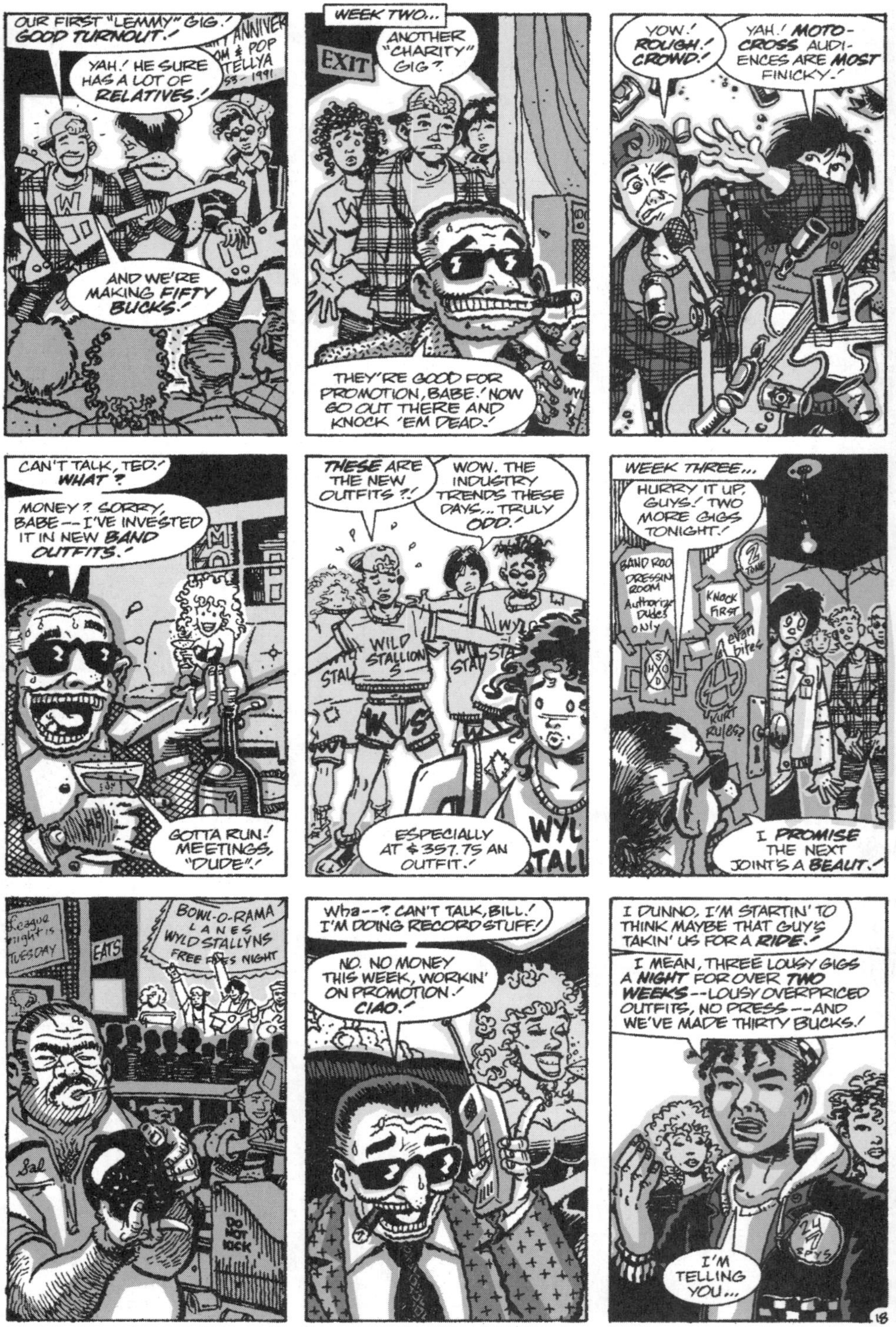
OUR FIRST "LEMMY" GIG! GOOD TURNOUT!
YAH! HE SURE HAS A LOT OF RELATIVES!
AND WE'RE MAKING FIFTY BUCKS!
WEEK TWO...
EXIT
ANOTHER "CHARITY" GIG?
THEY'RE GOOD FOR PROMOTION, BABE! NOW GO OUT THERE AND KNOCK 'EM DEAD!
YOW! ROUGH! CROWD!
YAH! MOTO-CROSS AUDI-ENCES ARE MOST FINICKY!
CAN'T TALK, TED! WHAT?
MONEY? SORRY, BABE--I'VE INVESTED IT IN NEW BAND OUTFITS!
GOTTA RUN! MEETINGS, "DUDE"!
THESE ARE THE NEW OUTFITS?!
WOW. THE INDUSTRY TRENDS THESE DAYS... TRULY ODD!
WILD STALLION S
ESPECIALLY AT $357.75 AN OUTFIT!
WEEK THREE...
HURRY IT UP, GUYS! TWO MORE GIGS TONIGHT!
KNOCK FIRST
I PROMISE THE NEXT JOINT'S A BEAUT!
League night is TUESDAY
EATS
BOWL-O-RAMA LANES WYLD STALLYNS
Wha--? CAN'T TALK, BILL! I'M DOING RECORD STUFF!
NO. NO MONEY THIS WEEK, WORKIN' ON PROMOTION! CIAO!
I DUNNO, I'M STARTIN' TO THINK MAYBE THAT GUY'S TAKIN' US FOR A RIDE!
I MEAN, THREE LOUSY GIGS A NIGHT FOR OVER TWO WEEKS--LOUSY OVERPRICED OUTFITS, NO PRESS--AND WE'VE MADE THIRTY BUCKS!
I'M TELLING YOU...

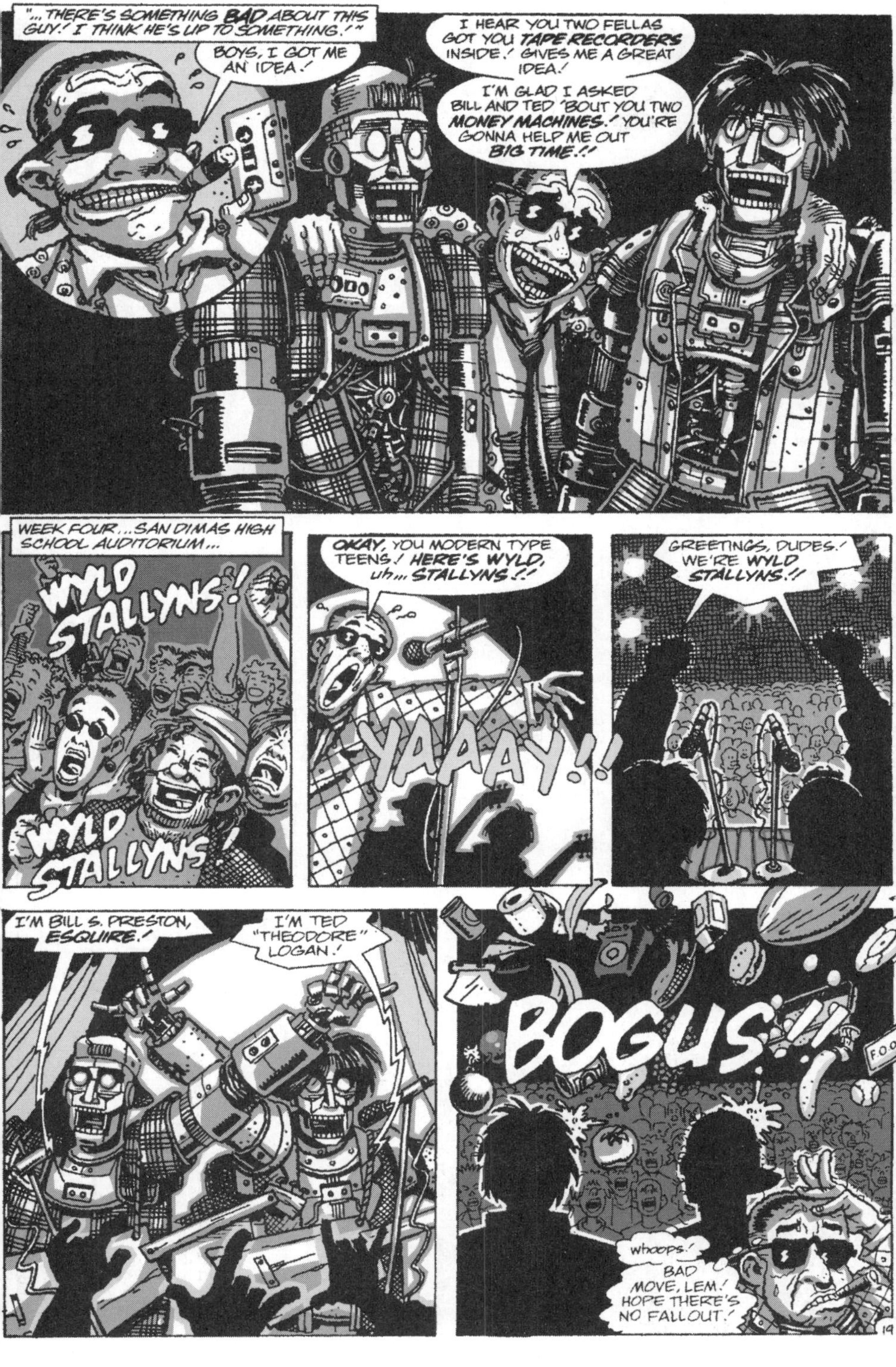
"...THERE'S SOMETHING BAD ABOUT THIS GUY! I THINK HE'S UP TO SOMETHING!"
BOYS, I GOT ME AN' IDEA!
I HEAR YOU TWO FELLAS GOT YOU TAPE RECORDERS INSIDE! GIVES ME A GREAT IDEA!
I'M GLAD I ASKED BILL AND TED 'BOUT YOU TWO MONEY MACHINES! YOU'RE GONNA HELP ME OUT BIG TIME!!
WEEK FOUR...SAN DIMAS HIGH SCHOOL AUDITORIUM...
WYLD STALLYNS!
WYLD STALLYNS!
OKAY, YOU MODERN TYPE TEENS! HERE'S WYLD, uh... STALLYNS!!
YAAAAY!!
GREETINGS, DUDES! WE'RE WYLD STALLYNS!!
I'M BILL S. PRESTON, ESQUIRE!
I'M TED "THEODORE" LOGAN!
BOGUS!!
F.O.O.M
whoops!
BAD MOVE, LEM! HOPE THERE'S NO FALLOUT!

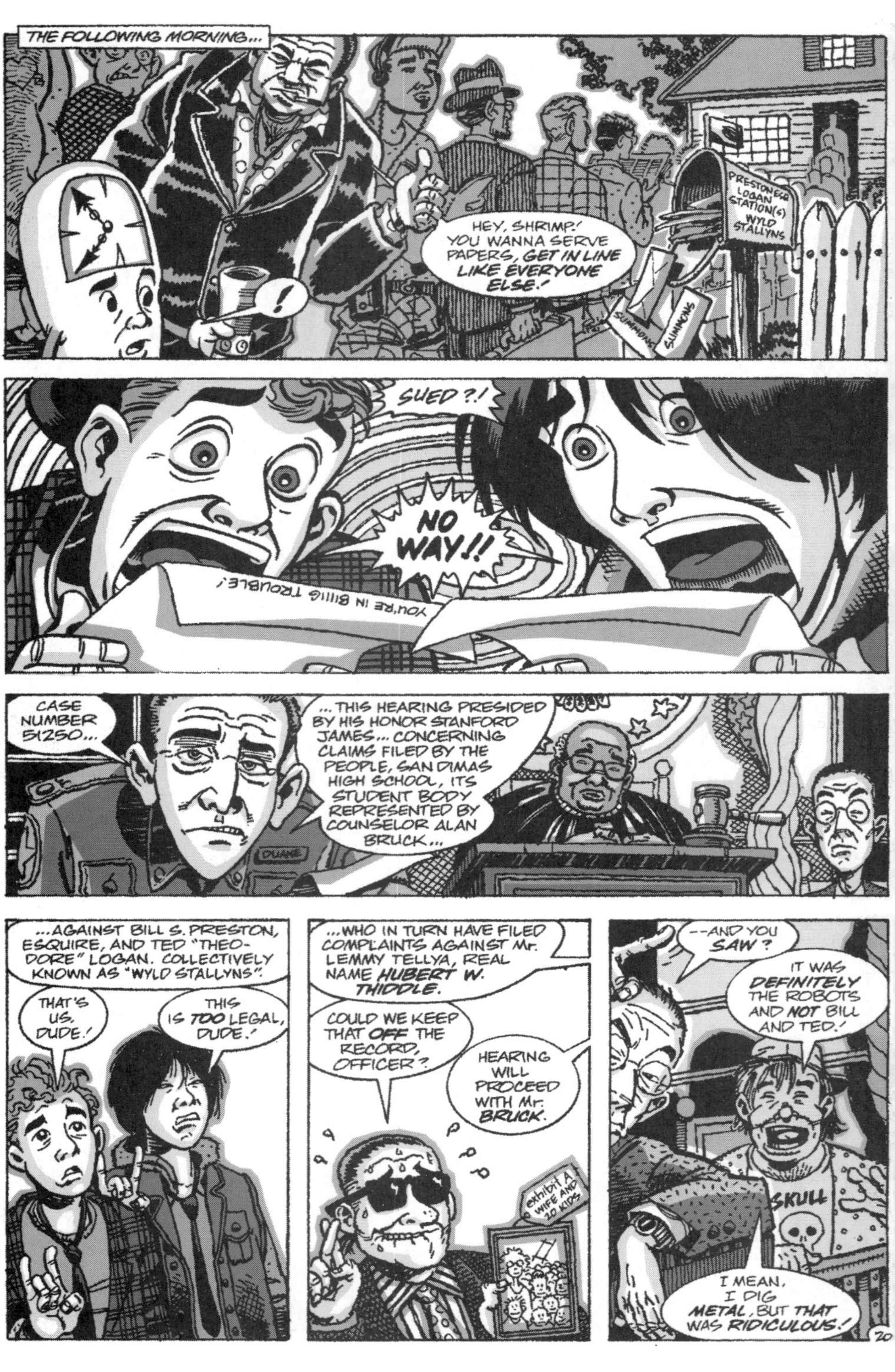
THE FOLLOWING MORNING...
PRESTON ESQ
LOGAN
STATION(S)
WYLD STALLYNS
HEY, SHRIMP! YOU WANNA SERVE PAPERS, GET IN LINE LIKE EVERYONE ELSE!
!
SUMMONS
SUMMONS
SUED?!
NO WAY!!
YOU'RE IN BIIIG TROUBLE!
CASE NUMBER 51250...
...THIS HEARING PRESIDED BY HIS HONOR STANFORD JAMES... CONCERNING CLAIMS FILED BY THE PEOPLE, SAN DIMAS HIGH SCHOOL, ITS STUDENT BODY REPRESENTED BY COUNSELOR ALAN BRUCK...
DUANE
...AGAINST BILL S. PRESTON, ESQUIRE, AND TED "THEODORE" LOGAN. COLLECTIVELY KNOWN AS "WYLD STALLYNS".
THAT'S US, DUDE!
THIS IS TOO LEGAL, DUDE!
...WHO IN TURN HAVE FILED COMPLAINTS AGAINST Mr. LEMMY TELLYA, REAL NAME HUBERT W. THIDDLE.
COULD WE KEEP THAT OFF THE RECORD, OFFICER?
HEARING WILL PROCEED WITH Mr. BRUCK.
exhibit A WIFE AND 20 KIDS
--AND YOU SAW?
IT WAS DEFINITELY THE ROBOTS AND NOT BILL AND TED!
SKULL
I MEAN, I DIG METAL, BUT THAT WAS RIDICULOUS!

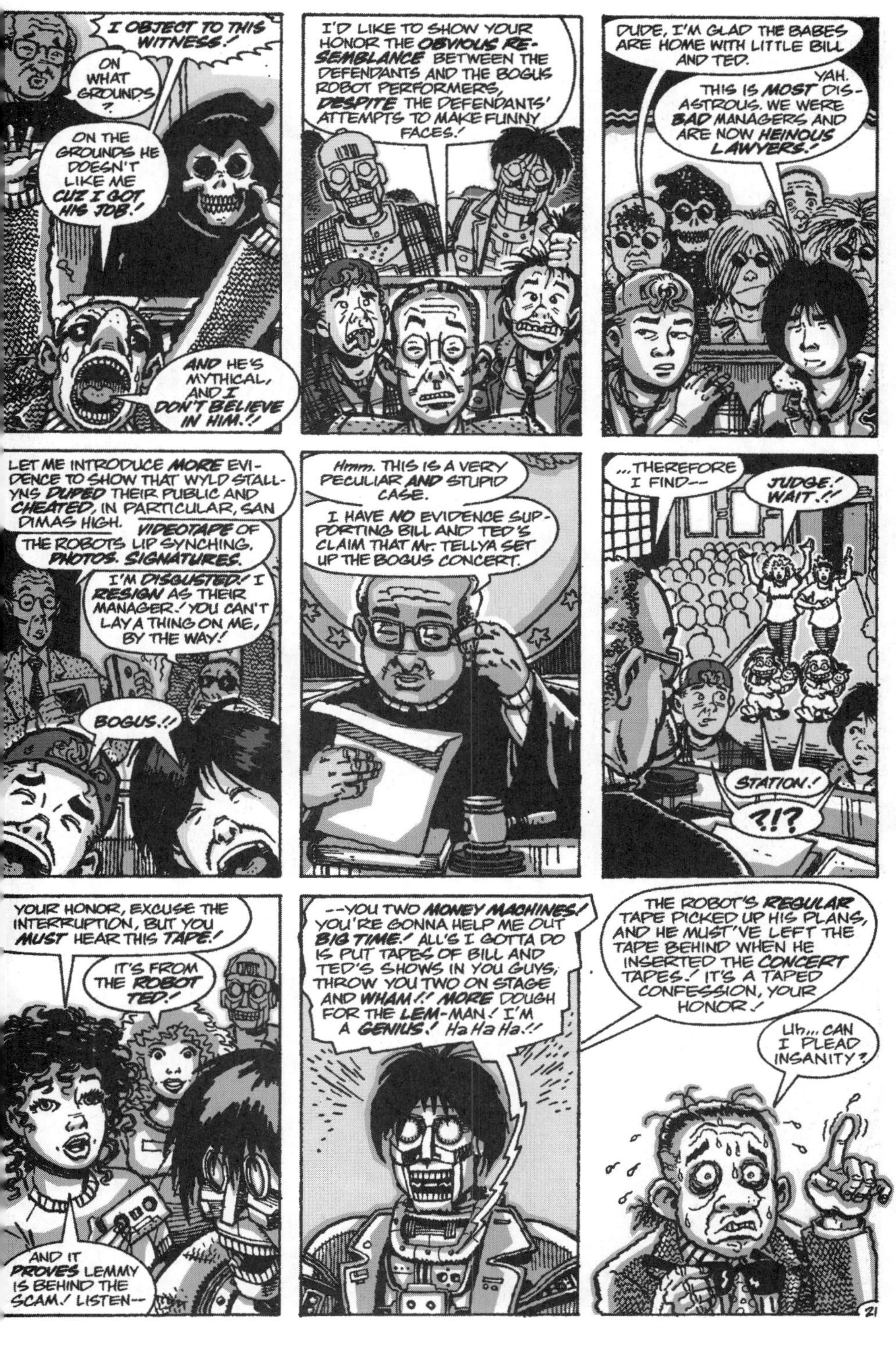
I OBJECT TO THIS WITNESS.!
ON WHAT GROUNDS ?
ON THE GROUNDS HE DOESN'T LIKE ME CUZ I GOT HIS JOB.!
AND HE'S MYTHICAL, AND I DON'T BELIEVE IN HIM.!!
I'D LIKE TO SHOW YOUR HONOR THE OBVIOUS RESEMBLANCE BETWEEN THE DEFENDANTS AND THE BOGUS ROBOT PERFORMERS, DESPITE THE DEFENDANTS' ATTEMPTS TO MAKE FUNNY FACES.!
DUDE, I'M GLAD THE BABES ARE HOME WITH LITTLE BILL AND TED.
YAH. THIS IS MOST DISASTROUS. WE WERE BAD MANAGERS AND ARE NOW HEINOUS LAWYERS.!
LET ME INTRODUCE MORE EVIDENCE TO SHOW THAT WYLD STALLYNS DUPED THEIR PUBLIC AND CHEATED, IN PARTICULAR, SAN DIMAS HIGH. VIDEOTAPE OF THE ROBOTS LIP SYNCHING. PHOTOS. SIGNATURES.
I'M DISGUSTED.! I RESIGN AS THEIR MANAGER.! YOU CAN'T LAY A THING ON ME, BY THE WAY!
BOGUS.!!
Hmm. THIS IS A VERY PECULIAR AND STUPID CASE.
I HAVE NO EVIDENCE SUPPORTING BILL AND TED'S CLAIM THAT Mr. TELLYA SET UP THE BOGUS CONCERT.
...THEREFORE I FIND--
JUDGE.! WAIT.!!
STATION.!
?!?
YOUR HONOR, EXCUSE THE INTERRUPTION, BUT YOU MUST HEAR THIS TAPE.!
IT'S FROM THE ROBOT TED.!
AND IT PROVES LEMMY IS BEHIND THE SCAM.! LISTEN--
--YOU TWO MONEY MACHINES.! YOU'RE GONNA HELP ME OUT BIG TIME.! ALL'S I GOTTA DO IS PUT TAPES OF BILL AND TED'S SHOWS IN YOU GUYS, THROW YOU TWO ON STAGE AND WHAM.!! MORE DOUGH FOR THE LEM-MAN.! I'M A GENIUS.! Ha Ha Ha.!!
THE ROBOT'S REGULAR TAPE PICKED UP HIS PLANS, AND HE MUST'VE LEFT THE TAPE BEHIND WHEN HE INSERTED THE CONCERT TAPES.! IT'S A TAPED CONFESSION, YOUR HONOR.!
Uh... CAN I PLEAD INSANITY?

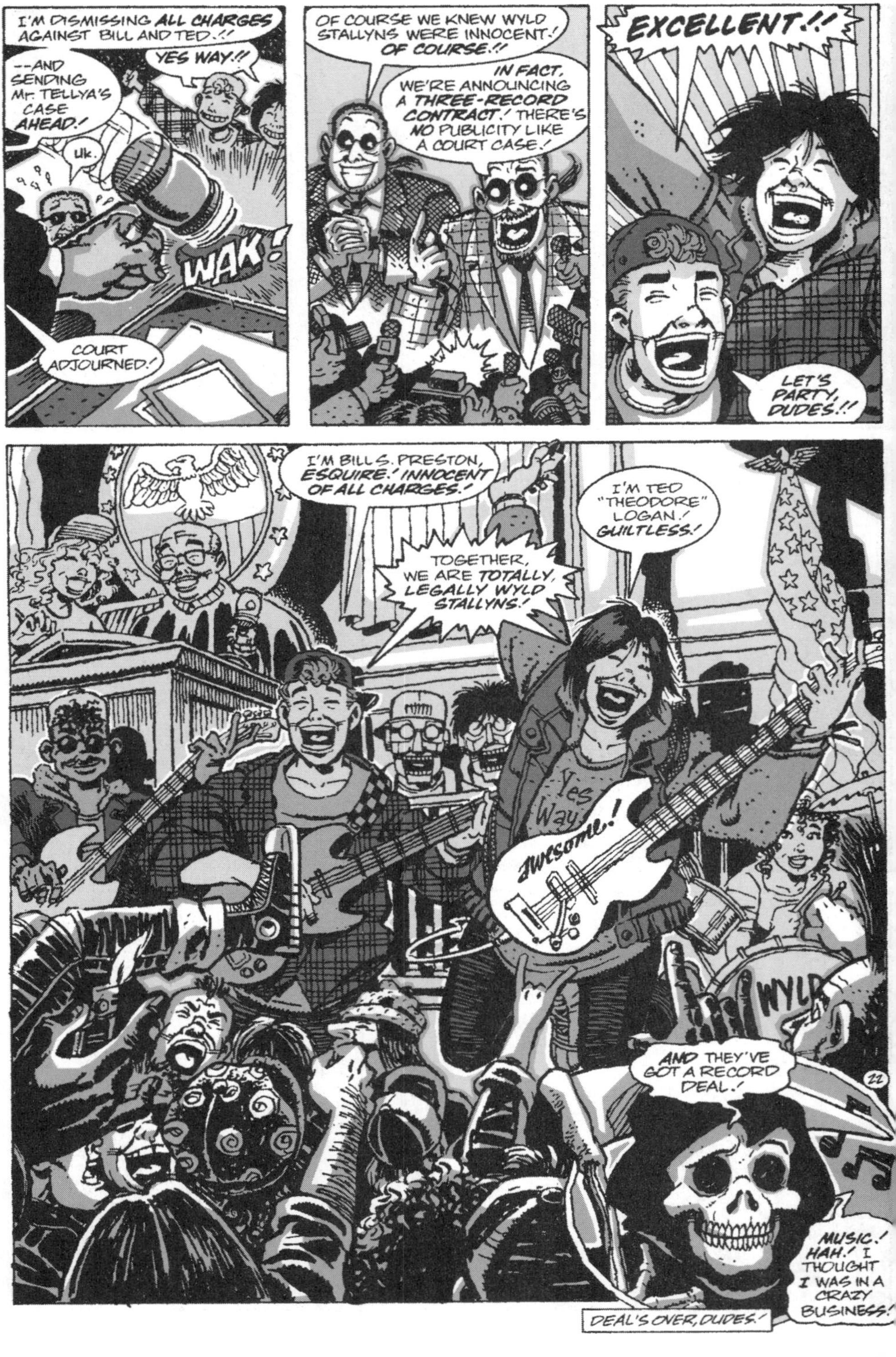
I'M DISMISSING ALL CHARGES AGAINST BILL AND TED!!
YES WAY!!
--AND SENDING Mr. TELLYA'S CASE AHEAD!
Uk.
WAK!
COURT ADJOURNED!
OF COURSE WE KNEW WYLD STALLYNS WERE INNOCENT! OF COURSE!!
IN FACT, WE'RE ANNOUNCING A THREE-RECORD CONTRACT! THERE'S NO PUBLICITY LIKE A COURT CASE!
EXCELLENT!!!
LET'S PARTY, DUDES!!
I'M BILL S. PRESTON, ESQUIRE! INNOCENT OF ALL CHARGES!
I'M TED "THEODORE" LOGAN! GUILTLESS!
TOGETHER, WE ARE TOTALLY, LEGALLY WYLD STALLYNS!
Yes Way
Awesome!
WYLD
AND THEY'VE GOT A RECORD DEAL!
22
MUSIC! HAH! I THOUGHT I WAS IN A CRAZY BUSINESS!
DEAL'S OVER, DUDES!

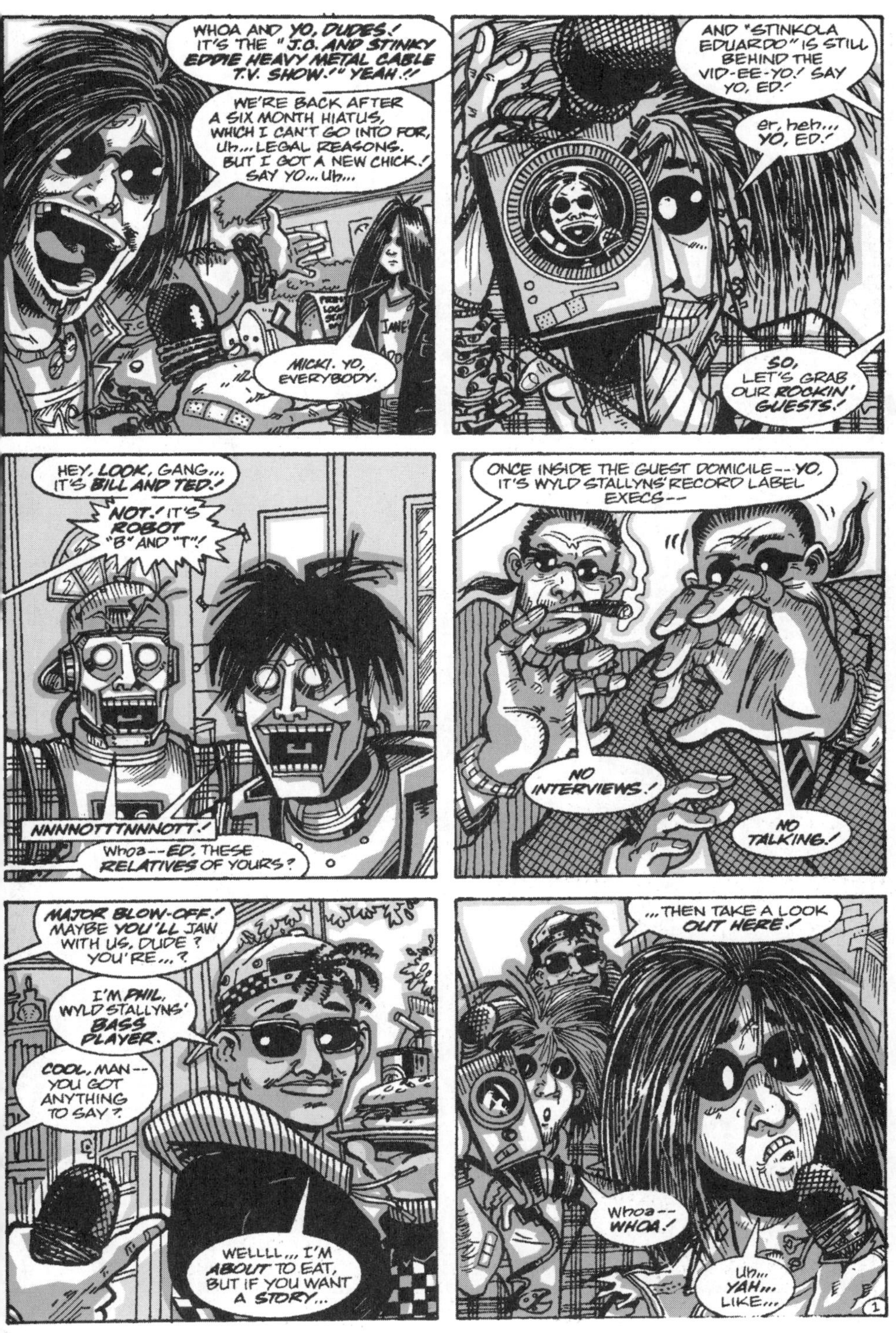
WHOA AND YO, DUDES! IT'S THE "J.O. AND STINKY EDDIE HEAVY METAL CABLE T.V. SHOW!" YEAH!!
WE'RE BACK AFTER A SIX MONTH HIATUS, WHICH I CAN'T GO INTO FOR, Uh... LEGAL REASONS. BUT I GOT A NEW CHICK! SAY YO... Uh...
MICKI. YO, EVERYBODY.
AND "STINKOLA EDUARDO" IS STILL BEHIND THE VID-EE-YO! SAY YO, ED!
er, heh... YO, ED!
SO, LET'S GRAB OUR ROCKIN' GUESTS!
HEY, LOOK, GANG... IT'S BILL AND TED!
NOT! IT'S ROBOT "B" AND "T"!
NNNNOTTTNNNOTT!
Whoa--ED, THESE RELATIVES OF YOURS?
ONCE INSIDE THE GUEST DOMICILE-- YO, IT'S WYLD STALLYNS' RECORD LABEL EXECS--
NO INTERVIEWS!
NO TALKING!
MAJOR BLOW-OFF! MAYBE YOU'LL JAW WITH US, DUDE? YOU'RE...?
I'M PHIL, WYLD STALLYNS' BASS PLAYER.
COOL, MAN-- YOU GOT ANYTHING TO SAY?
WELLLL... I'M ABOUT TO EAT, BUT IF YOU WANT A STORY...
...THEN TAKE A LOOK OUT HERE!
Whoa-- WHOA!
Uh... YAH... LIKE...

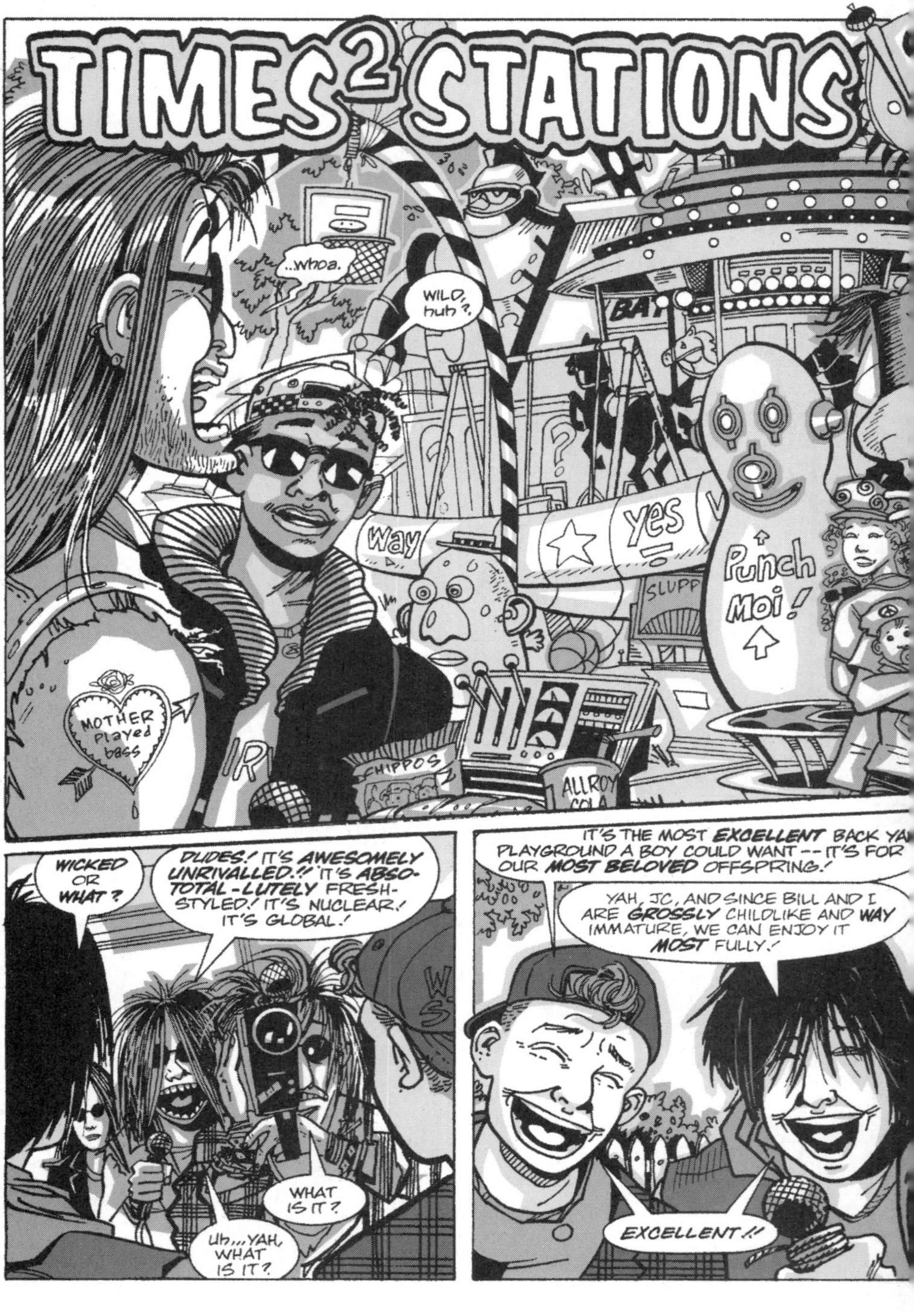

TIMES² STATIONS
...whoa.
WILD, huh ?.
way
yes
Punch Moi !
SLUPP
MOTHER played bass
CHIPPOS
ALLROY COLA
WICKED OR WHAT ?
DUDES! IT'S AWESOMELY UNRIVALLED!! IT'S ABSO-TOTAL-LUTELY FRESH-STYLED! IT'S NUCLEAR! IT'S GLOBAL!
WHAT IS IT ?
Uh,,, YAH, WHAT IS IT ?
IT'S THE MOST EXCELLENT BACK YA PLAYGROUND A BOY COULD WANT -- IT'S FOR OUR MOST BELOVED OFFSPRING!
YAH, JC, AND SINCE BILL AND I ARE GROSSLY CHILDLIKE AND WAY IMMATURE, WE CAN ENJOY IT MOST FULLY!
EXCELLENT!!

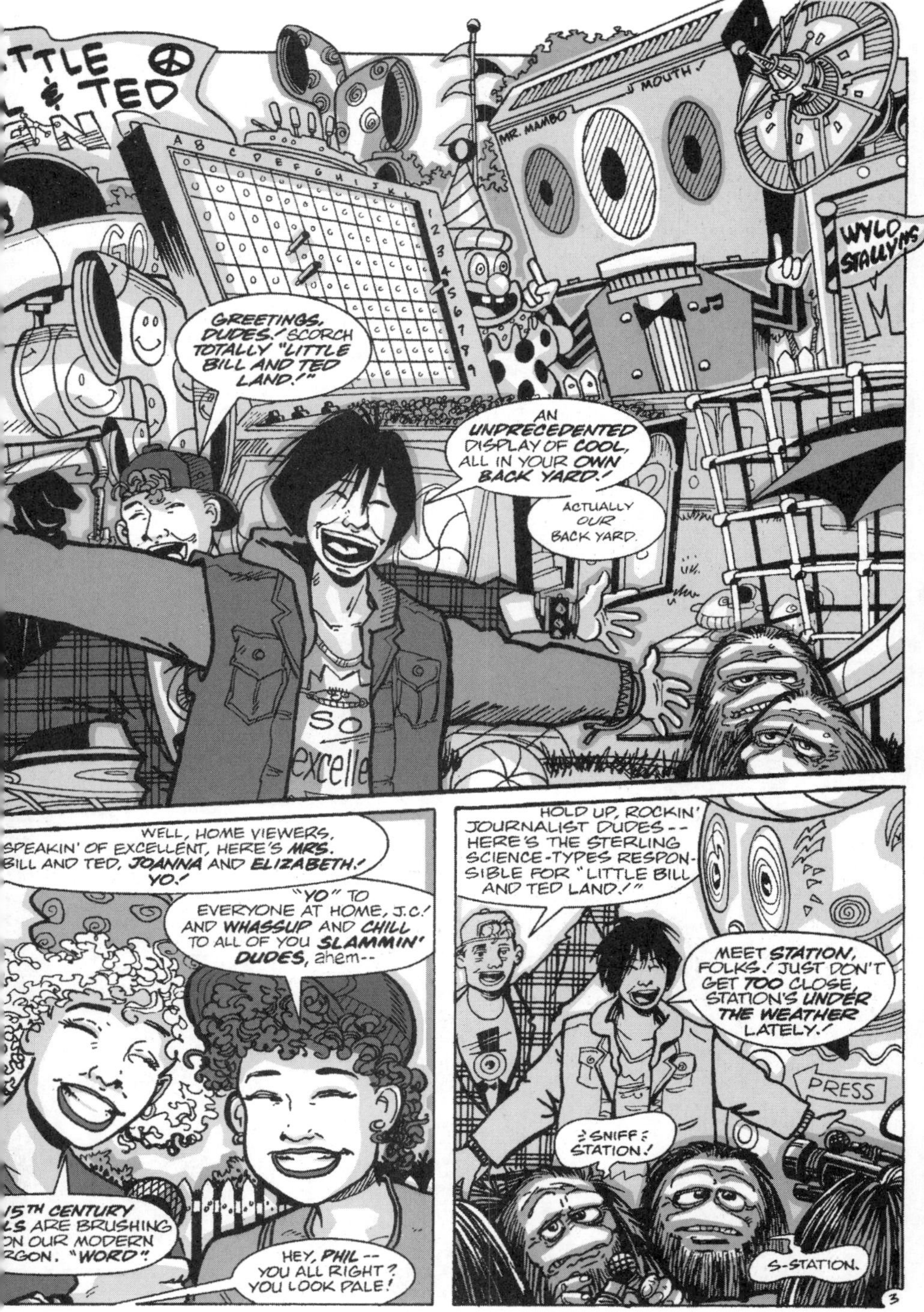
MR. MAMBO
MOUTH!
WYLD STALLYNS
GREETINGS, DUDES! SCORCH TOTALLY "LITTLE BILL AND TED LAND!"
AN UNPRECEDENTED DISPLAY OF COOL, ALL IN YOUR OWN BACK YARD!
ACTUALLY OUR BACK YARD.
WELL, HOME VIEWERS, SPEAKIN' OF EXCELLENT, HERE'S MRS. BILL AND TED, JOANNA AND ELIZABETH! YO!
"YO" TO EVERYONE AT HOME, J.C.! AND WHASSUP AND CHILL TO ALL OF YOU SLAMMIN' DUDES, ahem--
15TH CENTURY LS ARE BRUSHING ON OUR MODERN RGON. "WORD".
HEY, PHIL-- YOU ALL RIGHT? YOU LOOK PALE!
HOLD UP, ROCKIN' JOURNALIST DUDES-- HERE'S THE STERLING SCIENCE-TYPES RESPONSIBLE FOR "LITTLE BILL AND TED LAND!"
MEET STATION, FOLKS! JUST DON'T GET TOO CLOSE, STATION'S UNDER THE WEATHER LATELY!
PRESS
SNIFF STATION!
S-STATION.

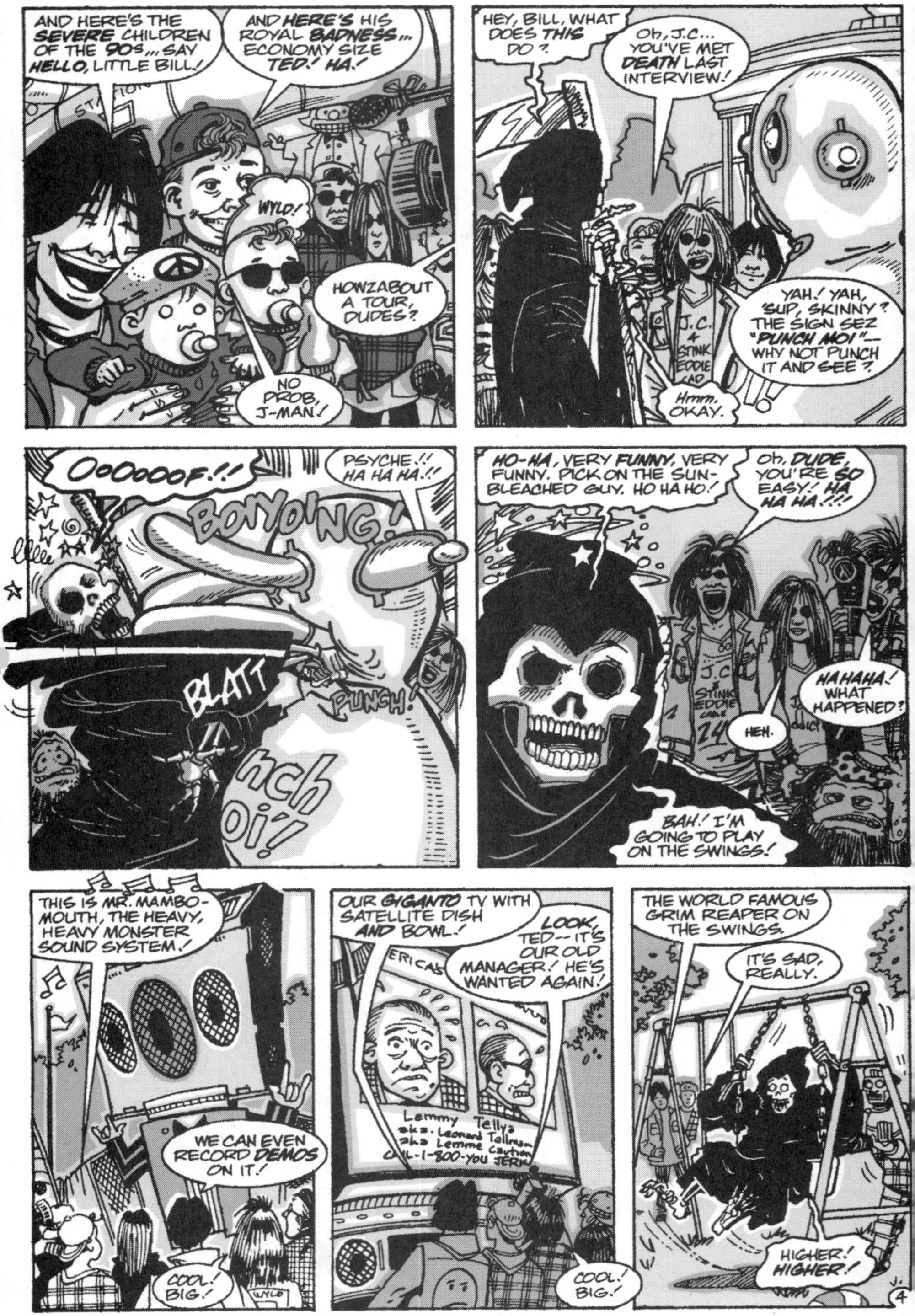
AND HERE'S THE SEVERE CHILDREN OF THE 90s... SAY HELLO, LITTLE BILL!
AND HERE'S HIS ROYAL BADNESS... ECONOMY SIZE TED! HA!
WYLD!
HOWZABOUT A TOUR, DUDES?
NO PROB, J-MAN!
HEY, BILL, WHAT DOES THIS DO?
Oh, J.C... YOU'VE MET DEATH LAST INTERVIEW!
J.C. 4 STINK EDDIE
YAH! YAH, 'SUP, SKINNY? THE SIGN SEZ "PUNCH MOI"— WHY NOT PUNCH IT AND SEE?
Hmm. OKAY.
OOOOOOOF!!
PSYCHE!!! HA HA HA!!
BOYOING!
BLATT
PUNCH!
nch oi!
HO-HA, VERY FUNNY, VERY FUNNY. PICK ON THE SUN-BLEACHED GUY. HO HA HO!
Oh, DUDE, YOU'RE SO EASY! HA HA HA!!!
HA HA HA! WHAT HAPPENED?
HEH.
BAH! I'M GOING TO PLAY ON THE SWINGS!
THIS IS MR. MAMBO-MOUTH, THE HEAVY, HEAVY MONSTER SOUND SYSTEM!
WE CAN EVEN RECORD DEMOS ON IT!
COOL! BIG!
WYLD
OUR GIGANTO TV WITH SATELLITE DISH AND BOWL!
LOOK, TED-- IT'S OUR OLD MANAGER! HE'S WANTED AGAIN!
Lemmy Tellya
aka. Leonard Tallman
aka Lemme Caution
1-800-YOU JERK
COOL! BIG!
THE WORLD FAMOUS GRIM REAPER ON THE SWINGS.
IT'S SAD, REALLY.
HIGHER! HIGHER!

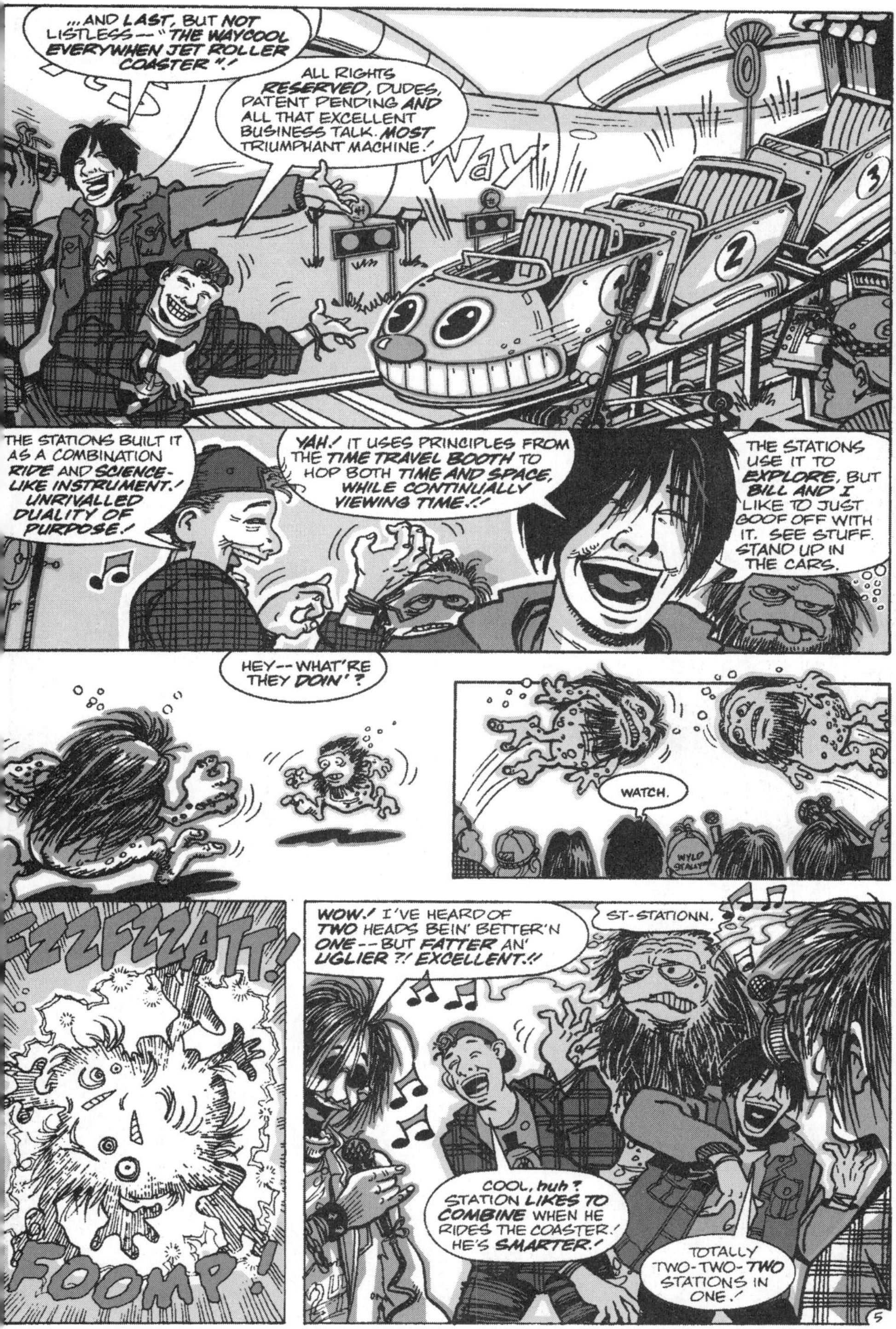
...AND LAST, BUT NOT LISTLESS -- "THE WAYCOOL EVERYWHEN JET ROLLER COASTER"!
ALL RIGHTS RESERVED, DUDES, PATENT PENDING AND ALL THAT EXCELLENT BUSINESS TALK. MOST TRIUMPHANT MACHINE!
WAY!
THE STATIONS BUILT IT AS A COMBINATION RIDE AND SCIENCE-LIKE INSTRUMENT! UNRIVALLED DUALITY OF PURPOSE!
YAH! IT USES PRINCIPLES FROM THE TIME TRAVEL BOOTH TO HOP BOTH TIME AND SPACE, WHILE CONTINUALLY VIEWING TIME!!
THE STATIONS USE IT TO EXPLORE, BUT BILL AND I LIKE TO JUST GOOF OFF WITH IT. SEE STUFF. STAND UP IN THE CARS.
HEY--WHAT'RE THEY DOIN'?
WATCH.
ZZZFZZATT!
FOOMP!
WOW! I'VE HEARD OF TWO HEADS BEIN' BETTER'N ONE--BUT FATTER AN' UGLIER?! EXCELLENT!!
ST-STATIONN.
COOL, huh? STATION LIKES TO COMBINE WHEN HE RIDES THE COASTER! HE'S SMARTER!
TOTALLY TWO-TWO-TWO STATIONS IN ONE!

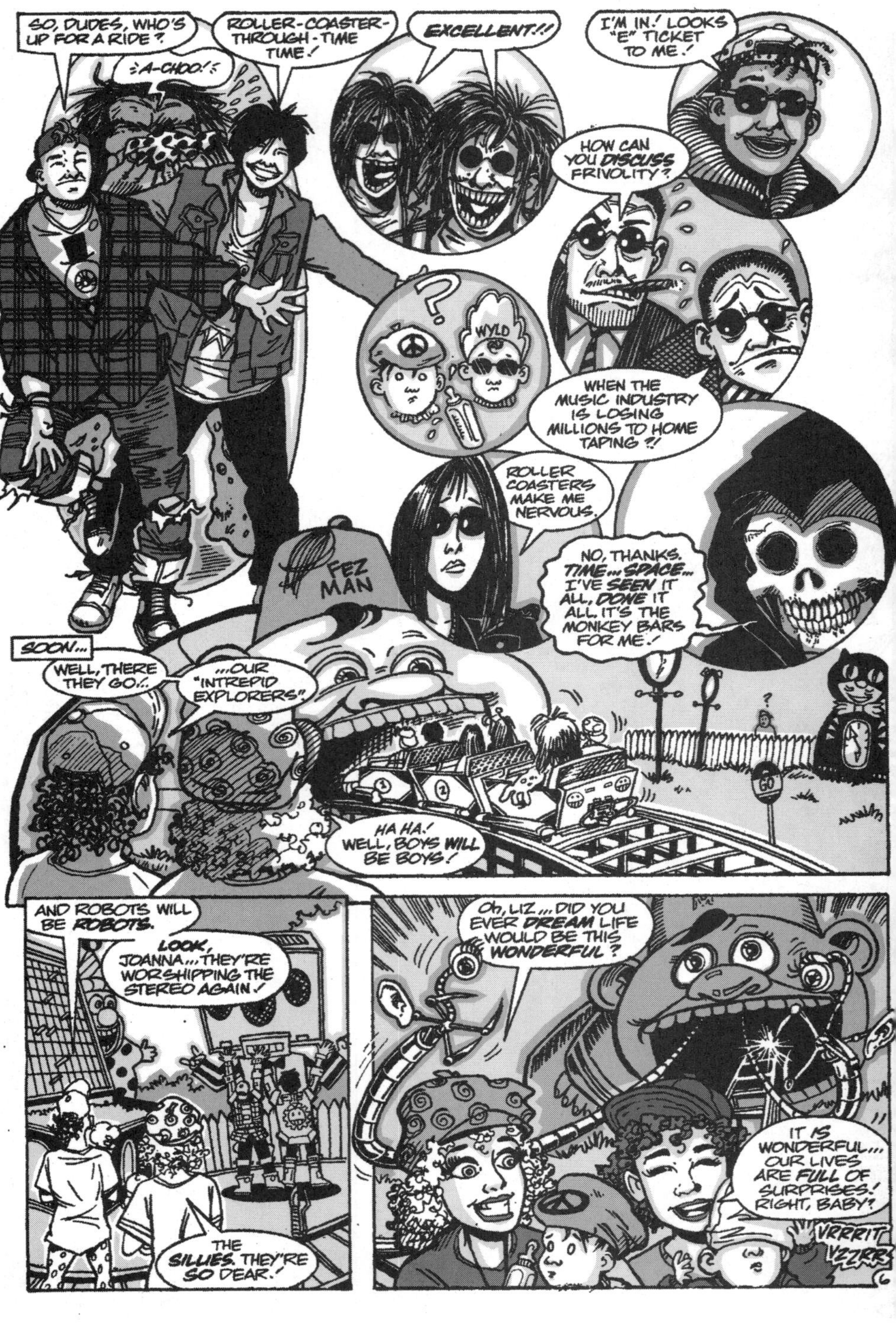

SO, DUDES, WHO'S UP FOR A RIDE?
A-CHOO!
ROLLER-COASTER-THROUGH-TIME TIME!
EXCELLENT!!!
I'M IN! LOOKS "E" TICKET TO ME!
HOW CAN YOU DISCUSS FRIVOLITY?
WYLD
WHEN THE MUSIC INDUSTRY IS LOSING MILLIONS TO HOME TAPING?!
ROLLER COASTERS MAKE ME NERVOUS.
FEZ MAN
NO, THANKS. TIME... SPACE... I'VE SEEN IT ALL, DONE IT ALL. IT'S THE MONKEY BARS FOR ME!
SOON...
WELL, THERE THEY GO...
...OUR "INTREPID EXPLORERS".
HA HA! WELL, BOYS WILL BE BOYS!
AND ROBOTS WILL BE ROBOTS.
LOOK, JOANNA... THEY'RE WORSHIPPING THE STEREO AGAIN!
THE SILLIES. THEY'RE SO DEAR!
Oh, LIZ... DID YOU EVER DREAM LIFE WOULD BE THIS WONDERFUL?
IT IS WONDERFUL... OUR LIVES ARE FULL OF SURPRISES! RIGHT, BABY?
VRRRIT
VZZRR

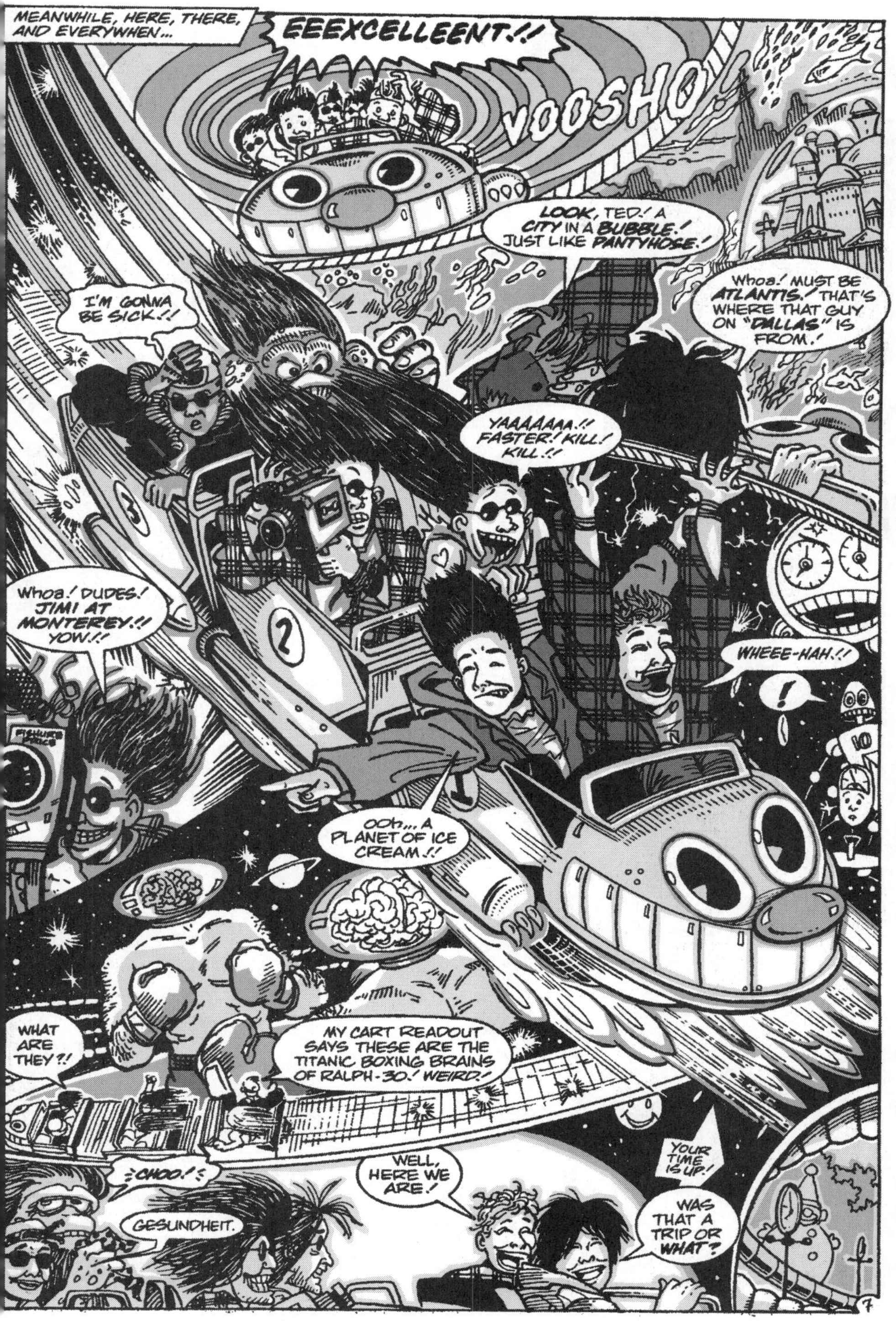

MEANWHILE, HERE, THERE, AND EVERYWHEN...
EEEXCELLEENT.!!
VOOSHOO
LOOK, TED! A CITY IN A BUBBLE! JUST LIKE PANTYHOSE!
I'M GONNA BE SICK!!
Whoa! MUST BE ATLANTIS! THAT'S WHERE THAT GUY ON "DALLAS" IS FROM!
YAAAAAAA!! FASTER! KILL! KILL!!
Whoa! DUDES! JIMI AT MONTEREY!! YOW!!
WHEEE-HAH!!
!
Ooh... A PLANET OF ICE CREAM!!
WHAT ARE THEY?!
MY CART READOUT SAYS THESE ARE THE TITANIC BOXING BRAINS OF RALPH-30! WEIRD!
YOUR TIME IS UP!
CHOO!
GESUNDHEIT.
WELL, HERE WE ARE!
WAS THAT A TRIP OR WHAT?

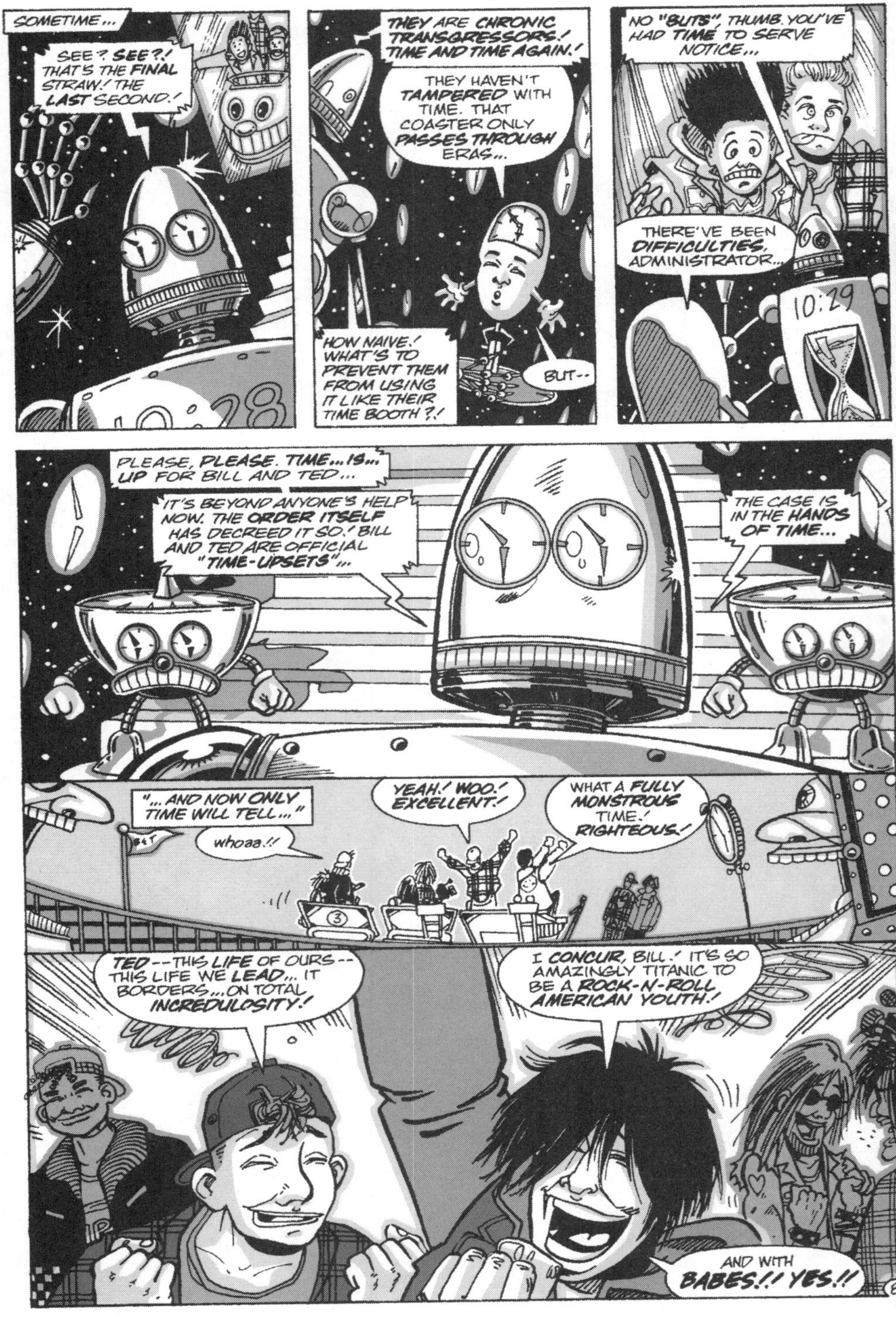
SOMETIME...
SEE? SEE?! THAT'S THE FINAL STRAW! THE LAST SECOND!
THEY ARE CHRONIC TRANSGRESSORS! TIME AND TIME AGAIN!
THEY HAVEN'T TAMPERED WITH TIME. THAT COASTER ONLY PASSES THROUGH ERAS...
HOW NAIVE! WHAT'S TO PREVENT THEM FROM USING IT LIKE THEIR TIME BOOTH?!
BUT--
NO "BUTS", THUMB. YOU'VE HAD TIME TO SERVE NOTICE...
THERE'VE BEEN DIFFICULTIES, ADMINISTRATOR...
10:29
PLEASE, PLEASE. TIME...IS... UP FOR BILL AND TED...
IT'S BEYOND ANYONE'S HELP NOW. THE ORDER ITSELF HAS DECREED IT SO! BILL AND TED ARE OFFICIAL "TIME-UPSETS"...
THE CASE IS IN THE HANDS OF TIME...
"...AND NOW ONLY TIME WILL TELL..."
whoaa!!
YEAH! WOO! EXCELLENT!
WHAT A FULLY MONSTROUS TIME! RIGHTEOUS!
TED--THIS LIFE OF OURS--THIS LIFE WE LEAD... IT BORDERS...ON TOTAL INCREDULOSITY!
I CONCUR, BILL! IT'S SO AMAZINGLY TITANIC TO BE A ROCK-N-ROLL AMERICAN YOUTH!
AND WITH BABES!! YES!!

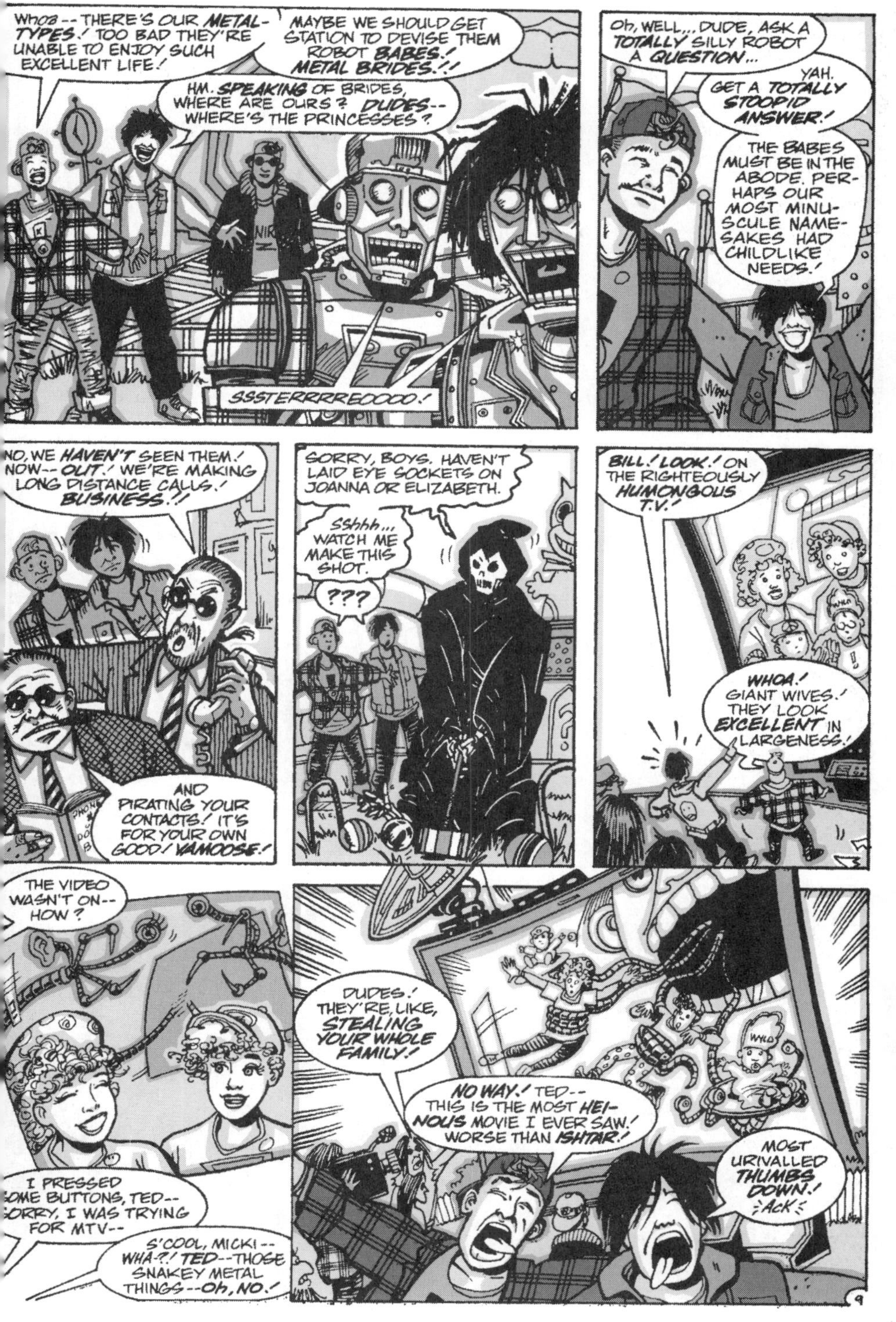
Whoa -- THERE'S OUR METAL-TYPES! TOO BAD THEY'RE UNABLE TO ENJOY SUCH EXCELLENT LIFE!
MAYBE WE SHOULD GET STATION TO DEVISE THEM ROBOT BABES! METAL BRIDES!!
HM. SPEAKING OF BRIDES, WHERE ARE OURS? DUDES--WHERE'S THE PRINCESSES?
SSSTERRRRREOOOOO!
Oh, WELL... DUDE, ASK A TOTALLY SILLY ROBOT A QUESTION...
YAH. GET A TOTALLY STOOPID ANSWER!
THE BABES MUST BE IN THE ABODE. PER-HAPS OUR MOST MINU-SCULE NAME-SAKES HAD CHILDLIKE NEEDS!
NO, WE HAVEN'T SEEN THEM! NOW-- OUT! WE'RE MAKING LONG DISTANCE CALLS! BUSINESS!!
AND PIRATING YOUR CONTACTS! IT'S FOR YOUR OWN GOOD! VAMOOSE!
SORRY, BOYS. HAVEN'T LAID EYE SOCKETS ON JOANNA OR ELIZABETH.
Sshhh... WATCH ME MAKE THIS SHOT.
???
BILL! LOOK! ON THE RIGHTEOUSLY HUMONGOUS T.V.!
WHOA! GIANT WIVES! THEY LOOK EXCELLENT IN LARGENESS!
THE VIDEO WASN'T ON-- HOW?
I PRESSED SOME BUTTONS, TED-- SORRY, I WAS TRYING FOR MTV--
S'COOL, MICKI-- WHA-?! TED--THOSE SNAKEY METAL THINGS--Oh, NO!
DUDES! THEY'RE, LIKE, STEALING YOUR WHOLE FAMILY!
NO WAY! TED-- THIS IS THE MOST HEI-NOUS MOVIE I EVER SAW! WORSE THAN ISHTAR!
MOST URIVALLED THUMBS DOWN! ACK

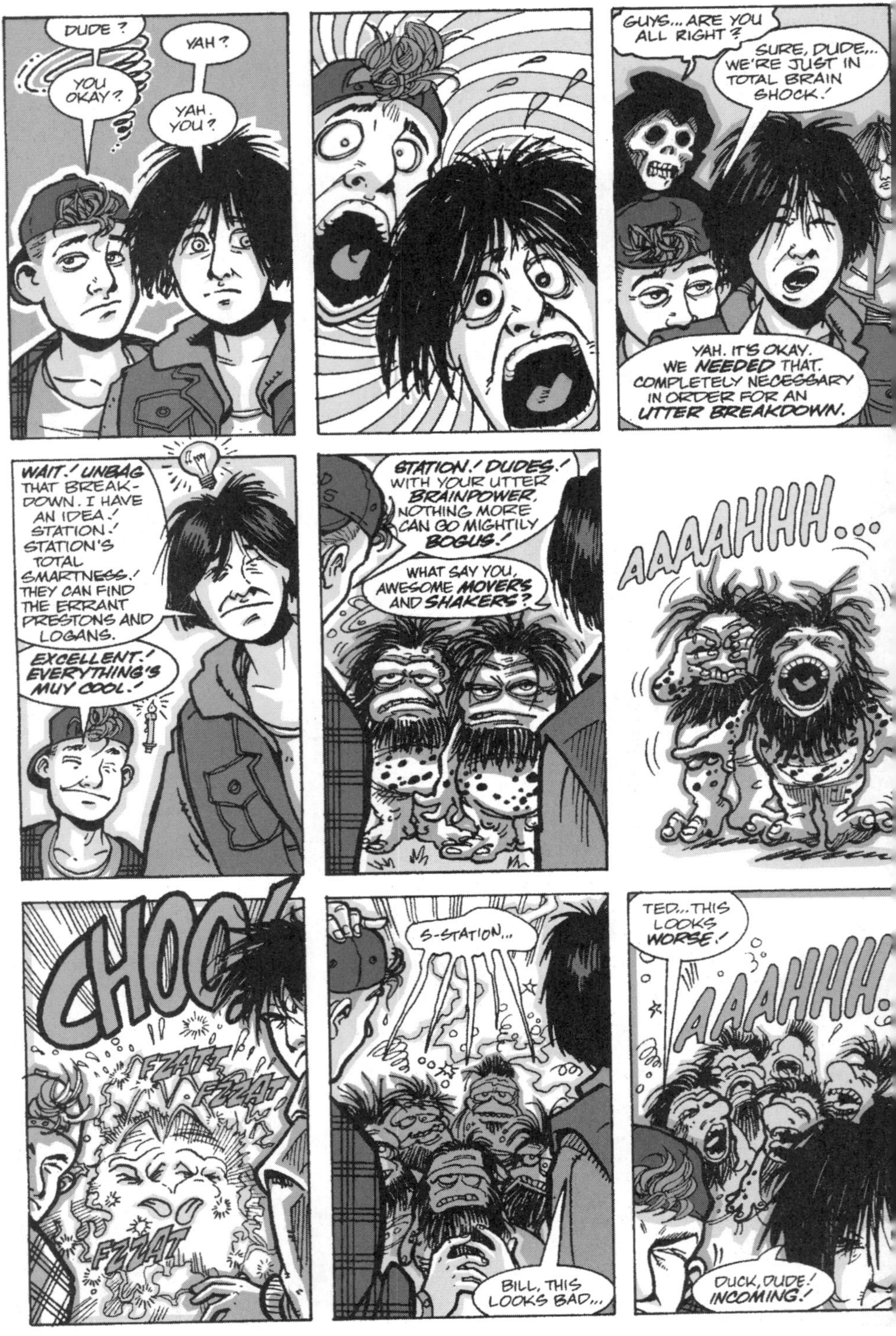
DUDE?
YOU OKAY?
YAH?
YAH. YOU?
GUYS... ARE YOU ALL RIGHT?
SURE, DUDE... WE'RE JUST IN TOTAL BRAIN SHOCK!
YAH. IT'S OKAY. WE NEEDED THAT. COMPLETELY NECESSARY IN ORDER FOR AN UTTER BREAKDOWN.
WAIT! UNBAG THAT BREAK-DOWN. I HAVE AN IDEA! STATION! STATION'S TOTAL SMARTNESS! THEY CAN FIND THE ERRANT PRESTONS AND LOGANS.
EXCELLENT! EVERYTHING'S MUY COOL!
STATION! DUDES! WITH YOUR UTTER BRAINPOWER, NOTHING MORE CAN GO MIGHTILY BOGUS!
WHAT SAY YOU, AWESOME MOVERS AND SHAKERS?
AAAAHHH...
CHOO!
FZZAT
FZZAT
FZZAT
S-STATION...
BILL, THIS LOOKS BAD...
TED... THIS LOOKS WORSE!
AAAHHH!
DUCK, DUDE! INCOMING!

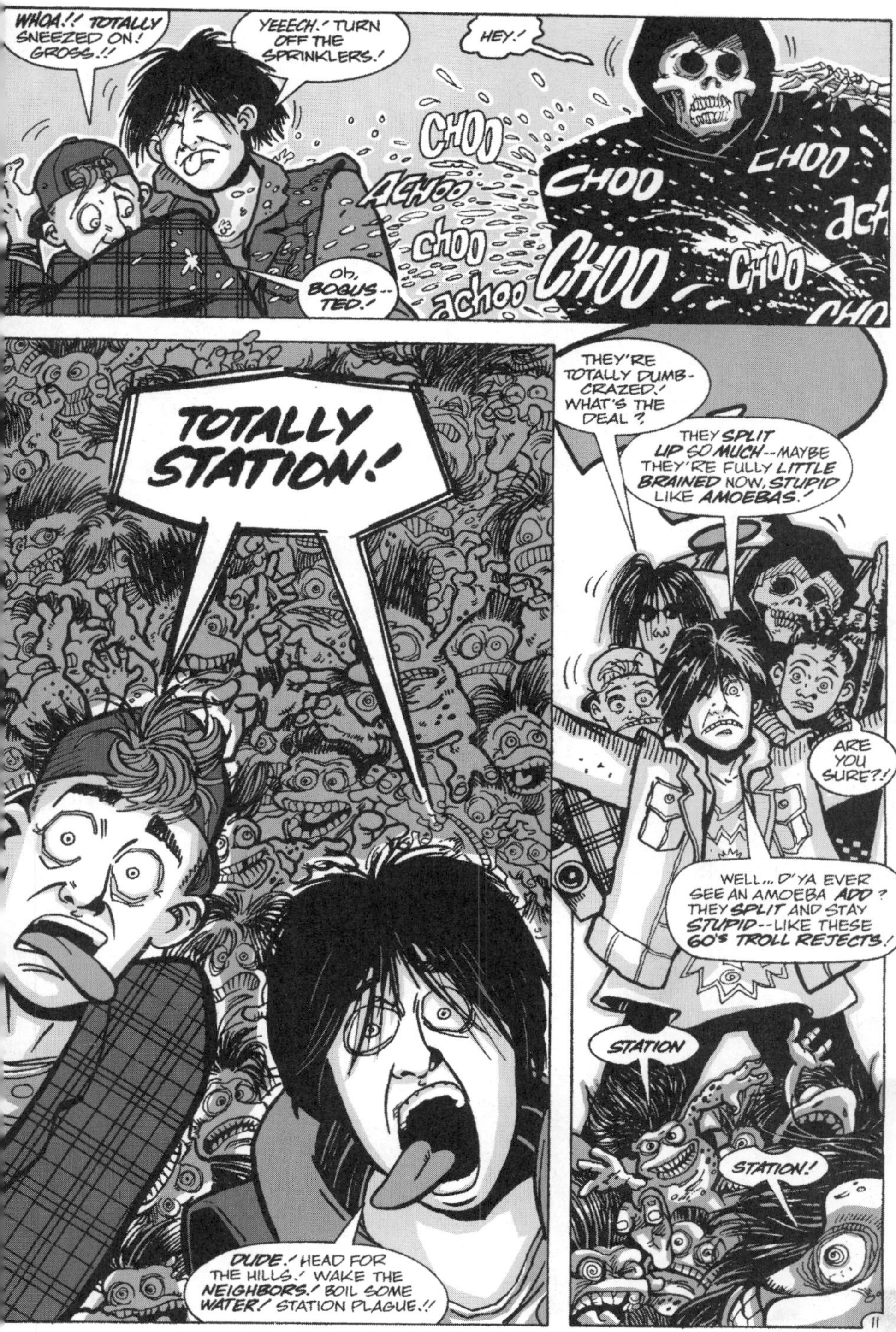
WHOA!! TOTALLY SNEEZED ON! GROSS!!
YEEECH! TURN OFF THE SPRINKLERS!
HEY!
Oh, BOGUS-- TED!
ACHOO
CHOO
choo
achoo
CHOO
CHOO
CHOO
ach
CHOO
CHOO
TOTALLY STATION!
DUDE! HEAD FOR THE HILLS! WAKE THE NEIGHBORS! BOIL SOME WATER! STATION PLAGUE!!
THEY'RE TOTALLY DUMB-CRAZED! WHAT'S THE DEAL?
THEY SPLIT UP SO MUCH--MAYBE THEY'RE FULLY LITTLE BRAINED NOW, STUPID LIKE AMOEBAS!
ARE YOU SURE?!
WELL... D'YA EVER SEE AN AMOEBA ADD? THEY SPLIT AND STAY STUPID--LIKE THESE 60's TROLL REJECTS!
STATION
STATION!

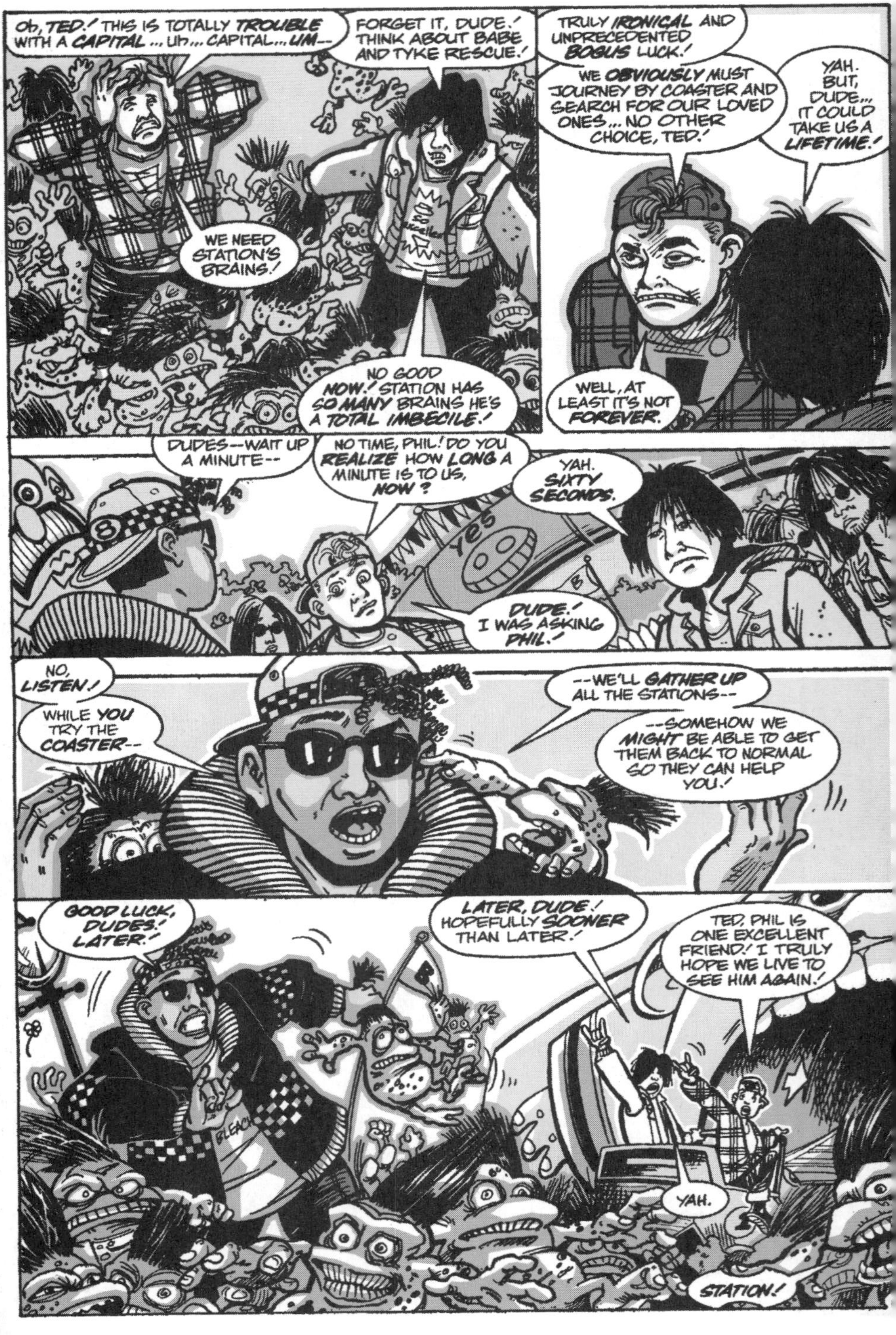

Oh, TED! THIS IS TOTALLY TROUBLE WITH A CAPITAL ... Uh... CAPITAL... UM--
FORGET IT, DUDE! THINK ABOUT BABE AND TYKE RESCUE!
WE NEED STATION'S BRAINS!
NO GOOD NOW! STATION HAS SO MANY BRAINS HE'S A TOTAL IMBECILE!
TRULY IRONICAL AND UNPRECEDENTED BOGUS LUCK!
WE OBVIOUSLY MUST JOURNEY BY COASTER AND SEARCH FOR OUR LOVED ONES... NO OTHER CHOICE, TED!
YAH. BUT, DUDE... IT COULD TAKE US A LIFETIME!
WELL, AT LEAST IT'S NOT FOREVER.
DUDES--WAIT UP A MINUTE--
NO TIME, PHIL! DO YOU REALIZE HOW LONG A MINUTE IS TO US, NOW?
YAH. SIXTY SECONDS.
DUDE! I WAS ASKING PHIL!
NO, LISTEN!
WHILE YOU TRY THE COASTER--
--WE'LL GATHER UP ALL THE STATIONS--
--SOMEHOW WE MIGHT BE ABLE TO GET THEM BACK TO NORMAL SO THEY CAN HELP YOU!
GOOD LUCK, DUDES! LATER!
LATER, DUDE! HOPEFULLY SOONER THAN LATER!
TED, PHIL IS ONE EXCELLENT FRIEND! I TRULY HOPE WE LIVE TO SEE HIM AGAIN!
YAH.
STATION!

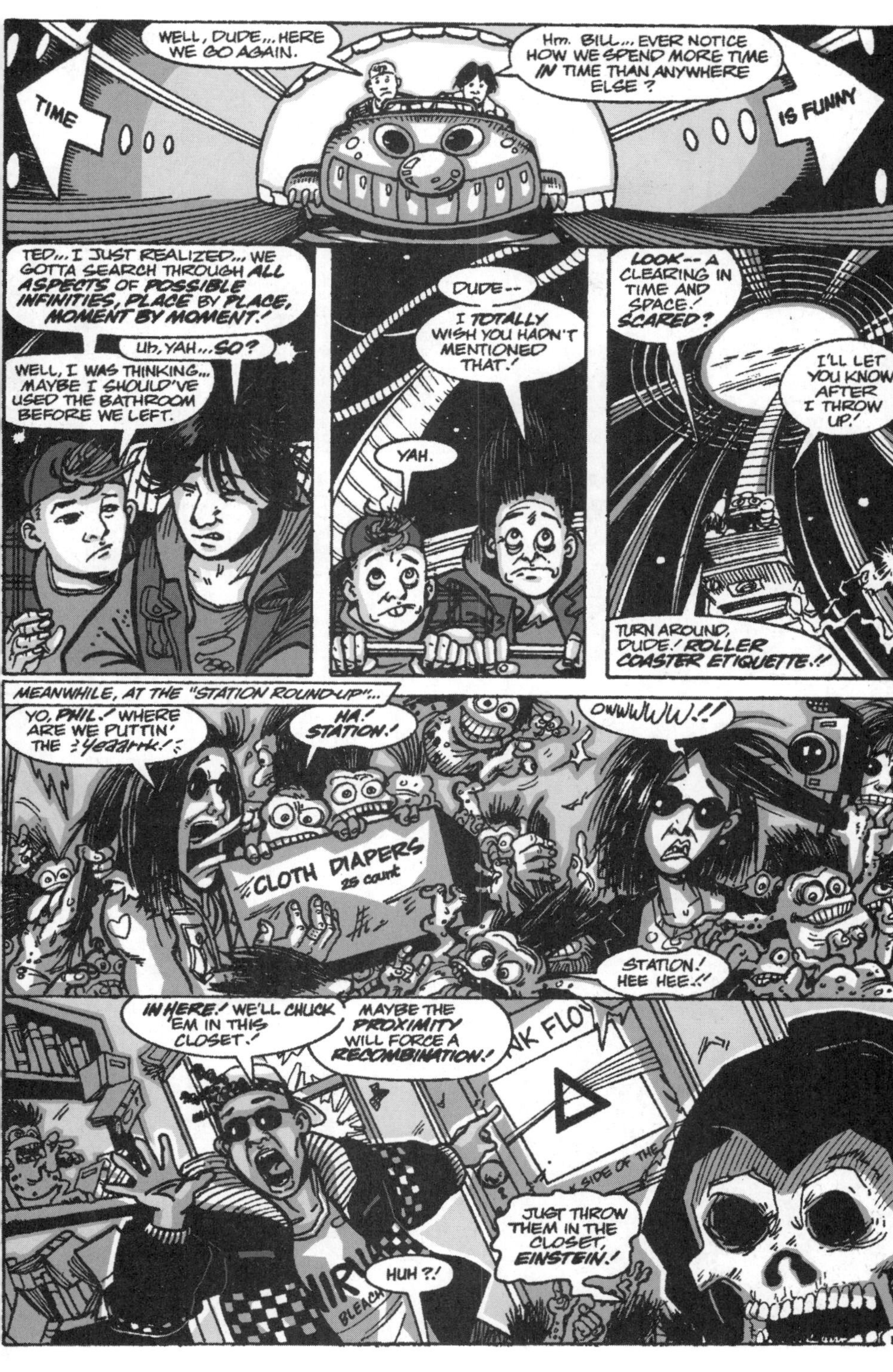

WELL, DUDE... HERE WE GO AGAIN.
Hm. BILL... EVER NOTICE HOW WE SPEND MORE TIME IN TIME THAN ANYWHERE ELSE?
TIME
IS FUNNY
TED... I JUST REALIZED... WE GOTTA SEARCH THROUGH ALL ASPECTS OF POSSIBLE INFINITIES, PLACE BY PLACE, MOMENT BY MOMENT!
Uh, YAH... SO?
WELL, I WAS THINKING... MAYBE I SHOULD'VE USED THE BATHROOM BEFORE WE LEFT.
DUDE--
I TOTALLY WISH YOU HADN'T MENTIONED THAT!
YAH.
LOOK-- A CLEARING IN TIME AND SPACE! SCARED?
I'LL LET YOU KNOW AFTER I THROW UP!
TURN AROUND, DUDE! ROLLER COASTER ETIQUETTE!!
MEANWHILE, AT THE "STATION ROUND-UP"...
YO, PHIL! WHERE ARE WE PUTTIN' THE Yeaarrk!
HA! STATION!
OWWWWW!!
CLOTH DIAPERS
25 count
STATION! HEE HEE!!
IN HERE! WE'LL CHUCK 'EM IN THIS CLOSET!
MAYBE THE PROXIMITY WILL FORCE A RECOMBINATION!
NK FLO
SIDE OF THE
JUST THROW THEM IN THE CLOSET, EINSTEIN!
HUH?!
BLEACH

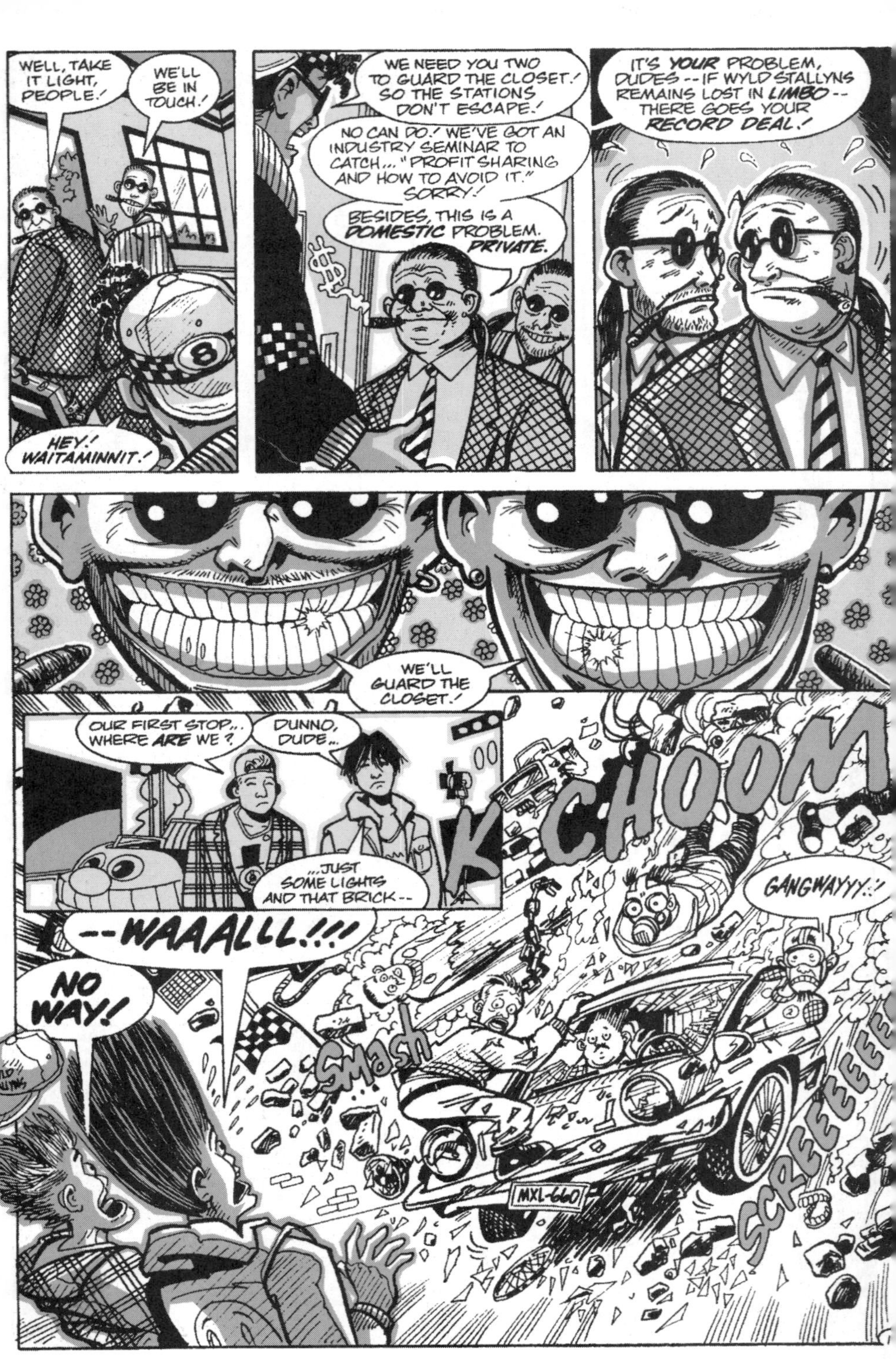
WELL, TAKE IT LIGHT, PEOPLE.!
WE'LL BE IN TOUCH.!
HEY.! WAITAMINNIT.!
WE NEED YOU TWO TO GUARD THE CLOSET.! SO THE STATIONS DON'T ESCAPE.!
NO CAN DO.! WE'VE GOT AN INDUSTRY SEMINAR TO CATCH... "PROFIT SHARING AND HOW TO AVOID IT." SORRY.!
BESIDES, THIS IS A DOMESTIC PROBLEM. PRIVATE.
IT'S YOUR PROBLEM, DUDES -- IF WYLD STALLYNS REMAINS LOST IN LIMBO -- THERE GOES YOUR RECORD DEAL.!
WE'LL GUARD THE CLOSET.!
OUR FIRST STOP... WHERE ARE WE ?
DUNNO, DUDE...
...JUST SOME LIGHTS AND THAT BRICK --
--WAAALLL.!!!!
NO WAY!
KCHOOM
GANGWAYYY.!.!
SMASH
SCREEEEEE
MXL-660
WYLD STALLYNS

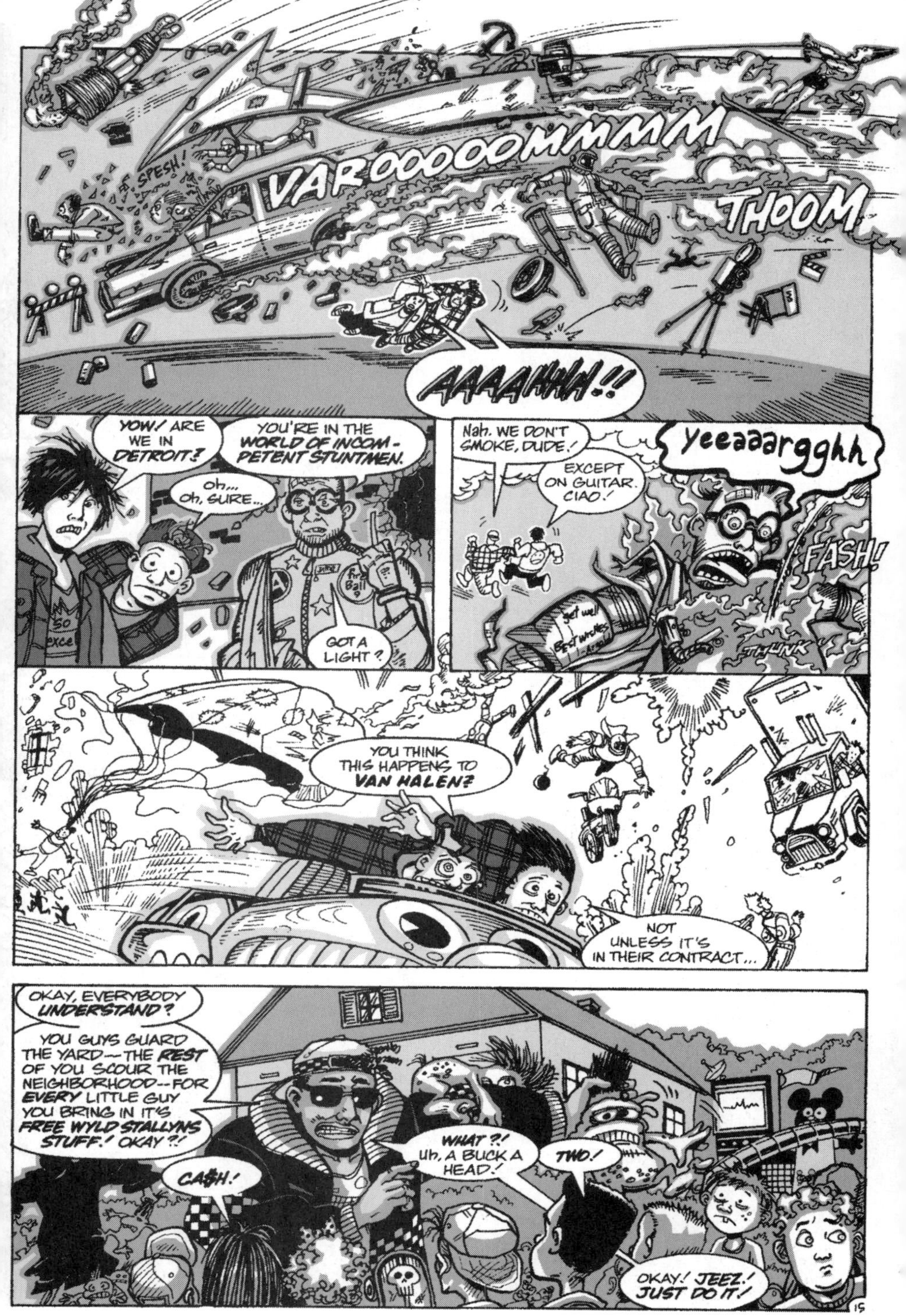

SPESH!
VAROOOOOOMMMMM
THOOM
AAAAHHH!!
YOW! ARE WE IN DETROIT?
YOU'RE IN THE WORLD OF INCOMPETENT STUNTMEN.
oh... oh, SURE...
GOT A LIGHT?
Nah. WE DON'T SMOKE, DUDE!
EXCEPT ON GUITAR. CIAO!
yeeaaargghh
FASH!
get well
Best wishes
THUNK
YOU THINK THIS HAPPENS TO VAN HALEN?
NOT UNLESS IT'S IN THEIR CONTRACT...
OKAY, EVERYBODY UNDERSTAND?
YOU GUYS GUARD THE YARD-- THE REST OF YOU SCOUR THE NEIGHBORHOOD-- FOR EVERY LITTLE GUY YOU BRING IN IT'S FREE WYLD STALLYNS STUFF! OKAY?!
CA$H!
WHAT?! Uh, A BUCK A HEAD!
TWO!
OKAY! JEEZ! JUST DO IT!

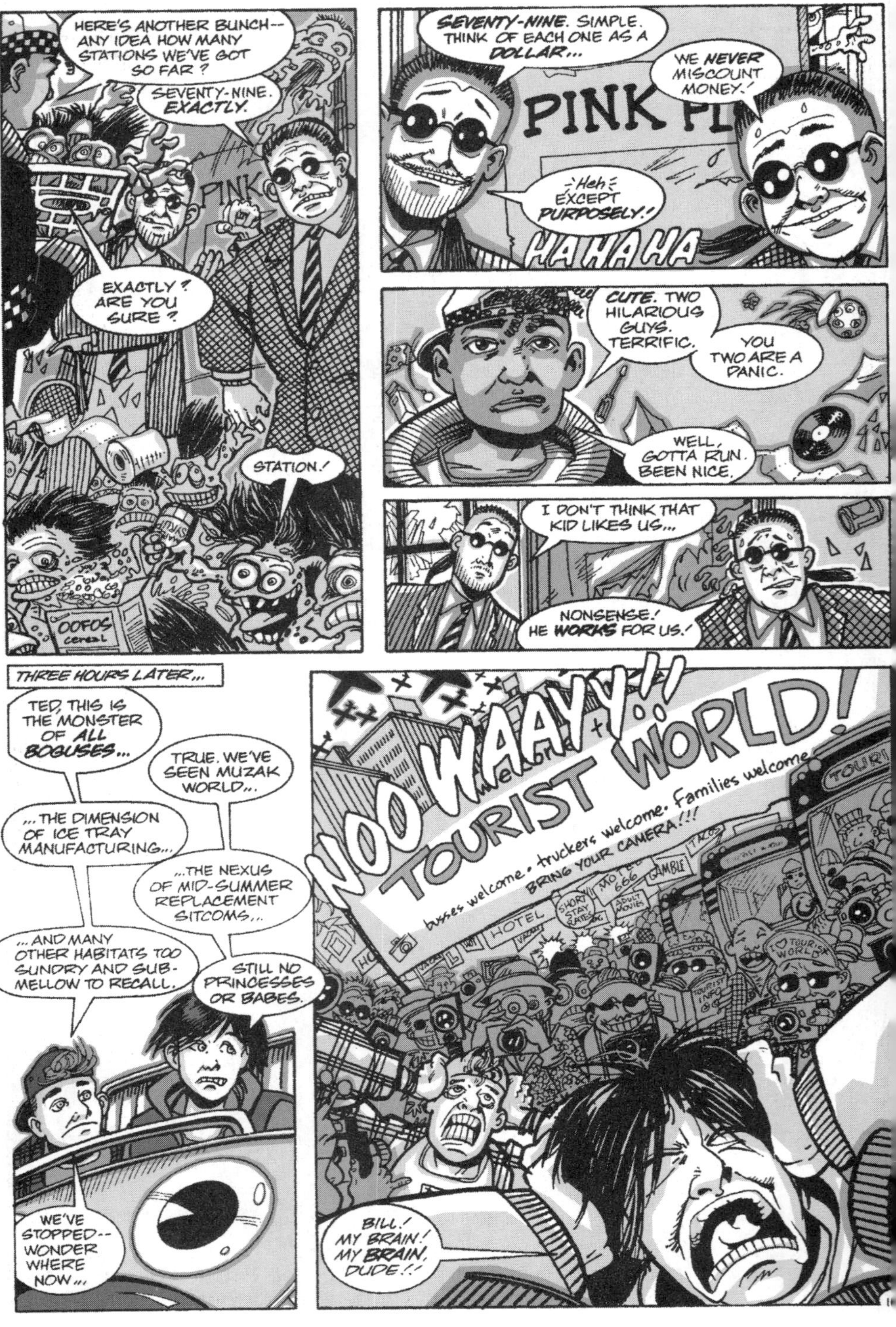

HERE'S ANOTHER BUNCH-- ANY IDEA HOW MANY STATIONS WE'VE GOT SO FAR?
SEVENTY-NINE. EXACTLY.
PINK
EXACTLY? ARE YOU SURE?
STATION!
OOFOS cereal
SEVENTY-NINE. SIMPLE. THINK OF EACH ONE AS A DOLLAR...
WE NEVER MISCOUNT MONEY!
PINK PI
-Heh- EXCEPT PURPOSELY!
HAHAHA
CUTE. TWO HILARIOUS GUYS. TERRIFIC.
YOU TWO ARE A PANIC.
WELL, GOTTA RUN. BEEN NICE.
I DON'T THINK THAT KID LIKES US...
NONSENSE! HE WORKS FOR US!
THREE HOURS LATER...
TED, THIS IS THE MONSTER OF ALL BOGUSES...
TRUE. WE'VE SEEN MUZAK WORLD...
...THE DIMENSION OF ICE TRAY MANUFACTURING...
...THE NEXUS OF MID-SUMMER REPLACEMENT SITCOMS...
...AND MANY OTHER HABITATS TOO SUNDRY AND SUB-MELLOW TO RECALL.
STILL NO PRINCESSES OR BABES.
WE'VE STOPPED-- WONDER WHERE NOW...
NOO WAAAYY!!
TOURIST WORLD!
busses welcome. truckers welcome. Families welcome
BRING YOUR CAMERA!!!
HOTEL
GAMBLE
ADULT MOVIES
SHORT STAY RATES
BILL! MY BRAIN! MY BRAIN, DUDE!!

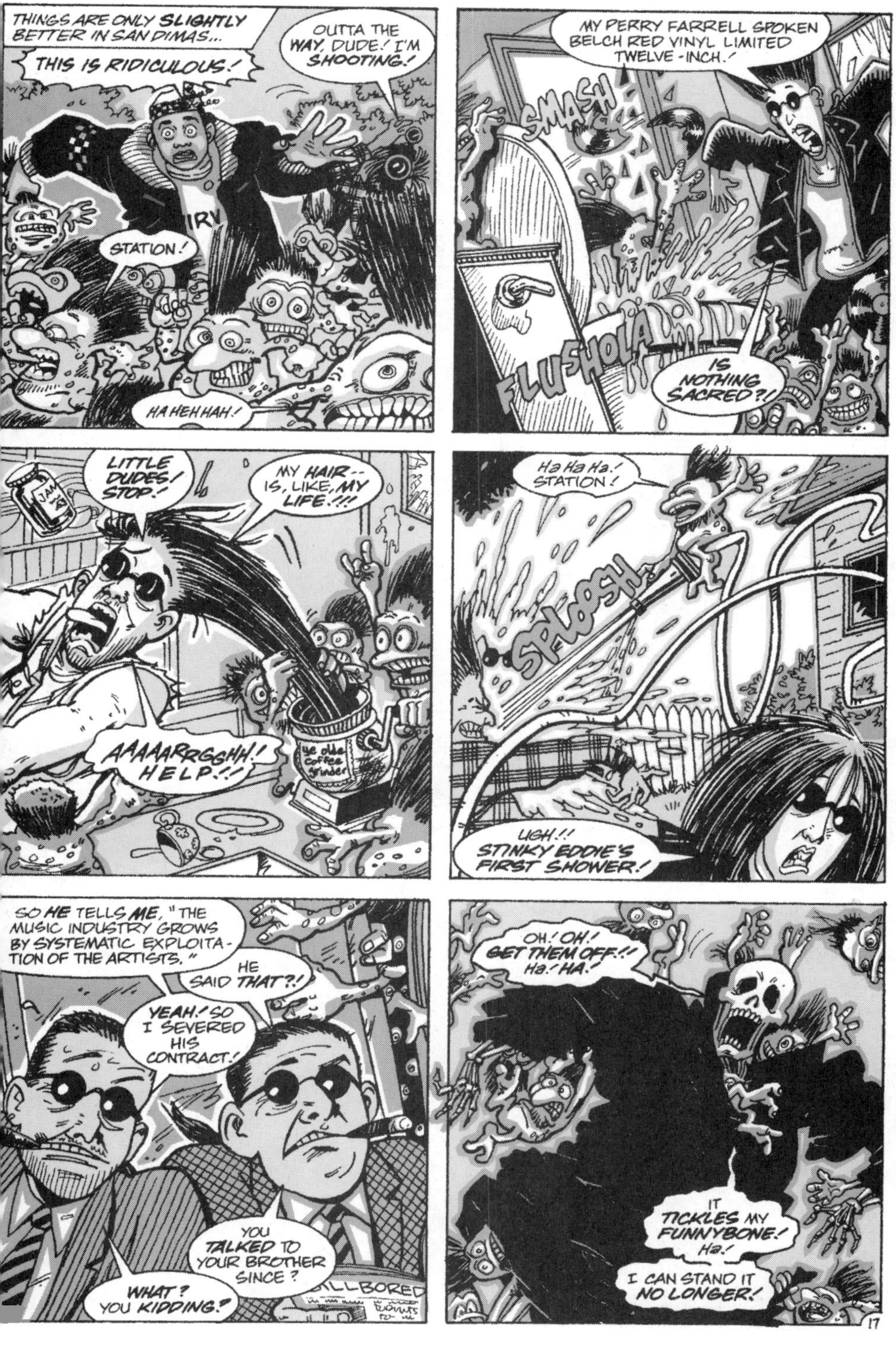
THINGS ARE ONLY SLIGHTLY BETTER IN SAN DIMAS...
THIS IS RIDICULOUS!
OUTTA THE WAY, DUDE! I'M SHOOTING!
STATION!
HA HEH HAH!
MY PERRY FARRELL SPOKEN BELCH RED VINYL LIMITED TWELVE-INCH!
SMASH
FLUSHOLA
IS NOTHING SACRED?!
LITTLE DUDES! STOP!
MY HAIR-- IS, LIKE, MY LIFE!!!
JAM
ye olde coffee grinder
AAAAARRGGHH! HELP!!!
Ha Ha Ha! STATION!
SPLOOSH
UGH!!! STINKY EDDIE'S FIRST SHOWER!
SO HE TELLS ME, "THE MUSIC INDUSTRY GROWS BY SYSTEMATIC EXPLOITATION OF THE ARTISTS."
HE SAID THAT?!
YEAH! SO I SEVERED HIS CONTRACT!
YOU TALKED TO YOUR BROTHER SINCE?
WHAT? YOU KIDDING?
BILLBORED
OH! OH! GET THEM OFF!!! Ha! HA!
IT TICKLES MY FUNNYBONE! Ha!
I CAN STAND IT NO LONGER!

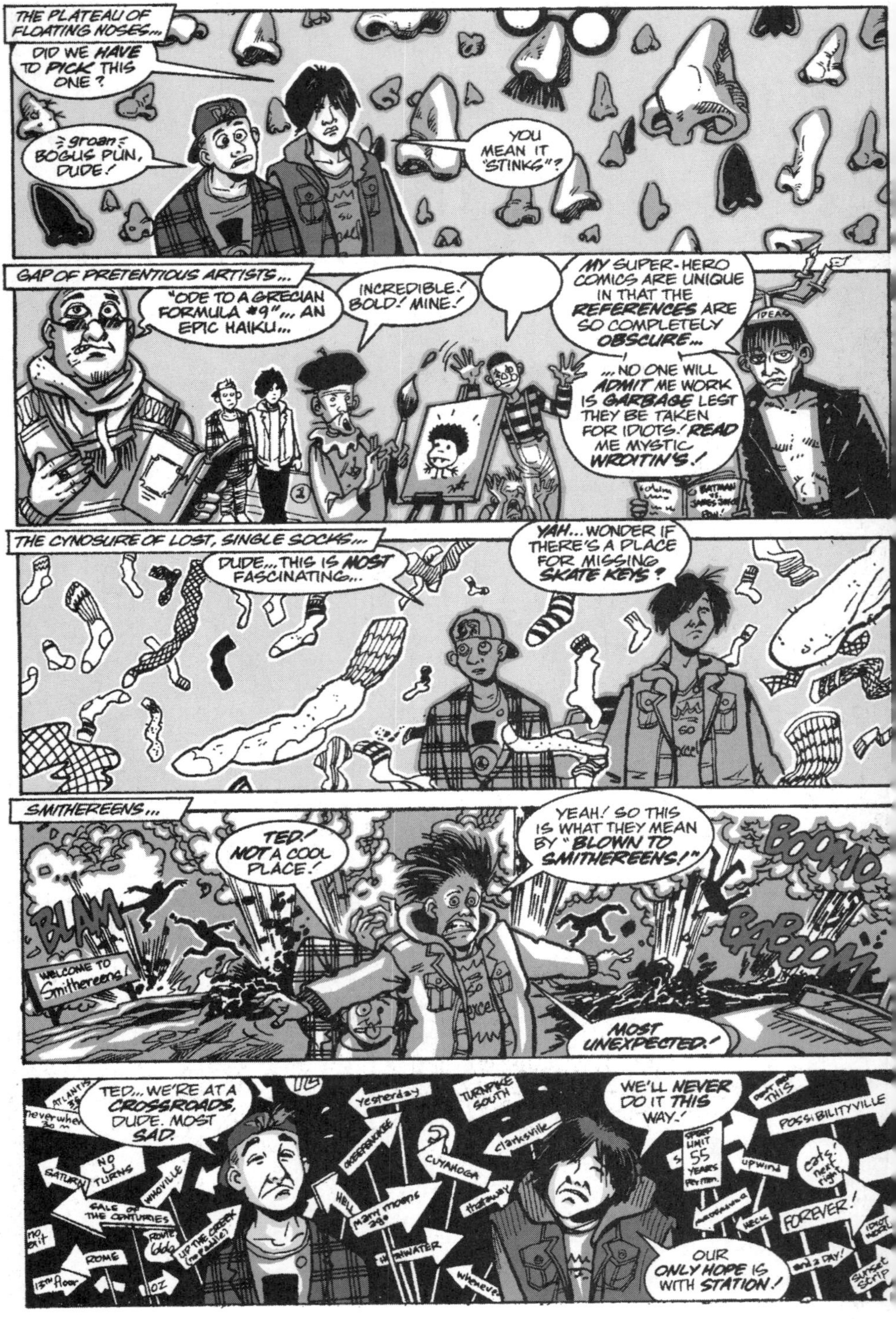
THE PLATEAU OF FLOATING NOSES...
DID WE HAVE TO PICK THIS ONE?
groan BOGUS PUN, DUDE!
YOU MEAN IT "STINKS"?
GAP OF PRETENTIOUS ARTISTS...
"ODE TO A GRECIAN FORMULA #9"... AN EPIC HAIKU...
INCREDIBLE! BOLD! MINE!
MY SUPER-HERO COMICS ARE UNIQUE IN THAT THE REFERENCES ARE SO COMPLETELY OBSCURE...
...NO ONE WILL ADMIT ME WORK IS GARBAGE LEST THEY BE TAKEN FOR IDIOTS! READ ME MYSTIC WROITIN'S!
IDEA
THE CYNOSURE OF LOST, SINGLE SOCKS...
DUDE... THIS IS MOST FASCINATING...
YAH... WONDER IF THERE'S A PLACE FOR MISSING SKATE KEYS?
SMITHEREENS...
TED! NOT A COOL PLACE!
YEAH! SO THIS IS WHAT THEY MEAN BY "BLOWN TO SMITHEREENS!"
BLAM
BOOM
BAROOM
WELCOME TO Smithereens!
MOST UNEXPECTED!
TED... WE'RE AT A CROSSROADS, DUDE. MOST SAD.
WE'LL NEVER DO IT THIS WAY!
Yesterday
TURNPIKE SOUTH
POSSIBILITYVILLE
NO U TURNS
SATURN
WHOVILLE
CUYAHOGA
clarksville
SPEED LIMIT 55 YEARS
upwind
HELL
SALE OF THE CENTURIES
no exit
ROME
OZ
13th floor
FOREVER!
OUR ONLY HOPE IS WITH STATION!

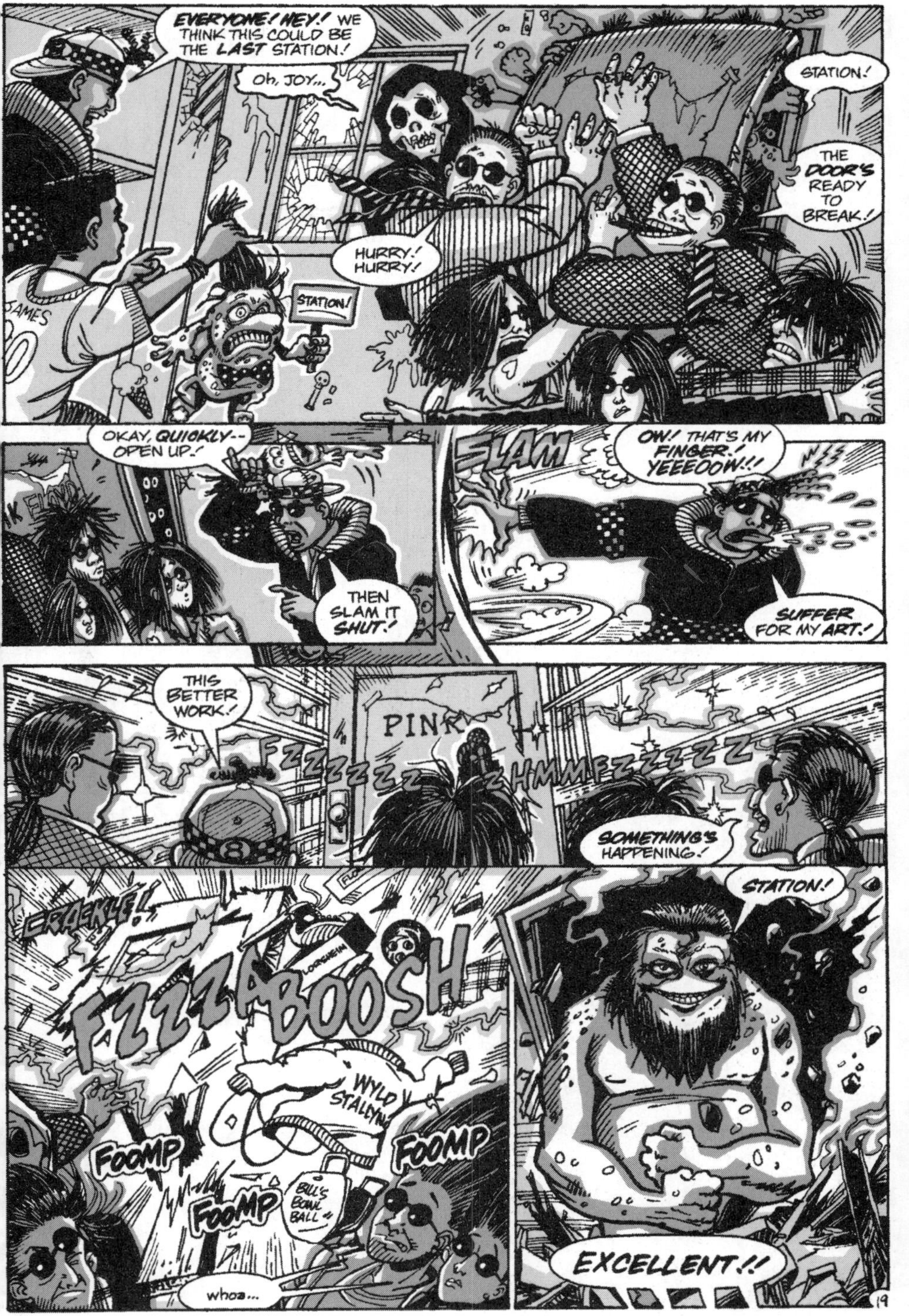
EVERYONE! HEY! WE THINK THIS COULD BE THE LAST STATION!
Oh, JOY...
STATION!
THE DOOR'S READY TO BREAK!
HURRY! HURRY!
STATION!
JAMES
OKAY, QUICKLY-- OPEN UP!
THEN SLAM IT SHUT!
SLAM
OW! THAT'S MY FINGER! YEEEOOW!!!
SUFFER FOR MY ART!
THIS BETTER WORK!
PINK
FZZZZZZ HMMFZZZZZZZ
SOMETHING'S HAPPENING!
CRACKLE!
FZZZABOOSH
WYLD STALLYNS
FOOMP
FOOMP
FOOMP
BILL'S BOWL BALL
whoa...
STATION!
EXCELLENT!!

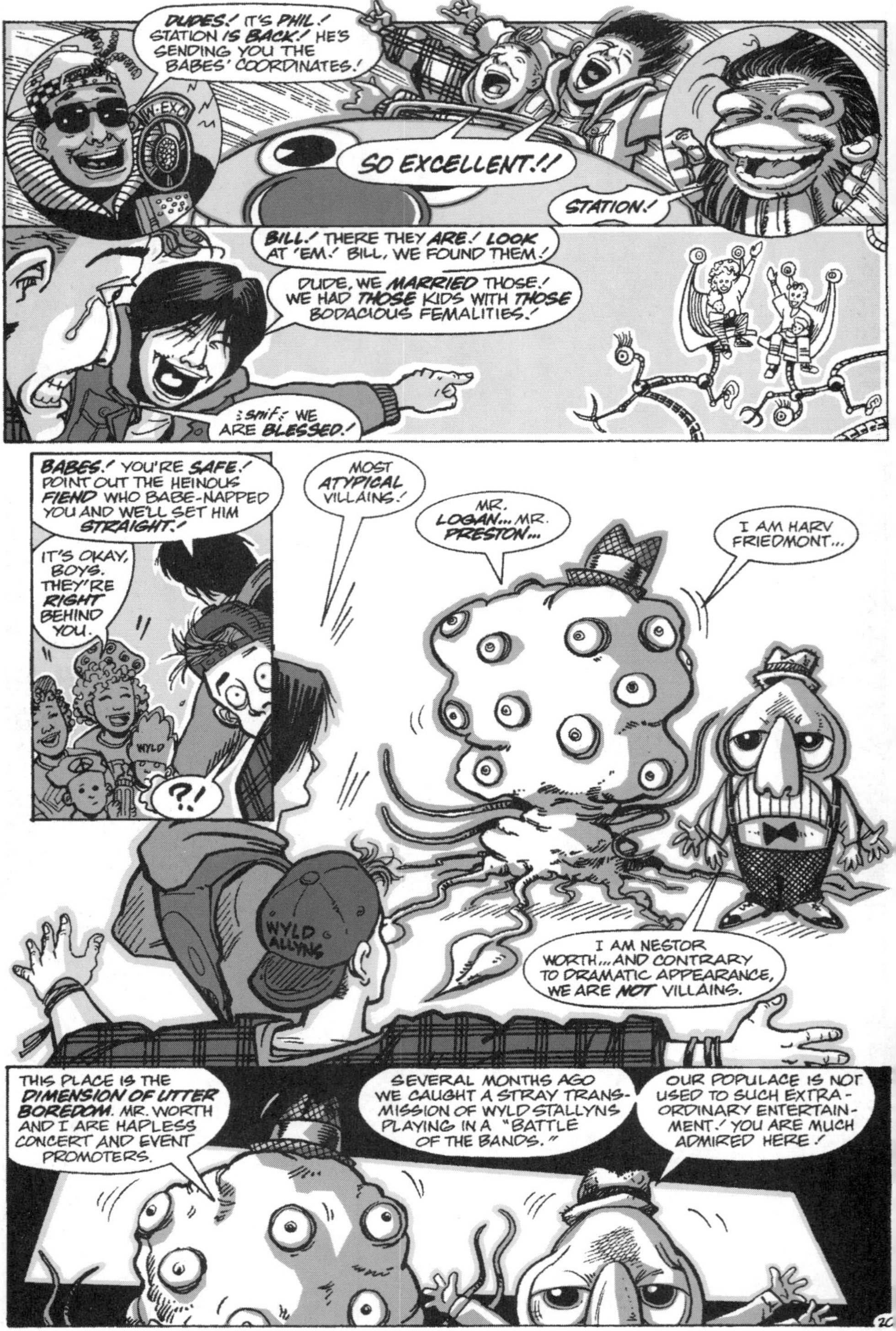

DUDES! IT'S PHIL! STATION IS BACK! HE'S SENDING YOU THE BABES' COORDINATES!
W-EXC
SO EXCELLENT!!
STATION!
BILL! THERE THEY ARE! LOOK AT 'EM! BILL, WE FOUND THEM!
DUDE, WE MARRIED THOSE! WE HAD THOSE KIDS WITH THOSE BODACIOUS FEMALITIES!
:snif: WE ARE BLESSED!
BABES! YOU'RE SAFE! POINT OUT THE HEINOUS FIEND WHO BABE-NAPPED YOU AND WE'LL SET HIM STRAIGHT!
IT'S OKAY, BOYS. THEY'RE RIGHT BEHIND YOU.
WYLD
?!
MOST ATYPICAL VILLAINS!
MR. LOGAN... MR. PRESTON...
I AM HARV FRIEDMONT...
WYLD ALLYNS
I AM NESTOR WORTH... AND CONTRARY TO DRAMATIC APPEARANCE, WE ARE NOT VILLAINS.
THIS PLACE IS THE DIMENSION OF UTTER BOREDOM. MR. WORTH AND I ARE HAPLESS CONCERT AND EVENT PROMOTERS.
SEVERAL MONTHS AGO WE CAUGHT A STRAY TRANSMISSION OF WYLD STALLYNS PLAYING IN A "BATTLE OF THE BANDS."
OUR POPULACE IS NOT USED TO SUCH EXTRA-ORDINARY ENTERTAINMENT! YOU ARE MUCH ADMIRED HERE!

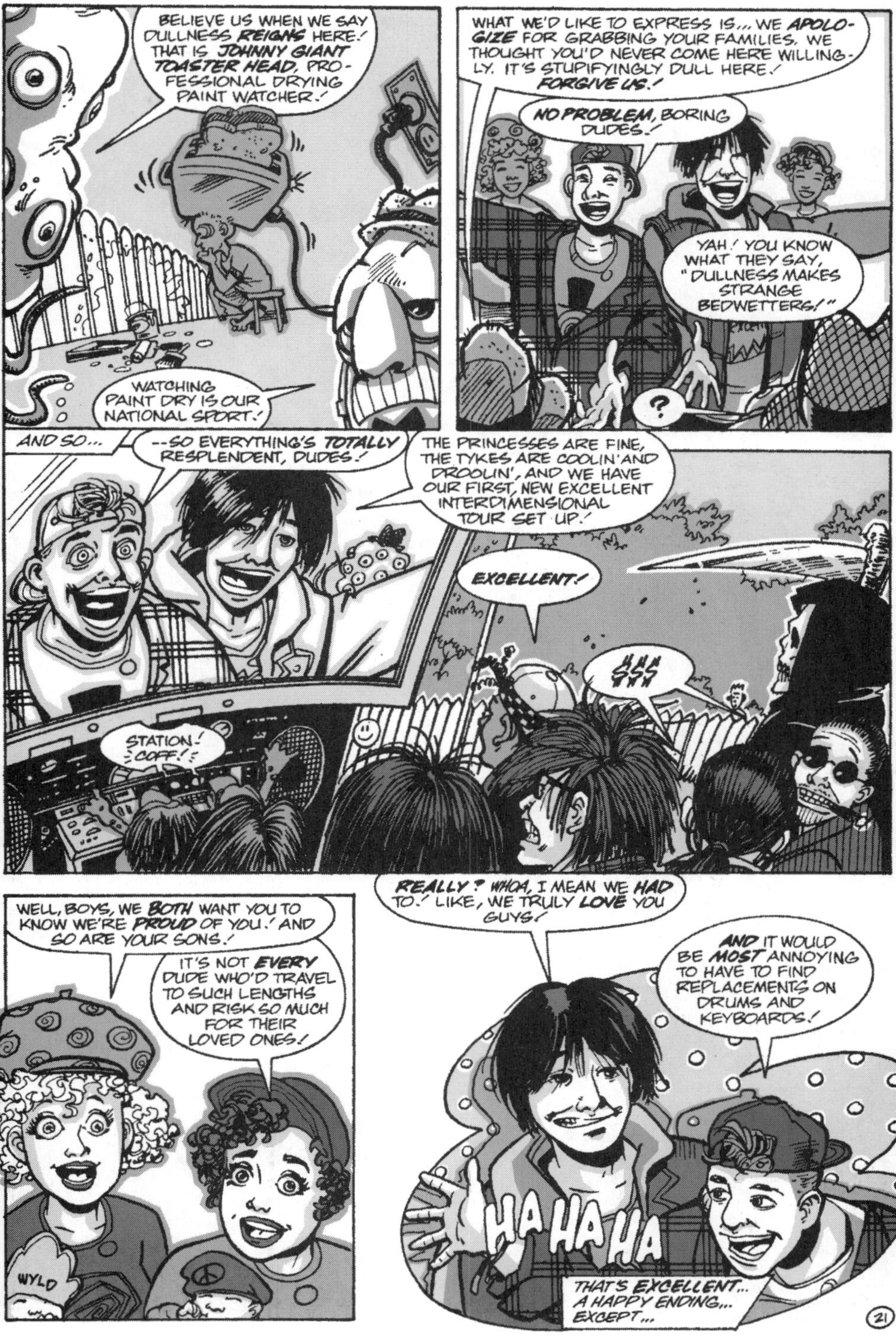
BELIEVE US WHEN WE SAY DULLNESS REIGNS HERE! THAT IS JOHNNY GIANT TOASTER HEAD, PROFESSIONAL DRYING PAINT WATCHER!
WATCHING PAINT DRY IS OUR NATIONAL SPORT!
WHAT WE'D LIKE TO EXPRESS IS... WE APOLOGIZE FOR GRABBING YOUR FAMILIES. WE THOUGHT YOU'D NEVER COME HERE WILLINGLY. IT'S STUPIFYINGLY DULL HERE! FORGIVE US!
NO PROBLEM, BORING DUDES!
YAH! YOU KNOW WHAT THEY SAY, "DULLNESS MAKES STRANGE BEDWETTERS!"
?
AND SO...
--SO EVERYTHING'S TOTALLY RESPLENDENT, DUDES!
THE PRINCESSES ARE FINE, THE TYKES ARE COOLIN' AND DROOLIN', AND WE HAVE OUR FIRST, NEW EXCELLENT INTERDIMENSIONAL TOUR SET UP!
EXCELLENT!
HAA SSS SHH
STATION! COFF!
WELL, BOYS, WE BOTH WANT YOU TO KNOW WE'RE PROUD OF YOU! AND SO ARE YOUR SONS!
IT'S NOT EVERY DUDE WHO'D TRAVEL TO SUCH LENGTHS AND RISK SO MUCH FOR THEIR LOVED ONES!
REALLY? WHOA, I MEAN WE HAD TO! LIKE, WE TRULY LOVE YOU GUYS!
AND IT WOULD BE MOST ANNOYING TO HAVE TO FIND REPLACEMENTS ON DRUMS AND KEYBOARDS!
HA HA HA
THAT'S EXCELLENT... A HAPPY ENDING... EXCEPT...
WYLD

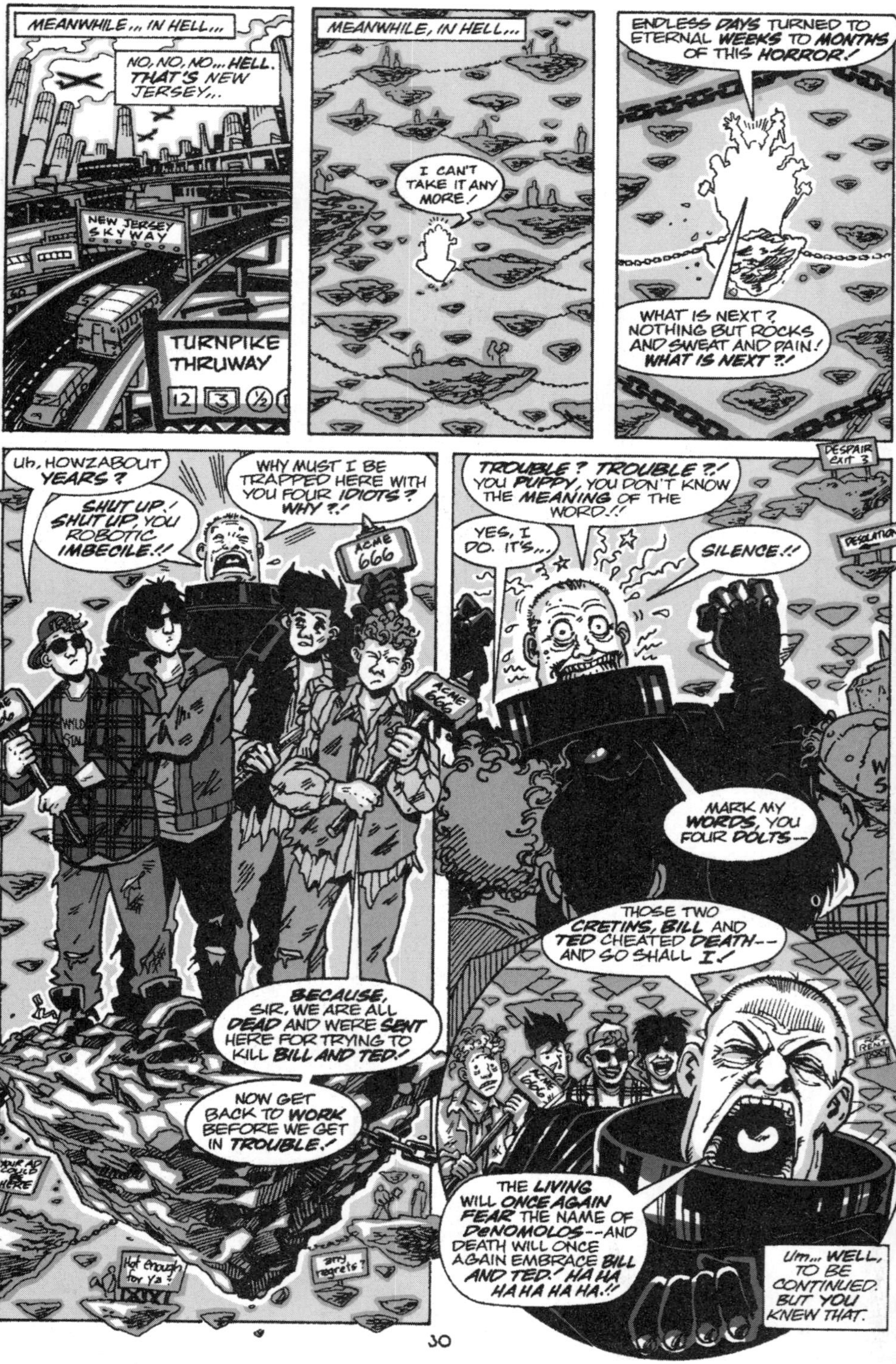
MEANWHILE... IN HELL...
NO, NO, NO... HELL. THAT'S NEW JERSEY...
NEW JERSEY SKYWAY
TURNPIKE THRUWAY
12 3 1/2
MEANWHILE, IN HELL...
I CAN'T TAKE IT ANY MORE!
ENDLESS DAYS TURNED TO ETERNAL WEEKS TO MONTHS OF THIS HORROR!
WHAT IS NEXT? NOTHING BUT ROCKS AND SWEAT AND PAIN! WHAT IS NEXT?!
Uh, HOWZABOUT YEARS?
SHUT UP! SHUT UP, YOU ROBOTIC IMBECILE!!
WHY MUST I BE TRAPPED HERE WITH YOU FOUR IDIOTS? WHY?!
ACME 666
BECAUSE, SIR, WE ARE ALL DEAD AND WERE SENT HERE FOR TRYING TO KILL BILL AND TED!
NOW GET BACK TO WORK BEFORE WE GET IN TROUBLE!
Hot enough for Ya?
any regrets?
DESPAIR EXIT 3
DESOLATION
TROUBLE? TROUBLE?! YOU PUPPY, YOU DON'T KNOW THE MEANING OF THE WORD!!
YES, I DO. IT'S...
SILENCE!!
MARK MY WORDS, YOU FOUR DOLTS--
THOSE TWO CRETINS, BILL AND TED CHEATED DEATH-- AND SO SHALL I!
THE LIVING WILL ONCE AGAIN FEAR THE NAME OF DeNOMOLOS--AND DEATH WILL ONCE AGAIN EMBRACE BILL AND TED! HA HA HA HA HA HA!!
Um... WELL, TO BE CONTINUED. BUT YOU KNEW THAT.

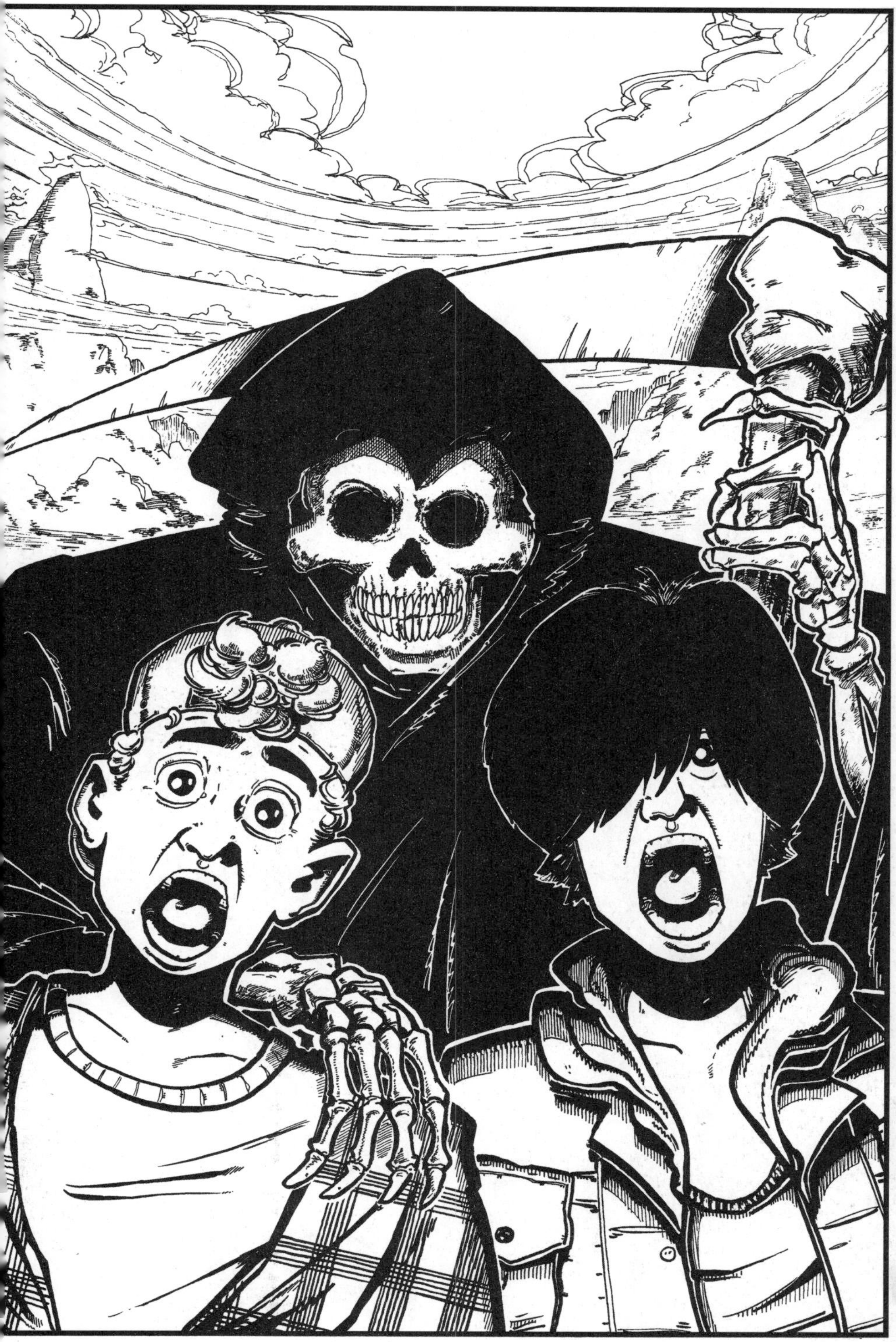

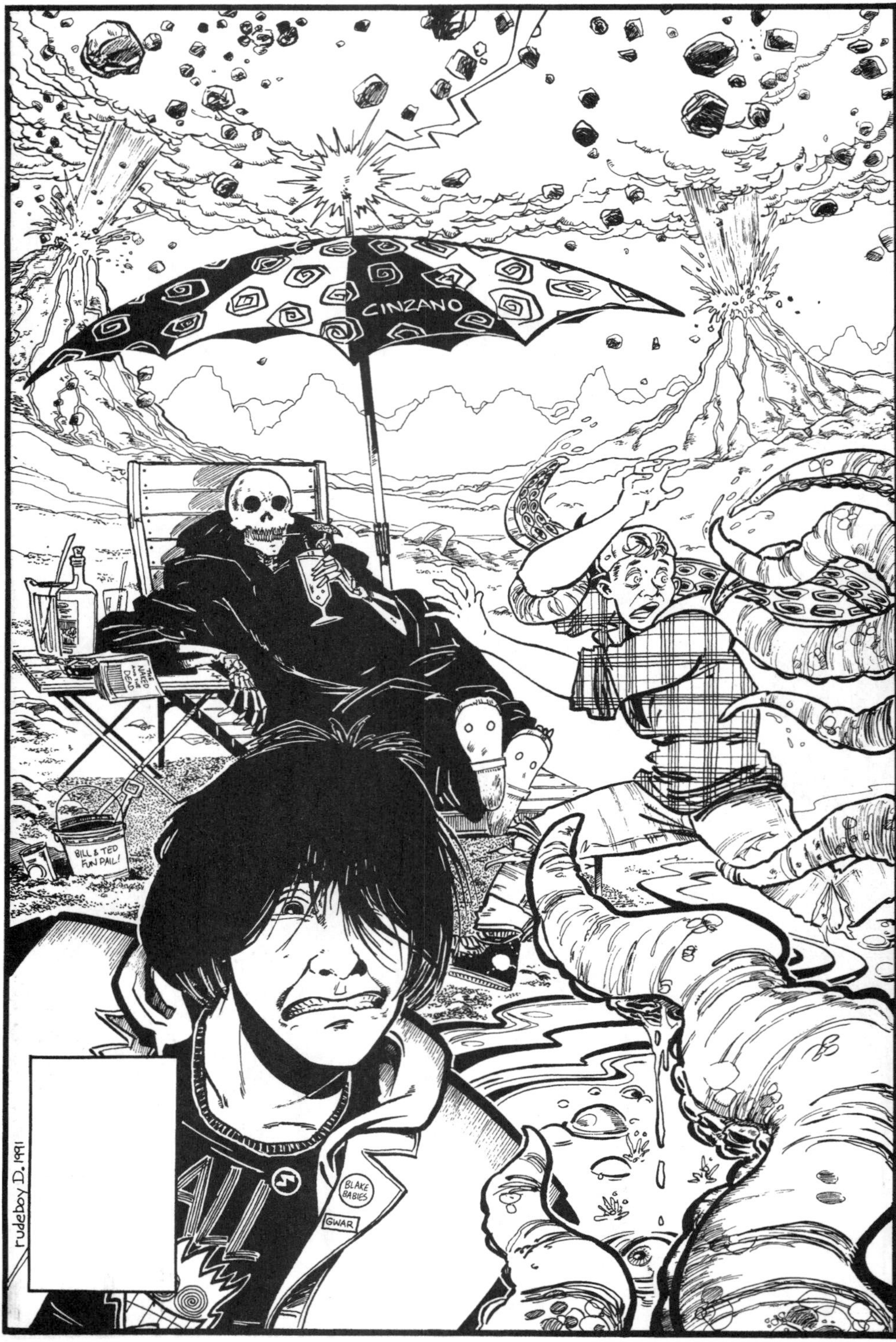
CINZANO
THE NAKED AND THE DEAD
BILL & TED FUN PAIL!
BLAKE BABIES
GWAR
rudeboy D. 1991

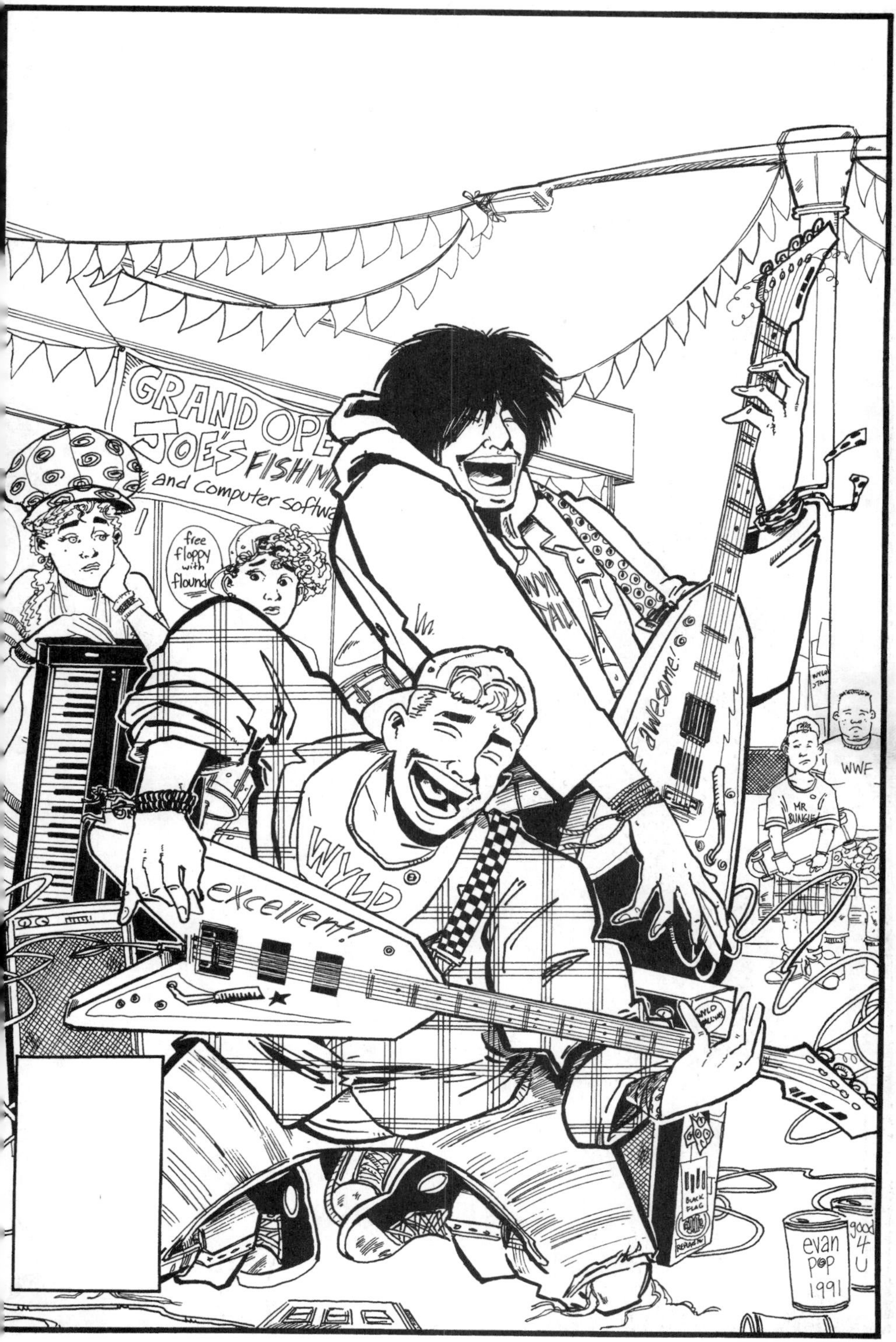

GRAND OPE
JOE'S FISH M
and computer softw
free floppy with floundr
WYLD STALL
awesome!
excellent!
WYLD
WWF
MR BUNGLE
BLACK FLAG
evan pop 1991
good 4 U

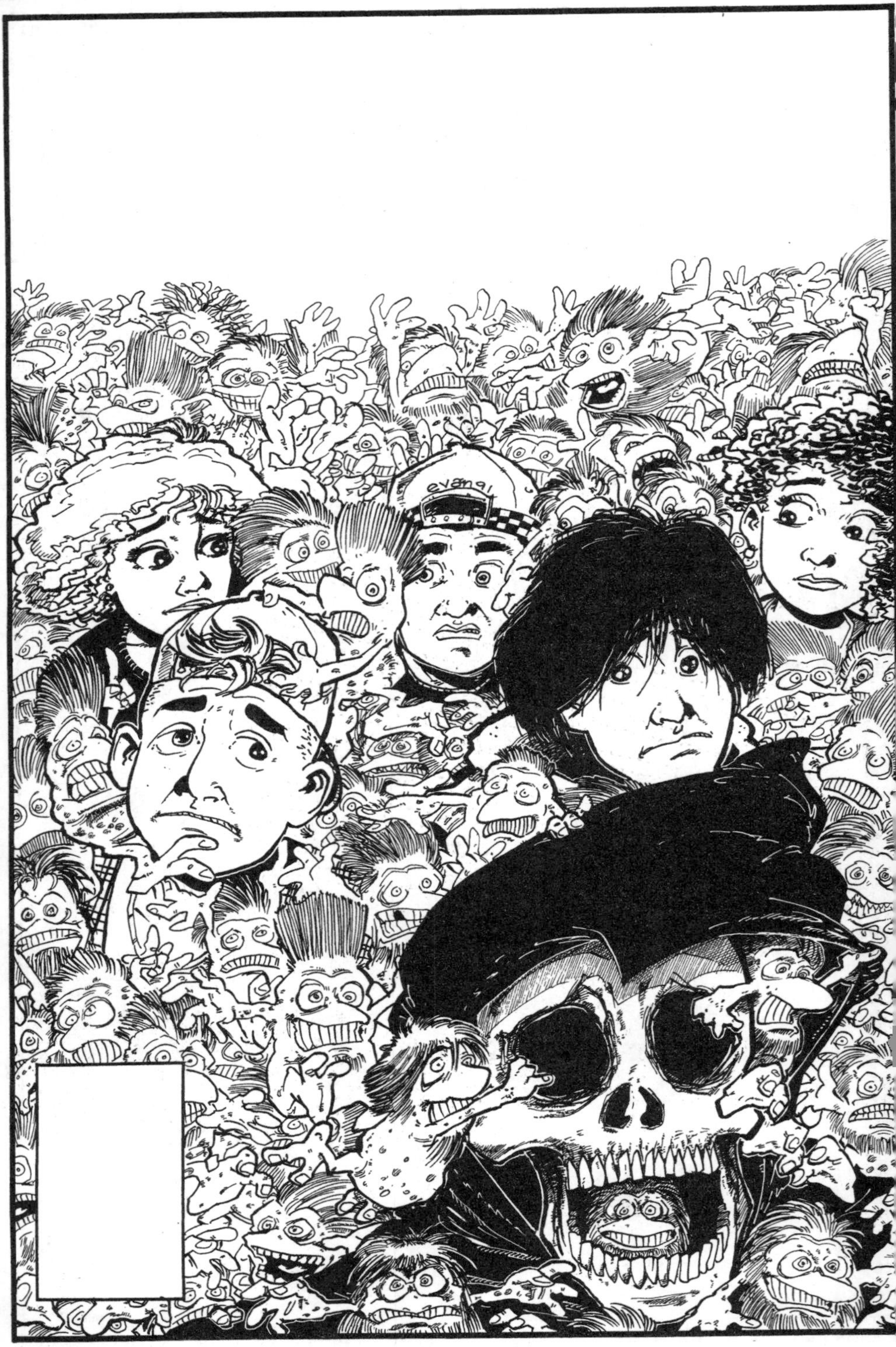
evan91